Cultural Diversity

A Primer for the Human Services

Third Edition

Jerry V. Diller

THOMSON
™
BROOKS/COLE

Australia • Brazil • Canada • Mexico • Singapore
Spain • United Kingdom • United States

THOMSON
*

™
BROOKS/COLE

Cultural Diversity: A Primer for the Human Services, **Third Edition**
Jerry V. Diller

Senior Acquisitions Editor: Marquita Flemming
Assistant Editor: Jennifer Walsh
Editorial Assistant: Samantha Shook
Marketing Manager: Meghan McCullough
Marketing Communications Manager: Tami Strang
Content Project Manager, Editorial Production: Rita Jaramillo
Creative Director: Rob Hugel
Art Director: Vernon Boes

Print Buyer: Nora Massuda
Permissions Editor: Roberta Broyer
Production Service: International Typesetting and Composition
Copy Editor: Joan Flaherty
Cover Designer: Nancy Nimoy
Cover Printer: Thomson/West
Compositor: International Typesetting and Composition
Printer: Thomson/West

Printed in the United States of America
1 2 3 4 5 6 7 10 09 08 07 06

Library of Congress Control Number: 2006906345

ISBN 0-495-12764-7

Thomson Higher Education
10 Davis Drive
Belmont, CA 94002-3098
USA

For more information about our products, contact us at:
Thomson Learning Academic Resource Center
1-800-423-0563

For permission to use material from this text or product, submit a request online at **http://www.thomsonrights.com.**
Any additional questions about permissions can be submitted by e-mail to **thomsonrights@thomson.com.**

Contents

Preface

The previous editions of *Cultural Diversity: A Primer for the Human Services* were well received by students and faculty alike. In them I tried to speak honestly and directly to the reader about the kinds of knowledge, awareness, and skills necessary for effectively working with culturally different clients. The book's accessibility, personal style, anecdotal and clinical examples, and broad range of topics make it a popular introductory text for both students in training and professionals in the field. Especially popular were the interviews with Providers of Color and a White ethnic on how to work with clients from communities. Their honest sharing of personal experiences, cultural knowledge, and clinical suggestions seemed to engage the reader and make the topic of becoming culturally competent come alive.

Much has happened in the realm of cultural diversity and intergroup relations since *Cultural Diversity: A Primer for the Human Services* first appeared in print. Ethnic populations in the United States have continued to grow at an astounding rate. There has been a significant move toward conservatism in politics and a worsening economic climate. Both have contributed to a backlash against immigration and efforts to promote equity and social justice. And the terrorist attack of September 11, 2001, and war in Iraq have changed our very perception of the world and our place in it, ushering in widespread suspicion and animosity toward Arab and Muslim peoples. These trends have made the United States a more dangerous place for those who are culturally different and further underline the need for cultural competence in human service providers.

The second edition of the text included a number of changes and additions. Statistical demographics of the Communities of Color were updated to include data from the 2000 U.S. census. Sections on the development of self-esteem in Children of Color and models of racial identity development were significantly expanded, as was the introductory culture-specific material that precedes each interview. The material on privilege and racial consciousness in Whites was moved to Chapter 3, and Chapter 13: "Working with White Ethnic Clients: An Interview with the Author," focusing on clinical work with American Jews, was expanded to parallel the chapters on working with Clients of Color that precede it. There was also a new concluding chapter, Chapter 15, entitled "Some Closing Thoughts," which served as a summary and compendium of suggestions of where to pursue cultural competence further. The end of the book contained a glossary with definitions of italicized terms in the text and a bibliography of suggested readings on various topics in diversity. Finally, with each text, students were given a free four-month subscription to InfoTrac© College Edition, an online library of hundreds of journals and periodicals.

The third edition of the text offers several substantial additions in response to the suggestions of instructors and students. First, I have added summaries and suggested activities to all chapters to enhance learning and interaction with the material. I have expanded Chapter 6, "Mental Health Issues," to include a section on trauma and added a new Chapter 9, "Addressing Ethnic Conflict, Genocide, and Mass Violence," which explores healing in the aftermath of racial and ethnic strife. A conservative estimate holds that there are currently 53 wars and military conflicts taking place on our planet, most of which have strong ethnic or colonial components. There is a desperate need for research and intervention by skilled professional helpers who can offer culturally competent services to heal both the individual victims who have been traumatized and the societies that have been skewed by hatred and the desire for revenge. I have also significantly expanded Chapter 8, "Critical Issues in Working with Culturally Different Clients," to include an in-depth conceptual analysis of cross-cultural therapeutic work, an expanded section on assessment, and two detailed, interactive, case studies. Finally, two new interviews have been added, one with Roberto Almanzan, a Mexican American counselor, and another with Veronique Thompson, an African American psychologist.

■ A Word About Diversity

Human beings are diverse in a variety of ways: race, ethnicity, language, culture, gender, socioeconomic class, age, sexual orientation, religion, ablism and disability, and more. Each must be fully appreciated and accounted for in order to understand the complexity of human behavior. This is no small task, however, because each affects the individual differently and operates by a unique set of rules and dynamics. No single text can adequately and comprehensively cover all forms of diversity. The present book focuses on working with clients from different racial and ethnic groups. Diversity within these groups is discussed throughout the book. The decision to highlight only race and ethnicity in this text is pragmatic and in no way minimizes the import of gender, class, age, sexual preference, and so on. Rather, it underlines the fact that each deserves its own text to do it justice. There are even those who argue that covering too many forms of diversity in a single treatment tends to be superficial and minimize the importance of each. For those who would like to read further on other forms of diversity, I have included a selected bibliography arranged by areas of diversity.

■ Acknowledgments

A book like this is not written in a vacuum. I would first like to thank my daughters, the lights of my life, Becca and Rachel, whose support kept me going and whose encouragement allowed me to complete the dream of writing this book.

And to Carole Diller, for her help in supporting my escape to Berkeley, where this book was written.

A number of indispensable people made writing this book possible. Stuart W. Cook, Tom Vernon, Harrie Hess, Gil Davis, Zalman Schachter-Shalomi, Ed Diller, and Nevitt Sanford were early teachers who taught me about race, ethnicity, and my own Jewish tradition. More recent teachers include Bob Cohen, Manny Foreman, Martin Acker, Reuben Cota, Jack Lawson, and Guadalupe Quinn. In particular, Leland Robison shared with me the richness of his Rom tradition. Saul Siegel, Myrna Holden, Deb Johnson, and Carol Stone provided helpful feedback on early drafts of the work. At Brooks/Cole I am thankful for the help of Marquita Flemming, Samantha Shook, and Roberta Boyer who offered useful support, creative ideas, and enormous help in taking care of a variety of details and small but necessary tasks. Special thanks to the following people who served as readers and reviewers of the text:

Reviewer	Affiliation
William McDowell	Marshall University
Johnny Sanders	Winthrop University
Margaret Miller	Boise State U
Stacie Robertson	Southern Illinois U
Emma Lucas-Darby	Carlow U
Brian Ogawa	Washburn U
Sandra Chesborough	St. Cloud State U

And finally, special thanks to my colleagues: Veronique Thompson, Roberto Almanzan, Dan Hocoy, and Jack Lawson. They generously took time out from very busy schedules and lives to share their expertise as interviewees in the chapters on working with Clients of Color. I chose them as much for their very special human qualities as for their expert knowledge.

Jerry V. Diller

1 Introduction

I once worked at a university counseling center that was baffled by the fact that very few of the university's rather sizable Asian student population ever sought treatment. In the hope of remedying the situation, the center invited Asian student leaders to visit the counseling center to learn about available services. After a very polite but unproductive meeting, I overheard one of the students commenting to another, "This place looks like a hospital. Why would anyone want to come here? This is where people come to die." No one on the staff had ever considered that the remodeled health center with its hospital-like rooms might deter clients from seeking help or that in some cultures hospitals are places people go to die and are thus to be avoided.

Contained in this simple scenario is the crux of a serious problem currently facing *human service providers*. How can one hope to offer competent services cross-culturally when one lacks basic knowledge about the people one hopes to serve? Ethical guidelines of all human services professions expressly forbid discriminating against clients on the basis of race and ethnicity. However, although some efforts are being made in this direction, professional organizations have neither clearly defined what culturally competent services should look like nor developed methods of censuring those who provide services without the requisite skills. The reality is that most service providers regularly, though unknowingly, discriminate against culturally different clients by lacking the skills and knowledge necessary to serve them properly.

This fact is reflected in research that consistently shows that community facilities and services are underused by culturally different clients, especially those of Color. The following are a number of reasons for this:

- Mainstream agencies may inadvertently make clients feel uncomfortable or unwelcome, as in the opening scenario.
- Clients may not trust the motives or abilities of providers because of past experiences with the system.
- Clients may believe they will not be understood culturally or will not have their needs met in a helpful manner.
- Clients may be unfamiliar with the kinds of services available or come from a culture in which such services are perceived very differently.

Each of these possibilities is sufficient to deter culturally different clients, who as a group tend to have especially high mental health needs, from seeking treatment or help.

1

The purpose of this book is to sensitize providers and those learning to be providers to the complex issues involved in *cross-cultural service delivery*. Only when culturally sensitive services are routinely available will utilization rates of public facilities among culturally different clients begin to approach those of mainstream White groups. Providers, as professionals, are expected to demonstrate expertise and competence in the services they offer. Cross-cultural service delivery should be no less an area to be mastered. Only by gaining the requisite knowledge and skills necessary to be "culturally competent" can human service providers hope to actualize their professional commitment to nondiscrimination and equal access for all clients.

Discrimination in this context involves more than merely refusing to offer services to those who are racially or ethnically different. It also includes the following:

- Being unaware of one's own prejudices and how they may inadvertently be communicated to clients.
- Being unaware of differences in cultural style, interactive patterns, and values, and how these can lead to miscommunication.
- Being unaware that many of the theories taught during training are culturebound.
- Being unaware of differences in cultural definitions of health and illness as well as the existence of traditional cultural healing methods.
- Being unaware of the necessity of matching treatment modalities to the cultural style of clients or of adapting practices to the specific cultural needs of clients.

Of equal importance to effective cross-cultural service delivery is developing empathy and an appreciation for the life experience of those who are culturally different in the United States. Why do so many culturally different clients harbor fears and mistrust of providers and others who represent the system? Why are so many angry and frustrated? Why do many culturally different people tend to feel tenuous and conflicted about their traditional identities? Why is parenting for these clients such a major challenge? What is the source of the enormous stress that is the ongoing experience of many culturally different clients? And why do they so often feel that majority group members have very little awareness of or concern for the often harsh realities of their daily lives? Without keen insight into the complex answers to these questions, well-meaning professionals cannot hope to serve their clients sensitively.

Providers are, by training, familiar with the inner workings of the system and thus able to gain access to it on behalf of clients. However, special care must be taken in this regard. First, there is the danger that culturally different clients may, as a result of interacting with providers and the system, be unintentionally socialized into the ways of the dominant culture. For example, in working with women from traditional cultures, it is important for them to understand that becoming more independent and assertive, a frequent outcome of counseling with mainstream women, can prove highly problematic when reentering the traditional world. Culturally competent providers educate their clients as to the service alternatives available, as well as the possible con-sequences, and then allow them to make informed choices. Such providers also make use of and collaborate with traditional indigenous healers when useful or supportive to the client. A second danger is dependence. Culturally different clients are especially susceptible, given their more limited knowledge of mainstream culture. As the conduit to the system, providers may unknow-ingly perpetuate dependence rather than help these clients learn to function independently.

Often, for example, it is easier and more expedient to arrange referrals for clients than teach them how to do it for themselves. Helping is most useful, however, when it facilitates clients' interaction with the system on their own terms and in light of their cultural values and needs. In the literature, this is called *empowerment* and involves supporting and encouraging clients to become their own advocates.

Providers and clients from culturally different backgrounds do not come together in a vacuum. Rather, each brings a certain amount of baggage about the ethnicity of the other. Clients, for example, may initially feel mistrust, anger, fear, suspicion, or deference in the presence of the provider. Providers, in turn, may respond with feelings of superiority, condescension, discomfort, fear, or inadequacy. Each may also perceive the other in terms of cultural stereotypes. Such reactions may be subtle or covered up, but one can be sure they will be there and, for a time at least, get in the way of forming a working alliance. Projections such as these fade with time as client and provider come to know each other as individuals instead of stereotypes. The least helpful thing that a provider can do at this point, however, is to take these reactions person-ally and respond defensively. A much better strategy is to acknowledge their existence and raise them as a topic for discussion. Research shows that clients of all backgrounds are most comfortable with professionals from their own culture. Unfortunately, there is a serious shortage of non-White providers, and Clients of Color find themselves working with dominant group professionals. This is where cultural competence comes in. It is my belief and experience that basic trust can develop cross-culturally, but it is not easy. It requires the right skills, a sincere desire to help, a willingness to openly acknowledge and discuss racial and ethnic differences, and a healthy tolerance for being tested.

This book focuses on working with clients from different cultures. Its prin-ciples, however, are applicable in a variety of helping situations where provider and client come from qualitatively different backgrounds. This is even true for members of the same cultural group. Differences in class, gender, age, geogra-phy, social and political leanings, and ableness can lead to such diverse life expe-riences that members of the same group may feel they have little in common.

A middle-class White provider, for example, growing up in a major Eastern city may experience difficulties similar to those just described when working with poor Whites from the rural South. Likewise, providers and clients from different cultural backgrounds who share similar demographics of class, gender, geography, and so forth may feel that they have much in common upon which to build a working relationship.

I use a number of different terms in referring to culturally different clients and do so consciously. Anyone familiar with this field is aware of the power of such terms. They possess, first of all, subtle connotations and at times implicit value judgments. They have often been used as means of oppressing and demeaning devalued groups, but they can also serve as powerful sources of empowerment and pride. It is not surprising that ethnic group members pay very serious attention to the ways in which they label themselves and are labeled by others. Finding out what term is preferable is a matter of respect, and if providers are in doubt, they should just ask clients what name they prefer. I have never seen anyone offended by that question. I have, however, repeatedly watched providers unintentionally alienate clients through their use of outdated and demeaning terms like "Orientals" or insensitive general references such as "you people."

Consider the following terms, which are used in this text:

- *Cultural diversity* refers to the array of differences among groups of people with definable and unique cultural backgrounds.
- *Culturally different* implies that the client and provider come from different cultures. It suggests no value judgment as to the superiority of one culture over the other, only that the two have been socialized in very different ways and may likely find communication problematic.
- *Culture* is viewed as a lens through which life is perceived. Each culture, through its differences (in language, values, personality and family patterns, worldview, sense of time and space, and rules of interaction), generates a phenomenologically different experience of reality. Thus, the same situation, (e.g., an initial counseling session at a community mental health center) may be experienced and interpreted very differently depending on the cultural background of individual clients and providers.
- *Ethnic group* is any distinguishable people whose members share a common culture and see themselves as separate and different from the majority culture. The observable differences—whether physical, racial, cultural, or geographic—frequently serve as a basis for discrimination and unequal treatment of a minority ethnic group within the larger society.
- *Racial group*, or *race*, is a biologically isolated, inbreeding population with a distinctive genetic heritage. Socially, the concept of race has created many difficulties. In general, I avoid the concept of race as a definer of group differences (with the exception of talking about the development of racial awareness and consciousness in People of Color). The distinction between race as a social and biological category is discussed in chapter 4.
- *People of Color and Clients of Color* refer to non-White clients.
- *Communities of Color* are collectives of non-Whites who share certain physical (racial), cultural, language, or geographic origins/features. In naming specific Communities of Color, I try to use the term or referent that is most current and acceptable to members of that group (although there is always some debate within communities about what names are most acceptable). In relation to Clients and Communities of Color, the following

terms are generally used: *African Americans, Latinos/as, Native Americans* or *Native Peoples*, and *Asian Americans* or *Asians*. In quotes and references to research, terms are used as they appear in the original text.

- *Whites* refer to members of the dominant or majority group whose origins are Northern European.
- *White ethnics* refer to dominant or majority group members whose origins are not Northern European.

This book is written from a perspective that assumes that there are certain psychological characteristics and experiences that all ethnically and culturally different clients share. First is the experience of belonging to a group that is socially stigmatized and the object of regular discrimination and derision. Second is the stress and harm this causes to the psyche and the resulting adaptations, some healthy and empowering and others unhealthy and dysfunctional, that ethnic individuals and families must make in order to survive. Third is the stress and harm that result from problems regularly associated with prejudice and racism (e.g., poverty, insufficient health care, crime, and drug abuse). Not all cultures or individuals within cultures, however, experience these factors with equal intensity. Each society, in its inner workings, designates certain groups as primary scapegoats and others as secondary. In the United States, for example, People of Color have traditionally been the primary object of derision. In Europe, on the other hand, it has been Jews and the Rom (Gypsies). There religion rather than race defined primary minority status. Fourth is the fact that problems in *ethnic* or *racial identification* are often evident in non-White and White ethnic clients. Ethnic and racial identification refers to two related processes. First is the attachment that individuals feel to their cultural group of origin. Second is the awareness or consciousness that individuals have of the impact that race or ethnicity has had on their lives. In one form or another, most clients from ethnic minorities exhibit some modicum of these four factors and thus share their dynamics.

It is also important that providers be aware of the diversity that exists both across and within ethnic groups. Each group, first of all, has its unique history in the United States. As a result, somewhat different problems have emerged for each around its status as a culturally different group. People of Color, for example, are set apart primarily by the color of their skin and differences in racial features. As a consequence, they may struggle with concerns over body image and the possibility of "passing" for White. Many Latinos/as and Asians have immigrated from traditional homelands and face ongoing dilemmas regarding assimilation, bilingualism, and the destruction of traditional family roles and values. Native Americans, as victims of colonization in their own land, have experienced destruction of traditional ways and identities and struggle to come to grips with these losses. African Americans have faced a similar psychological dislocation due to slavery. Whites in minority ethnic groups, in turn, find themselves suspended between worlds. They are culturally different, yet perceived, and often wish to be perceived, as part of the majority.

These ethnically specific circumstances shape and determine the kinds of problems for which clients seek help.

Differences among clients in the same ethnic group (be it class, age, gender, ableness, language, etc.) can also be extensive. The surest indicator of cultural insensitivity is the belief that all members of a particular group share all characteristics and circumstances. A recently arrived migrant worker from central Mexico, poor and barely able to speak English, faces life challenges very different from those of a similarly aged man from a wealthy Chilean family, born in the States, well educated, and working as a banker. The first task of any cross-cultural worker is to carefully assess the client's demographic and cultural situation. Some of the following information may be critical in determining the situation and needs of a culturally different client: place of birth, number of generations in the United States, family roles and structure, language spoken at home, English fluency, economic situation and status, amount and type of education, amount of acculturation, traditions practiced in the home, familiarity and comfort with Northern European lifestyle, religious affiliation, and community and friendship patterns.

The culturally competent provider not only seeks such information but also is aware of its possible meaning. The migrant worker just described may be in need of financial help, unfamiliar with the system, homesick, fearful of authorities, traditional and macho in his attitudes, and possibly abusing drugs or alcohol. His Chilean counterpart is more likely to be concerned with issues of cultural than economic survival—how ethnicity is affecting him in the workplace, parental concern over his acculturation, changing roles with his wife and children, balancing success with retaining traditional ways, and differing patterns of alcohol and drug use.

I bring to this text both my own perspective on ethnicity and my experience as an American Jew and White ethnic. The autobiographical material that I share in chapter 13 should make it quite clear that these are not merely academic issues for me. Like so many other racial and ethnic group members, I have struggled personally with conflicts over group belonging and identity.

This has taught me both the complexity of the issues that are the focus of this book and the fact that becoming culturally competent is indeed a lifelong process that needs constant monitoring. It is important for you to know, as someone beginning to learn in this field, that even those of us who have gained some competence in working cross-culturally never stop struggling with these issues. It is just part and parcel of the process of becoming culturally competent.

I have worked in intergroup relations for more than 20 years: teaching courses on multicultural issues in counseling, consulting with various public and private agencies and institutions, and doing clinical work with a wide range of ethnic populations. Yet, I still grow uneasy when I am put in the position of speaking about those who are culturally different from me. To this end, I have written the chapters dealing with the broader conceptual issues, drawing on research as well as examples from my experience, and have invited experts from the four Communities of Color to speak about working with clients from their respective groups. I am still learning about my own culture and heritage, so how can I presume to speak authoritatively about the culture of others?

I have called this work a "primer." According to Webster, a primer is a book of elementary or basic principles. This book's intention is to provide you with basic principles, sensitivities, and knowledge that will lay a foundation for becoming a culturally competent professional. The chapters that follow explore different aspects of cultural diversity:

- Chapter 2, "What It Means to Be Culturally Competent," discusses the need for cultural competence, the skill areas it comprises, and the kind of benefits gained by providers who choose to pursue it.
- Chapter 3, "Understanding Racism, Prejudice, and White Privilege," describes the dynamics of racism and prejudice as they operate at individual, institutional, and cultural levels and how they may impinge on the helping relationship. I also highlight the notion of White privilege as well as ways in which Whites structure and protect their racial attitudes.
- Chapter 4, "Understanding Culture and Cultural Differences," focuses on the elusive concept of "culture"—its various dimensions, how to make sense of and deal with cultural differences, and the meaning of multiculturalism.
- Chapter 5, "Children and Parents of Color," is the first of three chapters that focus on the psychological experience of People of Color or what has been called *ethnic psychology*. Chapter 5 discusses developmental issues peculiar to children from oppressed racial and ethnic backgrounds, the challenges to parenting these children, and issues related to biracial or bicultural families.
- Chapter 6, "Mental Health Issues," deals with various mental health factors that have particular relevance for culturally different clients. Included are discussions of racial and ethnic identity development in adults, acculturation, stress, trauma, and substance abuse.
- Chapter 7, "Bias in Service Delivery," explores various sources of bias in cross-cultural service delivery as well as ways of adapting human service delivery to the specific cultural needs of clients.
- Chapter 8, "Working with Culturally Different Clients," directs attention to the process of beginning work with culturally different clients and provides a conceptualization of cross-cultural work as well as guidelines and specific hands-on information for doing so.
- Chapter 9, "Addressing Ethnic Conflict, Genocide, and Mass Violence," looks at the extreme consequences of ethnic and racial hatred as well as models for healing both the traumatized victim/survivor and the society in which it occurred.
- Chapters 10–13 provide culturally specific information on four Communities of Color in the United States. In each, an expert indigenous to that community—Latinos/as (chapter 10), Native Americans (chapter 11), African Americans (chapter 12), and Asian Americans (chapter 13)—highlights key

issues and differences of which providers working with clients from their respective cultures should be aware. An interview format is used.

- Chapter 14, "Working with White Ethnic Clients: An Interview with the Author," focuses attention on work with White ethnic clients, using American Jews as a case in point.
- Chapter 15, "Some Closing Thoughts," summarizes basic notions about cultural competence and suggests ways in which you can continue learning about cross-cultural service delivery.

2 What It Means to Be Culturally Competent

▮ Demographics

The demographics of the United States have been changing dramatically, and central to these changes is a significant increase in non-White populations. Atkinson, Morten, and Sue (1993) refer to this trend that began in the 1980s as the "diversification" of America. The statistics speak for themselves. Between 1980 and 1992, for example, the relative percentages of population increase for ethnic groups were as follows: Asian and Pacific Islander, 123.5%; Hispanic, 65.3%; Native American/Eskimo/Aleut, 30.7%; African American, 16.4%; and non-Hispanic White, 5.5%. These percentages represent not only a sizable increase in the actual numbers of People of Color in the United States, but also a significant decline in the relative percentage of Whites from almost 80% to less than 75%. Healey (1995) suggests that "if this trend continues, it will not take many generations before 'non-Hispanic Whites' are a numerical minority of the population" (p. 12).

Estimates for the future bear out Healey's prediction. Riche's (2000) projections for the next 50 years, based on 2000 U.S. Census data, are summarized in Table 2–1. Most noteworthy is the growth of Hispanics to 24% of the population, the growth of Asians to 9% of the population, and the reduction of non-Hispanic Whites to 53%. It is further estimated that by 2060 non-Hispanic Whites will represent less than 50% of the population. By 2100, Hispanics alone will represent 33% of the U.S. population, and non-Whites 60% of that population. Such changes are even more dramatic for certain subpopulations and regions of the United States. By 2030, for example, half of all elementary school age children in the United States will be Children of Color. In California (a clear pacesetter for diversity), such parity was reached in 1990, when one out of every four school-aged children came from homes where English was not the primary language and one out of every six was born outside of the United States. And by 2020, four states—New Mexico, Hawaii, California, Texas—and Washington, D.C., will have "minority majority" populations.

Two factors—immigration and birthrates—are particularly responsible for these dramatic changes. The last 30 years of the twentieth century have seen an unprecedented wave of immigration to the United States, with yearly numbers rising to 1 million. Unlike earlier immigration patterns, however, the new arrivals are primarily non-European: approximately one third from Asia and one third from South and Central America. In 1998, for example, while 9%

■ **TABLE 2–1**   Projected Percentages of Ethnic Groups in U.S. Population

Group	1999 (%)	2020 (%)	2050 (%)
Non-Hispanic Whites	72	64	53
African Americans	12	13	13
Hispanics	12	17	24
Asians	4	6	9
Native Americans	1	1	1*

Note. Adapted from "America's Diversity and Growth: Signposts for the 21st Century" by M. F. Riche, 2000, *Population Bulletin, 55* (2).

*While statistics for Native Americans are projected to remain below 1% of the population, actual numbers will triple during this period.

of all citizens in the United States were foreign born, 63% of Asian American citizens and 35% of Hispanic citizens were foreign born. Differential birthrates of ethnic groups in the United States are equally skewed. Birthrates of Hispanic populations tend to be approximately 1.7 times that of Whites, and Asian Americans anywhere from 3 to 7 times greater depending on the specific subpopulation.

Opportunity 2000, a study of projections for the work force in the year 2000, commissioned by the U.S. Department of Labor and carried out by the Hudson Institute (1988), showed similar trends. It accurately estimated that the labor market would grow smaller, older, and, most interesting for our purposes, significantly more diverse. Only 15% of new entrants into the job market are native-born White males, although this group has traditionally accounted for 47% of the workforce. People of Color constitute 29% of the current workforce, women 42%, and immigrants 22%. Statistics for People of Color entering the workforce in 2005 represent a twofold increase over the previous decade. Unfortunately, projections suggest that these growing numbers will be of little help to urban, African American, and Latino males, who may actually experience a decline in available jobs if their work-related skills do not keep up with the growing demand for increased technical knowledge.

And for the first time in the 2000 Census, there was an attempt to identify multiracial individuals. The result was that 6.8 million people, or 2.4% of the population of the United States, reported multiracial backgrounds. Of these, 93% reported only two races. Thirty-two percent of this group reported being White and "Some Other Group"; 16%, White and American Indian or Alaska Native; 13%, White and Asian; and 11%, White and Black or African American (Jones and Smith, 2001).

■ Reactions to the Changing Demographics

What has been the reaction to this growing diversification? First, White America has clearly felt threatened by these changes. The sheer increase in non-White numbers has stimulated a widespread political backlash. Most prominent has been a rise in anti-immigrant sentiment and legislation and a strong push to repeal affirmative action practices, which were instituted over the last several decades to level out the economic and social playing fields for People of Color.

As economic times have worsened for White working and middle classes, frustration has increasingly been directed at non-White newcomers who have been blamed for "taking our jobs" and told to "go back to where you came from if you're not willing to speak English." In a similar vein, White supremacist, militia, and anti-government groups, playing on racial hatred and a return to "traditional values" and "law and order," have attracted growing numbers. The result has been a society even further polarized along color lines. People of Color, in turn, have sensed in their growing numbers an ultimatum to White America: "Soon you won't even have the numerical majority. How can you possibly continue to justify the enormous injustice and disparity?" For those in the helping professions, a major implication of these new demographics is a radically different client base. More and more, providers will be called on to serve clients from diverse cultures. Job announcements increasingly state: "bilingual and bicultural professionals preferred" and "cross-cultural experience and sensitivity a requirement." There is, at the same time, a growing awareness that it is not sufficient to merely channel these new clients into the same old structures and programs or to hire a few token Professionals of Color. Rather, a radical reconceptualization of effective helping vis-à-vis those who are culturally different and how it occurs is needed.

At the center of such a renewed vision is the notion of *cultural competence.*

■ A Model of Cultural Competence

In its broadest context, cultural competence is the ability to effectively provide services cross-culturally. According to Cross (1988), it is a "set of congruent behaviors, attitudes, and policies that come together in a system, agency, or among professionals and enable that system, agency, or those professionals to work effectively in cross-cultural situations" (p. 13). It is not a new idea. It has been called "ethnic sensitive practice" (Devore and Schlesinger, 1981), "crosscultural awareness practice" (Green, 1982), "ethnic competence" (Green, 1982), and "ethnic minority practice" (Lum, 1986) by human service providers. It has been referred to as "intercultural communication" (Hoopes, 1972) by those working in international relations and "cross-cultural counseling" (Petersen, Draguns, Lonner, and Trimble, 1989) and "multicultural counseling" (Ponterotto, Casas, Suzuki, and Alexander, 1995) in the field of counseling psychology.

What is new, however, is the projected demand for such services and the urgent need for a comprehensive model of effective service delivery.

The work of Cross, Bazron, Dennis, and Isaacs (1989) on cultural competence offers a good example of such an evolving model. Cross is the executive director of the National Indian Child Welfare Association in Portland, Oregon. For over a decade, he and his associates have attempted to articulate an effective, reality-based, and comprehensive approach to cross-cultural service delivery.

Cross et al. begin by asserting that cultural competence, whether in a system, agency, or individual professional, is an ideal goal toward which to strive. It does not occur as the result of a single day of training, a few consultations with experts, reading a book, or even taking a course. Rather, it is a developmental process that depends on the continual acquisition of knowledge, the development of new and more advanced skills, and an ongoing self-evaluation of progress. Cross et al. further believe that a culturally competent care system must rest on a set of unifying values, or what might be called "assumptions," about how services are best delivered to People of Color. These values share the notions that being different is positive, that services must be responsive to specific cultural needs, and that they be delivered in a way that empowers the client. According to Cross et al., a culturally competent care system

- respects the unique, culturally defined needs of various client populations.
- acknowledges culture as a predominant force in shaping behaviors, values, and institutions.
- views natural systems (family, community, church, healers, etc.) as primary mechanisms of support for minority populations.
- starts with the "family," as defined by each culture, as the primary and preferred point of intervention.
- acknowledges that minority people are served in varying degrees by the natural system.
- recognizes that the concepts of "family," "community," and the like are different for various cultures and even for subgroups within cultures.
- believes that diversity within cultures is as important as diversity between cultures.
- functions with the awareness that the dignity of the person is not guaranteed unless the dignity of his or her people is preserved.
- understands that minority clients are usually best served by persons who are part of or in tune with their culture.
- acknowledges and accepts that cultural differences exist and have an impact on service delivery.
- treats clients in the context of their minority status, which creates unique mental health issues for minority individuals, including issues related to self-esteem, identity formation, isolation, and role assumption.
- advocates for effective services on the basis that the absence of cultural competence anywhere is a threat to competent services everywhere.
- respects the family as indispensable to understanding the individual because the family provides the context within which the person functions and is the primary support network of its members.
- recognizes that the thought patterns of non-Western peoples, though different, are equally valid and influence how clients view problems and solutions.
- respects cultural preferences that value process rather than product and harmony or balance within one's life rather than achievement.
- acknowledges that when working with minority clients process is as important as product.
- recognizes that taking the best of both worlds enhances the capacity of all.

- recognizes that minority people have to be at least bicultural, which in turn creates its own set of mental health issues such as identity conflicts resulting from assimilation, and so forth.
- functions with the knowledge that behaviors exist that are adjustments to being different.
- understands when values of minority groups are in conflict with dominant society values.

(From *Towards a Culturally System of Care* by T. L. Cross, B. J. Bazron, K. W. Dennis, & M. R. Isaacs, pp. 22–24. Georgetown University Child Development Center, Washington, DC. Reprinted by permission of the author.)

Taken together, these assumptions provide the psychological underpinnings of a truly cross-cultural model of service delivery. First, they are based on the experience of People of Color and those who have worked intimately with them. Second, they take seriously notions that are not typically included in dominant culture service models. These notions include the impact of cultural differences on mental health; the family and community as a beginning point for treatment; agency accountability to its constituent community; and biculturalism as an ongoing life experience for People of Color. Third, they provide a yardstick against which existing agencies can measure their own treatment philosophy and assumptions.

Assessing Agency Cultural Competence

Cross et al. (1989) have also defined a developmental continuum along which agencies differ and can be assessed according to their ability to deal effectively with cultural differences in their clients.

At one extreme are agencies that they describe as exhibiting "cultural destructiveness." Included are those whose policies and practices are actively destructive to cultures and their members. Although it is difficult to find examples of such blatant practices today, it is important to realize that "historically, some agencies have been actively involved in services that have denied people of color access to their natural helpers and healers, removed children of color from their families on the basis of race, or purposely risked the well-being of minority individuals in social and medical experiments without their knowledge or consent" (Cross et al., 1989, p. 14).

"Cultural incapacity" is the designation given to the next set of agencies along the continuum. These providers, although not intentionally destructive, lack the capacity to help People of Color and their communities. In the process of doing their work, they routinely perpetuate societal biases, beliefs in racial inferiority, and paternalism. In addition, they tend to discriminate in hiring practices, send messages that People of Color are not valued or welcome, and usually have lower expectations for these clients.

Agencies exhibiting "cultural blindness," the third group of providers, try to be unbiased in their approach but do so by asserting that race and culture make no difference in how they provide services and then proceed to apply a dominant cultural approach to all clients. They routinely ignore the cultural strengths and uniqueness of People of Color, encourage assimilation, and tend to blame victims rather than society for their problems.

More to the positive end of the continuum, providers move into a phase Cross et al. call "cultural precompetence." Such agencies are sincere in their efforts to become more multicultural but have had difficulty in making progress. They realize they have problems in serving minority ethnic group clients and have discovered this fact through ineffectual efforts at better serving a single ethnic population. They tend to lack a realistic picture of what is involved in becoming culturally competent and often succumb to either a false sense of accomplishment or a particularly difficult failure. In addition, they tend to fall prey to tokenism and put unrealistic hopes in the hiring of one or two Professionals of Color whose cultural competence they tend to overestimate. It is probably fair to say that the majority of human service agencies today are culturally precompetent, with some still functioning at the level of cultural incapacity.

The last two points on the continuum, which are still probably more hypothetical than real in today's service world, represent increasing levels of cultural competence. Agencies that possess "basic cultural competence" are well versed in the five skill areas believed to be essential to competent cross-cultural service delivery (to be described shortly). Such agencies also "work to hire unbiased employees, seek advice and consultation from the minority community, and actively decide what they are and are not capable of providing minority clients" (Cross et al., 1989, p. 17). Finally, "cultural proficiency," the positive endpoint of the continuum, refers to providers who, in addition to those qualities exhibited in basic cultural competence, advocate more broadly for multiculturalism within the general health care system and are engaged in original research on how to serve culturally different clients better and its dissemination.

Table 2–2 offers a summary of these six levels.

Having defined this continuum, Cross et al. are quick to point out that movement from one stage to the next takes significant effort. It requires a determined reshuffling of agency attitudes, policies, and practices; the implementation of skill development for all staff; and the serious involvement of all agency personnel: board members, policymakers, administrators, practitioners, and consumers alike. You may find it useful to consider where agencies with which you are familiar might be placed on this continuum and why.

Individual Cultural Competence Skill Areas

Turning their attention to the development of cultural competence in individual practitioners, Cross et al. (1989) define five basic skill areas necessary for effective cross-cultural service delivery. Each can be assessed on its own continuum, although growth in one tends to support positive movement in the others. It is believed that these skills must infuse not only the provider's work but also the general climate of agencies and the health care system as a whole.

These skill areas must be taught, supported, and, even more basically, introduced as underlying dimensions of everyday functioning within agencies.

■ **TABLE 2–2**   Continuum of Cultural Competence in Agencies

Level of Cultural Competence	Typical Characteristics
Cultural Destructiveness	Policies and practices are actively destructive of Communities and Individuals of Color.
Cultural Incapacity	Policies and practices unintentionally promote cultural and racial bias; discriminate in hiring; do not welcome, devalue, and hold lower expectations for Clients of Color.
Cultural Blindness	Attempt to avoid bias by ignoring racial and cultural differences (all clients are treated the same), yet adopt a mainstream approach to service delivery. Ignore cultural strengths of clients, encourage assimilation, and participate in victim blame.
Cultural Precompetence	Have failed at attempts toward greater cultural competence due to limited vision of what is necessary. Either hold false sense of accomplishment or overwhelmed by failure. Tend to depend on tokenism and overestimate impact of isolated Staff of Color.
Basic Cultural Competence	Incorporate five basic skill areas into ongoing process of agency. Work to hire unbiased staff, consult with Communities of Color, and actively assess who they can realistically serve.
Cultural Proficiency	Exhibit basic cultural competence, advocate for multiculturalism throughout the health care system, carry out original research on how to better serve Clients of Color, and disseminate findings.

Note. Adapted from *Towards a Culturally Competent System of Care* by Cross, Bazron, Dennis, and Isaacs, 1989. Washington, DC: Georgetown University Child Development Center.

The first skill area, for example, involves being aware of and accepting differences. For providers, this means respecting differences in their clients. At an agency level, however, a similar commitment to accepting and valuing diversity must also be evident in the clinical practices that are adopted, in the philosophy that is shared, and in the relationship between colleagues and with associates from other parts of the care system.

Awareness and Acceptance of Differences. A first step toward cultural competence involves developing an awareness of the ways in which cultures differ and realizing that these differences affect the helping process. While all people strive to meet the same basic psychological needs, they differ greatly in how they have learned to do so. Cultural differences exist in values, styles of communication, perception of time, meaning of health, community, and so on. In attuning one's efforts to work with clients from other cultures, acknowledging and looking at differences are as important as highlighting similarities. The discovery of exactly what dimensions of living vary with culture is an ever-evolving drama. Each individual begins life with a singular experience of culture that is taken for reality itself. Only with exposure to additional and differing cultural realities does one begin to develop an appreciation for the diversity in human behavior.

Equally critical to becoming aware of differences is accepting them. Rokeach (1960), in his analysis of the sources of prejudice, goes so far as to suggest that differences in beliefs and cultural views, rather than a reaction to race per se, are at the heart of racial antipathy. Most difficult is accepting cultural ways and values that are at odds with our own. For instance, as a success-oriented, hyperpunctual client of Northern European ancestry, I might find it very difficult to accept the perpetual "lateness" of individuals who belong to cultures where time is viewed as flexible and inexact. What eventually emerges in providers who are moving toward cultural competence, however, is a broadening of perspective that acknowledges the simultaneous existence of differing realities that requires neither comparison nor judgment. All exist in their own right and are different. Further along the continuum is a position where differences are not merely accepted but truly valued for the richness, perspective, and complexity they offer. A culturally competent practitioner actively and creatively uses these differences in the service of the helping process.

Self-awareness. It is impossible to appreciate the impact of culture on the lives of others, particularly clients, if one is out of touch with his or her own cultural background. Culture is a glue that gives shape to life experience, promoting certain values and experiences as optimal and defining what is possible. As a skill area, self-awareness involves understanding the myriad ways that culture impacts human behavior. "Many people never acknowledge how their day-to-day behaviors have been shaped by cultural norms and values and reinforced by families, peers, and social institutions. How one defines 'family,' identifies desirable life goals, views problems, and even says hello are all influenced by the culture in which one functions" (Cross, 1988, p. 2).

In addition, the skill of self-awareness requires sufficient self-knowledge to anticipate when one's own cultural limits are likely to be pushed, foreseeing potential areas of tension and conflict with specific client groups and accommodating them. If my day is tightly scheduled, as is the case in most agencies, and it is in the nature of my clients' culture to be late, I must find a strategy for meeting with them that allows me to remain true to my cultural values and concurrently allows them to do the same. Cultural self-awareness is an especially difficult task for many White providers who grew up in households where intact cultural pasts have been lost. What remains instead are bits and pieces of cultural identity and personal history that were long ago cut loose from extended family, traditions, and community and, as a result, lack meaning. Without such a felt sense of the role of culture in the lives of People of Color, certain areas of client experience become difficult to empathize with and understand.

Dynamics of Difference. Related to self-awareness is what Cross et al. (1989) call the "dynamics of difference." When client and provider come from different cultures, there is a strong likelihood that sooner or later they will miscommunicate by misinterpreting or misjudging the other's behavior. An awareness of the dynamics of difference involves knowing what can go wrong in cross-cultural communication and knowing how to set it right. Cultural miscommunication has two general sources: experiences either the client or practitioner has had with members of the other's group and the nature of current political relations between groups. Mexican immigrants, for example, tend to be hypervigilant in relation to anyone who is perceived as either White or authoritative. Or, given tensions between African Americans and Jews in the United States that emerged in the 1960s and 1970s a helping relationship between an African American provider and a Jewish client, or vice versa, might prove initially problematic. Dynamics of difference also involve differences in cultural style. If a teacher from a culture that interprets direct eye contact as a sign of respect works with a student who has been taught culturally to avert eye contact as a sign of deference, there is a good chance that the teacher will come away from their interaction with erroneous impressions of the student. If providers are prepared for the possibility of such cross-cultural miscommunication, they are better able to immediately diagnose a problem and more quickly set things back on track.

Knowledge of the Client's Culture. Cross et al. (1989) also believe that it is critical for providers to familiarize themselves with a client's culture so that behavior may be understood within its cultural context. Many serious mistakes can be avoided if only one would preface each attempt at analyzing client motivation or behavior by considering what it might mean within the context of the client's cultural group. Similarly, other kinds of cultural information can be clinically useful. "Workers must know what symbols are meaningful, how health is defined and how primary support networks are configured" (Cross, 1988, p. 4). Interpreting the behavior of someone who is culturally different without considering cultural context or ethnocentricity (i.e., from one's own cultural perspective) is fraught with danger as the following anecdote amply demonstrates.

Several years ago, during a period of particularly heavy immigration from Southeast Asia, Children's Protective Services received a rash of abuse reports on Vietnamese parents whose children had come to school with red marks all over their bodies. A bit of cultural detective work quickly turned up the fact that the children had been given an ancient remedy for colds called "cupping," which involves placing heated glass cups on the skin, leaving harmless red marks for about a day. The resulting fallout was a group of irate Vietnamese parents, always hyperattentive to the needs of their children, being deeply insulted by accusations of bad parenting and several workers feeling rather foolish about their cultural ignorance. Given the variety of populations that must be served and the diversity that exists within each of them, it is not reasonable to expect any single provider to be conversant in the ways of all cultures and subcultures. However, it is possible to learn to identify the kind of information that is required to understand what is going on in the helping situation and have available the use of cultural experts with whom one can consult.

Adaptation of Skills. The fifth skill area involves adapting and adjusting generic helping practices (that in reality, as we shall see, have their roots in the dominant cultural paradigm) to accommodate cultural differences. Such adaptations can take a variety of forms. Treatment goals can be altered to better fit cultural values. For example, a Chinese family may not feel comfortable working toward an outcome that involves greater assertiveness in their children. The style of interaction in which the helping process is carried out can be adjusted to something that is more familiar to the client. In many cultures, for instance, healing practices are highly authoritative and directive, with advice freely given by experts. Some clients only respond to healers by showing deference.

The definition of who is a family member, and thus should be included in treatment, can also vary greatly from culture to culture. Family therapy with African Americans, for instance, usually involves the inclusion of multiple generations as well as nonbiological family members such as good friends and neighbors. Time and place of meeting can be modified to fit the needs of those who could not ordinarily be available during traditional hours or would find it difficult or threatening to come to a professional office far from their community. Finally, treatment topics can be expanded to include issues that are unique to culturally different clients. Dealing with racism, resolving conflicts around assimilation and acculturation, and clarifying issues of ethnic identity are three examples. These five individual skill areas are summarized in Table 2–3.

■ **TABLE 2–3**   Summary of Individual Cultural Competence Skill Areas

Skill Area	Definition
Awareness and Acceptance	Culturally competent providers are aware of the existence of cultural differences, accept their reality and value, and actively and creatively use them in the service of helping.
Self-awareness	Culturally competent providers appreciate the impact of their own ethnicity and racial attitudes on potential clients and actively work to limit the impact of such factors.
Dynamics of Difference	Culturally competent providers are aware of likely areas of potential cross-cultural miscommunication, misinterpretation, and misjudgment; anticipate their occurrence; and have the skills to set them right.
Knowledge of Client's Culture	Culturally competent providers actively educate themselves in regard to a client's culture in order to understand behavior in its own cultural context. They also actively seek consultation with indigenous experts when necessary.
Adaptation of Skills	Culturally competent providers adapt and adjust generic helping practices to accommodate cultural differences to better meet the needs and goals of culturally different clients.

Note. Adapted from *Towards a Culturally Competent System of Care* by Cross, Bazron, Dennis, and Isaacs, 1989. Washington, DC: Georgetown University Child Development Center.

Defining Professional Standards

Arredondo, Toporek, Brown, Jones, Locke, Sanchez, and Stadler (1996) offer a somewhat different approach to defining individual cultural competence. Building on the work of Sue, Arredondo, and McDavis (1992), they describe a set of professional multicultural competencies that will "become a standard for curriculum reform and training of helping professionals" (p. 477).

As yet, however, no professional helping association has formally accepted such standards as part of their ethical guidelines, thereby compelling "ethical responsibility." What currently exist vis-à-vis standards of cultural competence in professional codes such as that of the American Counseling Association (1995) are general prescriptions of "nondiscrimination" and "respecting differences" (Section A.2) as well as "boundaries of competence" (Section C.2). But without specific guidelines as to what cultural competence specifically looks like, how is one to achieve, assess, or enforce it? According to Sue et al. (1992), this problem "represents one of the major shortcomings of our profession" (p. 481).

The framework that the two groups have developed defines three areas of characteristics of culturally skilled counselors, borrowed from Sue and Sue (1990). First, such counselors "understand their own worldviews, how they are the product of their cultural conditioning, and how it may be reflected in their counseling and work with racial and ethnic minorities" (p. 481). Second, they "understand and share the worldviews of their culturally different clients with respect and appreciation" (p. 481). Third, they "use modalities and define goals consistent with the life experiences and cultural values of clients" (p. 481). Next, each of these three general characteristics—counselor awareness of own assumptions, values, and biases; understanding the worldview of the culturally different client; and developing appropriate intervention strategies and techniques—is broken down into three dimensions that underlie them: attitudes and beliefs, knowledge, and skills. Nine competence areas (three characteristics by three dimensions) are thus defined as basic to a culturally skilled counselor or helper.

Counselor Awareness of Own Cultural Values and Biases
Beliefs and Attitudes

- Culturally skilled counselors believe that cultural awareness and sensitivity to one's own cultural heritage is essential.
- Culturally skilled counselors are aware of how their own cultural background and experiences, attitudes, and values and biases influence psychological processes.
- Culturally skilled counselors are able to recognize the limits of their multicultural competency and expertise.
- Culturally skilled counselors recognize their sources of discomfort with differences that exist between themselves and clients in terms of race, ethnicity, and culture.

Knowledge

- Culturally skilled counselors have specific knowledge about their own racial and cultural heritage and how it personally and professionally affects their definitions and biases of normality-abnormality and the process of counseling.
- Culturally skilled counselors possess knowledge and understanding about how oppression, racism, discrimination, and stereotyping affect them personally and in their work. This allows individuals to acknowledge their own racist attitudes, beliefs, and feelings. Although this standard applies to all groups, for White counselors it may mean that they understand how they may have directly or indirectly benefited from individual, institutional, and cultural racism as outlined in White identity development models.
- Culturally skilled counselors possess knowledge about their social impact upon others. They are knowledgeable about communication style differences, how their style may clash or foster the counseling process with Persons of Color or others different from themselves, and how to anticipate the impact it may have on others.

Skills

- Culturally skilled counselors seek out educational, consultative, and training experiences to improve their understanding and effectiveness in working with culturally different populations. Being able to recognize the limits of their competencies, they (a) seek consultation, (b) seek further training or education, (c) refer out to more qualified individuals or resources, or (d) engage in a combination of these strategies.
- Culturally skilled counselors are constantly seeking to understand themselves as racial and cultural beings and are actively seeking a nonracist identity.

Counselor Awareness of Client's Worldview

Attitudes and Beliefs

- Culturally skilled counselors are aware of their negative and positive emotional reactions toward other racial and ethnic groups that may prove detrimental to the counseling relationship. They are willing to contrast their own beliefs and attitudes with those of their culturally different clients in a nonjudgmental fashion.
- Culturally skilled counselors are aware of the stereotypes and preconceived notions that they may hold toward other racial and ethnic minority groups.

Knowledge

- Culturally skilled counselors possess specific knowledge and information about the particular group with which they are working. They are aware of the life experiences, cultural heritage, and historical background of their culturally different clients. This particular competency is strongly linked to the minority identity development models available in the literature.

- Culturally skilled counselors understand how race, culture, ethnicity, and so forth may affect personality formation, vocational choices, manifestation of psychological disorders, help-seeking behavior, and the appropriateness or inappropriateness of counseling approaches.
- Culturally skilled counselors understand and have knowledge about sociopolitical influences that impinge upon the life of racial and ethnic minorities.
- Culturally skilled counselors understand how immigration issues, poverty, racism, stereotyping, and powerlessness may affect self-esteem and self-concept in the counseling process.

Skills

- Culturally skilled counselors should familiarize themselves with relevant research and the latest findings regarding mental health and mental disorders that affect various ethnic and racial groups. They should actively seek out educational experiences that enrich their knowledge, understanding, and cross-cultural skills for more effective counseling behavior.
- Culturally skilled counselors become actively involved with minority individuals outside the counseling setting (e.g., community events, social and political functions, celebrations, friendships, neighborhood groups) so that their perspective of minorities is more than an academic or helping exercise.

Culturally Appropriate Intervention Strategies
Attitudes and Beliefs

- Culturally skilled counselors respect clients' religious and/or spiritual beliefs and values, including attributions and taboos, because these affect worldview, psychosocial functioning, and expressions of distress.
- Culturally skilled counselors respect indigenous helping practices and respect help-giving networks among communities of color.
- Culturally skilled counselors value bilingualism and do not view another language as an impediment to counseling (monolingualism may be the culprit).

Knowledge

- Culturally skilled counselors have a clear and explicit knowledge and understanding of the generic characteristics of counseling and therapy (culture-bound, class-bound, and monolingual) and how they may clash with the cultural values of various cultural groups.
- Culturally skilled counselors are aware of institutional barriers that prevent minorities from using mental health services.
- Culturally skilled counselors have knowledge of the potential bias in assessment instruments and use procedures and interpret findings in a way that recognizes the cultural and linguistic characteristics of the clients.

- Culturally skilled counselors have knowledge of family structures, hierarchies, values, and beliefs from various cultural perspectives. They are knowledgeable about the community where a particular cultural group may reside and the resources in the community.
- Culturally skilled counselors should be aware of relevant discriminatory practices at the social and community level that may be affecting the psychological welfare of the population being served.

Skills

- Culturally skilled counselors are able to engage in a variety of verbal and nonverbal helping responses. They are able to send and receive both verbal and nonverbal messages accurately and appropriately. They are not tied down to only one method or approach to helping but recognize that helping styles and approaches may be culture-bound. When they sense that their helping style is limited and potentially inappropriate, they can anticipate and modify it.
- Culturally skilled counselors are able to exercise institutional skills on behalf of their clients. They can help clients determine whether a "problem" stems from racism or bias in others (the concept of healthy paranoia) so that clients do not inappropriately personalize problems.
- Culturally skilled counselors are not averse to seeking consultation with traditional healers or religious and spiritual leaders and practitioners in the treatment of culturally different clients when appropriate.
- Culturally skilled counselors take responsibility for interacting in the language requested by the client and, if not feasible, make appropriate referrals. A serious problem arises when the linguistic skills of the counselor do not match the language of the client. This being the case, counselors should (a) seek a translator with cultural knowledge and appropriate professional background or (b) refer to a knowledgeable and competent bilingual counselor.
- Culturally skilled counselors have training and expertise in the use of traditional assessment and testing instruments. They not only understand the technical aspects of the instruments but also are aware of the cultural limitations. This allows them to use test instruments for the welfare of the culturally different clients.
- Culturally skilled counselors should attend to as well as work to eliminate biases, prejudices, and discriminatory contexts in conducting evaluations and providing interventions, and should develop sensitivity to issues of oppression, sexism, heterosexism, elitism, and racism.
- Culturally skilled counselors take responsibility for educating their clients to the processes of psychological intervention, such as goals, expectations, legal rights, and the counselor's orientation.

(From "Operationalization of the Multicultural Counseling Competencies" by P. Arredondo, R. Toporek, S. P. Brown, J. Jones, D. C. Locke, J. Sanchez, and H. Stadler, *Journal of Multicultural Counseling and Development*, 3, January 1996, 42–78. Copyright 1996. Reprinted with permission.)

Professional Guidelines for Multicultural Service In addition to defining professional competencies, as in Arrendondo et al. (1996), the American Psychological Association (2002) has gone even further in policing the profession vis-à-vis culture by creating broader guidelines for professional conduct of psychologists. In their *Guidelines on Multicultural Education, Training, Research, and Organizational Change for Psychologists,* the APA defines a broad range of professional activities for careful scrutiny. The following guidelines provide a sense of the breadth of coverage:

- Psychologists are encouraged to recognize that, as cultural beings, they may hold attitudes and beliefs that can detrimentally influence their perceptions of and interactions with individuals who are ethnically and racially different from themselves.
- Psychologists are encouraged to recognize the importance of multicultural sensitivity/responsiveness, knowledge, and understanding about ethnically and racially different individuals.
- As educators, psychologists are encouraged to employ the constructs of multiculturalism and diversity in psychological education.
- Culturally sensitive psychological researchers are encouraged to recognize the importance of conducting culture-centered and ethnical psychological research among persons from ethnic, linguistic, and racial minority backgrounds.
- Psychologists strive to apply culturally appropriate skills in clinical and other applied psychological practices.
- Psychologists are encouraged to use organizational change processes to support culturally informed organizational (policy) development and practices.

A comparison of the models of Cross et al. (1989), Arredondo et al. (1996), and the American Psychological Association (2002) shows significant overlap in the kinds of development and learning they see as essential for those who hope to move toward cultural competence. You may find it valuable to consider the specific categories of these different models and assess where you might currently fall. Of late, there has been an increase in the availability of good training programs and courses designed to develop such skill areas. These learning experiences use a variety of process and interactive techniques including self-exploratory and self-assessment exercises (such as those included in the activities sections of each chapter), immersion in alternative cultural environments, and observation and on-the-job training in culturally competent agencies.

■ Why Become Culturally Competent?

In the past, gaining what is now called cultural competence was an ethical decision undertaken by practitioners with a particularly strong moral sense of what was right and fair. Usually, such individuals sought training with the express purpose of working with specific cultural groups, and they gravitated to minority agencies. Mainstream providers, with their predominantly White client base, had little reason to pursue cultural competence. But today the picture is quite different. All agencies are seeing more culturally diverse clients walk through their doors, and it may not be long before cultural competence becomes a professional imperative. In time, cultural competence may be a routine requirement for all jobs, not just those in the helping professions. If the *Opportunity 2000* projections (Hudson Institute, 1988) are correct and over 50% of the new entrants into the job market will be People of Color, most Americans will find themselves in close working relationships with colleagues who are culturally different.

Whether it is a matter of working under a superior who is a Person of Color, supervising others from different backgrounds, or retaining good relations with colleagues who are culturally different, being skilled in cross-cultural communication will increasingly be an asset. Given the dramatic diversification currently under way in the United States, gaining cultural competence may someday reach a status comparable to that of computer literacy. Twenty-five years ago, computer skills were an isolated novelty. Today it is difficult to compete successfully in any job market without them. The same may eventually be true of cultural competence.

■ The Fear and Pain Associated with Moving Toward Cultural Competence

It is my experience that most people are rather apprehensive of learning about race and ethnicity, and they approach the topic with some reluctance and even dread. The same may be true for you. When I start a new class, the tension in the room is palpable. Students don't know what to expect. Race is a dangerous subject for everyone. People can come unglued in relation to it. White students wonder if they will be attacked, called racists, and made to feel guilty. Students of Color wonder if the class is "going to be for real" or just another "exercise in political correctness." Everyone wonders whether they will really be able to speak their minds, whether things might get out of control and, if so, whether I will be able to handle it. Their concerns are understandable.

What is more familiar are accusations and attacks, name-calling, and long, endless diatribes. Consider the diatribes about racial profiling, affirmative action, anti-immigrant legislation, and differing perspectives on terrorism.

What one doesn't hear about or talk about, and what must become a focus of attention if there is ever going to be any positive change in this arena, is the psychological pain and suffering caused by racism and the ways in which everyone is touched by it. I cannot help but think of these past students and their stories:

- The young White woman who was traumatized as a young child when her mother found her innocently touching the face of their African American maid

- The Latina girl who was never the same after being accused of stealing the new bike that her parents had scrimped and saved to buy for her
- The Jewish man who discovered at the age of 25 that his parents had been hiding from him the fact that they were Jews
- The Asian woman, adopted at birth by White parents, who could not talk to them about how difficult it was for her living in an all-White world
- The White woman consumed by guilt because of what she felt to be an irrational fear of African American and Latino men

There is clearly as much fear and nervousness about letting out such feelings as there is about the unknowns of working with clients from other cultures.

I try to alleviate the anxiety by reviewing the ground rules and assumptions that define how we will interact in class. My intention is to create a safety zone where students can talk about race in ways that cannot be talked about in normal daily life. The following guidelines are clearly spelled out at the beginning of the course:

- There will be no name-calling, labeling, or blaming one another. There are no heroes or villains in this drama; no good people or bad. Each of us harbors negative reactions toward those who are different. It is impossible to grow up in a society and not take on its prejudices. So, it is not a matter of whether one is a racist or not. We all are. Rather, it is a question of what negative racial attitudes one has learned so far and, from this moment on, what one is willing to do about them.
- Everything that is said and divulged in this classroom is confidential, and it is not to be talked about with anyone outside of here. Students often censure, measure their words, and are less than honest in what they say out of fear of either looking bad or having their personal disclosures treated insensitively or as gossip.
- As much as possible, everyone will personalize his or her discussion and talk about personal experiences. There is much denial around racism that serves as a mechanism for avoiding responsibility. Only by personalizing the subject and speaking in the first person, rather than the third, can this be avoided.
- You can say whatever you believe. This may, in turn, lead to conflict with others. That is okay. But you must be willing to look at it, take responsibility for your words, and learn from what ensues. Anything that happens during class is a learning opportunity. It can and may be analyzed as part of the process. The class is a microcosm of the outer racial world with all of its problems, and as such, honest interaction in class can shed valuable light on the dynamics of intergroup conflict.

Most students have serious questions about race and ethnicity that need to be answered or experiences in relation to them that must be processed and better understood. Significant learning about race and ethnicity cannot proceed without this happening. Opportunities to do so are rare, but only through such occasions can growth and healing begin. Once some safety has been established, the floodgates open and students become emboldened by the frank comments of others to share what is really on their minds. These are the kind of concerns that emerge:

- Why do so many immigrants to America refuse to learn English? If they want to live here and reap the benefits, the least they should be willing to do is learn our language. My parents came over from Italy. They were dirt poor but made successful lives for themselves. They didn't have all this help. I really don't understand why it should be any different for People of Color.

- This is all really new to me. I grew up in a small town in rural Oregon. There was one Black family, but they stayed to themselves mostly. It's confusing, and to be perfectly honest, it is also pretty scary. There's just so much anger. If I had a Client of Color, I'm not sure I would know what to say or do.

- My biggest issues are with Black men. I try to be supportive of them and understand the difficulties they face. But when I see them always with White women, overlooking me and my sisters and all we have to offer, I get really angry.

- To be perfectly honest, I hate being White. I feel extremely guilty about what we have done to People of Color and don't know how to make up for it. I don't feel I have any culture of my own. We used to joke about being Heinz 57–variety Americans. And I envy People of Color for all of their culture and togetherness. We tried practicing some Native American ways, but that didn't seem exactly right, and besides, we were never made to feel very welcome.

- I've come to realize how much racial hatred there was in my family while I was growing up, and this disturbs me greatly. I find it very hard to see my parents in this negative light and don't know what to do with all of this.

- It's gotten pretty hard being a White male these days. You've always got to watch what you say, and as far as getting a job, forget it. There's a whole line of women and minorities and disabled in front of you. I guess I sort of understand the idea of affirmative action, but just because I'm White doesn't mean I have it made. I find it very difficult just getting by financially. I don't see where all of this privilege is.

- I just can't buy all this cultural stuff. People are just people, and I treat everyone the same. I grew up in an integrated neighborhood. I always had a lot of Black and Latino friends and never saw them as different. Frankly, I think all of this focus on differences is creating the problem.

- I'm Jewish but am finding it hard to discover where I fit in all of this. I don't feel White, but everyone treats me and classifies Jews as White. I was very involved in the Civil Rights Movement a number of years ago; even worked down in the South for a summer registering voters. But that seems so far away, and now Blacks hate Jews. What did we do?

- I'm in this class because I have to be. I don't need to take a class on racism. I've lived it all my life. White people don't get it. They just don't want to see, and no class is going to open their eyes. What I'm not willing to do is be a token Person of Color in here.

Moving toward cultural competence is hard emotional work. Personal issues such as those just described have to be given voice and worked through.

Students need good answers to their questions and support in finding solutions to personal conflicts with the material. Each of five skill areas described by Cross et al. (1989) represents a new set of developmental challenges. It is as if a whole new dimension of reality—that of culture—has been introduced into a student's phenomenological world. Old beliefs about oneself, others, and what one does and does not have in common must be examined and adjusted where necessary. There are, in addition, vast amounts of information to learn and new cultural worlds to explore. Perhaps most exciting, however, are the ways in which one's mind has to stretch and grow to incorporate the implications of culture. Students who have progressed in their learning about cultural matters often speak of a transformation that occurs in the ways they think about themselves and the world.

Bennett (1993) has tried to describe these cognitive changes. Of particular interest is the qualitative shift that occurs in a person's frame of reference— what Bennett describes as movement from *ethnocentrism* to *ethnorelativism*. In typical ethnocentric thinking, culturally different behavior is assessed in relation to one's own cultural standards; it is good or bad in terms of its similarity to how things are done in one's own culture. In ethnorelative thinking, "cultures can only be understood relative to one another and . . . particular behavior can only be understood within a cultural context . . . cultural difference is neither good nor bad, it is just different . . ." (p. 26). People who make this shift increase their empathic ability and experience greater ease in adopting a process orientation toward living. When the actions of others are not assessed or judged, but just allowed to exist, it is far easier to enter into their felt experience and thereby empathize with them. Similarly, realizing that behavior, values, and identity itself are not absolute, but rather constructed by culture, frees one to appreciate more fully the ongoing process of living life as opposed to focusing entirely on its content or where one is going or has been. These skills not only transform how people think but also prepare them for working more effectively with culturally different clients.

■ Speaking Personally About Cultural Competence

An old adage states: "You get as much out of something as you put into it." The same is true for pursuing cultural competence and using this book as a beginning. There is much useful information in the pages that follow that cannot help but contribute to your growth as a provider of cross-cultural services. And that is certainly worth the "price of admission." But it can also be the start of a journey that can change you in deep and unpredictable ways. As suggested earlier, engaging in the serious pursuit of cultural competence can be transformational, not so much in a religious sense, but rather in a perceptual one.

Black and white thinking will eventually be replaced by relational and process thinking. You will, in time, think very differently than you do now. I can also guarantee that, at times, if you pursue a deeper understanding of culture, you will be disturbed and disoriented and find yourself feeling very lost and alone. I can remember the first time I experienced cultural relativity and realized that what I had for my entire life taken to be absolute reality, the underpinnings of my world, was in reality relative. It came from reading the books of Alan Watts on Zen Buddhism and beginning to explore meditation. What I found so disturbing and unsettling was the realization that there was more than one way to understand reality. I was never quite the same again, as if the center of my consciousness had shifted somewhat and everything looked a little different. It is an unhinging aspect of the journey, to say the least, that will often be repeated in mini-versions as one continues to delve into cultural material.

Two qualities will make a difference in how you relate to this book and ultimately in the pursuit of cultural competence. The first is self-honesty. There is an aspect of ethnocentrism that is self-delusional. It seeks to hide the fact that human experience can be relative and that there might be "another show in town." As will become evident in chapter 3, there is also in all of us a strong tendency to deny and hide from consciousness the negative feelings we hold about race, ethnicity, and cultural differences. Together these tendencies conspire to keep us in the dark. Only by pushing oneself to critically engage the concepts and material of this book and to discover precisely how they have played themselves out in the confines of one's life can the power of cultural competence be truly appreciated. The second quality is a sustained commitment. The kind of learning that leads to cultural competence is long-term. It is as much process as content, tends to be cumulative in nature, and is, as Cross et al. (1989), Sue et al. (1992), and Bennett (1993) jointly point out, highly developmental. This means that the you may go through various predictable stages of growth, emotion, and change. This book is only a beginning. What happens next—what additional cultural learning experiences you seek and the extent to which you seriously engage in providing services cross-culturally—is up to you.

■ Summary

We are currently experiencing a diversification of American society. This includes both a sizable increase in the actual numbers of People of Color in the United States and a decline in the relative percentage of Whites. Projections suggest that these trends will only increase. By 2060, for example, non-Hispanic Whites will represent less than 50% of the population. Two factors are primarily responsible for these changes in demographics: immigration rates and birthrates. The implications for our human services and mental health systems are staggering. Increasingly, we will be asked to provide services to individuals from non-majority cultures, those born outside of the United States, and those for whom English is not the primary language. Adequately serving these populations requires more than merely color-coding or applying bandages to a system designed for a monocultural White population. In its place, we must establish a new vision of serviced delivery based on the notion of cultural competence.

Cultural competence is the ability to effectively provide helping services cross-culturally. It can reside in individual practitioners, in agencies, and in a system of care. It is generally defined by an integrated series of awarenesses and attitudes, knowledge areas, and skills. Cross et al. (1989) offer a comprehensive model of effective cross-cultural service delivery. They define the underlying assumptions of such a model, levels of agency competence, and individual practitioner competence skill areas. The latter includes awareness and acceptance of difference, self-awareness, understanding the dynamics of difference, knowledge of the individual's culture, and ability to adapt skills to changing cultural needs and demands. Arredondo et al. (1996) define a series of professional multicultural competencies revolving around three themes: counselor awareness of own cultural values and biases, counselor awareness of client's worldview, and culturally appropriate intervention strategies. The American Psychological Association (2002) offers a set of comprehensive guidelines for multicultural practice among psychologists. Becoming culturally competent is increasingly a professional imperative and will eventually become a basis for hiring. Increasingly, human service practitioners will find themselves working with clients and colleagues who are culturally different.

Moving toward cultural competence is an emotionally demanding process that does not occur overnight or with a single course or workshop. There are few places in which it is safe to speak openly and honestly about ethnicity and race. Everyone has been personally hurt by prejudice and racism, Whites as well as People of Color. Developing cultural competence requires looking at the pain and suffering racism has caused as well as looking at one's own attitudes and beliefs. Gaining cultural competence can also provide enormous personal growth in the form of increased self-awareness, cultural sensitivity, nonjudgmental thinking, and broadened consciousness.

■ Activities

This and subsequent chapters end with various activities that will help you understand the chapter's material in deeper and more personal ways. Some of these are self-assessment exercises and activities. A theme that reverberates through the beginning chapters of this book is the critical nature of self-awareness. Again, it is not just a question of whether you hold racist attitudes and stereotypes or if you are involved with practices of institutional or cultural racism. We all do and are. Rather, the issue is discovering in what ways your thinking as a provider is slanted racially, how this affects your role as helper, and what you can do to change it. The exercises in this book are meant to stimulate increased self-awareness. They are useful in countering natural tendencies toward denial, avoidance, and rationalization in matters of race and ethnicity. They will be productive to the extent that you take them seriously, give sufficient time to process and complete each thoroughly, and approach them with honesty and candor.

1. *Keep a cultural journal.* As you study about race, culture, and ethnicity, you will begin to notice these issues more broadly in school, in work, and in

your personal life. It is a matter of becoming aware of what has always been there. One method of optimizing such learning is to keep a journal of your observations throughout the term or semester and regularly review past entries. You will also notice that observations stimulate questions. Also make note of these, and consider how you will go about answering these questions.

2. *Observe and analyze an organization's cultural competence.* This exercise will help you identify dynamics and aspects of racism and cultural insensitivity in organizations and agencies. Choose an agency or organization with which you are familiar. It may be one in which you are currently working or volunteering or one you are familiar with from the past. Answer the following questions, some of which may require you to do research or seek additional information.

   a. How many People of Color or other minority ethnic group members work in this organization, and what kind of jobs do they hold?
   b. How are people hired or brought into the organization? Is there anything about this process or what might be required that may differentially affect People of Color or other ethnic group members?
   c. Does the organization promote cultural diversity? Do any mission statements, plans, or projections in this direction exist? Can you discern any unwritten feelings or attitudes that prevail around race and ethnicity within the organization? Has it done anything specific to promote greater diversity?
   d. How would you describe the organizational culture? Do you feel that members of various Communities of Color would be comfortable entering and being a part of it? Specify your answers by group and explain in detail. How do you think your co-workers or fellow volunteers would react to the entry of a Person of Color?
   e. How is the organization run? Who has the power? Who makes decisions? Is there anything about the organization's structure that makes it accessible or inaccessible to People of Color?
   f. What does it feel like working or volunteering in this organization? Are there unique or unusual rules, policies, and styles of working? Would you say that the organization's culture is predominantly Euro-American? Explain.
   g. If it is a service organization or agency, who are its clients? Are there any efforts being made (or have there ever been any efforts) to broaden the racial and ethnic composition of the clientele?

You may find it particularly informative to have co-workers or fellow volunteers answer these questions and then compare answers or use the questions as stimuli for discussing the cultural competence of the organization.

3

Understanding Racism, Prejudice, and White Privilege

Ron Takaki (1993) begins his book *A Different Mirror* by recounting a simple but powerful incident. While riding in a taxi from the airport to a hotel in a large Eastern city for a conference on multiculturalism, the cab driver engaged Takaki in casual conversation. After the usual discussion of weather and tourism, the driver asked, "How long have you been in this country?" Takaki winced and then answered, "All my life . . . I was born in the United States . . . My grandfather came here from Japan in the 1880s. My family has been here, in America, for over a hundred years." The cab driver, obviously feeling uncomfortable, explained, "I was wondering because your English is excellent!" (p. 1).

Encapsulated in this incident are the basic feelings that fuel racial tensions in the United States. The cab driver was giving voice to a belief shared by the majority of White Americans that this country is European in ancestry and White in identity and that only those who share these characteristics truly belong. All others, no matter how long they have resided here, are viewed and treated with suspicion and relegated to the status of outsider. Takaki's wince tells the other side of the story. People of Color who also call the United States home are deeply disturbed by their second-class citizenry. Being reminded of their unequal and unwanted status is a daily occurrence. This country, they argue, has grown rich on the labor of successive generations of immigrants and refugees, and our reward should be the same as Whites—full citizenship and equal access to resources as guaranteed in the Constitution. The situation is only exacerbated by White America's seeming indifference to the enormous injustice that exists in the system. Cross-cultural service delivery is most usefully viewed against this backdrop.

The helping relationship is, after all, a microcosm of broader society and, as such, is susceptible to the same racial tensions and dynamics. It is suggested in chapter 2 that cultural competence depends on self-awareness and this includes, above all, an awareness of the attitudes and prejudices that providers bring to their work. Neither provider nor client exists in a vacuum. Rather, both carry into the helping situation prejudices and stereotypes about the other's ethnicity; if unaddressed, these biases cannot help but interfere with communication. In this chapter you will learn about the dynamics of racism: its structure and meaning, the functions it serves for the individual and for society, how it operates psychologically, and why it is so resistant to change. The chapter ends with a self-assessment tool: a series of exercises intended to help you explore personal prejudices, stereotypes, and attitudes toward specific ethnic groups.

■ Defining and Contextualizing Racism

According to Wijeyesinghe, Griffin, and Love (1997), *racism* is "the systematic subordination of members of targeted racial groups who have relatively little social power . . . by members of the agent racial group who have relatively more social power" (p. 88). It is supported simultaneously by individuals, the institutional practices of society, and dominant cultural values and norms. Racism is a universal phenomenon that exists across cultures and tends to emerge wherever ethnic diversity and perceived or real differences in group characteristics become part of a struggle for social power. In the case of the United States, African Americans, Latinos/as, Native Americans, and Asian Americans—groups we have been referring to as People of Color—have been systematically subordinated by the White majority.

There are four important points to be made initially about racism:

1. Prejudice and racism are not the same thing. Allport (1954) defines *prejudice* as an "antipathy," that is, a negative feeling, either expressed or not expressed, "based upon a faulty and inflexible generalization which places [a group of people] at some disadvantage not merited by their actions" (p. 10). Thus, prejudice is a negative, inaccurate, rigid, and unfair way of thinking about members of another group. All human beings hold prejudices. This is true for People of Color as well as for majority group members. But there is a crucial difference between the prejudices held by Whites and those held by People of Color. Whites have more power to enact their prejudices, and therefore negatively impact the lives of People of Color, than vice versa. It is not that members of one group can garner more animosity than the other. Rather, it is the fact that one group (in this case, Americans of Northern European descent), because of its position of power, can more fully translate its negative feelings into real social, political, economic, and psychological consequences for the targeted group. Because of this difference, the term *racism* is used in relation to the racial attitudes and behavior of majority group members. Similar attitudes and behaviors on the part of People of Color are referred to as prejudice and discrimination (a term commonly used to mean actions taken on the basis of one's prejudices). Another way of describing this relationship is that prejudice plus power equals racism.

2. Racism is a broad and all-pervasive social phenomenon that is mutually reinforced at all levels of society. In this regard, J. M. Jones (1972) distinguishes three levels of racism: individual, institutional, and cultural. *Individual racism* refers to "the beliefs, attitudes and actions of individuals that support or perpetuate racism" (Wijeyesinghe et al., 1997, p. 89). *Institutional racism* involves the manipulation of societal institutions to

give preferences and advantages to Whites and at the same time restrict the choices, rights, mobility, and access of People of Color. While individual racism resides within the person, the institutional variety is wired into the very fabric of social institutions: into their rules, practices, and procedures. Some forms of institutional racism are subtle and hidden; others are overt and obvious. All, however, serve to deny and limit access to those who are culturally different. *Cultural racism* is the belief that the cultural ways of one group are superior to those of another. In the United States, it takes the form of practices that "attribute value and normality to White people and Whiteness, and devalue, stereotype, and label People of Color as 'other,' different, less than, or render them invisible" (Wijeyesinghe et al., 1997, p. 93). Cultural racism can be found both in individuals and in institutions. In the former, it is often referred to as *ethnocentrism*. Each level of racism supports and reinforces the others, and together they contribute to its general resistance to change. Later sections of this chapter explore the workings of each in depth as well as inquire into their relevance for providers working with culturally different clients.

3. People tend to deny, rationalize, and avoid discussing their feelings and beliefs about race and ethnicity. Often, these feelings remain unconscious and are brought to awareness only with great difficulty. It is hard to look at and talk about race because there is so much pain and hurt involved. Children's natural curiosity about human differences is quickly tainted and turned into negative judgments and discomfort. They, often imperceptibly, pick up parental prejudices with little awareness (at least at first) that the racial slurs and remarks that come so easily cut to the very core of their victim's self-esteem.

   In a society so riddled with racial tensions, everyone is eventually hurt by racism. Accompanying the pain, there is always enormous anger, and anger, whether held inside or directed toward someone else, is hard to deal with.

4. When such emotions become overwhelming, people defensively either turn off or distance themselves from the source of their feelings. Such defenses become habitual, and they are usually firmly in place by adulthood, effectively blocking emotion around the topic of race. An interesting dynamic exists around empathizing with those who have been the target of racism. When young children hear the stories of People of Color, they tend to deeply and sincerely feel with the storyteller. "We are really sorry that you had to go through that" is the most common reaction of children. By the time one reaches adulthood, however, the empathy is often gone. Instead, reactions tend to involve minimizing, justifying, rationalizing, or other forms of emotional blocking. Human service providers are no less susceptible to such defensive behavior, but they must force themselves to look inward if they are sincere in their commitment to work effectively cross-culturally. For this reason, this chapter concludes with a set of activities and exercises aimed at stimulating self-awareness.

■ Individual Racism and Prejudice

The burning question that arises when one tries to understand the dynamics of individual racism is: Why is it so easy for individuals to develop and retain racial prejudices? As suggested earlier, racism seems to be a universal phenomenon that transcends geography and culture. Human groups have always exhibited it, and if human history is any lesson, they always will. The answer, according to Allport (1954), lies in the fact that racial prejudice has its roots in the "normal and natural tendencies" of how human beings think, feel, and process information. For instance, people tend to feel most comfortable with those who are like them and to be suspicious of those who are different. They tend to think categorically, to generalize, and to oversimplify their views of others. They tend to develop beliefs that support their values and basic feelings and avoid those that contradict or challenge them. And they tend to scapegoat those who are most vulnerable and subsequently rationalize their racist behavior. In short, it is out of these simple human traits and tendencies that racism grows.

Traits and Tendencies Supporting Racism and Prejudice

The idea of in-group and out-group behavior is a good place to begin. There seems to be a natural tendency among all human beings to stick to their own kind and to separate themselves from those who are different. One need not attribute this fact to any nefarious motives; it is just easier and more comfortable to do so. Ironically, inherent in this tendency to love and be most comfortable with one's own are the very seeds of racial hatred. As Allport (1954) suggests, "We prize our mode of existence and correspondingly underprize or actively attack what seems to us to threaten it" (p. 26). Thus, what is different can always be, and often is, perceived as a threat. The tendency to separate oneself from those who are different only intensifies the threat because separation limits communication and, thus, heightens the possibility of misunderstanding. With separation, knowledge of the other also grows vague, and this vagueness seems to invite distortion, the creation of myths about members of other groups, and the attribution of negative characteristics and intent to them.

Prejudice is also stimulated by the human proclivity for categorical thinking. It is a basic and necessary part of the way people think to organize perceptions into cognitive categories and to experience life through these categories. As one grows and matures, certain categories become very detailed and complex; others remain simplistic. Some become charged with emotions; others remain factual. Individuals and groups of people are also sorted into categories. These "people" categories can become charged with emotion and vary greatly in complexity and accuracy. On the basis of these categories, human beings make decisions about how they will act toward others.

For example, I have the category "Mexican." As a child, I remember seeing brown-skinned people in an old car at a stoplight and being curious about who and what they were. As we drove by, my father mumbled, "Dirty, lazy Mexicans," and my mother rolled up the window and locked her door. This and a variety of subsequent experiences, both direct and indirect (e.g., comments by others, the media, what I read, etc.), are filed away as part of my Mexican category and shape the way I think about, feel, and act toward Mexicans.

But it is even more complicated than this because categorical thinking by its very nature leads to oversimplification and prejudgment. Once a person has been identified as a member of an ethnic group, he or she is experienced as possessing all of the categorical traits and emotions internally associated with that group. I may believe, for instance, that Asian Americans are very good at mathematics and that I hate them because of it. If I meet individuals I identify as Asian American, I will both assume that they are good at mathematics and find myself feeling negative toward them.

Related is the concept of stereotype. Weinstein and Mellen (1997) define *stereotype* as "an undifferentiated, simplistic attribution that involves a judgment of habits, traits, abilities, or expectations . . . assigned as a characteristic of all members of a group" (p. 175). For instance, Jews are short, smart, and money-hungry; Native Americans are stoic and violent and abuse alcohol. Implied in these stereotypes is that all Jews are the same and all Native Americans are the same (i.e., share all characteristics). Ethnic stereotypes are learned as part of normal socialization and are amazingly consistent in their content. As a classroom exercise, I ask students to list the traits they associate with a given ethnic group. Consistently, the lists they generate contain the same characteristics down to minute details and are overwhelmingly negative. One cannot help but marvel at society's ability to transmit the subtlety and detail of these distorted ethnic caricatures. Not only does stereotyping lead to oversimplification in thinking about ethnic group members, but it also provides justification for the exploitation and ill treatment of those who are racially and culturally different. Because of their negative traits, they deserve what they get. Because they are seen as less than human, it is easy to rationalize ill treatment of them.

Categorical thinking and stereotyping also tend to be inflexible, self-perpetuating, and highly resistant to change. Human beings go to great lengths to avoid new evidence that is contrary to existing beliefs and prejudices.

Situations where old beliefs may be challenged or where contrary information might be found are avoided. In a similar manner, people holding like views are sought out as a means of reinforcing existing beliefs. That is why segregated housing and neighborhoods were such an effective means of perpetuating the racial status quo. Often when contrary information is encountered, it is unconsciously manipulated so as to leave ethnic categories unaffected. Say, for instance, I believe that African Americans are lazy. But one day, a new employee, an African American, is hired in my office, and I have never seen anyone work as hard or as diligently as this person. So how do I make sense of this fact, given my beliefs about African American laziness? What I do is treat him as an exception; that is, he is not like other African Americans. Allport (1954) calls this "re-fencing." Contrary information is, thus, briefly acknowledged. But by excluding this exception to my general stereotype ("He is really not like other African Americans"), I can retain my beliefs about African Americans in light of seemingly contradictory evidence.

A similar phenomenon involves the distortion of perceptions. Social psychologists have amply demonstrated that individuals perceive and remember material that is consonant with their attitudes and beliefs (Allport, 1954). They have shown that perceptions can be distorted to avoid the introduction of contrary information. A classic example is the recall of ambiguous pictures. Pictures are shown to subjects at such high speeds that they can barely perceive the content. The more ambiguous the exposure, the easier it is for the subject to distort perception so as to support existing prejudices. Thus, an individual with extremely negative attitudes toward African Americans, when shown a drawing of an African American man being followed by a White man carrying a sticklike object in one hand, may report seeing an African American with a knife or club chasing a White man.

Psychological Theories of Prejudice

Psychologists, such as Allport, suggest that the factors just discussed—ingroup and out-group behavior, categorical thinking and stereotyping, avoidance, and selective perception—together set the stage for the emergence of racism. But without the existence of some form of internal motivation, an individual's potential for racism remains largely dormant. In a similar manner, Wijeyesinghe et al. (1997) distinguish between active and passive racism: the extent to which an individual actively engages in or advocates violence and oppression against People of Color as opposed to taking a more covert and passive stand. Various theories have been offered regarding the psychological motivation behind prejudice and racism. In reality, there does not seem to be a single theory that can adequately explain the impetus toward racism in all individuals. More likely, there is some truth in all of the theories that follow, and in the case of any given individual, one or more of these may be at work. (The summary of theories that follows derives largely from Allport, 1954.)

Probably the most widely held theory of prejudice is known as the *frustration-aggression-displacement hypothesis.* This theory holds that as people move through life they do not always get what they want or need and, as a result, experience varying amounts of frustration. Frustration, in turn, creates aggression and hostility, which can be alternately directed at the original cause of frustration, directed inward at the self, or displaced onto a more accessible target. Thus, if my boss reprimands me, I go home and take it out on my wife, who in turn yells at the kids, who then kick the dog. Such displacement, according to the theory, is the source of racism. How does one choose an appropriate target for displacement? There are a number of competing theories. Williams (1947) believes that the target must be "visible and vulnerable." Dollard (1938) sees any group with which one is in competition as a potential target. Still others believe that the target often symbolizes certain attributes that the individual detests. Another theory holds that societal norms dictate the acceptable targets for displacement. Finally, there is the belief that the choice of targets depends on the "analytic" mechanism of projection. Individuals displace their hostility on groups who possess "bad" attributes, which are in reality unconsciously similar to attributes they detest in themselves. The irrationality of displacement requires the person to find a justification for his or her hatred. This is often done by creating myths about why the group being discriminated against really deserves such treatment or by drawing on existing stereotypes, negative traits, and theories of inferiority. During the period of American slavery, for example, many slave owners asserted that African Americans were subhuman and incapable of caring for themselves, and because of this, slavery was actually a benign and kindly institution.

A second theory holds that prejudice is part of a broader, global personality type. The classical example is the work of Adorno, Frankel-Brunswik, Levinson, and Sanford (1950) on what has become known as the *authoritarian personality*. Growing out of the horrors of World War II and the willingness of so many to collaborate and "merely follow orders," Adorno and his colleagues postulated the existence of a global bigoted personality type manifesting a variety of traits revolving around personal insecurity and a basic fear of everything and everyone different. Such individuals are believed to be highly repressed and insecure and to experience low self-esteem and high alienation. In addition, they tend to be highly moralistic, nationalistic, and authoritarian; to think in terms of black and white; to have a high need for order and structure; to view problems as external rather than psychological; and to feel anger and resentment against members of all ethnic groups.

Another theory suggests that racial prejudice evolves within a society to promote certain economic and political objectives, for example, slavery or the economic use of various immigrant labor populations such as the Chinese in building the Western railroad. Prejudicial attitudes evolve after the fact, created to justify the economic or social injustice.

A fourth theory holds that individuals adopt prejudicial attitudes as a means of buoying up their own self-esteem by viewing members of other groups as inferior.

A fifth theory attributes prejudice to social norms rather than individual motivation. It suggests that racial hatred is determined and sanctioned according to the dictates of specific geographic regions that have traditions of prejudice against given ethnic groups. Individuals residing in those regions internalize prejudices during socialization as a way of adjusting to a social norm of their community.

A final theory argues that prejudice is based not so much on racial differences as on perceived dissimilarities in belief systems (i.e., people tend to dislike those who think differently than they do).

All of these theories share the idea that through racist beliefs and actions individuals meet important psychological and emotional needs. To the extent that this process is successful, their hatred remains energized and reinforced. Within such a model, the reduction of prejudice and racism can occur only when alternative ways of meeting emotional needs are found.

Somebodies and Nobodies. A somewhat different approach to understanding the motivation behind prejudice and racism is offered by Fuller (2003). He suggests that underlying all of the "isms," that is, racism, sexism, classism, and so on, is the phenomenon of rankism. *Rankism* is the persistent abuse and discrimination based on power differences in rank or hierarchy. The experience of being ranked above or below others, which Fuller refers to as being a somebody or a nobody, exists throughout our social system and persists "in the presence of an underlying difference of rank signifying power." Somebodies receive recognition and experience self-satisfaction and pride in themselves; nobodies face derision and experience indignity and humiliation. Somebodies use the power associated with their rank to improve or secure their situation to the disadvantage of the nobodies below them. Fuller argues that a person's self-esteem and identity are based on the recognition and appreciation that he or she receives and that a lack of recognition can have serious mental health consequences.

> As the hunger for recognition mounts, the undernourished may become desperate. An outcast starved for recognition who attacks others or himself is giving expression to the unendurable indignity of feeling inconsequential . . . Chronic recognition deficiencies can culminate in recognition disorders (like eating disorders) that are so severe, they take the form of aggressive behavior—even war and genocide . . . Recognition is not about whether we are a somebody or nobody, but rather about whether we feel we're taken for a somebody or a nobody. The willingness of others to acknowledge us is a measure of their respect. Unrecognized, we feel rejected; we're cast as non-persons, pawns in other people's employ. Recognized, we count, we matter, we may even find ourselves in charge. (Fuller, 2003, pp. 49–50)

Implications for Providers

What does all of this information about individual racism have to do with human service providers? Put most directly, it is the source or at least a contributing factor to many problems for which culturally different clients seek help. Some clients present problems that revolve around dealing with racism directly. They live with it on a daily basis. Relating to the racism they encounter in a healthy and non-self-destructive manner is, therefore, a major challenge. To be the continual object of someone else's hatred as well as that of an entire social system is a source of enormous stress, and such stress takes its psychological toll. It is no accident, for example, that African American men suffer from and are at particularly high risk for stress-related physical illnesses.

Other clients present with problems that are more indirect consequences of racism. A disproportionate number of People of Color find themselves poor and with limited resources and skills for competing in a White-dominated marketplace. The stress caused by poverty places people at high psychological risk. More affluent People of Color are no less susceptible to the far-reaching consequences of racism. Life goals and aspirations are likely blocked or at least made more difficult because of the color of their skin. There is a saying among Professionals of Color that one has to be twice as good as one's White counterpart to make it. This, too, is a source of inner tension, as are the doubts a Professional of Color may have as to whether he or she received a job or promotion because of ability or skin color.

It is critical that providers become aware of the prejudices that they hold as individuals. (Exercises at the end of this chapter, if undertaken with honesty and seriousness, can provide valuable insight into your feelings and beliefs about other racial and ethnic groups.) Without such awareness, it is all too easy for providers to confound their work with their prejudices. For example, if I think stereotypically about Clients of Color, it is very likely that I will define their potential too narrowly, miss important aspects of their individuality, and even unwittingly guide them in the direction of taking on the very stereotyped characteristics I hold about them. My own narrowness of thought will limit the success I can have working with culturally different clients. It is critical to remember that prejudice often works at an unconscious level and that professionals are susceptible to its dynamics. It is also critical to be aware that, after a lifetime of experience in a racist world, Clients of Color are highly sensitized to the nuances of prejudice and racism and can identify it very quickly. Finally, it is important to re-emphasize that professional codes of conduct consider it unethical to work with a client with whom one has a serious value conflict. Prejudice and racism are such value conflicts.

■ Institutional Racism

Consider the following statistics from Hacker (1992) about African Americans in the United States:

- Of the prisoners in the United States, 45.3% are African Americans.
- 44.8% of African American children live below the poverty level.
- Life expectancy of African Americans is 93% that of Whites.
- The infant mortality rate for African American babies is twice that of White babies.
- African Americans are 7 times more likely to contract tuberculosis, 2.5 times more likely to get diabetes, and 1.40 times more likely to suffer from heart disease than Whites.
- The income of African American families is 58% that of White families.
- The unemployment rates among African Americans is 2.76 times that of Whites.
- African Americans are overrepresented in low-pay service occupations (e.g., nursing aides and orderlies, 30.7%) and underrepresented among professionals (e.g., architects, 0.9%).
- Whites are 1.92 times more likely to have attended 4 or more years of college than African Americans.
- In the state of Illinois, 83.2% of African American children attend segregated schools.

These are the consequences of institutional racism: the manipulation of societal institutions to give preferences and advantages to Whites and at the same time restrict the choices, rights, mobility, and access of People of Color. In each of these varied instances, African Americans are seen at a decided disadvantage or at greater risk compared to Whites. The term *institution* refers to "established societal networks that covertly or overtly control the allocation of resources to individuals and social groups" (Wijeyesinghe et al., 1997, p. 93). Included are the media, the police, courts and jails, banks, schools, organizations that deal with employment and education, the health system, and religious, family, civil, and governmental organizations. Something within the fabric of these institutions causes discrepancies such as those just listed to occur on a regular and systematic basis.

In many ways, institutional racism is far more insidious than individual racism because it is embedded in bylaws, rules, practices, procedures, and organizational culture. Thus, it appears to have a life of its own and seems easier for those involved in the daily running of institutions to disavow any responsibility for it.

Determining Institutional Racism

How does one go about determining the existence of institutional racism? The most obvious manner is through the reports of victims themselves—those who regularly feel its effects, encounter differential treatment, and are given only limited access to resources. But such firsthand reports are often held suspect and are too easily countered by explanations of "sour grapes" or "they just need to pull themselves up by their own bootstraps" by those who may not, for a variety of reasons, want to look too closely at the workings of racism.

A more objective strategy is to compare the frequency or incidence of a phenomenon within a group to the frequency within the general population. One would expect, for example, that a group that comprises 10% of this country's population would provide 10% of its doctors or be responsible for 10% of its crimes. When there is a sizable disparity between these two numbers (i.e., when the expected percentages don't line up, especially when they are very discrepant), it is likely that some broader social force, such as institutional racism, is intervening.

One might alternatively argue that something about members of the group itself, rather than institutional racism, is responsible for the statistical discrepancy. Such explanations, however, with the one exception of cultural differences (to be described), must be assessed very carefully because they are frequently based on prejudicial and stereotypical thinking. For instance, members of Group X consistently score lower on intelligence tests than do dominant group members. One explanation may be that members of Group X are intellectually inferior. However, there has long been debate over the scientific merit of taking such a position that has yet to prove anything more than the fact that proponents who argue on the side of racial inferiority in intelligence tend to enjoy the publicity they inevitably receive. An alternative and more scientifically compelling explanation is that intelligence tests themselves are culturally biased and, in addition, favor individuals whose first language is English.

There are indeed aspects of a group's collective experience that do predispose members to behave or exhibit characteristics in a manner different from what would be expected statistically. For instance, because of ritualistic practices, Jews tend to experience relatively low rates of alcoholism. Therefore, it is not surprising to find that the percentage of Jews suffering from alcohol abuse is disproportionately lower than their representation in the general population.

Such differences, however, tend to be cultural rather than biological.

Consciousness, Intent, and Denial

Institutional racist practices can be conscious or unconscious and intended or unintended. "Conscious or unconscious" refers to the fact that people working in a system may or may not be aware of the practices' existence and impact. "Intended or unintended" means that the practices may or may not have been purposely created, but they nevertheless exist and substantially affect the lives of People of Color. A similar distinction was made early in the Civil Rights Movement between de jure and de facto segregation. The former refers to segregation that was legally sanctioned and the existence of actual laws dictating racial separation. De jure segregation was, thus, both conscious and intended. De facto segregation, on the other hand, implies separation that exists in actuality or after the fact but may not have been consciously created for racial or other purposes.

It is important to distinguish among consciousness, intent, and accountability. I may have been unaware that telling an ethnic joke could be hurtful, and I might not have intended any harm; however, I am still responsible for the consequences of my actions and the hurt that may result. Similarly, someone I know works in an organization that unknowingly excludes People of Color from receiving services, and it was never his or her intention to do so. But again, intention does not justify consequences, and as an employee of that institution, he or she should be aware of its actions. Thus, lack of intent or awareness should never be regarded as justification for the existence of or compliance with institutional or individual racism.

Although denial is an essential part of all forms of racism, it seems especially difficult for individuals to take personal responsibility for institutional racism.

- First, institutional practices tend to have a history of their own that may precede the individual's tenure in the organization. To challenge or question such practices may be presumptuous and beyond one's power or status. Or one might feel that he or she is merely following the prescribed employee practices or a superior's dictates and, thus, cannot fairly be held responsible for them. Similar logic is offered in discussions of slavery and White responsibility. "I never owned slaves; neither did my ancestors. That happened 150 years ago. Why should I be expected to make sacrifices in my life for injustices that happened long ago and were not of my making?"
- Second, people tend to feel powerless in relation to large organizations and institutions. Sentiments such as, "You can't fight city hall" and "What can

one person do?" seem to prevail. The distribution of tasks and power and the perception that decisions are made "above" contribute further to feelings of powerlessness and alienation.

- Third, institutions are by nature conservative and oriented toward keeping the status quo. Change requires far more energy and is generally considered only during times of serious crisis and challenge. Specific procedures for effecting change are seldom spelled out, and important practices tend to be subtly yet powerfully protected.

- Fourth, the practices of an institution that support institutional racism (i.e., that keep People of Color out) are multiple, complicated, mutually reinforcing, and, therefore, all the more insidious. Even if one were to undertake efforts to change sincerely, it is often difficult to know exactly where to begin.

To provide a better sense of the complexity with which institutional racism asserts itself, I would like to share two very different case studies.

 ## *Case Study 1*

The first is an excerpt from a cultural evaluation of Agency X focusing on staffing patterns. The purpose of the project was to assess the organization's ability to provide culturally sensitive services to its clients and to make recommendations as to how it might become more culturally competent. Although the report does not directly point to instances of institutional racism in staffing practices, they become obvious as one reads through the text and its recommendations.

Currently, People of Color are underrepresented on the staff of Agency X. In the units under study, only two workers are of Color: a Latino and an African American male. Neither are supervisors. In the entire office, only seven staff members are of Color: two Latino/as, one African American, and three Asian Americans. Two of the Asian Americans are supervisors. There are no People of Color in higher levels of management. An often-cited problem is the fact that there are few minority candidates on the state list from which hiring is done. To compensate requires special and proactive recruitment efforts to get People of Color on the lists as well as the creation of special positions and other strategies for circumventing such lists. At a systems level, attention must be given to screening practices that may inadvertently and unfairly reject qualified minority candidates. While parity in numbers of Staff of Color to population demographics should be an important goal, holding to strict quotas misses the point of cultural competence. The idea is to strive for making the entire organization, all management and staff, more culturally competent, that is, able to work effectively with those clients who are culturally different. Nor is it reasonable to assume that all Staff of Color will be culturally competent. While attempting to add more Staff of Color, it is highly useful to fill the vacuum through the use of community resources and professionals hired specifically to provide cultural expertise.

In general, the staff interviewed were found to be in need of cultural competence training. This would include awareness of broader issues of culture and cross-cultural communication, history and cultural patterns of specific minority cultures, and implications of cultural differences for the provision of client services. Especially relevant was knowledge of normal vs. dysfunctional family patterns within different cultural groups so that culturally sensitive and accurate assessments might be carried out. In moving towards a family support model within the agency, as was indicated by several staff members during our interviews, it is critical to understand family dynamics of a given family from the perspective of its culture of origin as opposed to a singular, monocultural Euro-American perspective. Also evident was a basic conflict within the organization between treatment and corrections models of providing services. Staff adhering to the latter tended to devalue the importance of cultural differences in working with Clients of Color and tended to see Youth of Color as using racism and cultural differences as an excuse for not taking responsibility for their own behavior.

White staff members report the following needs and concerns in regard to working with Children of Color: need help in identifying culturally appropriate resources and placements; discomfort in dealing with issues of race; don't know the right questions to ask; families often unwilling to discuss or acknowledge race as an issue; the need for more and better training; lack of knowledge about biracial children; and the need for a better understanding of the role of culture in the service model they use.

Staff of Color did not report any experiences of overt discrimination and felt respected by their colleagues. They believed that Agency X was, in fact, trying to deal with the problem of cultural diversity, but that this interest was of rather recent vintage and motivated primarily by political and legal concerns. They also suggested that the liberal climate of the organization did much to justify a pervasive attitude that "we treat everyone the same" and "I know good service provision and can deal with anyone." Together such attitudes often served as an excuse for not dealing directly with cultural differences in clients. They also stated that cultural diversity was experienced by some co-workers as an extra burden, requiring extra work from them. As in most work situations, the Staff of Color did experience some distance from co-workers. The onus of keeping up good relations was often felt to be on the Person of Color to put their White co-workers at ease. Staff of Color we interviewed were subject to especially high burnout potential and needed their own resources and support outside the organization. We found both Staff of Color in the units under investigation to be especially strong and competent individuals who were particularly stretched thin between their regular duties and their roles within the organization as cultural experts.

The recent hiring of a Latino professional by Agency X, as a means of dealing with a growing Spanish-speaking population, deserves some comment. The need to provide services to this population has been well documented by the demand that has already arisen for his services. We are concerned, however, that the way in which the position was created will eventually lead to

(continued)

burnout and failure and that much more support for the position must be consciously and systematically provided. We perceive an expectation from within and from outside the organization that this individual will be able to "do it all"—help organize an advisory board and provide services to it, do outreach to the Latino/a community, be an in-house cultural expert, be an advocate with other agencies and a referral source for all Latino/a members of the community, and carry a full caseload of Latino/a and non-Latino/a families. The work demands are already cutting into personal time, and as he deals with other agencies and realizes the lack of culturally relevant services available elsewhere, he becomes even further burdened.

Providing culturally competent services to the Latino/a community, as Agency X is now trying to do, will merely open the floodgates of additional demands for services. The current position holder suggested: "The agency doesn't realize that this is only the tip of the iceberg." It is likely that Agency X will soon be faced with adding bicultural, bilingual staff to meet the growing need. In this regard two caveats should be offered. First, culturally sensitive workers and those assigned caseloads of individuals from non-Euro-American cultures tend to work most effectively and creatively when they are allowed maximum flexibility, leeway, and discretion in how they carry out their duties. Rules and policies established in the context of serving Euro-American clients may be of little help and possibly obstructive to working with culturally different groups. Second, the existence of a defined cultural expert in an organization should not be viewed in any way as a justification for not actively pursuing the cultural competence of the agency in general and its staff.

 Case Study 2

The second case study, drawn from the work of Oakland psychiatrist Terry A. Kupers, deals with prisons, mental health, and institutional racism. Kupers (1999) argues that a disproportionate number of mentally ill individuals reside in prison, receive limited or no treatment, and decompensate as a result of the trauma and stress of life behind bars. These same conditions cause previously normal inmates to regularly experience "disabling psychiatric symptoms as well" (p. xvii). Especially dramatic is the impact of these conditions on Prisoners of Color.

According to Kupers, "Racism permeates the criminal justice system" (p. 94). People of Color are more likely than Whites to be stopped, searched, arrested, represented by public defenders, and receive harsh sentences. Incarceration rates are badly distorted as 50% of the current prison population is African American, 15% is Latino/a, and Native Americans are dramatically overrepresented in relation to their numbers in the general population. It is estimated that by the year 2020, one third of African Americans and one quarter of Hispanics aged 18 to 34 years will be

in the criminal justice system. The numbers grow even more disproportionate as the level of incarceration becomes more severe. For example,
minimum security units are primarily White, "whereas the supermaxi-
mum security units contain up to 90 or 95% blacks and Latinos" (p. 95).

The prisons themselves are replete with racial tensions, and "racial lines
are drawn sharply" within the institutions (p. 93). For their own protection,
prisoners self-segregate along racial lines and gangs dominate the political
landscape. When tensions rise in the prison yard, inmates "quickly join the
largest group of their own race they can reach" (p. 96). Some analysts suggest that racial tensions are kept alive within the system as a means of social
control, and that there are many little things that keep Blacks and Whites
angry at each other. The bottom line, according to Kupers, is that "race matters very much, to everyone" (p. 96).

Located primarily in rural settings, a majority of prison staff is White,
as are those who sit on hearing and appeals panels. In general, they lack
experience and knowledge of People of Color and tend to view racially different prisoners in stereotypical ways. Complaints of racial discrimination
among guards are rampant. Jobs, supervisory positions, and training tend
to be doled out along racial lines with the more prestigious and better
paying ones going to White inmates. At times, practices are just plain cruel.
Kupers tells the story of an African American inmate who was "confined in
a cell covered with racist graffiti" (p. 98). Although there are "good" guards,
inmates complain that codes "among correctional officers" make it difficult "to interfere when a 'bad cop' is harassing or brutalizing a prisoner"
(pp. 98–99). There are even accusations of guards inciting interracial and
gang violence.

Prison life cannot help but remind Prisoners of Color of the injustices
and discriminations they have experienced in the outside world. Kupers
feels that there is good reason for Prisoners of Color to fear being abused
because of race behind bars and that such fear "creates psychiatric symptoms" (p. 103). Stable prisoners are traumatized, and those with histories of
mental illness tend to deteriorate and become self-destructive. When victimized by racism, the former report feeling frustrated and full of rage,
despair, and powerless. If they cannot hold on to sanity by remaining in contact with family and community or planning for release, the result is often
lethargy and/or acting out in fits of defiance. Kupers reports observing significant "anxiety, depression, panic attacks, phobias, nightmares, flash-
backs, and uncontrollable rage reactions" in these prisoners (pp. 104–105).
The plight of less stable Prisoners of Color is even more precarious.

In the face of persistent and significant racism, they decompensate.
Especially frequent are two patterns of emotional breakdown, depending
on the prisoner's mental history. Some are driven to clinical depression
due to increasing cycles of hopelessness and despair. Others, in the grip
of ever increasing rage, move toward ego disintegration and psychosis.

(continued)

In both cases, the breakdown tends to be progressive as the correctional staff responds to the increasingly symptomatic behavior with more oppressive measures. Finally, in relation to treatment, Prisoners of Color are more likely to be labeled "paranoid" and "disruptive," punished by being sent to "lock-up" rather than treated, and medicated as opposed to receiving psychotherapy or admittance to prison mental health programs. Kupers summarizes his findings vis-à-vis institutional racism in prison as follows: "Prisoners of Color are doubly affected by racial discrimination behind bars. Racism plays a big part in the evolution and exacerbation of their psychiatric symptomology, and they are more likely than whites to be denied adequate mental health services" (p. 111).

Implications for Providers

What, then, are the implications of institutional racism for human service providers? First and foremost, the vast majority of providers work in agencies and organizations that may suffer in varying degrees from institutional racism. To the extent that the general structure, practices, and climate of an agency make it impossible for Clients of Color to receive culturally competent services, the efforts of individual providers, no matter how skilled, are drastically compromised.

It is just not possible to divorce what happens between a provider and clients from the larger context of the agency. Culturally different clients may avoid seeking services from an agency once they are familiar with its practices. (Such information travels very quickly within a community.) If they must come, their willingness to trust and enter a working relationship with the individual provider to whom they are assigned is seriously diminished.

Again, their work with individual staff members is affected by how clients perceive and experience the agency as a whole. In their eyes, the provider is always a part of the agency and perceived as responsible for what it does. Finally, the ability to do what is necessary to meet the needs of a culturally different client may be limited by the rules and atmosphere of the workplace. Are there support, resources, and knowledgeable supervision for working with culturally different clients? Is the provider afforded enough flexibility to adapt services to the cultural demands of clients from various cultural groups? If the answer to either of these questions is no, then the provider must be willing to try to initiate changes in how the organization functions—its structure, practices, climate—so that it can be supportive of efforts to provide more culturally competent services.

■ Cultural Racism

Closely associated with institutional racism is cultural racism—the belief that the cultural ways of one group are superior to those of another. Whenever I think of cultural racism, I remember a Latino student once telling a class about painful early experiences in predominantly White schools:

> One day a teacher was giving us a lesson on nutrition. She asked us to tell the class what we had eaten for dinner the night before. When it was my turn, I proudly listed beans, rice, tortillas. Her response was that my dinner had not included all of the four major food groups and, therefore, was not sufficiently nutritious. The students giggled. How could she say that? Those foods were nutritious to me.

Institutions, like ethnic groups, have their own cultures: languages, ways of doing things, values, attitudes toward time, standards of appropriate behavior, and so on. As participants in institutions, people are expected to adopt, share, and exhibit these cultural patterns. If they don't or can't, they are likely to be censured and made to feel uncomfortable in a variety of ways. In the United States, the cultural form that has been adopted by and dominates all social institutions is White Northern European culture. The established norms and ways of doing things in this country are dictated by the various dimensions of this dominant culture. Behavior outside its parameters is judged bad, inappropriate, different, or abnormal. Thus, the eating habits with which my student was raised in his Latino home, in that they differed from what White culture considers nutritious, were judged unhealthy and he was made to feel bad and ashamed because of it. Herein lies the real insidiousness of cultural racism—those who are culturally different must either give up their own ways, and thus a part of themselves, and take on the ways of majority culture or remain perpetual outsiders. (Some people believe it is possible to be bicultural, that is, to learn the ways and function comfortably in two very different cultures. This idea is discussed in chapter 5.) Institutional and cultural racism are thus two sides of the same coin. Institutional racism keeps People of Color on the outside of society's institutions by structurally limiting their access. Cultural racism makes them uncomfortable if they do manage to gain entry. Its ways are foreign to them, and they know that their own cultural traits are judged harshly.

Wijeyesinghe et al. (1997) offer the following examples of cultural racism:

- Holidays and celebrations: Thanksgiving and Christmas are acknowledged officially on calendars. "Traditional" holiday meals, usually comprising foods that represent the dominant culture, have become the norm for everyone. . . . Holidays associated with non-European cultures are given little attention in United States culture.
- Personal traits: Characteristics such as independence, assertiveness, and modesty are valued differently in different cultures.
- Language: "Standard English" usage is expected in most institutions in the United States. Other languages are sometimes expressly prohibited or tacitly disapproved of.
- Standards of dress: If a student or faculty member dresses in clothing or hairstyles unique to their culture, they are described as "being ethnic," whereas the clothing or hairstyles of Europeans are viewed as "normal."
- Standards of beauty: Eye color, hair color, hair texture, body size, and shape ideals exclude most People of Color. For instance, black women who

have won the Miss America beauty pageant have closely approximated white European looks.

■ Cultural icons: Jesus, Mary, Santa Claus, for example, are portrayed as White. The devil and Judas Iscariot, however, are often portrayed as Black. (p. 94)

Implications for Providers

Cultural racism has relevance for human service providers in several ways. First, it is important that providers be aware of the cultural values that they, as professionals, bring to the counseling session and acknowledge that these values may be different from and even at odds with those of their clients. This is especially true for White providers working with Clients of Color. It is not unusual for Clients of Color to react to White professionals as symbols of the dominant culture and to initially act out their frustrations with a society that so systematically negates their cultural ways. Second, all helping across cultures must involve some degree of negotiation around the values that define the helping relationship. Most important, therapeutic goals and the general style of interaction must make sense to the client. Yet, at the same time, they must fall within the broad parameters of what the provider conceives as therapeutic. Most likely, the provider will have to make significant adaptations to standard methods of helping to fit the needs of the culturally different client. Third is the realization that traditional training as helping professionals and the models that inform this training are themselves culture-bound and have their roots in dominant Northern European culture. As such, what exactly are the values and cultural imperatives that providers bring to the helping relationship? And what relevance do these have for clients whose cultural worldview might be very different? Cultures differ greatly in how they view healing and how they conceive of the helping process. The notion of seeking professional help from strangers makes little sense in many cultures. Similarly, questions of what is healthy behavior and how one treats dysfunction vary greatly across cultures. Given all of this cultural variation and the ethnocentricity of traditional helping models and methods, helping professionals must answer for themselves a number of very knotty questions. Is it possible, for example, to expand culture-bound models so they can become universally applicable (i.e., appropriately applied multiculturally)? And if so, what would such a model look like? Or is there, perhaps, some truth to the contention of many minority professionals that something in the Northern European dominant paradigm is inherently destructive to traditional culture, and radically different approaches to helping must be forged for each ethnic population? These questions are addressed in chapter 4.

■ Racial Consciousness Among Whites

White Privilege

In a very heated classroom discussion of diversity, several White male students complained bitterly: "It has gotten to a point where there's no place we can just be ourselves and not have to watch what we say or do all the time." The rest of the class—women and ethnic minorities—responded in unison: "Hey, welcome to the world. The rest of us have been doing that kind of self-monitoring all of our lives." What these men were feeling was a threat to their privilege as men and as Whites, and they did not like it one bit. Put simply, *White privilege* encompasses the benefits that are automatically accrued to European Americans just on the basis of their skin color. Most insidious is that, to most Whites, it is all but invisible. For them, it is so basic a part of daily experience and existence, and so available to everyone in their "world," that it is never acknowledged or even given a second thought. Or at least, so it seems.

If one digs a little deeper, however, there is a strong element of defensiveness and denial. Whites tend to see themselves as individuals, just "regular people," part of the human race, but not as members of a racial group. They are, in fact, shocked when others relate to them racially (i.e., as "White"). In a society that gives such serious lip service to ideas of equality and equal access to resources ("With enough hard work, anyone can succeed in America" or "Any child can nurture the dream of someday being president"), it is difficult to acknowledge one's "unearned power," to borrow McIntosh's (1989) description.

It is also easier to deny one's White racial heritage and see oneself as colorless than to allow oneself to experience the full brunt of what has been done to People of Color in this country in the name of White superiority. Such awareness demands some kind of personal responsibility. If I am White and truly understand what White privilege means socially, economically, and politically, then I cannot help but bear some of the guilt for what has happened historically and what continues to occur. If I were to truly "get it," then I would have no choice but to give up my complacency, try to do something about it, and ultimately find myself with the same kind of discomfort and feelings as the men in my class. No one easily gives up power and privilege.

It is easy, as Whites, to feel relatively powerless in relation to others who garner more power than they do because of gender, class, age, and so forth and thereby deny holding any privilege. As Kendall (1997) points out, one need only look at statistics regarding managers in American industry. While White males constitute 43% of the work force, they hold 95% of senior management jobs. White women hold 40% of middle management positions compared to Black women and men who hold 5% and 4%, respectively. Having said all of this, it is equally important to acknowledge that as invisible as White privilege is to most European Americans, that is how clearly visible it is to People of Color. To them, we are White, clearly racial beings, and obviously in possession of privilege in this society. That they don't see it is, in fact, mind-boggling to most People of Color because to them race and racial inequity are ever-present realities. To deny them must seem either deeply cunning or bordering on the verge of psychosis.

At a broader level, White privilege is infused into the very fabric of American society, and even if they wish to do so, Whites cannot really give it up. Kendall (1997) enumerates some reasons for this:

- It is "an institutional (rather than personal) set of benefits."
- It belongs to "all of us, who are white, by race."
- It bears no relationship to whether we are "good people" or not.

- It tends to be both "intentional" and "malicious."
- It is "bestowed prenatally."
- It allows us to believe "that we do not have to take the issues of racism seriously."
- It involves the "ability to make decisions that affect everyone without taking others into account."
- It allows us to overlook race in ourselves and to be angry at those who do not.
- It lets me "decide whether I am going to listen or hear others or neither." (pp. 1–5)

McIntosh (1989) offers a number of examples of experiences that Whites, as people of privilege, can count on in their daily existence. These are listed in Table 3–1. The opposite conditions of these examples represent the daily experience of People of Color in the United States.

What can be done about White privilege? Mainly, individuals can become aware of its existence and the role it plays in their lives. It cannot be given away. Denying its reality or refusing to identify as White, according to Kendall (1997), merely leaves us "all the more blind to our silencing of people of color" (p. 6). By remaining self-aware and challenging its insidiousness within oneself, in others,

---

- **TABLE 3–1**   Typical Experiences of Privileged **Whites**

- If I should need to move, I can be pretty sure of renting or purchasing housing in an area that I can afford and in which I would want to live.
- I can be pretty sure that my neighbors in such a location will be neutral or pleasant to me.
- I can go shopping alone most of the time, pretty well assured that I will not be followed or harassed.
- I can turn on the television or look at the front page of the newspaper and see people of my race widely represented.
- When I am told about our national heritage or about "civilization," I am shown that people of my color made it what it is.
- I can be sure that my children will be given materials that testify to the existence of their race.
- I can go into a music shop and count on finding the music of my race represented; go into a supermarket and find the staple foods that fit with my cultural traditions; and go into a hairdresser's shop and find someone who can cut my hair.
- Whether I use checks, credit cards, or cash, I can count on my skin color not to work against the appearance of financial responsibility.
- I am never asked to speak for all the people of my racial group.
- I can be pretty sure that if I ask to talk to "the person in charge," I will be facing a person of my race.
- I can take a job with an affirmative action employer without having co-workers on the job suspect that I got it because of race.
- If my day, week, or year is going badly, I need not ask of each negative episode or situation whether it has racial overtones.
- I can choose blemish color or bandages in "flesh" color and have them more or less match my skin.

Note. Adapted from "White Privilege: Unpacking the Invisible Knapsack" by P. McIntosh, 1989, *Peace & Freedom* (July/August), pp. 10–12.

and in societal institutions, it is possible to begin to address the denial and invisibility that are its most powerful foundation. Like becoming culturally competent, fighting racism and White privilege, both internally and externally, is a lifelong developmental task.

White Racial Attitude Types

Rowe, Behrens, and Leach (1995) offer a framework for understanding how White, European Americans think about race and racial differences. Their research has generated seven attitude structures or types that Whites can adopt vis-à-vis race and People of Color.

The authors describe the first three types (avoidant, dependent, dissonant) as unachieved and the remaining four (dominative, conflictive, integrative, reactive) as achieved. The distinction between unachieved and achieved refers to the extent to which racial attitude is "securely integrated" into the person's general belief structure, in other words, how firmly it is held versus how easily it can be changed.

Unachieved attitude structures reflect the fact that individuals either have not thought about race and ethnicity or lack real commitment to any position. "Avoidant" types tend to ignore, minimize, or deny the importance of race in relation to both their own ethnicity and that of non-Whites. Whether out of fear or just convenience, they merely avoid the topic. The following sample statement typifies such a position:

> Minority issues just aren't all that important to me. We just don't get involved in that sort of thing. I really am not interested in thinking about those things. (p. 228)

Unlike the avoidant types, "dependent" types hold some position but merely have adopted it from significant others (often from as far back as childhood). Therefore, it remains unreflected, superficial, and easily changeable. The following is a typical dependent response:

> My thinking about minorities is mainly influenced by my (friends, family, husband/wife), so you could say I mainly learned about minorities from (them, him/her). That's why my opinion about minorities is pretty much the same as (theirs, his/hers). (p. 228)

The third unachieved type of attitude, "dissonant," is held by individuals who are uncertain about what they believe. They lack commitment to their position and are, in fact, open to new information even if it is dissonant. Their position may result from a lack of experience or knowledge, may indicate incongruity between new information and a previously held position, or may reflect a transition between positions. The following statement is typical of a dissonant attitude:

> I used to feel I knew what I thought about minorities. But now my feelings are really mixed. I'm having to change my thinking. I'm not sure, so I'm trying to find some answers to questions I have about minorities. (p. 229)

Rowe et al. (1995) next define four types of racial attitude that they consider as having reached an achieved status (i.e., sufficiently explored, committed to, and integrated into the individual's general belief system). "Dominative" attitudes involve the belief that majority group members should be allowed to dominate those who are culturally different. They tend to be held by people who are ethnocentric, use European American culture as a standard for judging the rightness of others' behavior, and devalue and feel uncomfortable with non-Whites, especially in closer personal relationships. These are the classic bigots. The following statement is exemplary:

> The truth about minorities is that they are kind of dumb, their customs are crude, and they are pretty backward compared to what Whites have accomplished. Besides that they are sort of lazy. I guess they just aren't up to what Whites are. I wouldn't want a family member, or even a friend of mine, to have a close relationship with a minority. You may have to work near them, but you don't have to live close to one. (p. 229)

A variation on this theme is the "conflictive" attitude, held by individuals who, although they wouldn't support outright racism or discrimination, oppose efforts to ameliorate the effects of discrimination such as affirmative action. They are conflicted around the competing values of fairness, which requires significant change, and retaining the status quo, which says that I am very content with the way things are. Consider the following example:

> There should be equal chances to better yourself for everyone, but minorities are way too demanding. The media is always finding something they say is unfair and making a big deal out of it. And the government is always coming up with some kind of program that lets them get more than they deserve. We shouldn't discriminate against minorities, but tilting things in their favor just isn't fair. White ethnic groups didn't get a lot of government help, and the minorities of today shouldn't expect it either. (pp. 229–230)

Individuals who possess "integrative" attitudes tend to be pragmatic in their approach to race relations. They have a sense of their own identity as Whites and at the same time favor interracial contact and harmony. They further believe that racism can be eradicated through goodwill and rationality. The following is reflective of an integrative attitude:

> Integration is a desirable goal for our society, and it could significantly improve problems relating to prejudice and discrimination if people would keep an open mind and allow it to work. Race and culture is not a factor when I choose my personal friends. I'm comfortable around minority people and don't mind being one of a few Whites in a group. In fact, I wouldn't mind living next to minority people if their social class were similar to mine. I think we will need racial harmony for democracy to be able to function. (p. 230)

The final attitude delineated by Rowe et al. is called "reactive" and involves a rather militant stand against racism. Such individuals tend to identify with People of Color, may feel guilty about being White, and may romanticize the racial drama. They are, in addition, very sensitive to situations involving discrimination and react strongly to the inequities that exist in society, as in this statement:

> Our society is quite racist. It is really difficult for minority people to get a fair deal. There may be some tokenism, but businesses won't put minorities in the top positions. Actually, qualified minority people should be given preference at all levels of education and employment to make up for the effects of past discrimination. But they don't have enough power to influence the government, even though it's the government's responsibility to help minority people. It's enough sometimes to make you feel guilty about being White. (p. 230)

According to the authors, these are the most frequently observed forms of White attitudes toward race and race relations. The unachieved types are most changeable; by definition, they have not been truly integrated into the person's worldview. The four achieved forms are more difficult to change, but under sufficient contrary information or experience, they can be altered. When that does occur, it usually involves a process of change during which the individual looks a lot like those who are in the dissonant mode. A summary of Rowe et al. can be found in Table 3–2.

A Model of White Racial Identity Development

Helms (1995) offers a somewhat different approach to understanding how Whites experience and relate to race in America through her model of White racial identity development. Rather than suggest a series of independent attitude statuses, as do Rowe et al., she envisions a developmental process (defined by a series of stages or statuses) through which Whites can move to recognize

■ **TABLE 3–2**   Racial Attitude Types and Statuses

Types	Status	Summary
Avoidant	Unachieved	Ignore, minimize, or deny race
Dependent	Unachieved	Adopt positions of significant others
Dissonant	Unachieved	Lack commitment and change position easily
Dominative	Achieved	Adopt classic bigotry
Conflictive	Achieved	Oppose efforts at social justice
Integrative	Achieved	Stand militantly against racism
Reactive	Achieved	Open to change through goodwill and rationality

Note. Adapted from "Racial/Ethnic Identity and Social Consciousness: Looking Back and Looking Forward" by W. Rowe, J. T. Behrens, & M. M. Leach, 1995, in *Handbook of Multicultural Counseling* (pp. 218–235), edited by J. P. Ponterotto, J. M. Casas, L. A. Suzuki, & C. M. Alexander, Thousand Oaks, CA: Sage Publications, Inc.

and abandon their privilege. According to Helms, each status or stage is supported by a unique pattern of psychological defense and means of processing racial experience. A statement typical of someone at that developmental level is presented following the description of each stage.

The first stage, "contact status," begins with the individual's internalization of the majority culture's view of People of Color as well as the advantages of privilege. Whites at this level of awareness have developed a defense Helms calls "obliviousness" to keep the issue of race out of consciousness. Bollin and Finkel (1995) describe contact status as the "naïve belief that race does not really make a difference" (p. 25).

> I'm a White woman. When my grandfather came to this country, he was discriminated against, too. But he didn't blame Black people for his misfortune. He educated himself and got a job; that's what Blacks ought to do. If White callers (to a radio station) spent as much time complaining about discrimination as your Black callers do, we'd never have accomplished what we have. You all should just ignore it. (p. 185)

The second stage, "disintegration status," involves "disorientation and anxiety provoked by unresolved racial moral dilemmas that force one to choose between own-group loyalty and humanism" (p. 185). It is supported by the defenses of suppression and ambivalence. At this stage, the person has encountered information or has had experiences that led him or her to realize that race in fact does make a difference. The result is a growing awareness of and discomfort with White privilege.

> I myself tried to set a nonracist example (for other Whites) by speaking up when someone said something blatantly prejudiced—how to do this without alienating people so that they would no longer take me seriously was always tricky—and by my friendships with Mexicans and Blacks who were actually the people with whom I felt most comfortable. (p. 185)

"Reintegration status," the third stage, is defined by an idealization of one's racial group and a concurrent rejection and intolerance for other groups. It depends on the defenses of selective perception and negative out-group distortion for its evolution. Here, the White individual attempts to deal with the discomfort by emphasizing the superiority of White culture and the natural deficits in Cultures of Color.

> So what if my great-grandfather owned slaves. He didn't mistreat them and besides, I wasn't even here then. I never owned slaves. So, I don't know why Blacks expect me to feel guilty for something that happened before I was born. Nowadays, reverse racism hurts Whites more than slavery hurts Blacks. At least they got three square (meals) a day. But my brother can't even get a job with the police department because they have to hire less qualified Blacks. That (expletive) happens to Whites all the time. (p. 185)

The fourth stage, "pseudoindependence status," involves an "intellectualized commitment to one's own socioracial group and deceptive tolerance of other groups" (p. 185). It is grounded in the processes of reshaping reality and selective perception. The individual has, at this point, developed an intellectual acceptance of racial differences and espouses a liberal ideology of social justice but has not truly integrated either emotionally.

> Was I the only person left in America who believed that the sexual mingling of the races was a good thing, that it would erase cultural barriers and leave us all a lovely shade of tan? . . . Racial blending is inevitable. At least, it may be the only solution to our dilemmas of race. (p. 185)

A person functioning in the "immersion/emersion status," fifth along the continuum, is searching for a personal understanding of racism as well as insight into how he or she benefits from it. As a part of this process, which has as its psychological base hypervigilance and reshaping, there is an effort to redefine one's Whiteness. Entry into this stage may have been precipitated by being rejected by Individuals of Color and often includes isolation within one's own group in order to work through the powerful feelings that have been stimulated.

> It's true that I personally did not participate in the horror of slavery, and I don't even know whether my ancestors owned slaves. But I know that because I am White, I continue to benefit from a racist system which stems from the slavery era. I believe that if White people are ever going to understand our role in perpetuating racism, then we must begin to ask ourselves some hard questions and be willing to consider our role in maintaining a hurtful system. Then, we must try to do something to change it. (p. 185)

The final stage, "autonomy status," involves "informed positive socioracial-group commitment, use of internal standards for self-definition, and capacity to relinquish the privileges of racism" (p. 185). It is supported by the psychological processes of flexibility and complexity. Here, the person has come to peace with his or her Whiteness, separating it from a sense of privilege, and is able to approach those who are culturally different without prejudice.

> I live in an integrated (Black–White) neighborhood and I read Black literature and popular magazines. So, I understand that the media presents a very stereotypic view of Black culture. I believe that if more of us White people made more than a superficial effort to obtain accurate information about racial groups other than our own, then we could help make this country a better place for all people. (p. 185)

Helms's model of White identity development parallels models of racial identity development for People of Color that are introduced in chapter 6. Both involve consciousness raising, that is, becoming aware of and working through unconscious feelings and beliefs about one's connection to race and ethnicity. The goal of identity development in each group is, however, different.

For People of Color, it involves a cumulative process of "surmounting internalized racism in its various manifestations," while for Whites, it has to do with the "abandonment of entitlement" (1995, p. 184). What the two models share is a process wherein the person (of Color or White) sheds internalized racial attitudes and social conditioning and replaces these with greater openness and appreciation for racial and cultural identity as well as cultural differences.

Identity Development in the Classroom

Ponterotto (1988), drawing parallels with the earlier work of both Helms (1985) and Cross (1971), describes "the racial identity and consciousness development process" of White participants in a multicultural learning environment, an educational setting that may well be similar to that in which you may find yourself.

Ponterotto identifies four stages through which students proceed:

- pre-exposure
- exposure
- zealot-defensive
- integration

In the "pre-exposure stage," the student "has given little thought to multicultural issues or to his or her role as a White person in a racist and oppressive society" (p. 151). In the "exposure stage," students are routinely confronted with minority individuals and issues. They are exposed to the realities of racism and the mistreatment of People of Color, examine their own cultural values and how they pervade society, and discover that the "mistreatment extends into the counseling process" and that "the counseling profession is ethnocentrically biased and subtly racist" (p. 152). These realizations tend to stimulate both anger and guilt—anger because they had been taught that counseling was "value free and truly fair and objective" and guilt because holding such assumptions had probably led them to perpetuate this subtle racism themselves.

In the "zealot-defensive stage," students tend to react in one of two ways—either overidentifying with ethnic minorities and the issues they are studying or distancing themselves from them. The former tend to develop a strong "prominority perspective" (p. 152), and through it, are able to manage and resolve some of the guilt feelings. The latter, on the other hand, tend to take the criticism very personally and by way of defense withdraw from the topic, becoming "passive recipients" (p. 153) of multicultural information. In the real world, such a reaction leads to avoidance of interracial contact and escape into same-race associations. In classes, however, where students are a "captive audience," there is greater likelihood that the defensive feelings will be processed and worked through as the class proceeds.

In the final "integration stage," the extreme reactions of the previous stage tend to decrease in intensity. Zealous reactions subside, and those students become more balanced in their views. Defensiveness is slowly transformed, and students tend to acquire a "renewed interest, respect, and appreciation for cultural differences" (p. 153). Ponterotto, however, is quick to point out that there is no guarantee that all students will pass through all four stages, and some can remain stuck in any of the stages.

Becoming a Cultural Ally

White students, after participating in a class or workshop on cultural diversity, often ask how they can support People of Color in addressing racism and moving toward greater social justice. Relevant here is the concept of becoming a *cultural ally*. Bell (1997) suggests that Whites "have an important role to play in challenging oppression and creating alternatives. Throughout our history there have always been people from dominant groups who use their power to actively fight against systems of oppression . . . Dominants can expose the social, moral, and personal costs of maintaining privilege so as to develop an investment in changing the system by which they benefit, but for which they also pay a price" (p. 13). Wijeyesinghe, Griffin, and Love (1997) define an ally as a "white person who actively works to eliminate racism. This person may be motivated by self-interest in ending racism, a sense of moral obligation, or a commitment to foster social justice, as opposed to a patronizing agenda of 'wanting to help those poor People of Color'" (p. 98). These authors, along with Thompson (2005), describe the following characteristics of a cultural ally as one who

- acknowledges the privilege they receive as a member of the culturally dominant group;
- listens and believes the experiences of marginalized group members without diminishing, dismissing, normalizing, or making their experience invisible;
- is willing to take risks, try new behaviors, act in spite of own fear and resistance from other agents;
- is humble, does not act as an expert toward the marginalized group culture;
- is willing to be confronted about own behavior and attitudes and consider change;
- takes a stand against oppression even when no marginalized-group person is present;
- believes he or she can make a difference by acting and speaking out against social injustice;
- knows how to cultivate support from other allies; and
- works to understand his or her own privilege and does not burden the marginalized group to provide continual education.

White providers are encouraged to assess their own reactions to the concept of privilege and to locate their level of development in relation to the models offered by Rowe et al. and Helms. To what extent are you aware of the existence of White privilege? This is an important question because culturally different clients view and relate to White providers in light of their privilege. As suggested in previous chapters, one cannot help but be a magnet for the feelings and reactions that Clients of Color have toward White dominant culture and how it has treated them and those they love. It is important that providers struggle to fully grasp the meaning and ramifications of their privilege and to communicate this awareness to culturally different clients. Trust cannot evolve when two people live in perceptually different worlds. A key aspect of unacknowledged White privilege is its invisibility to Whites and its concurrent visibility to People of Color. To the extent that White providers can acknowledge the centrality of race to a non-White client and at the same time grasp the nature of their own attitude toward racial differences, the cultural distance between them can be reduced dramatically.

■ Summary

Racism is "the systematic subordination of members of targeted racial groups who have relatively little social power . . . by members of the agent racial group who have relatively more social power" (Wijeyesinghe, Griffin, and Love, 1997). Prejudice is a negative, inaccurate, rigid, and unfair way of thinking about members of another group. Racism equals prejudice plus power and exists on three levels: individual, institutional, and cultural. In general, people deny, rationalize, and avoid discussing feelings and beliefs about race and ethnicity.

Individual racism emerges out of the normal and natural tendencies of how people think, feel, and process information. In-group and out-group behavior, categorical thinking and stereotyping, avoidance, and selective perception set the stage for the emergence of racism. There are a variety of theories about the psychological motivation behind racist behavior. The frustration-aggression-displacement hypothesis and the authoritarian or global personality type are two of the most popular.

Institutional racism involves the manipulation of societal institutions to give preferences and advantages to White people and at the same time restrict the choices, rights, mobility, and access of People of Color. One method of identifying institutional racism involves comparing the frequency or incidence of a characteristic within a group with the group's general frequency within the population. Lack of intent or consciousness should never be regarded as justification for institutional racism. Although denial is typically at work in all forms of racism, it is especially difficult for individuals to take responsibility for institutional racism.

Cultural racism is the belief that the cultural ways of one group are superior to those of another. In most institutions in the United States, White Northern European culture has been adopted and dominates. Behavior outside of its parameters is judged as bad or inappropriate. To succeed, People of Color must give up their own ways, and thus a part of themselves, and take on the ways of majority culture, or remain perpetual outsiders.

White privilege refers to the benefits that are automatically accrued to European Americans merely on the basis of skin color. What is most insidious and surprising about such privilege is that it is largely invisible to the people who hold it. Most Whites tend to see themselves not as racial beings or members of a racial grouping, but as individuals. As such, they tend to deny or play down the import of race and ethnicity as social forces. One reason may be that it is difficult to acknowledge "unearned power" in a society that gives such powerful lip service to equality and equal access to resources. A second reason is that acknowledging the import of race and the obvious racial inequity in our society would lead to strong feelings of guilt and responsibility and a need to make amends. It is also easy for many European Americans to experience themselves as powerless in relation to class, gender, age, and so on, thereby downplaying the power they accrue in relation to their Whiteness.

Rowe, Behrens, and Leach (1995) offer a model of racial attitude types to describe the ways that European Americans think about and relate to race and racial differences. Helms (1995) offers a model of White racial-identity development that assumes the existence of five stages of a White individual's progress toward self-awareness and the abandonment of privilege. Based on teaching diversity in the college classroom, Ponterotto (1988) identified a progression of four stages that most students pass through as they become more culturally sensitive and competent. White individuals interested in supporting People of Color and reducing racism and promoting greater social justice might consider becoming a cultural ally.

■ Activities

1. *Explore personal experiences around race and ethnicity.* The following questions concern your experiences with ethnicity and cultural difference. Several ask you to identify a time or event in the past. Allow yourself to relax and visualize the time or event you have identified. Try to re-experience it as much as possible. When you are finished, describe the experience in writing or to a partner. Include how you felt at the time, how you feel about it now, how it affects you today, and any other associations, images, or strong feelings that may come up. Use as much time and detail as you find valuable.

   ■ When did you first become aware that people were different racially or ethnically?
   ■ When did you first become aware of yourself as a member of a racial or ethnic group?
   ■ When were you first made aware of people being treated differently because of their race or ethnicity?
   ■ When did you first become aware of being treated differently yourself because of your race or ethnicity?
   ■ When were you proudest being a member of the group to which you belong?
   ■ When were you least proud of being a member of the group to which you belong?
   ■ How do you identify yourself racially/ethnically? Culturally? How has your sense of race/ethnicity or culture changed over time?

- How would you describe the extent of your contact with people who are racially/ethnically different from you? How has this changed over time? If your contact is limited, why do you think it is that way?

  You can increase the intensity and learning value of these exercises by sharing your answers with someone else. After you have shared each answer, use it as a springboard for further soul-searching and personal discussions of each topic.

2. *Identifying your attitudes toward members of different racial and ethnic groups.* This exercise gives you an opportunity to verbalize and identify your experiences with, attitudes toward, and beliefs about members of different racial and ethnic groups. Answer the questions or carry out the activity in relation to each of the following groups toward which you feel an affinity or dislike: (a) African Americans, (b) Latinos/as, (c) Asian Americans, (d) Native Americans, (e) White Northern Europeans, (f) White ethnic groups (Jews, Irish, Italians, etc.).

- Describe in detail experiences you have had with members of this group.
- At present, how do you feel about members of this group (describe your reactions in detail and, if possible, relate them to specific experiences) and how has that changed over time?
- Are there characteristics, traits, or other things about members of this group that make it difficult for you to approach them?
- Without censoring yourself, generate a list of characteristics—one-word adjectives—that describe your beliefs and perceptions about members of this group.
- What reactions, feelings, thoughts, or concerns come to mind when you think about working professionally with members of this group?
- What kinds of answers, information, learning experiences, contact, and so forth do you need to become more comfortable with members of this group?

4 Understanding Culture and Cultural Differences

There is a Zen story about a millipede that is stopped by an earthworm and asked how it can possibly manage to walk with so many legs to coordinate. The next moment the millipede is lying on its back in a ditch, trying to figure out which leg to put in front of the next. Many Americans have become like that millipede vis-à-vis culture. My White students often complain that they have no culture. They know nothing and feel nothing about where they came from. What they mean, I believe, is that they lack the kind of connection to a cultural heritage and community that they see among People of Color and White ethnics, and they are jealous.

When culture is alive and vibrant, it provides the kind of inner programming that keeps the millipede walking along. It's always there—much of the time beyond awareness. It gives life structure and meaning. When it becomes fragmented, however, a central part of what it is, and what it can offer, gets lost. This chapter discusses a number of issues related to culture. What exactly is it, and how does it function in the life of a person? Why are social scientists finding it preferable to describe group difference in terms of culture rather than race? Along what cultural dimensions do groups differ, and in what ways do the cultures of Euro-Americans and People of Color clash? What happened to White culture? Are the theories that inform professional helping culture-bound, as some practitioners have suggested? And finally, is there such a thing as multicultural counseling (i.e., a single approach that can adjust itself to the needs of many cultural groups)? Answers to these questions provide a better understanding of the ways in which culture affects service delivery.

◼ What Is Culture?

Culture is a difficult concept to grasp because it is so basic to human societies and so intertwined with our very natures that its workings are seldom acknowledged or thought about by those who have internalized it. It is all-encompassing, like water to a fish, so that it remains largely preconscious and is obvious only when it is gone or has been seriously disturbed. Anthropological definitions point to certain aspects of it. *Culture* comprises traditional ideas and related values, and it is the product of actions (Kroeber & Kluckhohn, 1952); it is learned, shared, and transmitted from one generation to the next (Linton, 1945); and it organizes life and helps interpret existence (Gordon, 1964). I also like the notion of culture as the ways a people have learned to respond to life's problems. For instance, all human groups must deal with death. But the rituals and practices that have developed around it vary greatly from culture to culture. All these definitions lack, however, something that would be particularly helpful for the present purposes—a more felt sense of how culture functions within the individual. To get at this, the concept of paradigm is very useful.

Kuhn (1970) introduced the term *paradigm* to describe the totality of how a science conceives of the phenomena it studies. He argues that sciences change over time, not through the slow accumulation of knowledge (as was always taught in high school physics) but through paradigm shifts. A paradigm is a set of shared assumptions and beliefs about how the world works, and it structures the perception and understanding of the scientists in a discipline. For example, in physics, when Newton's theory of how physical matter operated no longer fit the accumulating evidence, it was eventually replaced by Einstein's theory of relativity, which was a qualitative shift in thinking. The new paradigm was a radical departure from its predecessor and gave physicists a totally different way of thinking about their work. Kuhn's idea is very engaging because it suggests that our beliefs (paradigms) define what we perceive and experience as real.

The notion of paradigm was quickly appropriated by psychologists to describe the cognitive worldview through which human beings perceive and relate to their world. Their paradigms, without people's being very aware of them, tell people how human existence works—what is possible and impossible, what the rules are, how things are done. In short, they shape an individual's experience of reality. People think through their paradigms, not about them. "I'll see it when I believe it" is an accurate description of how beliefs can give form to what is experienced as "real." People also grow emotionally attached to their paradigms and give up or change them only with great difficulty and discomfort. Having one's paradigm challenged is experienced as a personal threat, for ego gets invested in the portrayal of how things should be. Having one's paradigm shattered is akin to the chaos of psychosis. When the world no longer operates as it "should," one feels cut adrift from familiar moorings, no longer sure where one stands or who one is.

Culture is the stuff of which human paradigms are made. It provides them content—their identity, beliefs, values, and behavior. It is learned as part of the natural process of growing up in a family and community and from participating in societal institutions. These are the purveyors of culture.

In short, one's culture becomes one's paradigm, defining what is real and right. Different cultures, in turn, generate different paradigms of reality, and each is protected and defended as if a threat to it were a threat to a member's very existence. From this perspective, it is easy to understand why the imposition of a Northern European cultural paradigm onto the lives of People of Color, who possess and live by very different cultural paradigms, is experienced so negatively.

■ Culture Versus Race in the Definition of Group Differences

Before you learn about the various dimensions along which cultures differ, it is useful to take a short digression to discuss difficulties with the concept of race. Increasingly of late, social scientists have chosen to distinguish between human groups on the basis of culture rather than race. For example, when they refer to tribal subgroups within the broader racial category of Native Americans as separate ethnic groups, they are emphasizing cultural differences in defining group identity as opposed to biological or physical ones. I have followed a similar practice here by using terms such as *ethnic group* and *culturally different clients* to describe human diversity. Ethnic group was defined in chapter 1 as any distinguishable people whose members share a culture and see themselves as separate and different from the cultural majority.

The emphasis is on shared cultural material as a basis for identification. It is not likely that the concept of race and its usual breakdown into five distinct human groups will ever disappear. It is just too deeply ingrained in the fabric of American society. Rather, its importance as a social, as opposed to a biological, concept will increasingly be emphasized.

There are many serious problems with the concept of race, which Healey (1995) defines as "an isolated inbreeding population with a distinctive genetic heritage."

- Physical anthropologists have shown quite conclusively that what has always been assumed to be clear and distinct differences among the races are not very clear or distinct at all. In fact, it appears that there is as much variability in physical characteristics within racial groups as there is among groups. It is not uncommon, for example, to see a wide array of skin colors and physical features among individuals who are all considered members of one racial group. It is believed that there has been so much racial mixing throughout history that, today, groups that may have once been genetically distinct are no longer distinguishable.
- The term *race* has become so emotionally charged and politicized that it can no longer serve a useful role in scientific discussion.
- Racial categories have been used throughout U.S. history to simultaneously oppress People of Color, justify White privilege, and confuse racial politics. For example, U.S. Census classifications of race have changed regularly every decade from 1889 to the present. In 1890, for example, they included "White, Black, Mulatto, Quadroon, Octoroon, Chinese, Japanese, and Indian." The 2000 Census tracked the following racial groups: "White, Black, American Indian or Alaskan Native, Asian Indian, Chinese, Filipino, Japanese, Korean, Vietnamese, Native Hawaiian, and Guamanian or Chamorro." In addition, Spanish, Hispanic/Latino group membership has become a separate racial category, as has the acknowledgment of more than one racial background. Of particular interest in regard to such redefinitions

is the fact that they seem to parallel changes in immigration restrictions passed by Congress. An increased demand for entry into the United States from groups who are perceived as threats by the White establishment results in reduced immigration quotas.

- Defining race biologically and genetically opens the door for pseudoscientific arguments about intellectual and other types of inferiority among People of Color.
- The social reality of race in the United States does not conform to the existence of five distinct groups. Rather, only two bear any real social meaning: White and of Color. The notion of the great melting pot, for instance, was, in actuality, only about melting White ethnics. The myth was never intended to apply to People of Color. For White ethnics, upper mobility involved discovering and asserting their group's whiteness as a means of setting themselves apart from and above the Groups of Color who perpetually resided at the bottom of America's social hierarchy. When they first arrived in America, various White ethnic groups were met with prejudice and scorn and were merely tolerated because they represented a source of much needed cheap labor. In time, however, as they acculturated into the system, they discovered that they could progress most quickly by identifying themselves as White and by taking on the prejudices against People of Color, which were an intrinsic part of White culture.

For all of these reasons, it has become increasingly compelling to set aside the term *race* as a distinguishing feature among groups and to turn to cultural differences as a more useful and less controversial yardstick.

■ The Dimensions of Culture

Cultural paradigms define and dictate how human beings live and experience life. Brown and Landrum-Brown (1995) describe the dimensions along which cultures can differ. They refer to these differences as dimensions of "worldview." The content and specifics of each vary from culture to culture. It is because of these differences and our natural tendency toward ethnocentrism, which assumes everyone else views the world in the same way we do, that cross-cultural misunderstanding occurs. Brown and Landrum-Brown enumerate the following dimensions of culture, which are also summarized in Table 4-1.

- *Psychobehavioral modality* refers to the mode of activity most preferred within a culture. Do individuals actively engage their world (doing), more passively experience it as a process (being), or experience it with the intention of evolving (becoming)?
- *Axiology* involves the interpersonal values that a culture teaches. Do they compete or cooperate (competition vs. cooperation)? Are emotions freely expressed or held back and controlled (emotional restraint vs. emotional expressiveness)? Is verbal expression direct or indirect (direct verbal expression vs. indirect verbal expression)? Do group members seek help from others, or do they keep problems hidden so as not to shame their families (help seeking vs. "saving face")?

■ **TABLE 4-1** Worldview Positions

Worldview dimensions	Sample worldview positions
Psychobehavioral modality axiology (values)	Doing vs. being vs. becoming
	Competition vs. cooperation
	Emotional restraint vs. emotional expressiveness
	Direct verbal expression vs. indirect verbal expression
	Seeking help vs. "saving face"
Ethos (guiding beliefs)	Independence vs. interdependence
	Individual rights vs. honor and protect family
	Egalitarianism vs. authoritarianism
	Control and dominance vs. harmony and deference
Epistemology (how one knows)	Cognitive processes vs. affective processes (vibes)
	Intuition vs. cognitive and affective
Logic (reasoning process)	Either-or thinking vs. both-and thinking vs. circular
Ontology (nature of reality)	Objective material vs. subjective vs. spiritual and material
Concept of time	Clock-based vs. event-based vs. cyclical
Concept of self	Individual self vs. extended self

Note. From Brown, M. T., & Landrum-Brown, J. (1995). Counselor supervision: Cross-Cultural perspectives. In J. P. Ponterroto, J. M. Casas, L. A. Suzuki, & C. M. Alexander (Eds.), *Handbook of Multicultural Counseling* (pp. 263–287). Thousand Oaks, CA: Sage.

- *Ethos* refers to widely held beliefs within a cultural group that guide social interactions. Are people viewed as independent beings or as interdependent (independence vs. interdependence)? Is one's first allegiance to oneself or to one's family (individual rights vs. honor and protect family)? Are all individual group members seen as equal or is there an acknowledged hierarchy of status or power (egalitarianism vs. authoritarianism)? Are harmony, respect, and deference toward others valued over controlling and dominating them (control and dominance vs. harmony and deference)?
- *Epistemology* summarizes the preferred ways of gaining knowledge and learning about the world. Do people rely more on their intellectual abilities (cognitive processes), their emotions and intuition (affective processes, "vibes," intuition), or a combination of both (cognitive and affective)?
- *Logic* involves the kind of reasoning process that group members adopt. Are issues seen as being either one way or the other (either-or thinking)? Can multiple possibilities be considered at the same time (both-and thinking)? Or is thinking organized around inner consistency (circular)?
- *Ontology* refers to how a culture views the nature of reality. Is what's real only what can be seen and touched (objective material)? Is there a level of reality that exists beyond the material senses (subjective spiritual)? Or are both levels of reality experienced (spiritual and material)?
- *Concept of time* involves how time is experienced within a culture. Is it clock-determined and linear (clock-based)? Is it defined in relation to specific events (event-based)? Or is it experienced as repetitive (cyclical)?
- *Concept of self,* finally, refers to whether group members experience themselves as separate beings (individual self) or as part of a greater collective (extended self).

In relation to these dimensions of worldview or culture, each society evolves a set of cultural forms—ritual practices, behavioral prescriptions, and symbols—that support them. For example, a given culture stresses the doing mode on the first dimension. Certain kinds of child-rearing techniques tend to encourage directed activity. Parents differentially reinforce activity over passivity. They also model such behavior. Cultural myths portray figures high on this trait, and moral teachings stress its importance. The group's language likely favors active over passive voice. What makes a culture unique, then, is the particular profile of where it stands on each of these dimensions combined with the specific cultural forms it has evolved.

As will become apparent shortly, the dimensions of culture are not totally independent. Rather, some tend to cluster. In relation to *ethos*, for instance, beliefs concerning independence, individual rights, egalitarianism, and control and dominance tend to occur together in the belief system of a culture, as do interdependence, honor and family protection, authoritarianism, and harmony and deference. Such clusters tend to be mutually reinforcing. It will become clear that certain cultures share a number of dimensions. The Cultures of Color in the United States, for example, have many dimensional similarities and, as a group, differ considerably from Northern European culture.

Finally, it is important to note that each culture generates a unique felt experience of living. The quality of life differs in tone, mood, and intensity. The same is true for the kind of mental health issues that members must face as well as the emotional strengths they develop. A very dramatic example of this occurred many years ago. I was a graduate student running a personal growth group for students at a multicultural weekend retreat. The students who showed up for my group were all White with the exception of one young Latino man, who was really there to spend more time with one of the young women in the group. Such groups seldom attracted non-White participants because it was the belief of most Students of Color that it was a "White thing" and something that "Whites really needed." "As for us, we don't have any trouble relating to other people." The group was quite successful, and it did not take long until people were sharing deeply and talking about feelings of disconnection from parents, isolation, and loneliness. At a certain point, the young Latino man could contain himself no longer and said, "I don't understand what you are all talking about. I am part of a big extended family; there is always someone around. I can't imagine feeling alone or isolated." Only after that did I realize that what I had thought to be the "universal malaise" of loneliness and isolation was, in fact, a cultural experience and an artifact of the Northern European lifestyle.

■ Comparing Cultural Paradigms in America

M. Ho (1987) compares the cultural paradigm of White, European Americans to those of the four Cultures of Color on five dimensions, which overlap extensively with those of Brown and Landrum-Brown. It is worth reviewing these in some detail to appreciate the breadth of difference that does exist. It should be remembered, however, that these comparisons speak in generalities and may not fit or apply to individual group members, especially those who have acculturated. In addition, each of the five "racial" groups described is, in actuality, made up of numerous subgroups whose cultural content can differ widely. In the United States, for example, Manson and Trimble (1982) identified 512 federally recognized Native "entities" and an additional 365 state-recognized Indian tribes, each with its cultural uniqueness.

Nature and the Environment

Ho classifies the four Cultures of Color—Asian Americans, Native Americans, African Americans, and Latino/a Americans—as living in "harmony with" nature and the environment, whereas European Americans prefer "mastery over" them. For the former, the relationship is one of respecting and coexisting with nature. Human beings are seen as part of a natural order and, as such, must live respectfully and nonintrusively with other aspects of nature. To destroy a fellow creature is to destroy a part of oneself. On the other hand, European American culture views human beings as superior to the physical environment and entitled to manipulate it for their own benefit. The world is a resource to be used and plundered. In contrast, the Cultures of Color see the component parts of nature as alive and invested with spirit—to be related to respectfully and responsibly. Great value is placed on being ever attentive to what nature has to offer and teach. Out of such a perspective come notions such as the Native American idea of Turtle Island, a myth that views the non-human inhabitants of the continent as an interconnected system of animal spirits and archetypal characters. A "mastery" mentality results in environmental practices such as runaway logging, strip mining, and oil drilling as well as the impetus for institutions such as human slavery, which exploit "inferior" human beings for material gain.

Time Orientation

There is great diversity among the five cultural groups in regard to how they perceive and experience time. European Americans are dominated by an orientation toward the future. Planning, producing, and controlling what will happen are all artifacts of a future-time orientation. What was and what is are always a bit vague and subordinated to what is anticipated. At the same time, European Americans view time as compartmentalized and incremental, and as such, being on time and being efficient with one's time are positive values.

Asian and Latino/a cultures are described as past-present oriented. For both, history is a living entity. Ancestors and past events are felt to be alive and influencing present reality. The past flows imperceptibly into and defines the present. In turn, both Native Americans and African Americans are characterized as present oriented. Focus is directed toward current experience of the here and now, with less attention to what led up to this moment or what will become of it. As a group, and distinct from European American culture, the

Cultures of Color share a view of time as an infinite continuum and find it difficult to relate to the White "obsession" with being on time. Interestingly, each of these groups has evolved a term to describe its "looser" sense of time: "Colored people's time," "Indian time," "Asian time," and "Latin time." Invariably, time becomes an issue when non-Whites enter institutions where European American cultural values predominate. Lateness is often mistakenly interpreted by Whites as indifference, provocative, or symptomatic of a lack of basic work skills.

People Relations

Ho (1987) distinguishes European Americans as having an "individual" social focus compared to a "collateral" one for the four Cultures of Color. Individual behavior refers to actions undertaken to actualize the self; collateral behavior involves doing things not for oneself but in light of what they may contribute to the survival and betterment of family and community. These differences, in turn, become a basis for attributing value to different, and opposing, styles of interaction. European Americans, for example, are taught and encouraged to compete, to seek individual success, and to feel pride in and make public their accomplishments. Native Americans and Latino/a Americans, in particular, place high value on cooperation and strive to suppress individual accomplishment, boasting, and self-aggrandizement. Having pointed out this shared collateral focus, it is equally important to understand that the four Communities of Color differ significantly in their communication styles and the meaning of related symbols. Native Americans place high value on brevity in speech, while for African Americans, the ability to rap is treated as an art form. It is considered impolite in certain Asian American subgroups to say "no" or refuse to comply with a request from a superior. Among Latino/a Americans, deferential behavior and the communication of proper respect depend on perceived authority, age, gender, and class. And the same handshake can be given in one culture to communicate respect and deference and in another to show authority and power.

Work and Activity

On the dimension of work and activity (similar to Brown and Landrum-Brown's psychobehavioral modality), European Americans, Asian Americans, and African Americans are described as "doing" oriented compared to Native Americans and Latino/a Americans who are characterized as "being-becoming." Doing is an active mode. It involves initiating activity in pursuit of a given goal. It tends to be associated with societies where rewards and status are given on the basis of productivity and accomplishment. But even here, there are differences in motivation. European Americans' work and activity are premised on the idea of meritocracy—that hard work and serious effort ultimately bring the person financial and social success. Asian Americans, on the other hand, pursue activity in terms of its ability to confer honor on one's family and concurrently to avoid shaming them or losing face. African Americans fall somewhere between these two extremes. Being-in-becoming, in turn, is more passive, process oriented, and focused on the here and now. It involves allowing the world to present opportunities for activity and work rather than seeking them out or creating them. It is a mode of activity that can easily be misinterpreted from a doing perspective as "lazy" or "lacking motivation." On a recent trip to the Sinai in Egypt, one of my traveling companions was a hardworking lawyer from New York City, clearly high on the doing dimension. After spending several hours visiting a Bedouin village, he could barely contain his shock at how the men just sat around all day. Our guide, himself a Bedouin, suggested that they were not merely sitting, but thinking and planning. He explained, "There is a lot to think about: where to find water, missing goats, perhaps a new wife, maybe a little smuggling." This didn't satisfy the lawyer, however, who said, "I don't understand how they can get anything done without meetings. Give me six months and I'd have this whole desert covered with condos."

One last point. Activity and work, whether of the doing or becoming variety, must occur in the context of other cultural values. For example, in many cultures, work does not begin until there has been sufficient time to greet and properly inquire about the welfare of one's family. To do otherwise is considered rude and insensitive. In White, European American business culture, such activity would be seen as lazy, wasteful, and the shirking of one's responsibilities.

Human Nature

This dimension of culture deals with how groups view the essence of being human. Are people inherently good, bad, both, or somewhere in between? According to Ho (1997), African Americans and European Americans see human nature as both good and bad and as possessing both potentials. But for each, the meaning is quite different. In African American culture, where all behavior involves a collateral focus, or what Nobles (1972) calls "experiential communality," good and bad are defined in relation to the community. It is laudable if it benefits the community and bad if it does not. Thus, human nature is seen as existing in the interaction between the person and the group.

European American culture, on the other hand, sees good and bad as residing in the individual. Freud's view of human nature is an excellent example. The instinctive urges of the id are seen as a negative force that must be controlled. The ego and the superego are assigned this task and, as such, play a positive role in containing baser drives. In addition, Freud hypothesized a life instinct that is balanced by a death instinct. Thus, the two sides of human nature, the good and bad, are seen in constant opposition and conflict.

Ho describes Asian Americans, Native Americans, and Latino/a Americans as sharing a view of human nature as good. This tendency to attribute positive motives to others has at times proved less than helpful in interaction with members of the dominant culture. Early treaty negotiations between Native

American tribes and the U.S. government are a case in point. Tribal representatives entered these negotiations under the assumption that they were dealing with honest and honorable men and that whatever agreements were struck would be honored. By the time sufficient experience forced them to re-evaluate their assumptions, it was too late and their lands had been stolen. Similarly, in the workplace, when members of such groups exhibit helpfulness, generosity, and caring for their fellow workers (behavior that follows from an assumption that others are basically good), they are frequently viewed as naive, gullible, and in need of "smartening up."

Case Study 1
A Case of Cross-Cultural Miscommunication

Sue and Sue (1990) offer the following example of cross-cultural miscommunication:

> Several years ago, a female school counselor sought the senior author's advice about a Hispanic family she had recently seen. She seemed quite concerned about the identified client, Elena Martinez, a 13-year-old student who was referred for alleged peddling of drugs on the school premises. The counselor had thought that the parents "did not care for their daughter," "were uncooperative," and "were attempting to avoid responsibility for dealing with Elena's delinquency." When pressed for how she arrived at these impressions, the counselor provided the following information.
>
> Elena Martinez is the second oldest of four other siblings, ages 15, 12, 10, and 7. The father is an immigrant from Mexico and the mother a natural citizen. The family resides in a blue-collar neighborhood in San Jose, California. Elena had been reported as having minor problems in school prior to the "drug-selling incident." For example, she had "talked back to teachers," refused to do homework assignments, and had "fought" with other students. Her involvement with a group of Hispanic students (suspected of being responsible for disruptive school-yard pranks) had gotten her into trouble.
>
> Elena was well-known to the counseling staff at the school. Her teacher last year reported that she was unable to "get through" to Elena. Because of the seriousness of the drug accusation, the counselor felt that something had to be done, and that the parents needed to be informed immediately.
>
> The counselor reported calling the parents in order to set up an interview with them. When Mrs. Martinez answered the telephone, the counselor had explained how Elena had been caught on school grounds selling marijuana by a police officer. Rather than arrest her, the officer turned the student over to the vice principal, who luckily was present at the time of the incident. After the explanation, the counselor had asked that the parents make arrangements for an appointment as soon as possible. The meeting would be aimed at informing the parents about Elena's difficulties in school and coming to some decision about what could be done.

During the phone conversation, Mrs. Martinez seemed hesitant about choosing a time to come in and, when pressed by the counselor, excused herself from the telephone. The counselor reported overhearing some whispering on the other end, and then the voice of Mr. Martinez. He immediately asked the counselor how his daughter was and expressed his consternation over the entire situation. At that point, the counselor stated that she understood his feelings, but it would be best to set up an appointment for tomorrow and talk about it then. Several times the counselor asked Mr. Martinez about a convenient time for the meeting, but each time he seemed to avoid the answer and to give excuses. He had to work the rest of the day and could not make the appointment. The counselor stressed strongly how important the meeting was for the daughter's welfare and that the several hours of missed work [were] not important in light of the situation. The father stated that he would be able to make an evening session, but the counselor informed him that school policy prohibited evening meetings. When the counselor suggested that the mother could initially come alone, further hesitations seemed present. Finally, the father agreed to attend.

The very next day, Mr. and Mrs. Martinez and a brother-in-law (Elena's godfather) showed up together in her office. The counselor reported being upset at the presence of the brother-in-law when it became obvious he planned to sit in on the session. At that point, she explained that a third party present would only make the session more complex and the outcome counterproductive. She wanted to see only the family.

The counselor reported that the session went poorly with minimal cooperation from the parents. She reported, "It was like pulling teeth," trying to get the Martinezes to say anything at all.

Note. From *Counseling the Culturally Different,* 2e, by S. W. Sue & D. Sue, pp. 118–119. Copyright © 1990 John Wiley & Sons, Inc. Reprinted with permission.

Before proceeding with an analysis of this case, I encourage you to try to identify areas of cultural insensitivity in the reactions and behavior of the counselor.

This is a clear case of misunderstanding cultural differences. The counselor proceeds with her normal modus operandi, irrespective of the very obvious cultural differences that exist between her and the Martinez family. She misreads their reactions and intentions and draws erroneous and insulting conclusions about them as parents. She communicates these to the Martinezes, who immediately withdraw and become nonreactive. What are some of the assumptions she made and cultural artifacts that she missed?

- It is very possible that because of her ethnicity and her involvement with a group of other Hispanic students, Elena was being carefully watched as a potential troublemaker.
- The counselor appears unaware that in a traditional Mexican family, the wife would not make a decision without first consulting her husband, which she did by "whispering on the other end." Similarly, it is the husband who represents and talks for the family in a formal situation such as this.

- The counselor assumes that Mr. Martinez is indifferent about his daughter because he seemed reluctant to miss work on her behalf. She had no idea of what his work situation was or what the consequences of missing work might be for him and his family. But she assumes he, like any middle-class professional, can make himself available during the day and even presumes to moralize at him, something he is probably not used to from a woman, about several hours of missed work being more important than his daughter. But at the same time, she is unwilling to accommodate herself to the family's need for an evening session and hides behind bureaucratic rules to avoid doing so.
- The counselor thinks too narrowly about what constitutes a family, is used to dealing with nuclear as opposed to extended families and has no idea of the appropriateness of the brother-in-law's presence. Godfathers in Latino/a culture are responsible for the spiritual life of their godchildren and are expected to fill in for the father when the necessity arises. Elena was possibly in the midst of serious spiritual difficulties.

■ Are Theories of Helping Culture Bound?

In chapter 3, cultural racism was defined as the belief that the cultural ways of one group are superior to those of another. It can exist within the mind of an individual, as in the case of Elena's counselor, who seems largely unaware that she is imposing her cultural values on the Martinez family. Cultural racism can also assert itself through the workings of institutions such as the agencies in which most health care providers work and through the theories and practices they hold. Many researchers strongly believe that the assumptions and practices of mainstream service delivery are based on Northern European cultural values (Draguns, 1981; Kim & Berry, 1993; Sue & Sue, 1990). Because of this, serious questions exist as to whether practitioners trained in such a model can adequately serve culturally different clients.

Anthropologists draw a distinction between emic and etic approaches to working cross-culturally. *Emic* refers to looking at a culture through its indigenous concepts and theories. For example, making traditional healers available to Native American clients is an emic approach to service delivery. *Etic* means viewing a culture through "glasses" that are external to it. This is the strategy that the helping professions have adopted. It has been assumed that their approach has relevance for all people irrespective of their cultural backgrounds, but this may not be true. Some critics argue that since the helping profession has its origins and roots in Northern European ideas, values, and sensibilities, it cannot appropriately be applied to individuals who hold different cultural values and assumptions (Duran & Duran, 1995). They further contend that such models are at best "pseudoetic" (Draguns, 1981), which means that they naively misjudge the universality of their approach and that what really has been created are "emic approaches to counseling that are designed by and for middle-class European Americans" (Atkinson, Morten, & Sue, 1993, p. 54).

■ Key Aspects of the Helping Process

If one looks carefully at the assumptions and practices that are central to the helping professions as they currently exist, it becomes immediately clear that much is in conflict with the general worldview of non-White clients. Four key aspects of the helping process can be identified as especially problematic:

- importance of verbal expressiveness and self-disclosure
- setting long-term goals
- relative importance placed on changing the client versus changing the environment
- definition of what is mentally healthy

Verbal Expressiveness and Self-Disclosure

Most practitioners believe that verbal expressiveness and self-disclosure by clients are critical aspects of the helping process. The Cultures of Color do not, however, share this value or feel comfortable talking about themselves or disclosing personal material to relative strangers. Asian Americans, for example, learn emotional restraint at an early age and are expected to exhibit modesty in the face of authority as well as subtleness in dealing with personal problems (Atkinson, Whitely, & Gin, 1990; D. R. Ho, 1994). To reveal intimate details of one's life to strangers is seen as bringing shame on the family and is experienced as "losing face." Similarly, it has been shown that Native Americans and Latino/a Americans also feel threatened with the demand for such disclosure (Fleming, 1992; Vontress, 1981). For both, intimate sharing is done only with friends of long standing. Only European Americans seem comfortable revealing intimate details of their life to relative strangers. Foreign travelers to the United States are often shocked by the amount of personal information revealed to them by fellow passengers.

African Americans, in turn, tend to be suspicious of requests by White providers for intimate life details (Gordon, 1964; Sue & Sue, 1990). The African American community considers it dangerous and potentially self-destructive to not hide one's feelings from Whites until their trustworthiness can be assured. I am reminded of a very bizarre but sad incident when minority youth leaders, mostly African American, from a major urban area were taken to an isolated part of the Grand Canyon for a sensitivity training experience by a group of White professionals. Communication between the two groups broke down very quickly, and only when it was learned that the African American youth had come to believe that they had been taken there to be assassinated was it possible to defuse the situation. Helping professionals obviously need to be aware of how culturally different clients view their efforts at helping as well as careful in drawing conclusions about a client's reluctance to self-disclose. Such behavior is normative in many cultural groups and should not be interpreted as defensiveness or as reflecting depression, shyness, or passivity.

Setting Long-Term Goals

Psychodynamic approaches to counseling and other forms of helping place importance on long-term treatment planning. Helping is envisioned as a long-term, ongoing process where therapist and client interact in a rather unstructured situation with the aim of making significant changes in the client's inner psychology. Clients of Color, on the other hand, tend to be more action-oriented and desirous of concrete advice and immediate solutions to the problems for which they seek help (Sue & Sue, 1990). They seem to find directive as opposed to nondirective approaches most helpful and often express confusion or frustration around the idea of abstract, long-term goal setting. The differences may result from differing time orientations, a belief that the individual's purpose is to serve the collective (rather than the self), or the fact that "sitting around and talking" is a luxury they just can't afford or can't see as potentially helpful. Again, the helper must avoid the temptation to interpret their "reluctance" to go along with long-term goal planning as resistance.

Changing the Client Versus Changing the Environment

Practitioner and client can differ greatly in how they conceive and think about the change process: Is it important to change the client to fit his or her circumstances or vice versa? These orientations are referred to technically as *autoplastic* and *alloplastic* solutions. Helping clients cope with a difficult life situation by accommodating or adapting to it (i.e., changing themselves in that direction) is autoplastic; encouraging or teaching clients to impose changes on the external environment so that it better fits their needs is alloplastic.

Cultures of Color differ widely on this question. Asian American culture tends to stress a passive acceptance of reality and a transcendence of conflict by adjusting one's perceptions so that harmony can be achieved with the environment (D. R. Ho, 1994). African Americans, on the other hand, tend to point to a racist environment as the cause of many of their distresses and advocate changing it as opposed to themselves (Kunjufu, 1984). To this end, in the late 1960s, African American psychologists in the state of California called for and obtained a moratorium on testing minority children in the public schools (Bay Area Association of Black Psychologists, 1972). They argued that culturally biased psychological assessment was being used to funnel culturally different children into special education classes by White teachers and administrators who were not comfortable with their non-White ways. In a similar vein, Braginsky and Braginsky (1974) and others have called the helping profession to task for serving as a "handmaiden to the status quo" by encouraging culturally different clients to adapt their behavior to the demands of White institutions as opposed to encouraging their clients to pursue societal change. Northern European culture, for its part, tends to encourage the confrontation of obstacles in the environment that restrict one's freedom (Holtzman, Diaz-Guerrero, & Swartz, 1975).

What seems most influential in determining the stance a provider assumes is the general theoretical perspective he or she follows. Psychodynamic approaches, for example, locate problems and conflicts within the individual and dictate inner changes as the exclusive solution. More behaviorally and cognitively oriented theories do the opposite. They advocate changing the environment to change behavior.

Sue and Sue (1990) offer an interesting perspective on this question. They suggest that much client behavior can be understood as resulting from their beliefs about locus of control and locus of responsibility. *Locus of control* refers to whether individuals feel that they are in control of their own fate (internal control) or that they are being controlled externally (external control) and, therefore, whether their actions can change the external world. *Locus of responsibility* refers to whether individuals believe that they are responsible for their own fate (internal responsibility) or that they cannot be held responsible because there are more powerful forces at work (external responsibility). Sue and Sue propose four "worldviews" based on combining these two dimensions and argue that People of Color may exhibit any of the four. Generally, Northern European American helpers believe in internal control and internal responsibility—that clients are in control of their own fate, their actions do affect their outcomes, and success or failure in life is related to their personal characteristics and abilities. If this does not match a client's perception of how the world works, there are likely to be serious differences regarding treatment goals and just what constitutes helping.

Definitions of Mental Health

The human service professions have tended to adopt Northern European cultural definitions of what constitutes healthy and normal functioning. Self-reliance, autonomy, self-actualization, self-assertion, insight, and resistance to stress are seen as hallmarks of healthy adjustment and functioning (Saeki & Borow, 1985; Sue & Sue, 1990). These are the characteristics toward which clients are encouraged to strive. They are not, however, the same personal qualities that are valued in all cultures. For example, Asian American cultures value interdependence, inner enlightenment, negation of self, transcendence of conflict, and passive acceptance of reality (D. R. Ho, 1994). This view is largely antithetical to that of mainstream Western thought. What Asian American culture shares with the other three Cultures of Color, and what sets them apart from Northern European culture, is the diminished importance of individual autonomy and self-assertion. A similar idea is expressed in the way Native American culture views health and illness (Duran & Duran, 1995). Illnesses, both mental and physical, are thought to result from disharmony of the individual, family, or tribe from the ways of nature and the natural order. Healing can occur only when harmony is restored. This is the goal of traditional healing practices.

Another way to describe this important difference is the distinction between the individual and the extended self (Brown & Landrum-Brown, 1995). The individual self is characteristic of Northern European culture. It exists autonomously, is fragmented from its social context, and has as its goal personal survival and betterment. The self develops very differently in cultures that limit its narcissism and free expression. The term *extended self* is used to describe ego development in group members who conceive of themselves not as individuals but as part of a broader collective. All behavior occurs with an awareness of what its impact will be not on the self but, more important, on the larger social group of which the person is a part. Referring back to the axiology and ethos dimensions suggested by Brown and Landrum-Brown, the subvalues of competition, emotional restraint, direct verbal expression, and help seeking and the sub-beliefs of independence, individual rights, egalitarianism, and control and dominance (all typical of the Northern European cultural paradigm) represent ideas that support the existence of an individual self.

Similarly, their opposites (the subvalues of cooperation, emotional expressiveness, indirect verbal expression, and "saving face" and the sub-beliefs of interdependence, honor and family protection, authoritarianism, and harmony and deference), most typical of the worldview of the Communities of Color, are related to an extended self. Independence, for example, allows for greater self-assertion; interdependence allows for greater intergroup harmony. In speaking of the extended self, I am reminded of a former graduate Student of Color who, when introduced to a model of identity development in People of Color that described the final stage of growth as "transcending specific group identities," reacted: "This can't be right. How can they see this as optimal growth? The person is no longer a part of the community." Thus, practitioners must be aware of incongruence between their notion of what is healthy and where treatment should be leading and that of the client. Where differences exist, they must be respected, and great care must be taken not to project one's values onto the helping process and not to unintentionally judge a client's behaviors that vary from one's own standards as inferior and deficient.

■ Conflicting Cross-Cultural Service Models

What can a practitioner do about these potential areas of conflict? The easiest and most immediate answer is fairly simple—alter and adjust the helping model to accommodate the client(s). Recall from chapter 2 that one of the central skills associated with cultural competence is the ability to adapt mainstream practices to the needs of culturally different groups. For example, it does not seem unreasonable or impossible to expect providers to alter their expectations (especially in the early stages of working together) regarding self-disclosure, verbal openness, or fluency. The provider should also be able to adjust the type of interaction that occurs and, when helpful, move into a less ambiguous and more directive problem-solving mode. Similarly, it should be possible to adapt the provider's view of where change should take place (changing the individual vs. changing the environment) to align with the client's cultural tendencies and to rethink treatment goals and outcomes in light of the client's cultural beliefs.

Sue and Zane (1987) suggest two additional strategies for improving provider credibility. First is to ensure that clients feel that their problems or reasons for seeking help are understood by the provider in terms of their own cultural viewpoint. This involves both appreciating their worldview in terms of the intricacies of their cultural background and being able to communicate that awareness to them. Second is to ensure that clients get some immediate benefit or reinforcement from the helping process. This may involve advocating for them with another agency, teaching them some skill or practice that might help them navigate the system, or even directly intervening in a situation on their behalf. Although such interventions push the boundaries of what is considered appropriate among mainstream providers, it should be remembered that such helping practices were developed primarily for working with dominant culture clients. Such therapeutic guidelines may just not make cultural sense in relation to working with Clients of Color.

Certain critics, however, suggest that merely making adjustments to a predominantly Northern European model of helping is not sufficient. Approaching the problem of cross-cultural service delivery from such limited perspective seems like something akin to "rearranging the deck chairs on the Titanic." They argue that merely making cosmetic changes to a process that is, by its very nature, highly destructive to traditional people and their cultures does not get at the real heart of the problem. Duran and Duran (1995), for example, believe that Northern European culture and its application through Western psychology has been instrumental in fragmenting Native American culture and lifestyle. They further contend that inherent in the Northern European worldview is an inability to tolerate the existence of alternative ways of knowing and experiencing the world:

> The critical factor in cross-cultural psychology is a fundamentally different way of being in the world. In no way does Western thinking address any system of cognition other than its own. Given that Judeo-Christian belief systems include notions of the Creator putting human beings in charge of all creations, it is easy to understand why this group of people assumes that it also possesses the ultimate way of describing psychological phenomena for all of humanity. In reality, the thought that what is right comes from one worldview produces a narcissistic worldview that desecrates and destroys much of what is known as culture and cosmological perspective. (p. 17)

Diamond's (1987) work on "primitive" versus "civilized" societies offers a useful metaphor through which to compare the nature of traditional cultures (which include the Cultures of Color in the United States) with that of postmodern Northern Europe. Like Duran and Duran, Diamond contends that there is something fundamentally skewed within "civilized" culture—that something essential has been lost. Only through a careful analysis of the dimensions of traditional culture can one discern what those elements might be. Diamond summarizes eight characteristics of "primitive" culture that have been lost through the civilizing process:

- good psychological nurturance of the individual
- multiple and engaging relationships throughout the life cycle
- various forms of institutionalized deviance

- celebration and fusion of the sacred—within nature, society, and the individual—through ritual
- direct engagement with nature and natural processes
- direct and active participation in cultural forms
- equating goodness, beauty, and the natural environment
- socioeconomic support as a natural inheritance

One consequence of the breakdown of traditional culture vis-à-vis the civilizing process, according to Diamond (1987), was a radical increase in stress, dysfunction, and mental illness.

> These prominent features of primitive society should lead us to anticipate an exceedingly low incidence of the chronic characterological or psychoneurotic phenomena that seem to be growing with civilization. This reflects my own experience; I would add only that the disciplined expressiveness of primitive societies, together with traditional social and economic supports, also results in a greater tolerance of psychotic manifestations, or better, converts the latter into a normal, bounded human experience. (p. 171)

Diller (1991) documents a similar destructive tendency in contemporary Western culture. Specifically, he looks at Jewish emancipation in 19th-century Europe and describes how it psychologically altered and transformed traditional Jewish culture. The result was widespread fragmentation and the destruction of traditional Jewish values, ways, community, and identity.

> As chaos reigned supreme within the ghetto, it simultaneously intruded itself into the inner psyche of the assimilating Jew, rupturing previous bases for self-understanding and identity. The internal consequences were staggering. One major symptom was a fragmentation in the way people thought. Mind increasingly came to function independent of emotion and intuition, and the integrity of the Jewish self fell prey to self-consciousness and compartmentalization. With the Enlightenment, Jews became self-conscious about their own Jewishness and in time they grew alienated from it. In the ghetto, being a Jew was a given, a fact of life that required no further exploration. Jews uncritically followed customs and habits thousands of years old and participated in a lifestyle that defined all aspects of their existence. They questioned the fairness of God, the reasons for their sad plight and exile, but never the fact of who they were. A given becomes a matter of debate, an absolute becomes relative, only when there is an alternative available. Emancipation provided Jews with that alternative in the form of potential escape and assimilation, the possibility of no longer being Jews. In so doing, it forced them to inquire into the nature of their Jewishness, thereby objectifying it and setting them apart from it. By asking the questions: "Why am I a Jew and what does that mean?" by tasting of the tree of Knowledge as Adam

had, post-emancipation Jews set into motion a process which would eventually and permanently alienate them from the past. (p. 32)

Such concerns have led researchers in cross-cultural service delivery toward various strategies in seeking alternative models to the mere adaptation and adjustment of the Northern European helping paradigm. Three trends can be identified:

- Some theorists call for the creation of individual ethnic-specific (emic) models or "psychologies," each developed by providers and researchers from a given ethnic community. The aim is to define a unique and unbiased understanding of the mental health and treatment issues of each community. In arguing for the wisdom of a "Black psychology," for example, White (1972) contends that "principles and theories developed by white psychologists to explain the behavior of white people simply do not have sufficient explanatory power to account for the behavior of blacks" (p. 2). In a similar vein, C. Clark (1972) suggests the need for "creating an alternative framework within which black behavior may be differently described, explained, and interpreted" (p. 1). According to Jones (1972), Mosby "makes the case for qualitative differences in the life experiences of blacks which lead to differences in developmental, social, personal, intellectual, educational, and family functioning. Black Psychology would account for the differences" (p. 2). Each evolving model would dictate a unique and culturally sensitive approach specific to providing helping services to members of that community.
- A second approach, such as that suggested by Duran and Duran (1995), advocates for a return to traditional healing practices from the client's culture. Each Community of Color has, over time, developed its own conceptions of health and illness as well as unique indigenous healing practices. Availing oneself of such services, first of all, guarantees that the help being received has not been compromised by dominant cultural ways. Second, it provides an avenue for strengthening ethnic identity and cultural ties. Finally, offering such services is especially useful to clients who remain steeped in traditional cultural ways and values and for whom dominant United States culture has little relevance or feels unsafe.
- A logical compromise, at least for the present, is to include traditional healers and healing practices as part of a broad range of helping services within a community. Such a strategy, above all, provides a strong statement about the value of cultural diversity to the human services. Most culturally different clients, however, have experienced some level of acculturation or, to put it differently, are in varying degrees bicultural. For these individuals, a full return to traditional, cultural ways is probably neither possible nor desirable. More relevant to their situation is the use of models of helping that have been sensitively and extensively adapted to the cultural needs of their group by practitioners, either indigenous or culturally different, who are truly culturally competent.

As the demand for cross-cultural helping continues to grow and increasingly complex and effective strategies for serving culturally diverse clients are developed, it is just a matter of time before dominant forms of helping begin to lose their decidedly Northern European perspective and become increasingly infused and informed by the wisdom and values of a variety of other cultures. In other words, it will become more multicultural.

■ Summary

Culture is the conscious and unconscious content that a group learns, shares, and transmits from generation to generation that organizes life and helps interpret existence. A useful analogy for understanding culture is the concept of paradigm. A paradigm is a set of shared assumptions and beliefs about how the world works that structures an individual's perception and ideas about reality. Our paradigms, or worldviews, tell us what is possible and impossible, what the rules are, and how things are done. The culture into which a person is born and socialized defines the dimensions of his or her personal paradigm. Different cultures generate different paradigms and experiences of reality.

Increasingly, social scientists have chosen to distinguish among human groups on the basis of culture rather than race. For example, there seems to be as much variability in physical characteristics within traditional racial categories as among groups, and the social reality of race in the United States does not conform to the existence of five distinct racial groupings.

Brown and Landrum-Brown (1995) define eight dimensions along which cultures can vary. Each culture generates a unique profile along these various dimensions and, as a result, generates a unique experience of living and reality that is shared by members of the cultural group. Ho (1987) compares the five racial groups on various cultural dimensions including views of nature and the environment, time orientation, human relations, work, and activity.

Contemporary theories of helping and counseling are themselves culture bound, embodying the values and style of Northern European culture. Examples include an emphasis on verbal expression and self-disclosure, setting long-term goals, and changing the client rather than changing the environment, as well as definitions of mental health that emphasize individuality and self-assertion. Because of this, serious questions exist as to whether practitioners trained in such a paradigm can adequately serve culturally different clients. Each of these therapeutic objectives is in conflict with the cultural tendencies and values of the four Communities of Color.

Various strategies for creating adequate cross-cultural service delivery models have been suggested. Some theorists believe that it is possible to adjust and adapt existing dominant-group-oriented paradigms. Others feel that there is something inherently destructive to traditional peoples and cultures in the Northern European worldview and call for the creation of ethnic-specific psychologies. A third alternative is to use traditional healing practices from the client's culture. A reasonable compromise is the inclusion of traditional healers and healing practices as part of a broad range of helping services offered to a community.

■ Activities

1. *Explore your culture*. This exercise will help you become more aware of your cultural roots and identity. Answer the following questions (developed by Hardy and Laszloffy, 1995) in relation to each ethnic group that constitutes your culture of origin. You might need to seek additional information from parents or other relatives.

   a. What were the migration patterns of the group?
   b. If other than Native American, under what conditions did your family enter the United States (immigrants, political refugee, slave, etc.)?
   c. What were/are the group's experiences with oppression? What were/are the markers of oppression?
   d. What issues divide members within the same group?
   e. Describe the relationship between the group's identity and your national ancestry. (If the group is defined in terms of nationality, please skip this question.)
   f. What significance do race, skin color, and hair play within the group?
   h. What is/are the dominant religion(s) of the group? What role does religion and spirituality play in the everyday lives of members of the group?
   i. What role does regionality and geography play in the group?
   j. How are gender roles defined within the group? How is sexual orientation regarded?
   k. (1) What prejudices or stereotypes does this group have about itself?
      (2) What prejudices or stereotypes do other groups have about this group?
      (3) What prejudices or stereotypes does this group have about other groups?
   l. What role (if any) do names play in the group? Are there rules, mores, or rituals governing the assignment of names?
   m. How is social class defined in the group?
   n. What occupational roles are valued and devalued by the group?
   o. What is the relationship between age and values of the group?
   p. How is family defined in the group?
   q. How does this group view outsiders in general and mental health professionals specifically?
   r. How have the organizing principles of this group shaped your family and its members? What effect have they had on you? (Organizing principles are "fundamental constructs which shape the perceptions, beliefs, and behaviors of members of the group." For example, for Jews an organizing principle is "fear of persecution.")
   s. What are the ways in which pride/shame issues of the group are manifested in your family system? (Pride/shame issues are "aspects of a culture that are sanctioned as distinctively negative or positive." For example, for Jews a pride/shame issue is "educational achievement.")
   t. What impact will these pride/shame issues have on your work with clients from both similar and dissimilar cultural backgrounds?

u. If more than one group comprises your culture of origin, how are the differences negotiated in your family? What are the intergenerational consequences? How has this impacted you personally and as a therapist?

2. *Take a cultural self-inventory.* Review Brown and Landrum-Brown's (1995) dimensions of culture. Ask yourself where you fit on each dimension and from where in your cultural past this characteristic is likely to have derived. Are there ways that you have personally changed on any of these dimensions as you have grown and matured? How and why?

■ Introduction to Chapters 5 through 7

In the opening chapters of this book we have focused on two key aspects of cultural competence—understanding racism in its various forms and understanding culture and cultural differences—and seen how each shapes the way human service providers interact with culturally different clients. In chapters 5 through 7, we explore a slightly different question: How do race and culture in America shape the psychological experiences of Clients of Color? In chapter 5 we begin with a consideration of how child development and parenting issues are shaped and affected by race and culture. Chapter 6 inquires into issues of mental health. What kinds of psychological issues do Clients of Color struggle with? What factors in society place Clients of Color at special risk for mental and emotional problems? And what types of personal and social problems are likely to bring them into the helping situation? Chapter 7, in turn, looks at various forms of bias in the delivery of human services and inquires into why culturally different clients tend to underutilize and avoid mainstream providers.

5 Children and Parents of Color

This chapter explores various issues of child development and parenting that are affected by race and culture. The following three psychological scenarios, drawn from real therapeutic situations, highlight the kinds of differences, demands, and challenges that face Children and Parents of Color. Most striking is the complexity of dynamics that affect these families to which they must respond and adapt. Often, forces in the broader environment affect them in negative ways, requiring some form of creative intervention, treatment, or accommodation if they are to be allowed to proceed along a normal and healthy developmental course. Culturally competent interventions involve helping family members draw upon unique cultural strengths and attributes to creatively solve life problems through empowerment and the development of self-worth and resiliency.

■ Three Scenarios

Scenario 1. Clark (1963), in his early but seminal exploration of racial identity, describes the following situation of a Black child referred to therapy because of severe racial identity confusion. "'I got a sun-tan at the beach this summer,' a 7-year-old Negro [sic] boy repeated over and over again to a psychologist. His mother, he said, was white and his father was white and therefore he was a 'white boy.' His brown skin was the result of a summer at the beach. He became almost plaintive in his pleading, begging the adult to believe him" (p. 37). Clark goes on to comment more broadly on this phenomenon. "General studies of a thousand Negro [sic] psychiatric patients in a mental hospital and detailed case histories of eight of them revealed that Negro [sic] patients frequently had delusions involving the denial of their skin color and ancestry. Some of these patients insisted that they were white in spite of clear evidence to the contrary" (p. 49). Similarly, but more recently, Ho (1992) describes play therapy with an 8-year-old Korean girl, a recent immigrant, who appeared withdrawn, would not interact in class, and was underachieving. In play therapy, she chose several light-skinned and one dark-skinned dolls, forming the latter into a circle that would not allow the dark-skinned doll to enter. Periodically, one of the light-skinned dolls would physically knock down the dark-skinned one. She also put two adult dolls in a house and demolished it. The author interpreted her behavior as reflecting both feelings of inferiority to her light-skinned classmates and anger at her parents for making her an "outcast" in an unfamiliar white group (pp. 127–128).

The first part of this chapter addresses various issues of child development that appear especially influential in the lives of Children of Color.

You will learn how differences in cultural temperament are identifiable from birth and form the basis for personality development. You will explore the development of racial identity in children and see its effects on self-esteem. You will explore cultural and racial issues related to adolescent identity formation as well as differences in cultural learning styles and their impact on academic performance. Finally, you will learn some basics of providing clinical services to Children of Color.

Scenario 2. Ho (1992) also describes family therapy for an American Indian boy who had grown increasingly withdrawn and exhibited acting-out behavior, primarily in the form of glue sniffing. The boy's mother, who was Cherokee, blamed her son's behavior on marital discord and the father's, a Hopi, unwillingness to discipline their son. She reported that the father had always been "apathetic" toward his child-rearing responsibilities, especially in regard to discipline. The father, a "kind, soft-spoken, mild-mannered man," explained that in Hopi culture, the male moves in with the wife's family, and it is she and her family who retain primary responsibility for raising the children. He, in turn, is responsible for overseeing the rearing of her sister's children, especially the boys. Having acted upon this cultural prescription, he saw nothing amiss in his actions. With the father's permission, the therapist consulted an elder of the father's tribe who privately met with the father and advised him that "the taboo of shared parental responsibility" held in marriages within the tribe, and that he was free to take on a bigger parenting role with his own son (pp. 154–155).

The second section of chapter 5 focuses on issues of parenting in culturally diverse families. You will explore the extent to which family dynamics and structures can vary with culture; how Parents of Color can create a "buffer zone" between their child and the harmful effects of majority culture; the relationship between parenting styles and self-esteem; and how children can be prepared for the experience of racism.

Scenario 3. As part of my private practice, I once saw an interracial couple for marital problems. The husband, of Chinese American descent, and the wife, Irish American, disagreed bitterly about the role his mother should play in their lives. He said that it was normal in his culture for the mother of the family to give advice and guidance to the daughter-in-law and that, even though it might at times be a little "heavy-handed," it was done out of love and caring. He further believed his wife should be more tolerant out of respect for his culture. She, in turn, responded that she had spent the last ten years trying to recover from an abusive home situation and refused to subject herself to any further abuse from the mother-in-law no matter how pure her intentions or how normal such behavior might be in Chinese culture. "I married you, not your family, and don't feel it is fair or very loving to ask me to continue to subject myself to your mother's intrusive and abusive ways." The husband just lowered his eyes, as if embarrassed by what his wife was saying. With help, the couple came to see that their conflicting perceptions were as much cultural as personal, and thereby less threatening and more amenable to change.

The final section of chapter 5 deals with an increasingly important and underserved family system—bicultural parents and children. Remember that, for the first time in U.S. history, Census 2000 collected data on mixed-race individuals. In this section you will learn about the dynamics of bicultural couples, patterns of bicultural marital discord, and the unique developmental issues that face bicultural children in discovering who they are and where they fit socially.

■ Child Development

Temperament at Birth

The preceding chapters discuss the importance of cultural differences in the evolution of cultural styles. It is important to realize that such differences appear very early in life, provide a base for the development of cultural uniqueness, and are highly responsive to cultural differences in parenting practices. The emotional characteristics of children from different ethnic and cultural groups, for example, vary greatly from birth (Trawick-Smith, 1997). It is easy to discern dramatic differences in temperament and activity levels of newborns and infants. Freedman (1979) offers the following examples. White babies (of Northern European background) cry more easily and are harder to console than Chinese babies, who tend to adapt to any position in which they are placed. Navajo babies show even more calmness and adaptability than the Chinese. They calmly accept being placed on a cradleboard. White babies cry and struggle to get out of the strapped confinement. Japanese children, in turn, are far more irritable than either the Chinese or Navajo. Australian aboriginal babies react strongly, like Whites, to being disturbed, but are more easily calmed.

Differences are also found in the ways mothers and infants interact (Seifer, Sameroff, Barrett, & Krafchuk, 1994). There is far less verbal interaction between a Navajo mother and baby than between a White mother and baby. The Navajo mother is actually rather silent and gets her baby's attention via eye contact. White mothers talk to their children constantly and their children respond with great activity. The mothers are equally adept, however, at gaining their children's attention. According to Freedman, the differences result from the continual interplay of inherited genetic predispositions and patterns of cultural conditioning through child–parent interaction. Thus, children's genetic temperamental tendencies are reinforced by cultural learning about the proper way to respond emotionally, and the result is children who increasingly take on the temperamental style of their culture (Garcia Coll, 1990; Scarr, 1993).

Development of Racial Awareness

Children of Color face the same developmental tasks as any other children. They are, however, at more risk for experiencing instances of racism and prejudice, which can powerfully impact fragile, developing psyches. As a result, they may exhibit problems navigating certain developmental tasks of childhood because of the preponderance of negative messages they receive about themselves from the White world. Of particular importance are potential difficulties in developing unconflicted racial identities and internalizing positive self-esteem.

Children of Color are aware of racial differences (i.e., differences in skin color and facial and body features) as early as age 3 or 4, and by age 7, one can begin to discern the rudiments of a racial awareness (Aboud, 1988; Grant & Haynes, 1995). Majority group children, in comparison, are generally slower to develop a consciousness of the fact that they are White because race is not as central to their families' lives as it is to People of Color (York, 1991). *Racial identity* evolves in relation to the sequential acquisition of three learning processes. The first is *racial classification ability* (Aboud, 1987; Williams & Morland, 1976) and involves the child's learning to apply ethnic labels accurately to members of different groups. For example, in the classic doll studies designed by Clark and Clark (1947) to measure racial identity in African American children, the child is asked: "Show me the Black doll" or "Show me the White doll" when presented with dolls of different skin tones. The child who can accurately perform such labeling on a regular basis is ready to move on to the next stage of forming a *racial identification* (Aboud & Doyle, 1993). Put simply, racial identification involves a child's learning to apply the newly gained concept of race to him- or herself. According to Proshansky and Newton (1968), this process requires a kind of inner dialogue through which children learn that because of their skin color, they are members of a certain group (i.e., that the child is black or yellow or brown) and, as such, visibly different from others. Thus, racial identification results from an interaction between children's comparisons of their skin color with those of parents, siblings, and others and what they are told about who they are racially. The final stage, called *racial evaluation* by Proshansky and Newton, involves the creation of an internal evaluation of one's own ethnicity. It is how children come to feel about being black or yellow or brown. Racial evaluation develops as a child internalizes the various messages regarding his or her ethnicity received from significant others and society in general. By age 7, most ethnic children are aware of the negative evaluation that society places on members of their group (Thornton, Chatters, Taylor, & Allen, 1990).

Racial Awareness and Self-Esteem

Early studies of racial awareness by Clark and Clark (1947), Kardiner and Ovesey (1951), and Goodman (1952) found that African American children had difficulty successfully completing the last two stages just described. These children would either deny the fact that their skin was black (as in Scenario 1), devalue people with black skin and black culture in general, or do both. In addition, it was found that these same African American children often exhibited negative self-concepts. The authors concluded that such outcomes were inevitable for Children of Color. By living in White-dominated society, they could not help but internalize the negative attitudes and messages that bombarded them daily, and the resulting negative self-judgments would inevitably translate into a diminished self-image.

As the ethnic pride movements of the 1960s gained momentum, however, the inevitability of such conclusions was vehemently challenged. Some referred to this early work as the "myth of self-hatred" (Trawick-Smith & Lisi, 1994). Earlier studies were criticized as being methodologically weak or as reflecting an earlier psychological reality that was no longer accurate. New studies showed no differences in self-esteem between African American and White children (Powell, 1973; Rosenberg, 1979). In racially homogeneous settings, in fact, African American children scored higher than their White counterparts (Spencer & Markstrom-Adams, 1990). The more extensive their interaction with Whites and the White world, however, the lower were their self-concept scores. The accuracy of these newer findings was, in turn, challenged as too conveniently fitting the researchers' political agenda.

Clarifying the Question

In order to bring some clarity to this controversy, Williams and Morland (1976) carried out an empirically sound, longitudinal study of racial identity formation in African American (Afro) and White (Euro) children over a period of 12 years. Racial identity was assessed in the same cohort by four different measures administered at four different times during the 12-year period: during preschool, third grade, sixth grade, and junior high school. They published the following findings:

- In regard to racial classification ability (i.e., accurately applying racial labels to different racial groups), Williams and Morland found no differences between Euro and Afro (their terms) students. Both began regularly classifying race by ages 4 and 5, with high accuracy by 6 years.
- Racial identification (i.e., the ability to accurately apply racial labels to parents and self) was measured by asking children which of the various colored dolls (light- or dark-skinned) looked like them or a parent. Preschool Euro children chose the light-skinned figure 80% of the time and the dark-skinned figure 20%, whereas Afro preschoolers evenly distributed their choices between the dark- and light-skinned dolls 50/50. By the third grade, however, the Afro children were also choosing the dark-skinned figures 80% of the time, paralleling the differential responses of the same-aged Euro children. By junior high school, both groups were almost 100% accurate in their respective choices.
- Racial evaluation (i.e., assigning positive evaluation to one's own racial group) was assessed by asking the young subjects to choose a figure (light- or dark-skinned) in response to a description that included a positive or

negative adjective (e.g., choose the good parent). Both Euro and Afro preschoolers overwhelmingly assigned the positive features to the light-skinned figures (pro-Euro response) at a rate of 90% and 80%, respectively. These patterns repeated for both groups through late elementary school. In junior high school, however, the Afro students' responses changed dramatically to pro-Afro (i.e., positive adjectives assigned to dark-skinned figures), ending with a rate equal to that of Euro junior high students.

■ Racial acceptance (a second measure of racial evaluation) was measured by showing the subjects photos of dark- and light-skinned individuals and asking if they would like to play with this person. Euro preschoolers were significantly less accepting of Afro photos than Afro preschoolers were of Euro photos. In fact, Afro preschoolers accepted Euro pictures slightly more frequently than they did Afro photos. By elementary school and beyond, both Afro and Euro students grew increasingly less accepting of photos of the other group, with Afros always a bit more accepting than Euros.

By way of summary, Williams and Morland found that by third grade African American children were appropriately aware of their racial identity, accepted it, and preferred playmates from their own group. They did find African American preschoolers regularly making pro-Euro responses on all measures, which could be interpreted as indicating early identity confusion (as suggested in the pre-1960s studies discussed earlier). The authors, however, attribute this to response bias rather than any underlying pathology, and their interpretation seems to be borne out by the fact that with further socialization, and by the third grade, all except one of the measures showed group-appropriate responses. Regarding racial evaluation, however, there does seem to be lingering pro-White attitudes among Black youth until junior high school, when there is a dramatic reversal to predominantly pro-Afro responses. From these data, it seems likely that African American children do internalize to some extent the attitudes of society at large. But it is not clear from this study whether their pro-Euro preferences can be interpreted as indicative of negative feelings toward themselves or their own group. In any case, the effects are not lasting, and there doesn't seem to be any concurrent difficulty in racial identification itself. It is probably fair to say, however, that this is a critical period in the developmental life of Children of Color and may be problematic for the development of self-esteem as long as pro-Euro attitudes linger. A more recent study by Spencer and Markstrom-Adams (1990) supports these conclusions. See Table 5–1 for a summary of Williams and Morland's research.

Such studies clearly show that Children of Color regularly exhibit positive self-esteem and unconflicted racial identities. But this does not mean that racism poses any less risk for them. It simply implies that active measures must be taken to protect them, whether it be through Norton's (1983) notion of creating a buffer zone around the child or McAdoo's (1985) belief in the value of creating ethnic pride as a means of insulating the child psychologically from the experience of racism.

A final perspective on the impact of racism on self-esteem can be gleaned from interviews with People of Color who came to the United States as adults

■ **TABLE 5–1**   Racial Identity Formation in African American and
White Children

Measure of racial identity	Summary of findings
Racial classification ability (ability to accurately apply racial labels to different racial groups)	Develops in both Euro and Afro children by ages 4–5. High accuracy in all children in both groups by age 6.
Racial identification (ability to accurately apply racial labels to parents and self)	In preschool, Euro children exhibit 80% Euro response, and Afro children exhibit 50% Euro response. By third grade, Euros had 90% Euro response and Afros had 80% Afro response. By adolescence, both Euros and Afros had 100% group-appropriate choices.
Racial evaluation (ability to assign positive evaluation to one's own racial group)	In preschool, Euros exhibit 90% pro-Euro responses, and Afros exhibit 80% pro-Euro responses. Percentages remain the same until adolescence when Afro students reverse their preferences to 90% pro-Afro.
Racial acceptance (acceptance of playmates of a different race)	In preschool, Euros exhibit 50% acceptance of Afro playmates, and Afros exhibit 60% acceptance of Euro playmates. By third grade, both Euros and Afros show 80% preference for own race playmates.

Note. Adapted from *Race, Color and the Young Child* by J. E. Williams & J. K. Morland, 1976, Chapel Hill, NC: University of North Carolina Press.

after growing up in countries where they were in the racial majority (Diller, 1997). Only after they had arrived in this country did they have their first personal experiences with prejudice and racism. How did they respond? Their first reported reaction was shock and disbelief. Once they had sufficient time to process what had happened and to label it as a "racial attack," they were able to put up sufficient ego defenses to protect themselves emotionally as well as physically. They quickly learned to identify such situations before or as they happened and to deal with them quickly and effectively. They uniformly believed that it was only because of their own strong sense of self and well-developed ego defenses as adults that they were able to come out of these experiences relatively unharmed. When asked how they might have felt as children facing such experiences, they all indicated that they would have been overwhelmed and likely scarred in some essential way.

Adolescent Racial Identity

In her book *Why Are All the Black Kids Sitting Together in the Cafeteria?*, Tatum (1997) points out that race and racial identity issues become particularly salient when Children of Color enter adolescence. Changes in school groupings, dating, and broader participation in the social environment highlight the existence of racism and the need to understand "what it means for *me* to be a Black." With adolescence, there is a greater likelihood of encountering "experiences that may trigger an examination of their racial identity." Boy-girl events and interaction become much less racially diverse, and White peers seem less likely to understand or be able to provide support for the emerging Black identities. As a result, Adolescents of Color gravitate naturally to like-race peers and often adopt an "oppositional stance or identity," absorbing stereotyped images of being of Color and rejecting characteristics and behaviors that they see as White. "The anger and resentment that adolescents feel in response to their growing awareness of the systematic exclusion of Black people from full participation in U.S. society leads to the development of an oppositional social identity. This . . . both protects one's identity from the psychological assault of racism and keeps the dominant group at a distance" (p. 60). Tatum sees this attachment to the peer group as a "positive coping strategy" in the face of stress. It is not without its difficulties, however. Images of Blackness tend to be highly stereotyped, and academic success is often discounted as White. As we shall see in chapter 6, this stage of racial identity development, which Cross (1995) calls the "encounter" and entails a turning toward one's own group and a rejection of the majority and its values, is followed by the emergence of greater individualization and diversification of racial identity.

Earlier studies have also found different patterns of personal identity formation across ethnic groups. Hauser and Kasendorf (1983), for example, compared working-class urban African American and White adolescent boys in relation to the development of self-image. Building on the work of Erikson (1968), they explored the manner in which adolescents integrate various images of themselves into a coherent sense of self. For Erikson, adolescence is a time of self-exploration during which one tries to find a comfortable synthesis of past experience, sense of family, present questions and concerns, and hopes and plans for the future.

Hauser and Kasendorf found that African American adolescents formed a stable integration of self-images much earlier than did their White counterparts, who seemed to experience higher levels of confusion, disequilibrium, and personal exploration. In fact, it took the White youth all four years of high school to reach the same level of identity stability as the African American sample accomplished after one or two years. Compared to Whites, who exhibited greater variability and flexibility in content, African American adolescents showed a striking sameness in how they saw themselves. According to Erikson's model, the White youth were experiencing "identity progression and moratorium" (i.e., slow but steady movement toward a coherent definition of self with extensive confusion and time out for exploration). African American adolescents, on the other hand, were exhibiting "identity foreclosure" (i.e., stabilizing identities early with a premature closing off of possibilities in terms of content).

For many African American youth, rigid and fixed expectations were found in relation to images of themselves as future parents, fantasies of future accomplishment, and availability of positive role models. At the same time, Hauser and Kasendorf (1983) found that on a daily basis African American adolescents exhibited great capacity for coping with life. Current images of self reflected levels of negativity and hopelessness that differed little from those of their White counterparts. Times have changed, and there is clearly greater access for many People of Color to the financial and social resources that can translate into more positive future expectations for the self. Yet, studies such as Hauser and Kasendorf's demonstrate the detrimental effects poverty and racism can have on hopes and possibilities of youth.

A word of caution should be voiced about such studies, however. Erikson's (1968) model has its origins in Northern European culture and reflects a view of adolescence that may not be accurate or appropriate for all groups. Some anthropologists believe that the prolonged period of confusion and moratorium that typifies Western European adolescence is, in fact, a symptom of the loss of relevant rites of passage that are necessary for a firm sense of grounding and future role stability.

Academic Performance and Learning Styles

A final aspect of child development that has special relevance for Children of Color relates to academic performance in the schools. Research clearly demonstrates that Children of Color perform academically at a lower level than their White counterparts in the public school system (Tatum, 1997). Obgu (1978) attributes such differences to institutional racism. He distinguishes three types of ethnic minorities that differ in relation to success in academic performance. "Autonomous" groups, such as Jews, Amish, and Mormons, tend to be small in number and experience prejudice but not widespread oppression. They tend to possess distinctive cultural traits related to academic success, have many successful role models, and do well in academic performance. "Immigrant" groups, such as Koreans and Chinese, come to the United States voluntarily in order to improve life conditions, and although the majority culture may view them negatively, they do not hold those views of themselves. Living conditions in the United States are a marked improvement over what they experienced in their countries of origin, and if they were to grow dissatisfied here, there is always recourse to returning. In spite of cultural differences, their children perform well in school and on academic tests. The third group, what Obgu calls "castelike" minorities, includes African Americans, Latinos/as, and Native Americans who jointly experience disproportionate amounts of school failure. They are the objects of systematic racism and disadvantage both within and outside of the schools and, according to Obgu, often view school success not as a path to advancement but rather as "acting White" or "Uncle Tom" behavior.

A related factor in poor school performance is cultural differences in *learning styles*. Each culture has its characteristic manner of learning, and as children grow, they internalize a given learning style and become progressively more comfortable and proficient in its use. There is much evidence to show that poor school performance among ethnic group children is related to conflicts in learning style (i.e., the U.S. school system as an institution is based on and rewards a mode of learning that is characteristic of Northern European culture). See, for example, Anderson and Adams (1992). Those who are unable to adapt or to become comfortable interacting educationally in this mode are clearly at a disadvantage and likely to fail over time. When efforts have been made to adjust classroom interaction to the cultural needs of different groups, the results have shown dramatic increases in performance and school success (Wolkind & Rutter, 1985).

Cultural learning styles develop pragmatically. Native Americans, for example, developed a keen sense of visual observation out of necessity and in relation to the environment that was their home. Their survival depended on "learning the signs of nature," and thus observation became a central mode of learning: "watching and listening, trial and error" (Fleming, 1992). In addition, oral tradition is a primary mode of teaching values and traditional attitudes, and such storytelling was often stylized through the use of symbols, anthropomorphizing, and metaphor, a particularly powerful way of teaching complex concepts. Today, according to Fleming, "modern Indian children still demonstrate strengths in their ability to memorize visual patterns, visualize spatial concepts, and produce descriptions that are rich in visual detail and the use of graphic metaphor" (pp. 161–162).

Contrast this with the very different learning paradigm that is emphasized in White schools: auditory learning, conceptualization of the abstract, and a heavy emphasis on language skills. Similarly, African Americans (Hale-Benson, 1986), Hawaiians (Gallimore, Boggs, & Jordan, 1974), and Mexican Americans (Kagan & Madsen, 1972) exhibit learning styles that have a heavy relational component as opposed to the Northern European style, which emphasizes individualism and competition. Mexican American children, for example, are less willing than White students to enter rivalries or competition or to internalize a drive to perform well to meet the expectations of teachers. Similarly, Hawaiian children are not interested in forsaking their strong need to affiliate with peers for a more individualistic modality that reinforces goal-orientated behavior. Although children from these cultures might be able learn to process information in a manner consonant with majority culture, it is counter to their preferred mode of interacting. Put simply, it just feels foreign and unnatural; most Students of Color, rather than adapt, choose to shut down in a variety of ways and thereby exit the formal U.S. education system. The real task of education in a multicultural society is to broaden the dimensions of the classroom in order to make room for the learning styles of all students (Collett & Serrano, 1992). Similarly, human service providers should be aware of optimal learning styles for clients to maximize learning during the helping process.

Cultural Issues in Therapeutic Interventions with Children

Cultural competence in clinical interventions with Children of Color requires simultaneous attention to a number of variables. Especially important are (1) an expanded definition of family, (2) use of a nondeficit definition of family structure and process, (3) resiliency as a therapeutic goal, and (4) the reality of biculturalism in the life experience of most Children and Families of Color.

- A key to understanding and working with Families of Color is an appreciation for their extreme diversity (especially in relation to mainstream, White families). First of all, their form varies from culture to culture. As Gushue and Sciarra (1995) suggest, each culture has "differing ways of understanding 'appropriate' family organization, values, communication and behavior" (p. 588). For example, Mexican American families share certain general cultural forms. They tend to be hierarchical and male dominated, religious, traditionally sex typed, and often bilingual with deep extended family roots. But to push such generalizations too far is to enter into the realm of stereotyping. McGoldrick (1982), who almost single-handedly has crafted the interest in the importance of culture in working with families, argues that no two families are ever culturally the same. Each internalizes in its own way aspects of the group's cultural norms. Some become very important; others are disregarded. McGoldrick sees the latter as "starting points" for understanding a given family. She goes on to enumerate a variety of other factors that affect "the way ethnic patterns surface in families," Including acculturation, class, education, ethnic identity, reason for migration to the United States, language status, geographic location, and stage in the family life cycle when they migrated.

- It is vitally important that cultural differences in family structure and process not be interpreted as cultural "deficits." The Moynihan Report (Moynihan, 1965) on the status of the Black family refers to "the myth of the Black matriarchy" and is an excellent case in point. The report, which had great impact on public welfare policy in the 1960s and 1970s, implies that the strong influence of the mother in African American families is an aberration caused by racism. It further implies that with the coming of more equitable times, African American family structure would return to a more patriarchal form. Critics of the report argue that the existence of strong women in the African American family is instead a cultural artifact that belies greater role equality and flexibility for men and women than is true for White families. They further point to it as an example of the kind of creative and adaptive strategies and strengths that have emerged out of the African American family as a necessity for dealing with a hostile social environment. The critical conceptual difference here is seeing this phenomenon as a creative adaptation of a traditional African American cultural form and as a strength rather than a deficit.

- In a similar vein, resiliency has become an increasingly important metagoal in clinical work with Children of Color. Promoting resiliency involves strengthening personal characteristics in the child that will permit better coping in stressful situations. Myers and King (1985), for example, identify the following generic factors as critical to resiliency: an ability not to overreact to stress, specific coping and problem-solving skills, a history of success in coping with race-related situations, a perception of oneself as capable of manipulating the world and of controlling one's destiny, and a healthy and well-integrated sense of self. Obviously, such factors do not work in isolation but reinforce one another. Success in coping, for instance, leads to personal empowerment and feelings of competency, which in turn increase the probability of successes in adapting and coping. In looking at specific populations, Canino and Zayas (1997) found that Puerto Rican children, whom they define as "invulnerable," tend to exhibit more sociability, dominance, endurance, high energy, demonstrativeness, reflectiveness, and impulse control than those who are more at risk. Their research also points to the importance of ethnic identification, familistic values, and adaptation to biculturality as hedges against vulnerability to stress. Dupree, Spencer, and Bell (1997) in turn suggest the following guidelines for instilling resiliency in African American youth:

One of the goals of counseling with African American children and youth is to promote coping strategies under unique circumstances. Therefore one should avoid using methods that encourage clients to accept their negative environmental circumstances and adapt to such an environment. Methods providing information that promote the effective use of underutilized resources and resources that are typically unattainable within their community should be sought. Help-seeking strategies and greater social mobility will enable them to survive in their environment. (p. 258)

- All treatment planning by providers working with Children of Color should incorporate resiliency-inducing strategies as well as other forms of empowerment. A final metagoal that providers should strive to incorporate in work with Children of Color is comfort and success in dealing with culture conflict and biculturality. Pinderhughes (1989) underlines the importance of helping clients tolerate competing cultural values and practices by learning to reduce the conflict and confusion inherent to the bicultural condition. At times, such conflicts find their way into the therapeutic setting itself. Pinderhughes offers the example of a conflict between teachers and a child's parents over allowing the child to fight. The teacher reported:

A mother explained when I was questioning her values about allowing him to fight. "I'll take care of his behavior; you take care of his education. Where we live he has to be tough and be able to fight. I'm not going to stop that. You set your standards here and I'll see that he understands he has to abide by them." (p. 181)

Pinderhughes is describing the value of teaching the child to negotiate this duality—that inconsistencies between home and school, for example, are likely to be ongoing realities of the bicultural child's world and that he or she must learn to negotiate them. Rather than unintentionally create a conflict, providers must regularly monitor their own value judgments and treatment goals so as not to undermine

the children's ability to tolerate the inconsistency between home and school. What the children needed was a sense that while the values at school were different, those of their parents were not being undermined. The teachers . . . must be able to function as a bridge, respecting the children's cultural values while simultaneously upholding the values of the school. (p. 182)

In addition to these four variables critical to a culturally sensitive approach to working therapeutically with Children of Color, Ho (1992) summarizes a variety of other useful skills and guidelines organized in relation to phases of therapy. They are listed in Table 5–2.

■ **TABLE 5–2**   Guidelines for Therapeutic Intervention Skills with Ethnic
Minority Children

Intervention phase	Intervention skills
Precontact	Ability to realize the child's ethnic minority reality, including the effect of racism and poverty on the child
	Ability to understand the child's ethnicity, race, language, social class, and differences in minority status, such as refugees, immigrants, and native born
	Ability to objectify and make use of worker's own culture/ethnicity and professional culture (psychiatry, social work, psychology, etc.), which may be different from the child's culture and ethnicity
	Ability to be sensitive to the child's fear of racist or prejudiced orientation
Problem identification	Ability to understand and "tune in" to the child's cultural dispositions, behaviors, and family structures that may include close extended-family ties
	Ability to discuss openly racial/ethnic differences and issues and respond to culturally based cues
	Ability to adapt to the child's interactive style and language, conveying to the child that the worker understands, values, and validates his or her life strategies
	Ability to understand the child's help-seeking behavior, which includes the child's conceptualization of the problem and the manner by which the problem can be solved
Problem specification	Ability to use cultural mapping to ascertain the child's problem
	Ability to identify the ecosystemic sources (racism, poverty, prejudice) of a minority child's problems
	Ability to identify the links between ecosystemic problems and individual concerns and problems
	Ability to consider the implications of what is being suggested in relation to each child's cultural reality (unique dispositions, life strategies, and experiences)
Mutual goal formation	Ability to clearly delineate agency functions and respectfully inform the child of the worker's professional expectations of him or her
	Ability to formulate goals consistent with the child's emphasis on collectivism and interdependence
	Ability to differentiate and select from three categories of goals: situational stress (e.g., social isolation, poverty), cultural transition (e.g., conflictual family–school practices), and transcultural dysfunctional patterns (e.g., developmental impasses and repetitive interactional behavior)
	Ability to engage the child to formulate a goal that is problem or growth focused, structured, realistic, concrete, practical, and readily achievable
Problem solving	Ability to reaffirm the child's life skills and coping strategies within a bicultural environment
	Ability to frame the change within the traditional, culturally acceptable language
	Ability to suggest a change or new strategy as an expansion of the "old" cultural stress or problem-solving response
	Ability to apply new strategies that are consistent with the child's needs and problem, degree of acculturation, motivation for change, and comfort in responding to the worker's directives

■ **TABLE 5–2** *(Continued)*	
Intervention phase	**Intervention skills**
Termination	Ability to assess the accomplishment of therapeutic goals according to the child's collectivist culture
	Ability to reconnect and restore the child to his or her larger world or environment
	Ability to assist the child to incorporate the new changes in the child's original life strategy independent of the worker's interaction
	Ability to consider the child's concept of time and space in a relationship during termination and make sure the termination is natural and gradual

Note. From *Minority Children and Adolescents in Therapy* (pp. 28–29) by M. Ho, 1992, Thousand Oaks, CA: Sage Publications, Inc. Copyright © 1992 by Sage Publications, Inc. Reprinted with permission.

■ Parenting

Margaret Burroughs captures the dilemma that faces all Parents of Color in the opening lines of this poem:*

> What shall I tell my children who are black
> Of what it means to be a captive in this dark skin?
> Of how beautiful they are when everywhere they turn
> They are faced with abhorrence of everything that is black . . .

All parents face a similar task—that of creating a safe environment in which their child can move without harm through the various developmental tasks and stages that are part of growing up. In the case of mainstream White parents, threats to the child's health or safety, when they do exist, are random and unpredictable. Children of Color, however, are born into an environment in which they are systematically subjected to the harmful effects of racism. Parents of Color, having grown up under similar conditions, are aware of what awaits their children and of the fact that there is only so much they can do to protect them. What can Parents of Color do? First, they can create a buffer zone in which the child is protected from the negative attitudes and stereotypes of the broader society. Such a safety zone can increase the likelihood of instilling ethnic pride and a positive sense of self in the child. Second, Parents of Color can teach their children how to constructively deal with the emotions that are stimulated by the experience of racism. Third, they can prepare their children cognitively for what they will encounter in the world outside the buffer zone.

---

*Excerpt from poem "What Shall I Tell My Children Who Are Black?" by Margaret Burroughs. (Reprinted with permission of the author.)

Creating a Buffer Zone

Mainstream theories in social psychology hold that society's negative views and stereotypes of People of Color are directly reflected onto the psyches of Children of Color and internalized into their sense of self and identity. Other theorists, Norton (1983) for example, argue that messages sent by the child's more immediate environment of home, significant others, and community can mitigate those of the broader society and provide a basis for the internalization of positive ethnic identity and self-worth. For White children, there is generally little difference between the messages received from their immediate environment and those from society in general. For Children of Color, however, the situation may be very different, with the two systems offering conflicting messages. The family, in turn, can act as a buffer between children and society's negative evaluations of them, thus becoming the primary sculptor of feelings about self and a source of healthy self-esteem. In this regard, Norton raises a number of questions: "What happens in the interaction between black parents and their children in those stable nurturing families from any educational or socioeconomic level who manage to rear children with a strong sense of self? How and with what patterns do these families defy the 'mark of oppression'? How can we determine the strengths and healthy coping mechanisms in the interaction between black parents and their children?" (p. 188).

The idea of creating a buffer zone in which the child can develop without harmful intrusions from the outside is the essence of all good parenting. Young children need protection and nurturance until they are able to venture into the outside world with sufficient skills and abilities to protect themselves. Children of Color, being generally at risk, are in special need of good psychological grounding in a positive sense of self with which to go out into the world.

Research, for example, has correlated positive self-concept with effective social functioning, higher levels of cognitive development, and greater emotional health and stability (Curry & Johnson, 1990). The creation of a buffer zone (against racism and negative racial messages) can provide a place and time for such optimal personal growth. Psychological theories about the development of the self speak of mirroring and reflection and imply that children take in and make a part of themselves the reflected views of others (Wylie, 1961). If they are loved, they will love themselves; if they are demeaned or devalued, that is how they will come to feel about themselves. In this regard, K. B. Clark (1963) writes: "Children who are consistently rejected understandably begin to question and doubt whether they, their family, and their group really deserve no more respect from the larger society that they receive" (pp. 63–64). This is why the buffer zone is so critical. When Parents of Color can substitute the reflection of loving parents and significant others for that of a hostile environment that routinely negates the value of children because of their ethnicity, their children are likely to develop a positive sense of self.

Norton (1983) describes the ingredients for optimal (i.e., esteem-producing) parent–child interaction as follows: "Early consistent, loving, nurturing interaction is the ideal process of interaction leading to a good sense of self. The child who is loved, accepted and supported in appropriate reality-oriented functioning in relationship to others comes to love himself and to respect himself as someone worthy of love" (p. 185). The idea of a buffer zone should not, however, be limited merely to parents and family. The entire ethnic community with its various institutions can function in a similar way to protect its children. The African adage that "it takes an entire village to raise a child" is relevant here. The idea of ethnic separatism, such as that practiced by Black Muslims, is predicated on such a notion of creating a safe, supportive, and economically viable system that does not depend on Whites and, in fact, limits interaction with them and their institutions.

Parenting for Self-Esteem

Wright (1998) offers an interesting but controversial perspective on the relationships among parenting, race, and the nurturing of self-esteem. She believes that there are three crucial ways in which parents, especially African American parents, can support or negate their child's developing sense of self-worth.

- The first is disciplinary style. According to Wright, "many parents in the black community hold a . . . strong belief in the value of corporal punishment." Regardless of the reason for it—to follow the biblical injunction to not "spare the rod," because it is "cultural" for African Americans to use physical pain in disciplining their children and it "worked well for me," to "toughen" children in order to prepare them for life in a hostile world, because of the belief that African American children "need more severe discipline than the children of other races" and it is the only thing that works with them—physical punishment may erode self-esteem. Wright suggests that children learn less about internal control and self-regulation and more about fear and hostility from physical punishment. Most important, Wright believes that when Black children are spanked, for whatever reason, they may learn at the hands of their own caretakers a message that mimics, "the same message that white society . . . has traditionally sent to blacks" (1998, p. 131). Gentler discipline, on the other hand, may foster greater emotional health by sending a very different message—that the child is worthy of such treatment and respect. It is important to point out that many Black parents may take exception to Wright's views on corporal punishment.
- A second factor in the promotion of self-esteem, according to Wright, is parental closeness or distance. To the extent that parents can be present and emotionally involved in the daily life of their children, there is greater likelihood for the development of positive self-worth. At times, this has been a challenge for many in the African American community. The absence of fathers due to the cycle of poverty and racism; single-parent mothers torn between having to earn a living and being away from their children, often without the traditional African American extended support system; and, especially of late, the ravages of addictions on family life—all

threaten the emotional health of children who are touched by them. It is important to realize that when a parent is unavailable for whatever reason, children tend to blame themselves for the absence, often interpreting it as evidence of their own worthlessness. Such factors are highly related to socioeconomics.

- A final factor mitigating the development of self-worth is the parents' attitude toward race and life in general. Wright describes working with children who seem "unusually vulnerable to perceived and actual racism. Some of them obviously have to deal with an unusually heavy share of discrimination, but more often these children come from families who habitually blame their child's problems on race and who bring their children up to believe that they are victims because they are black" (1998, p. 6). Premature sensitization to racism before children are developmentally ready may take an enormous toll on their future ability to cope. Similarly, Wright raises concerns about the parents' basic attitude toward life distinguishing between attitudinal "impoverishment" and "enrichment." Seeing the glass as half empty or half full, in spite of one's level of disadvantage, is a perceptual habit that parents pass on to children that can play a major role in how they feel about themselves and their futures. This concern, like others raised by Wright, should be considered controversial, and some even view it as "blaming the victim."

Preparing the Child Emotionally for Racism

Poussaint (1972) offers some good insights into how to help children deal emotionally with the negative racial experiences they encounter. Speaking to the situation of African American parents, he first emphasizes that children should not be allowed to feel alone in their struggles. They must not only feel the support of their parents, peers, and teachers, but also understand that they are part of a long history of individuals who have similarly struggled against racism. Parents should model active intervention and mastery over the environment as well as help their children develop competence and the ability to achieve personal goals. If children can experience their parents as powerful, they gain a certain sense of power vicariously. They should generally be allowed to try to deal with racial situations on their own with parents prepared to intervene if necessary. It is the parents' job to be sure that the situation is resolved quickly and satisfactorily and, above all, that the child's self-esteem is protected.

Poussaint describes a number of counterproductive "compensatory mechanisms"—stances or strategies parents adopt as they prepare their children for life. Though well-intentioned, such efforts tend to create deleterious side effects and reflect parental insecurities around the issue of race.

- Some parents subject their children to a verbal regimen of "Black is beautiful," hoping to reinforce a strong sense of positive identity and self. Children, however, may begin to wonder why they are being asked to repeat the same phrases over and over again and may begin to feel that perhaps the compulsive need to do so actuality points to the possibility that maybe "Black is not so beautiful after all."

- Other parents assume an overly permissive stance, being too generous and accommodating with their children, as if to assuage their own guilt or make up for the harshness that the child will eventually encounter. The problem with this kind of strategy is that it does not allow children to test themselves and their abilities in the real world and thereby foster feelings of competence and self-worth.
- Still other parents are overly authoritarian. They feel that the best thing they can do for their children is to toughen them up, thus preparing them for the rigors of a hostile environment. This strategy, however, can lead to abuse, which teaches children to be abusive in their own right. It can also give them a green light to act out in the world.
- A final compensatory mechanism involves encouraging the child to remain passive and to avoid aggressive behavior of any kind, as if such a strategy would somehow mollify racial hatred.

Poussaint points out the importance of helping children learn to manage the righteous anger that they will feel as objects of racial hatred. Suppressing anger eventually leads to feelings of self-loathing and low self-esteem. Overgeneralized anger is counterproductive, leading nowhere and consuming a vast amount of undirected energy. Rather, a more balanced approach seems optimal: teaching children to assert themselves sufficiently, to display their anger appropriately, and to sublimate and channel much of it into constructive energy for actively dealing with the world. "Our job," Poussaint writes, "is to help our children develop that delicate balance between appropriate control and appropriate display of anger and aggression, love and hate" (1972, p. 110). He summarizes as follows: "As parents, we must try to raise men and women who are emotionally healthy in a society that is basically racist. If our history is a lesson, we will continue to survive. Many black children will grow up to be strong, productive adults. But too many others will succumb under the pressures of a racist environment. Salvaging these youngsters is our responsibility as parents" (p. 111).

Preparing the Child Cognitively for Racism

Equally important to creating a strong emotional base in children is helping them to understand racism. While many researchers have written on this topic, the early work of Lewin (1948) still offers the most compelling advice to parents vis-à-vis preparing their children to cognitively cope with the experiences of prejudice and discrimination.

- First, according to Lewin, never deny a child's ethnicity or underestimate the impact it will have on their lives. Some parents feel that it is best to put off discussions of racism as long as possible, thereby keeping the child naïve until it can no longer be avoided. There are real problems with this approach. It models, first of all, a kind of denial of reality that not only confuses children, but also sets them on a life course of passively dealing with their ethnic identity. Parents who choose to avoid discussions of race also tend to underestimate the level of a child's knowledge and thus avoid issues that have already become real and problematic. (Remember, as cited earlier, some ethnic children are aware of racial differences as early as 3 years of age, and by 7 years all are aware of the negative judgments that society holds about their group.) Children in fact welcome the opportunity to discuss race-related experiences, especially when an unspoken rule has been established within the family system to remain silent about race relations. Parents can thus unintentionally remove themselves as important resources for their children.

- Lewin (1948) also points out, using the analogy of adoption, that "learning the truth" can be much more damaging and hurtful the older the child is. In other words, the longer one lives with a given picture of reality, the more devastating it can be to have that reality shattered. Although Lewin's work focused primarily on assimilating Jews who could more easily hide their identities than most People of Color, his points about avoiding the topic of ethnicity are still well taken. As suggested earlier, it is clearly best to encourage children to bring up the subject and talk with them about it as it becomes an issue in their lives. Parents should answer questions as simply as possible and not overwhelm children with more knowledge than they currently need. More often than not, a small amount of information will suffice. Parents should answer questions in a manner that fits the child's level of cognitive development. Similarly, the child should not be overwhelmed emotionally with difficult information or stories. Preparing children for dealing with racism is not a single-time event. It is an ongoing developmental process. As they encounter racism in the real world, it should be discussed and processed, and as they mature, information and explanations should grow in depth and comprehensiveness.

- It is vital to help children develop strong and positive ethnic identities based on values inherent in group membership so as to internally counteract the negative experiences of being an object of prejudice. A statement of such a positive identity is: "I am Latino/a and come from a rich cultural tradition of which I am very proud. Sure, I experience a lot of racism, but that is just the way it is, although at times I get very angry. But I would never trade it for being White or anything else, even if it meant life would be a lot easier." An ethnic identity based solely on negative experiences is a very fragile thing that disappears as soon as the adversity is gone. If children are made to feel bad because of their differences, it is psychologically crucial that they possess positive feelings about who they are as people and as members of a group. Lacking such sources of self-esteem, they may likely reject group membership, identifying it as the source of all of their problems. Jewish parents, for example, are now beginning to realize that identities based exclusively on the experience of the Holocaust or a long history of oppression eventually drive their children from the fold.

- Racial hatred should always be presented as a social, and not as an individual or personal, problem. For example, "Why did Tommy call me that bad name? I didn't do anything to him." The answer to that might well be: "Of course, you didn't. Sometimes when people get angry or unhappy, they take it out on others who are different from them. There is something wrong with people when they do that." It is vital that children not come to believe, consciously or unconsciously, that something they did brought on the discriminatory behavior. Parents should never assume that a child has not personalized a negative racial experience. They must check it out. Young children, in their egocentric conception of the world, tend to take responsibility for most things that happen to them. Parents must actively intervene to assure themselves that such a conclusion is not drawn. I have sadly seen many instances where an ethnic child is transformed (e.g., from a very happy and carefree young person to one who is negative and sullen) by a single experience with hatred, and I believe that such damage could have been mitigated if the incident had been carefully worked through with the child. Parents must also be careful to not expect "special things or behaviors" from their children because of who they are racially or ethnically. Such expectations inadvertently communicate to the child responsibility for their own plight as well as the belief that better behavior could have averted the incident. This is a heavy burden to unintentionally place on a child.

- Children must learn that group membership is based not only on obvious physical or cultural features, but also on an "interdependence of fate." Members of ethnic groups often share the experience of mistreatment by society. Although this can serve to heighten intragroup solidarity, it is also possible for children to learn to vent their frustration on subgroups within their community, blaming them for the bad treatment that all group members experience. Such internalized racism can become a tyranny of its own and can lead to destructive intragroup wrangling and bickering. There do exist within some Communities of Color powerful caste systems based on lightness and darkness of skin color.

- Children must not learn to fear multiple group allegiances. If children are unnecessarily made to choose between alternative roles and group memberships, they will grow resentful and eventually find ways to get even with parents, often through the rejection of ethnicity. Some parents, for instance, are very critical of their children's attempts at being bicultural (i.e., trying to become competent in the ways of the dominant culture as well as their own). Fearful that their children will lose touch with traditional ways and values, they force them to choose. The result is usually severe family strife. The reverse may also occur—forcing children to acculturate into the mainstream culture can engender eventual resentment and yearning for identity.

- Parents must realize that a child's feelings about ethnicity and group belonging are most likely to model their own. If they themselves are in some way confused or conflicted about who they are ethnically, it is likely to be passed on. Poussaint (1972) made a similar point in relation to compensatory mechanisms in the previous section. If cycles of dysfunction are to be broken, they must be interrupted by parental awareness and healing.

■ Bicultural Children and Families

Bicultural families represent a little-understood, yet increasingly important subgroup in American society. Perkins (1994) estimates approximately a million interracially married couples in the United States, an increase of 250% from 1967 to 1987. Smolowe (1993) estimates that the increase in birthrate of multiracial children is 26 times that of any other group. Census 2000 data numbers multiracial individuals at 6.8 million or 2.4% of the population. In spite of these dramatic increases, a number of myths and distorted beliefs about bicultural children remain. This is not surprising given the fact that in 1967 there were still laws against interracial marriages in 16 states.

Kerwin and Ponterotto (1995) describe three of the most prevalent of these myths:

- Bicultural children turn out to be very tragic and marginal individuals.
- Bicultural children must choose to identify with only one of their parents' cultural groups.
- Bicultural children are very uncomfortable discussing their ethnic identity with others.

According to these authors, each of these myths is a distortion of the psychological reality:

- Bicultural children are quite capable of developing healthy ethnic identities and finding a stable social place for themselves.
- Contrary to being forced to choose one parent's ethnic affiliation over the other, healthy identity development in bicultural children involves an integration of both cultural backgrounds into a unitary sense of self that is an amalgam of both and yet uniquely different from either.
- Bicultural children welcome the opportunity to discuss and explore who they are ethnically.

Such myths are most likely sustained by individuals who are uncomfortable with the idea of bicultural relationships and who project their own discomfort onto the children.

There are two general forms of bicultural families: ones in which parents come from two or more different cultures and ones in which parents come from the same culture with a child adopted from another cultural group. Our treatment begins with a discussion of bicultural parental relationships and ends with a consideration of the unique dynamics related to cross-cultural adoption.

Bicultural Couples

Clinical work with bicultural spouses (as in Scenario 3 at the beginning of the chapter) yields a very informative psychological profile. First, bicultural couples tend to approximate extremes in healthy functioning. Some are very high functioning and bring to the relationship advanced communication skills, good cultural understanding of each other, and a strong motivation toward openness and working through difficulties. Others enter the relationship with a culturally different partner for unconscious reasons of which they are largely unaware and bring to the relationship very poor interpersonal skills and little insight.

Jacobs (1977) carried out extensive interviews with African and European American bicultural couples and their children. Because of sampling methods, parents in the study tended toward the higher functioning pole. All reported personal attraction as opposed to race as motivation for entering a bicultural relationship. Jacobs found that several spouses acknowledged a drive toward asserting autonomy as a secondary motive. For White spouses this tended to be autonomy from rigid and overcontrolling families, and for the African American spouses it represented "overcoming limits placed on them by racism." None of the 14 spouses felt any guilt over their relationships. Jacobs' couples were assessed as well differentiated from each other and, because of this, were able to allow their children to separate and individuate. The parents did suggest that it was easier to give their children autonomy because the child was experienced at "being different" and not exactly like either of them.

Only two of the seven White spouses reported acceptance by parents of their intention to intermarry. In contrast, all of the Black spouses reported families of origin as accepting of their partner choice. This data parallels previous research findings that Communities of Color tend to be more accepting of bicultural relationships and marriages than Whites. A notable exception to this tendency can be found among Asian American subgroups. White spouses reported an interesting sequence of reactions to parental rejection. After a period of initial anger, lasting anywhere from several months to several years, they were able to develop some empathy and understanding for the rejecting parents and moved toward re-establishment of contact and attachment. Spouses who exhibited unhealthy attachment patterns found it impossible to make such movement and efforts at reconciliation. They tended to be flooded with guilt over their marriage, were heavily preoccupied with race (the healthier couples were not so preoccupied), harbored serious prejudices of their own, and continued to act out behaviorally the same conflict that had drawn them into the interracial relationship in the first place.

Jacobs' bicultural couples also reported frequent focus on issues of race and ethnicity. Being in close and intimate interaction with someone who is culturally different cannot help but elicit racial material from both partners. Such issues must be discussed honestly and worked through if the marriage is to function. What exists in effect is a microcosm of race relations in the home with numerous opportunities to explore resolving cross-cultural problems. For example, Memmi (1966) suggests that during arguments between bicultural couples racial prejudices and stereotypes often surface in the heat of battle. Because of the hurtful nature of such attacks, resolution must be found. Jacobs (1977) also found that the interracial couples were more open to discussing topics of race and ethnicity than were either African American or White monocultural couples.

Bicultural couples tended to be rather isolated as a unit, often experiencing social rejection and preferring social contact with other bicultural couples who can more easily understand what they face in daily living. As a result, they often developed patterns of strong interdependence between them, which included an unwillingness to acknowledge problems or seek help as a unit. On the positive side, interdependence and isolation caused them to try harder to resolve conflicts on their own; on the negative, airing of problems could be experienced as a particular threat.

Finally, bicultural couples faced another challenge that monocultural couples were generally spared. They have to face not only personality differences and conflicts, but also the complex and difficult terrain of cultural differences. Interfaith couples, for example, Jewish and Christian, must agree on shared practices in the home and religious education. Bicultural Couples of Color in turn face stylistic, value, priority, and expectation differences that are cultural in origin. Northern Europeans, for instance, become quiet and distant during interpersonal conflicts and tend to move away from the partner, while individuals from more traditional cultures tend to become more verbal and emotional and move toward their partner in an effort to resolve conflicts. If problems are ever to be resolved by such bicultural couples, they must learn to accommodate their differences in style.

Patterns of Bicultural Relationships

Bicultural children are psychologically privy not only to reflections of conflicts and tensions within the broader society, but also to those that originate within the family. Difficulties in bicultural marriages represent a microcosm of the kinds of conflicts bicultural children face in their lives. Falicov (1986), for example, believes that cross-cultural marriages demand from each partner a kind of cultural transition. According to her, the couple must "arrive at an adaptive and flexible view of cultural differences that make it possible to maintain some individuated values, to negotiate conflictual areas, and even to develop a new cultural code that integrates parts of both cultural streams" (p. 431).

Falicov identifies the following three patterns of cultural tension with bicultural families as most frequent.

- First is what she calls "conflicts in cultural code." This involves cultural differences in how marriages are conceived and structured. Particularly important are differences in rules related to the inclusion and exclusion of others (especially extended family members) and the relative power and authority between spouses. In the hope of mutually adapting to each other's style, partners often minimize or maximize cultural differences. In either case, they tend to have only limited knowledge of the other's culture and are generally unable to carry out what Falicov sees as a necessary developmental task for the marriage—that of negotiating together a new cultural code that implies the melding of their different ways. She also points out that errors in this arena often stem from "ethnocentric or stereotyped views of the other." As a result of such limited knowledge, cultural differences may be "mistaken for negative personality traits" of the other.
- A second type of problem involves "cultural differences and permission to marry." Here, Falicov includes difficulties related to parental disapproval

of the relationship and cultural style issues such as the tendency toward enmeshment, which makes separating from family of origin a more conflictual task. She identifies two differing patterns of adaptation in couples who have not received emotional permission to marry. In the first, partners "maximize their differences and do not blend, integrate, or negotiate their values and life styles. They lead parallel lives, each holding on to their culture and/or family of origin. Often, the counterpoint of the marital distance is an excessive involvement of one or both parties with the family of origin. There may also be unresolved longings for the past ethnic or religious affiliations, even if these were of little importance previously" (Falicov, 1986, p. 440). This pattern is often accompanied by expectations and pressures for children to choose between parents and their respective families. A second pattern involves the opposite: a minimizing and denying of difference, which may take the form of either adopting a third and alternative culture style or cutting ties with culture and family altogether. One often sees in such couples an attitude of "us against them" (meaning the world) or "we only have each other." Structurally, rigid boundaries are constructed externally (especially with families of origin) and unclear boundaries internally. The resulting isolation is often internalized by the child.

- Falicov's third problem area in cross-cultural marriages is "cultural stereotyping and severe stress." In such situations, impending stress (e.g., the death of a parent) initiates a maximizing of cultural differences and stereotyping between partners. Falicov suggests that in this case cultural material that was previously dealt with constructively is now used as a defense against looking at other noncultural problems and that the resulting stress wears down the couple's ability to cope. Children in families reacting to stress in this manner may need extra help negotiating the pull of competing cultures. Teachers alerted to impending stress within bicultural families may need to be prepared to offer more than the usual care and empathy for such children. As we shall see next, the three patterns of cultural tension in marriage identified by Falicov exacerbate the kind of developmental tasks that the bicultural child must navigate.

Bicultural Children

Monocultural Children of Color will eventually face the realities of a hostile social environment, but bicultural children must also come to grips with their parents' interracial drama and the perpetually repeated question: "What are you?" Kich (1992) suggests that the interracial child represents not only the parents' racial differences but also a unique individual who must work through very personal identity issues related to their differences. Kerwin and Ponterotto (1995) summarize the development of racial identity in biracial children. In many ways, the process parallels that of monocultural Children of Color, but with the added task of simultaneously exploring two (or more) rather than a single ethnic heritage and then integrating these into a unique whole. Perhaps, the most salient point to remember in working with bicultural and multicultural children is that psychologically they are not merely reflections of their two or more sides but unique integrations of them.

Bicultural children on the average develop awareness of race and racial differences even earlier than monocultural Children of Color, usually by age 3 or 4. This is because they are exposed to such differences from birth in the confines of their own families. It is also likely that their parents are more attuned to these differences because of their interracial relationship. Upon entry into school, bicultural children are immediately confronted with questions that serve as major stimuli for their internal processing of "What are you?" Concurrently, they begin to experiment with labels for themselves. Children may create self-descriptions based on perceptions of their skin color (e.g., coffee and cream) or adopt parental terms (e.g., interracial).

In general, bicultural children are most successful moving through the identity formation process when race is openly discussed at home and parents are available to help sort out various issues of self-definition. Rate of development also depends on the amount of integration in their classrooms and the availability in school of role models from both cultural sides. During preadolescence, children begin to regularly use racial or cultural as opposed to physical descriptions of themselves. They are becoming increasingly aware of group differences other than skin color (physical appearance, language, etc.) and of the fact that their parents belong to distinct ethnic groups. Exposure to "racial incidents" and first-time entry into either integrated or segregated school settings also accelerate learning.

Adolescence is particularly problematic for bicultural children. It is a time of marked intolerance for differences both for children and their peers. There are likely to be strong pressures on bicultural adolescents to identify with one parent's ethnicity over the other: usually with the Parent of Color if one parent is White. Peers of Color push the adolescent to identify with them, and increasingly, Whites perceive and treat the bicultural adolescent as a Person of Color. Jacobs (1992) believes that vacillation between identification with one ethnicity and the simultaneous rejection of the other, followed by its opposite, is a natural part of identity formation in bicultural youth. Perhaps only by internalizing one aspect of the self at a time, and even vacillating between the two over the duration of adolescence and young adulthood, can there be any real integration of both identities. Dating begins in adolescence, and this fact accentuates race as a central life issue. It is not unusual for biracial youth to experience rejection because of their color or ethnicity, and such experiences are likely to have a great impact on their emerging sense of identity. Heightened sexuality of adolescence also stimulates questions such as, "If I become pregnant or make someone pregnant, what will the baby look like?" Bicultural women have a particularly difficult task meshing their body images with either of their bicultural physical types. Young Black women often opt out of mainstream society's "beauty contest" because of an inability to match mainstream standards. Ironically, this may lead to the establishment of a more realistic and healthy body image. Biracial women may be torn between the media image on one hand and her body image identity with her mother, if of Color, on the other.

Interactions between bicultural children and their parents are at times complex and conflictual. As children grow more mature and aware, they are increasingly confronted with and confused by the experience of being different. Some have described it as akin to "going crazy" or having no way of making sense out of how the world is reacting to them. Bicultural parents often have a difficult time understanding exactly what the child is going through. At the root of this misunderstanding is parents' tendency to see the child as an extension of themselves rather than as an amalgam of the couple. The realization by parents that their child sees himself or herself as something different from them can be quite anxiety provoking.

In family situations where one of the parents has detached from his or her group of origin, bicultural children tend to feel particularly protective of that parent. Similarly, where one of the parents is White, they may overly empathize with the Parent of Color when he or she is feeling bad or rejected because of racism. Divorce can be especially traumatic because it represents a severing of the two sides of a child's identity. Because of this a child may feel a real need to keep the warring parents together at any cost. Such dynamics are especially exacerbated if parents use race against each other. Nor is it uncommon for the child to take on the prejudices of individual parents during divorce. In single-parent families, difficulties can arise when the lone parent, usually the mother, feels great hostility toward the father for abandoning them and unconsciously turns her resentment toward the child as a visible reminder of the union. Similarly, parental and child resentment may emerge as subtle racism toward the missing parent.

Adopted Children

Bicultural adoption is a second source of bicultural families. Communities of Color have taken very strong stances against adoption and foster care across racial lines. Their feeling is that White parents are not capable of providing Children of Color with either adequate exposure and connection with their cultures of birth or training in how to deal with the racism they will eventually experience. Serious efforts have been made to sensitize and train adoptive parents in cultural competence as well as to encourage them to keep their child connected to his or her community of origin. There are, however, real questions as to whether such efforts can overcome cultural gaps, let alone a racially hostile social environment. White adoptive parents seldom understand the enormity of difference that their children face as People of Color. In addition, they often unconsciously deny differences that exist between themselves and their children. This puts children in a very difficult psychological position. They feel isolated in dealing with the very complex issues of race and ethnicity. There is, for example, the aforementioned sense of "going crazy," fostered by the enormous gulf between how they are being reacted to in the external social world and at home. Finally, it can become confusing for adopted Children of Color when their adopted parents simultaneously represent nurturance/emotional support on one side and oppression on the other. A process somewhat akin to the identity vacillation suggested by Jacobs (1992) may occur for these bicultural children as well.

■ Summary

The chapter begins with three short case studies, anticipating the three major sections of the chapter: child development and ethnicity, parenting in culturally diverse families, and biracial and bicultural children and families.

From birth, characteristics and development of children vary greatly across ethnic groups. Differences in reactivity, temperament, and mother–child interactions are most prominent. Children of Color are aware of racial differences as early as age 3; majority-group children are slower to develop awareness of their whiteness. Early studies suggested that Children of Color exhibited negative self-concepts and lower self-esteem (Clark & Clark, 1947). The "myth of self-hatred" has been challenged by subsequent researchers such as Williams and Morland (1976). Studies of personal identity formation in adolescence show that African American youth formed stable integration of self-images much earlier than did White youth, although they also exhibited identity foreclosure, a sign of premature closing off of possibilities of who they could become. Children of Color show higher achievement scores when learning activities are culturally relevant to their life experiences and when learning strategies fit cultural learning styles.

Parents of Color face the difficult task of creating safe environments for children who are systematically subjected to the harmful effects of racism. Creating "buffer zones" in homes and communities where children are protected from the negative attitudes and stereotypes of racism represents one strategy of helping. Developing ethnic pride is a second. Poussaint (1972) warned against "compensatory mechanisms" that parents may adopt to prepare their children for racism. Wright (1998) warned against the use of corporal punishment, emotional distancing, and blaming family problems exclusively on racism. Parents can prepare their children both cognitively and emotionally for what they will encounter outside of the buffer zone.

Families of Color tend to exhibit more diversity in their form and structure than do mainstream White families. It is critical to avoid interpreting cultural differences in family structure as cultural deficits. The example of the "Black matriarchy" is presented, with an emphasis on interpreting differences in family patterns as indicative of creative and adaptive development rather than as pathology.

Bicultural couples and families represent a growing and special subset of ethnic families. A number of myths about bicultural children are shown to be unfounded. Bicultural couples tend to exhibit either very healthy or extremely dysfunctional relationship patterns. The work of Jacobs (1977) is reviewed. Falicov (1986) pointed to three typical problems in bicultural martial discord: conflicts in cultural codes, difficulties in separating from families of origin, and cultural stereotyping of partners during times of crisis and stress.

Bicultural children face not only prejudice and racism but also the task of integrating two cultural identities; are aware of race and ethnicity earlier than monoethnic children; do best in environments where ethnicity is discussed openly; and receive help from parents in sorting out issues of self-definition. Adolescence is particularly difficult for bicultural children. Communities of Color have opposed the adoption of ethnic children across racial lines. This may be because adopted Children of Color often find themselves isolated and on their own in dealing with issues of race and ethnicity.

■ Activities

1. *Explore racial attitudes of your family of origin.* Divide into dyads or small groups. First, take turns sharing memories of the first time you became aware of racially or ethnically different people. Describe the experience and what it taught you about such differences. Next, talk about the racial attitudes of members of your family. What messages did your family communicate to you about race and ethnicity, prejudice, people who are culturally different, and so on? Finally, discuss differences in how such material was dealt with in your respective families and how these have affected you.

2. *Analyze race-related scenarios.* Read the following two scenarios and, drawing on the ideas and material presented in this chapter, analyze the diversity issues they pose and then answer the questions at the end of each. You can do this exercise individually or in dyads or small groups.

   a. You are a clinical social worker, seeing children and families in an agency located in a primarily African American neighborhood. One of your clients, an 8-year-old African American girl, accidentally disclosed to you that her parents used spankings to discipline her and her siblings. Once she realized what she had said, see quickly tried to retract it, clearly anxious about her statement, and then asked you to not say anything to her parents about it. When asked why, she said that her parents had told her there were certain things that she shouldn't talk about with the White social worker. As a mandated reporter, you know that you have a duty to report certain kinds of punishment to Child Protective Services. You are also aware from reading the present chapter and previous experience in the agency that African American families (for a variety of good reasons) tend to be mistrustful of CPS and other social services agencies, that there is a debate within their community about the use of physical punishment, and that many see it as an acceptable cultural practice. You are also aware that making the report or even talking with the parents might lead them to terminate treatment (and you have been making significant progress) as well as possibly putting their daughter at risk for further punishment. How might you proceed sensitively to protect the child, respect the cultural attitudes of the parents, and maximize the likelihood that the therapy would continue? Explain your reasoning and choices.

b. I was once awakened early in the morning to attend an emergency meeting of a Jewish religious school's board of directors. During the previous night, someone had broken into the school, made a mess of the place, sprawled anti-Semitic graffiti all over the walls, and destroyed and defaced religious articles and artwork. A night janitor had discovered the break-in, and board members were meeting to decide how to handle the situation. In the very heated and emotional discussion, some argued that the school should not be reopened the next morning but remain closed until all signs of the vandalism were removed. They felt that it would be too traumatic for the children, aged 5 through 12, to witness because they were not old enough to understand what had happened. One parent summarized this position as follows: "There will be plenty of time in their future for the children to learn about this kind of hatred." Others felt it was "never too early" and suggested that students be shown the school now and be given ample opportunity to talk about what had happened. Yet others favored exposing only the older children to what had happened or letting the choice be up to individual parents. Given the material presented in this chapter, how would you suggest they proceed and what issues do you see at stake in this hard decision?

c. You are a cultural consultant to a local adoption agency. Recently, the agency has been the object of lobbying and protests of their policy of open adoption by a local group made up of ethnic parents and professionals who oppose cross-racial adoption. The agency has always prided itself on its color blindness and commitment to find the best parent for the child, irrespective of race and ethnicity. You have been asked to advise the board, explain to them the position of the protestors, and take a position on which course would be in the best interest of these Children of Color. Also, if the board decides to continue cross-racial adoption, what guidelines for parent training might you suggest?

6 Mental Health Issues

In an extraordinary book entitled *Black Rage,* psychiatrists William Grier and Price Cobbs (1968) explore the enormous anger lurking below the surface of the African American patients who seek their help. They begin by describing the life circumstances of three patients. (1) Roy was an overachieving painter who had become impotent and unable to work after a fall from scaffolding. He sought help because there was no physical basis for his malaise or reason for the way his life had fallen apart after the accident. (2) Bertha entered treatment because of a severe depression. She was very dark-skinned, had grown up in the South, and had experienced a series of abusive relationships with working-class men who were far below her socially and intellectually. In treatment, she revealed deep feelings of self-hatred and self-deprecation and a self-image as Black, ugly, ignorant, and dirty. Her depression had become clinical after a marriage to a fellow professional and the birth of a child. (3) John was a highly trained professional with a severe anger problem that had lost him a series of good jobs. He sought treatment after entering a very promising executive training program in which he was doing poorly because of his discomfort in supervising and competing with White co-workers.

The patterns that these patients presented with were very typical of Grier and Cobbs's general African American clientele. All had been living reasonably functional lives until an emotional crisis knocked them down, and each had a difficult time recovering. Psychotherapy had revealed very negative self-perceptions that were deeply intertwined with their experiences as African Americans in the United States. According to the authors, African Americans, because of their circumstances of having to live in, adapt to, and survive in a hostile and racist world, are at perpetual risk for developing serious physical and emotional disorders. Most survive. Many even grow strong from it, but all pay an emotional price that may, with sufficient stress and personal difficulty, result in some type of psychological breakdown. For many, the ultimate consequence is depression and grief, which are understood by Grier and Cobbs to be nothing less than "hatred turned toward the self." But when these patients are helped to feel the depth of their sorrow, their grief begins to lift, and enormous anger is set free. According to the authors, African Americans stand at a precarious juncture, "delicately poised, not yet risen to the flash point, but rising rapidly nonetheless" (1968, p. 213). As if looking into a crystal ball, they anticipated a growing violence that has increasingly become a part of race relations in America since the 1970s.

This chapter focuses attention on mental health issues that plague People of Color. In it you will explore a number of factors, like the racism described by Grier and Cobbs, that put People of Color at risk for mental and emotional difficulties. Chapter 5 discusses some of the psychological issues related to child development and parenting in Communities of Color. Chapter 7 explores various sources of bias in the delivery of mental health services to People of Color and why, even when there is significant need, Clients of Color consistently avoid mental health services. These three chapters together provide a clear picture of the kinds of psychological issues culturally different clients struggle with and that they ultimately bring with them into the helping situation.

You will begin this chapter by exploring problems related to racial identification and group belonging in Adults of Color and gain an understanding of the evolution of ethnic identity conflict, paying special attention to recent models of racial identity development that have proved particularly useful in making sense out of cross-cultural interactions in the helping situation. In subsequent sections you will learn about the psychological impact of assimilation and acculturation, the role of stress as a mediator in the development of physical and emotional symptoms among People of Color, the psychology of trauma, and, finally, drug and alcohol use and their relationship to ethnicity. These various problems are interrelated and mutually sustaining.

■ Racial Identity and Group Belonging

The controversy over whether Children of Color regularly experience problems in group identification and low self-concept as a result of racism is discussed in some detail in chapter 5. The conclusion, based on several sources of evidence, is that they did not necessarily, but without sufficient and appropriate family and community support, Children of Color were certainly at risk for such problems. There is also a certain hesitancy among researchers to underestimate the deleterious effects of racism and the negative views that society in general holds of ethnic group members. In this section, this picture will be expanded to include identity difficulties in ethnic adults.

The Inner Dynamics of Ethnic Identity

The general term *identity* refers to the existence of a stable inner sense of who a person is and is formed by the successful integration of various experiences of the self into a coherent self-image. *Ethnic identity,* in turn, refers to that part of personal identity that contributes to one's self-image as an ethnic group member. Thus, when one speaks of African American identity, Native American identity, or Jewish identity, what is being referred to is the individual's subjective experience of ethnicity. What does the person feel, consciously and unconsciously, about being a member of his or her ethnic group? What meaning do individuals attach to their ethnicity? What does their behavior reflect about the nature of their attachment to the group? Answers to these questions are subsumed under the notion of ethnic identity.

Ethnic identity formation, like personal identity formation, results from the integration of various personal experiences one has had, for example, as an African American, Native American, or Jew, combined with the messages that have been communicated and internalized about ethnicity by various family members and significant others.

In general, ethnic identity can be categorized as *positive ethnic identification, negative ethnic identification,* or *ambivalent ethnic identification,* and individuals as positive, negative, and ambivalent identifiers (Klein, 1980). The latter two have also been referred to in the literature as internalized racism, internalized oppression, and racial self-hatred.

- As emphasized in the previous chapter, Children of Color, by the fact of being raised in a hostile and racist environment, are likely to have unpleasant experiences associated with their ethnicity. As these negative group-related experiences accumulate, it becomes increasingly difficult for the child, and later the adult, to integrate them into a coherent and positive sense of ethnic self. Instead, they are either actively rejected and disowned, and thus relegated to the unconscious and experienced as "not me" (negative identification) or allowed to remain conscious, but unintegrated. In time, they are likely to become a source of ambivalent feelings about the self as an ethnic group member (ambivalent identification). In this regard, Klein (1980) found that Jews with positive ethnic identities tend to be healthier psychologically and better adjusted than those with more conflicted feelings about their Jewishness. A similar logic would seem to hold for People of Color.

- Inner conflicts in ethnic identity, such as those just described, ultimately find expression in some form of overt behavior. In the case of negative identification (i.e., where aspects of the ethnic self are actively rejected or disowned), there is, first of all, a tendency in the individual to deny, avoid, or escape group membership in whatever ways possible. In Communities of Color, this is often referred to as "passing." It may include trying to change one's appearance so as not to look so typically ethnic, changing a name, moving to nonethnic neighborhoods, dating and marrying outside of the group, and taking on majority group habits, language, and affectations. Such behaviors are usually experienced as offensive within ethnic communities. In fact, specific derogatory terms have been created in each Communities of Color to describe such individuals: "Oreos" among African Americans, "coconuts" among Latinos/as, "apples" among Native Americans, and "bananas" among Asian Americans. All refer to such individuals as being of Color on the outside but White on the inside. As part of this rejection of ethnicity, one also finds the taking on of majority attitudes and habits, including the dominant culture's prejudices and stereotypes toward one's own group. For those who are unfamiliar with such patterns of "identity rejection and self-hatred," it is usually shocking to learn that some of the most virulent anti-Semites and racists can be Jews and Blacks, respectively.

- In relation to ambivalent identification, where rejecting tendencies exist concurrently with positive feelings about group membership, there is either vacillation between love and hate (where individuals move back and forth, pulling away from feeling too identified if they get too close and moving back toward the group if they grow too distant) or the simultaneous expression of contradictory positive and negative attitudes and behaviors. One form of accommodation is to compartmentalize ethnic identity (i.e., retain certain aspects and reject others). For instance, a Latino/a might refuse to speak Spanish or identify as a Catholic or marry within the group, but at the same time have strong preferences for native foods, prefer living in a barrio, and become involved in civil rights activities.

- However, psychological accommodations such as these tend to be precarious at best and often fall apart, or at least grow fragile, in relation to all forms of emotional upheaval and change. It is not uncommon, for example, for individuals to "rethink" their connection to ethnicity after the birth of a child, death of a parent or close relative, or a personal near-death experience. It is perhaps most accurate to conceive of ethnic identity formation as an ongoing and lifelong process. As such, it involves a series of internal psychological adaptations (that may eventually translate into changes in behavior) to an ever-changing complex of unfolding ethnic experiences. Generally, core conflicts around ethnicity that occur early in life continue to feed basic feelings of negativity or ambivalence and are difficult to resolve completely. But even here, there are instances when dramatic and significant changes toward positive identification do occur (Diller, 1991).

The three states of ethnic identification just described are summarized in Table 6–1.

■ **TABLE 6–1**   Summary of Ethnic Identification States

Ethnic identity state	Characteristic reactions
Positive identification	Accepts and integrates ethnic-related experiences
	Ethnic-related reactions are conscious
	Accepts ethnic self
	Positive group attachment
	Retains and celebrates ethnic ways and attitudes
Negative identification	Rejects and disowns ethnic-related experiences
	Ethnic-related reactions remain unconscious
	Reject aspects of ethnic self
	Denies, avoids, or escapes group membership
	Takes on majority ways and attitudes
Ambivalent identification	Vacillates between the reactions described for both
	positive and negative identification and/or
	compartmentalizes areas of ethnic content

Note. Adapted from *Jewish Identity and Self-esteem: Healing Wounds Through Ethnotherapy* by J. Klein, 1980, New York: Institute on Pluralism and Group Identity. Copyright © 1980 and *Freud's Jewish Identity: A Case Study in the Impact of Ethnicity* by J. V. Diller, 1991, Cranbury, NJ: Fairleigh Dickinson University Press. Copyright © 1991 held by Jerry V. Diller.

Models of Racial Identity Development

A somewhat different approach to understanding the evolution of racial or cultural consciousness is offered by various researchers (Atkinson, Morten, & Sue, 1993; Cross, 1995; Hardiman & Jackson, 1992; Helms, 1990) who began in the 1970s to develop what has come to be called "models of *racial identity development*." These models, which were first developed in relation to the experience of African Americans, assume that there are strong similarities in the ways all ethnic individuals from different groups respond to the experience of oppression and racism. It is believed, further, that there is a series of predictable stages that People of Color go through as they struggle to make sense out of the relationship to their own cultural group as well as to the oppression of mainstream culture.

Cross (1995), whose work is exemplary, hypothesizes five such stages of development. It is assumed that each Person of Color can be located in one of the five stages depending on his or her level of racial awareness and identity:

1. In Stage 1, called "pre-encounter," individuals are not consciously aware of the impact that race and ethnicity have had on their life experiences. They tend to assimilate, seek acceptance by Whites, exhibit strong preferences for dominant cultural values, and even internalize negative stereotypes of their own group. By de-emphasizing race and distancing themselves from other group members, they are able to deny their actual vulnerability to racism and sustain, as long as they are able, the myth of meritocracy and the hope of achievement unencumbered by racial hatred.

2. In Stage 2, "encounter," some event or experience shatters the individual's denial and sends him or her deep into confusion about his or her ethnicity. The person for the first time must consciously deal with the fact of being different and what this difference means. People of Color at this stage often speak of "waking up" to reality, realizing that ethnicity is an aspect of self that must be dealt with, and the enormity of what must be confronted out in the world.

3. Stage 3, "immersion–emersion," is characterized by two powerful feelings: first a desire to immerse oneself in all things "ethnic," for example, to celebrate all symbols of "Blackness," and to simultaneously avoid all contact with Whites, the White world, and symbols of that world. The result is at first an uncritical descent into Blackness, where everything Black is beautiful, and everything White is abhorrent. During this more separatist period, People of Color seek information about ethnic history and culture and surround themselves exclusively with "their own kind." The enormous anger that is generated during Stage 2 and lingers into Stage 3 slowly dissipates as the person grows increasingly focused on self-exploration, creating attachment within his or her ethnic world, and less in need of lashing out at the White world.

4. "Internalization," Stage 4 of the model, begins as the Person of Color becomes increasingly secure and positive in his or her sense of racial identity and less rigid in the attachment to group allegiances at the expense of personal

autonomy. Pro-ethnic attitudes become more "expansive, open, and less defensive." Although the person feels securely connected to his or her ethnic community, there also emerges a greater willingness to relate to Whites and members of other ethnic groups who are able to acknowledge and accept their ethnicity.

5. Stage 5, "internalization–commitment," represents a growing and maturing of the tendencies initiated in Stage 4. People of Color at Stage 5 have found ways of translating their personal ethnic identities into an active sense of commitment to social justice and change. According to Tatum (1992), the Stage 5 person is "anchored in a positive sense of racial identity," and can "proactively perceive and transcend race." Race has become an instrument for reaching out into the world, rather than an end in itself as in Stage 3 or a social reality to be denied or avoided as in Stage 1.

Separate racial identity models have been created in relation to each Community of Color. While some differences exist in the number of stages hypothesized, content of stages and process of movement from one stage to the next, the general process of identity development and change is the same across groups.

Atkinson, Morten, and Sue (1993) have reviewed these models and extrapolated four dimensions of change that they believe occur universally as the Person of Color moves through the stages. Specifically, they see changes in attitudes toward:

- the self
- others of the same ethnic group
- members of different ethnic groups
- dominant group members

In relation to attitudes toward the self, self-depreciating feelings are transformed into self-appreciation as one moves through the various stages. Attitudes toward one's own group change from group depreciating to group appreciating, with the disappearance of identity conflict and internalized oppression across stages. Attitudes toward other minorities move from discriminatory feelings to the eventual acceptance and appreciation of differences.

Attitudes toward dominant group members move from identifying with the majority through rejecting them to selective appreciation as the individual proceeds through the various stages. Atkinson, Morten, and Sue's progression of attitude changes across developmental stages is summarized in Table 6–2. It should be noted that they define five stages of development as opposed to the six stages posited by Cross (1995).

Racial Identity Development and the Helping Process

The value of these models of racial identity development to providers is twofold:

1. They educate and sensitize providers to the importance of cultural identity in understanding the experiences of People of Color.

■ **TABLE 6–2**   Minority Identity Development Model: Attitude Changes
Across Stages

Stages	Attitude toward self	Attitude toward others of same minority	Attitude toward others of different minority	Attitude toward dominant group
1—Conformity	Self-depreciating	Group-depreciating	Discriminatory	Group-appreciating
2—Dissonance	Conflict between self-depreciating and self-appreciating	Conflict between group-depreciating and group-appreciating	Conflict between dominant-held views of minority hierarchy and feelings of shared experience	Conflict between group-appreciating and group-depreciating
3—Resistance and Immersion	Self-appreciating	Group-appreciating	Conflict between empathy for other minority experiences and culturocentrism	Group-depreciating
4—Introspection	Concern with basis of self-appreciating	Concern with nature of unequivocal appreciation	Concern with ethnocentric basis for judging others	Concern with the basis of group depreciation
5—Synergetic	Self-appreciating	Group-appreciating	Group-appreciating	Selective appreciating

Note. Adapted from *Counseling American Minorities*, 4e (p. 34), by D. R. Atkinson, G. Morten, & D. W. Sue, 1999. Copyright © 1993 by W. C. B. Brown & Benchmark. Reprinted with permission.

2. They suggest that individuals at different stages of development may exhibit very different needs and values and may feel differently about what is supportive or therapeutic in the helping situation.

Various authors have differentiated the counseling needs that Clients of Color exhibit as they move through the five stages of racial identity development (Atkinson, Morten, & Sue, 1993; Sue & Sue, 1999).

■ Clients at Stage 1 tend to seek help for issues unrelated to ethnic identity and generally prefer working with White providers. According to Sue and Sue (1999), Stage 1 individuals are likely to feel threatened by direct explorations of race and ethnicity and tend to feel more comfortable with a "task-oriented, problem-solving approach." They also react differently to White and same-race providers. Stage 1 clients are likely to overidentify with and seek approval from the former, and direct hostility toward the latter as a symbol of what he or she is trying to reject. Both types of therapist, however, have a similar task of bringing to consciousness the topic of race and culture.

■ Clients at Stage 2 tend to be preoccupied with personal issues of race and identity, but at the same time are torn between fading Stage 1 beliefs and an emerging awareness of race consciousness. They seek counselors knowledgeable about their cultural group and tend to do best with counseling modes that allow maximum self-exploration. Sue and Sue (1999), however, point out that the person may still be more comfortable with a White therapist, as long as he or she is culturally aware.

■ Clients in Stage 3 are less likely to seek counseling. They tend to be absorbed in re-exploring and engaging in ethnic ways and see personal problems exclusively as the result of racism. If they must enter treatment, Counselors of Color are by far preferred. Sue and Sue (1999) offer the following suggestions in relation to Stage 3 clients. The therapist, whether White or of Color, will inevitably be seen as a "symbol of the oppressive society" and thus challenged. The least helpful response for either is to become defensive and take any attacks personally. "White guilt and defensiveness" on the part of White therapists will especially exacerbate client anger. Therapists must realize that they will be continually tested and often find that honest self-disclosure about matters of race is "a necessary requirement to establish credibility." Last, Sue and Sue (1999) suggest adopting strategies that are more "action oriented" and "aimed at external change" as well as group approaches when working with Stage 3 clients.

■ Clients in Stage 4 are struggling to balance group and personal perspectives and may seek counseling to help them sort out these issues. They may still prefer a counselor from their own group, but they can begin to conceive of receiving help from a culturally sensitive outsider. Sue and Sue (1999) point out that those in Stage 4 appear in many ways similar to those in Stage 1. They tend to experience conflict between identification with their group and the need to "exercise greater personal freedom." Unlike the Stage 1 person, however, reactions tend to be issue specific and do not challenge their positive attachment to the group. Approaches that emphasize self-exploration are particularly helpful in integrating group identity and personal concerns of the self.

■ Clients who have reached Stage 5, according to Atkinson et al. (1993), are again less in need of access to counseling. They have developed good skills at balancing personal needs and group obligations, have an openness to all cultures, and are able to deal well with racism when it is encountered. Their preference for a counselor, if needed, is most likely to be dictated by the personal qualities and attitudes of the counselor rather than by group membership.

Recall that in chapter 3 Helms's (1995) model of White identity development was introduced. Her model, which parallels and evolved from the work just described, enumerates stages of racial consciousness development in Whites and the eventual abandonment of entitlement. Just as it is useful to be able to identify the stage of identity development of individual Clients of Color, so too is it valuable to assess White helpers vis-à-vis Helms's model in order to train them better and match them with appropriate Clients of Color. According to Sue and Sue (1999), White providers will be most effective in cross-cultural service delivery when they have successfully worked through feelings about Whiteness and privilege. Such individuals, located in the highest stages of Helms's model, are able to experience their own ethnicity "in a nondefensive and nonracist manner." They also warn against mismatches, especially when the White therapist is at Stage 1 of Helms's model.

> A White therapist at the conformity level, for example, may cause great harm to culturally different clients. . . .The therapist may . . . a) reinforce a conformity client's feelings of racial self-hatred, b) prevent or block a dissonance client from looking at inconsistent feelings/attitudes/ beliefs, c) dismiss and negate resistance and immersion client's anger about racism . . . or d) perceive the integrative awareness individual as having a confused sense of self-identity. (p. 162)

■ Assimilation and Acculturation

Ethnic group members differ widely in the extent of their *assimilation* and *acculturation*. Conceptually, ethnic assimilation is the coming together of two distinct cultures to create a new and unique third cultural form. This is the myth of the "great melting pot," taken from a play by the same name, written by Jewish playwright Israel Zangwill at the beginning of the 20th century. It is referred to as a myth because it just never happened that way.

Gordon (1964) distinguishes several forms of assimilation:

- Acculturation involves taking on the cultural ways of another group, usually those of the mainstream culture.
- Structural assimilation means gaining entry into the institutions of a society. Gordon also refers to this as "integration."
- Marital assimilation implies large-scale intermarriage with majority group members.
- Identificational assimilation involves developing a sense of belonging and peoplehood with the host society.

It is probably most accurate to say that White ethnics—Irish, Italian, Jews, Armenians, and so forth—have assimilated into American society on all of these dimensions, but only to the extent that they have been willing to give up their traditional ways and values. People of Color, on the other hand, were never really considered part of the great melting pot and have remained structurally separate. They have, however, acculturated in varying degrees to the dominant Northern European culture. Thus, in the United States, assimilation has always been a one-way process perhaps, according to Healey (1995), better described as "Americanization" or "Anglo-conformity." Healey states:

> This kind of assimilation was designed to maintain the predominance of the British-type institutional patterns created during the early years of American society. Under Anglo-conformity there is relatively little sharing of cultural traits, and immigrants and minority groups are expected to adapt to Anglo-American culture as fast as possible. Historically,

Americanization has been a precondition for access to better jobs, higher education, and other opportunities. (p. 40)

Acculturation, again, is the taking on of cultural patterns of another group, in this case, dominant White culture. In relation to working with culturally different populations, acculturation has importance in two ways:

- It is critical to be able to assess the amount of acculturation that has taken place within any individual or family and, simultaneously, to discover to what extent and in what specific areas traditional attitudes, values, and behavior still remain. Without such a "reading," it is impossible to know what form of helping process is most appropriate and most effective with culturally different clients. Just knowing that a client is Latino/a in origin tells us very little about who the person is or how he or she lives. To know where the individual falls on a continuum from traditional identification to complete acculturation offers more information. It is important, however, not to confuse group membership with the degree of acculturation that has occurred, or as Sue and Zane (1987) warn, to "avoid confounding the cultural values of the client's ethnic group with those of the client" (p. 8).
- Acculturation can create serious emotional strain and difficulties for ethnic clients. A special term, *acculturative stress*, has been coined to refer to such situations. Take, for example, a newly arrived Vietnamese family. The children have learned English relatively quickly in comparison to their parents. As a result, they may end up translating for and becoming the spokespeople for the family. This is not a traditional role for Vietnamese children, who are trained to be very deferential to their elders. Nor is it natural within their tradition for children to be in a position to wield so much power. As the children Americanize, they feel increasingly less bound by traditional ways. The result is enormous stress on the family unit, as is usually the case when traditional cultural ways are compromised or lost as a result of immigration and acculturation.

Views of Acculturation

Researchers have long argued over how best to conceptualize the process of acculturation. Is it unidimensional or multidimensional? That is, does acculturation exist on a single continuum ranging from identification with the indigenous culture at one end to identification with the dominant culture at the other? Or does it make more sense to conceive of an individual's attachment to the two groups as independent of each other, with the possibility of simultaneously retaining an allegiance to one's traditional culture as well as to dominant American culture?

- The unidimensional view implies that as one moves toward dominant cultural patterns, there must be a simultaneous giving up of traditional ways. This approach has generated the notion of the "marginal" person, an ethnic group member who tries to acculturate into the majority but ends up in a perpetual limbo between the two cultures (Lewin, 1948; Stonequist, 1961).

Such individuals have transformed themselves too much to return to traditional ways, but at the same time, they cannot gain any real acceptance in the majority culture because of their skin color. A variety of symptoms has been attributed to such marginality: feelings of inferiority, depression, hyper-self-consciousness, restlessness and anomie, and a heightened sense of race consciousness.

- Other writers see acculturation as bi- or multidimensional. Proponents of such *biculturalism* believe that it is possible to live and function effectively in two cultures (T. L. Cross, 1988; Oetting & Beauvais, 1990; Valentine, 1971). Unlike the marginal person who is suspended between cultures with little real connection to either, the bicultural individual feels connected to both and picks and chooses aspects of each to internalize. Thus, in this view, it is possible for an Asian American to remain deeply steeped in a traditional lifestyle while interacting comfortably in the White world, perhaps in relation to work, some socializing, and political activity outside of the Asian American community. Problems with this notion arise when aspects of the two cultures are in clear conflict. For example, an immigrant Latina woman is forced to give up her traditional role and work outside of the home and yet tries to remain true to traditional sex roles. Even if she is able to integrate the two, it will be very difficult for her children, not having been fully enculturated in traditional ways, to do the same (Casas & Pytluk, 1995). It should also be pointed out that biculturalism is not seen as a virtue in all ethnic communities. Some view those who have become proficient in majority ways with contempt—as "turncoats" who have rejected and turned away from their own kind.

- A third perspective, typified by the work of Marin (1992), suggests that the impact of acculturation can be assessed best by discovering the kinds of material that have been gained or lost through acculturation. Marin distinguishes three levels of acculturation. The superficial level involves learning and forgetting facts that are part of a culture's history or tradition. The intermediate level has to do with gaining or losing more central aspects and behaviors of a person's social world (e.g., language preference and use, ethnicity of spouse, friends, neighbors, names given to children, and choice of media). The significant level of cultural material involves core values, beliefs, and norms that are essential to the very cultural paradigm or worldview of the person. For example, Marin (1992) points to Latino culture's values of "encouraging positive interpersonal relationships and discouraging negative, competitive and assertive interactions," "familialism," and "collectivism" (p. 239). When cultural values of this magnitude are lost or become less central, acculturation has reached a significant point, and one might wonder what remains of an individual's cultural attachment. For many Whites, traditional cultural ties progressively slipped away, generation by generation in America, according to Marin's model. The immigrant generation tended to trade more superficial cultural material. Their children, in turn, exchanged more immediate cultural material as they increasingly acculturated, and so forth.

Immigration and Acculturation

Acculturative stress is most pronounced during periods of transition, especially during and after significant migrations (e.g., to the United States) and the exposure and necessary adjustment to a new culture. Landau (1982) points to five factors that make the transition either easier or more difficult:

- The reasons for the migration and whether or not the original expectations and hopes were met
- The availability of community and extended family support systems
- The structure of the family and whether it was forced to assume a different form after migration (e.g., moving from extended family to exclusively nuclear)
- The degree to which the new culture is similar to the old (the greater the difference, the more substantial the stress)
- The family's general ability to be flexible and adaptive

According to Landau, when the stresses are severe, the support insufficient, and the family basically unhealthy, it is likely to try to compensate in one of three ways, each leading to further stresses and a compounding of existing problems. The family may isolate itself and remain separate from its new environment. It may become enmeshed and close its boundaries to the outside world, rigidify its traditional ways, and become overly dependent on its members. Or, the family may become disengaged, wherein individual family members become isolated from one another as they reject previous family values and lifestyle. Especially problematic is the situation in which family members acculturate at very different rates.

Perhaps the most common and problematic consequence of acculturation is the breakdown of traditional cultural and family norms. Among Latino/a immigrants, for instance, this may take the form of challenges to traditional beliefs about male authority and supremacy, role expectations for men, and standards of conduct for females. But such changes may not be limited to newer immigrants. Carrillo (1982) suggests that these same changing patterns are evident within the Latino/a community as a whole: "Clearly, Hispanics appear to be moving away from such strict concepts of role and authority within the family, and with this movement approaching new normative behavior for males and females" (p. 260).

Carrillo goes on to warn helping professionals to exhibit caution in assessing pathology, appropriateness, and inappropriateness in relation to Latino/a sex-role behavior and provides the following example:

> An Hispanic man who prefers the company of other men and who behaves in an authoritative manner with his wife may be manifesting his "machismo" rather than indicating personal pathology. Such behavior among other cultural groups may imply "latent homosexuality," or an "inferiority complex," or that the woman is masochistic and prefers to be a "martyr." Such is not necessarily the case among Hispanic groups. (1982, p. 261)

It is critical to be familiar with the norms of the group and subgroup of which the client is a member. This is not to say, however, that emotional problems do not develop as a result of cultural change. Quite the contrary. Carrillo (1982), in fact, points out a number of problems that can emerge in relation to the individual's "inability to accept, conform to or adhere to sex-role defined standards of conduct" (p. 258). For males, symptoms can include difficulties in relation to authority, preoccupation and anxiety over sexual potency, conflict over the need for role consistency, and depression and isolation over having to feel invincible. For females, it tends to include feelings of failure and depression over not being able to live up to the strict sex-role requirements that are placed on them as well as the somatization (development of bodily symptoms) of their frustration and rage.

Acculturation and Community Breakdown

A final dynamic worth exploring is the psychological consequences of the breakdown of communal support as a result of assimilation. As acculturation proceeds and individual group members feel less attached to traditional ways, they often choose to leave the community (or ghetto) in the hope of avoiding some of the hatred and animosity that are routinely directed toward the group. Lewin (1948), drawing on observations of highly assimilated German Jews prior to World War II, suggests a very different outcome than one would predict. Specifically, he found that by leaving the ghetto, acculturated individuals put themselves at greater risk of being the objects of prejudice and racial hatred than was true when they resided within the traditional community. Lewin writes:

> If we compare the position of the individual Jew in the Ghetto period . . . with his situation in modern times . . . we find that he now stands much more for and by himself. With the wider spread and scattering of the Jewish group, the family or the single individual becomes functionally much more separated. . . . In the ghetto he felt the pressure to be essentially applied to the Jewish group as a whole. . . . Now as a result of the disintegration of the group, he is much more exposed to pressure as an individual. . . . Even when the pressure on the whole group from without was weakened, that on the individual Jew was relatively increased. (pp. 153–155)

In other words, with acculturation and assimilation, the ability of the community to protect the individual is weakened, and efforts to avoid racial hatred by distancing oneself from group membership are likely to prove counterproductive.

■ Stress

A critical question that needs to be answered in order to understand the complex relationship between ethnicity and health is: How exactly does the negative impact of broad social factors, such as racism, acculturation, poverty, and so forth, get translated into the everyday physical and emotional distresses that disproportionately affect People of Color?

According to Myers (1982), the mechanism is stress. Put most simply, being without resources and the perpetual object of discrimination make life more stressful and, in turn, increase the risks of disease, instability, and breakdown. Myers begins his argument by suggesting that "for many blacks, particularly those who are poor, the critical antecedents appear to be the higher basal stress level and the state of high stress vigilance at which normative functioning often occurs" (p. 128). In other words, poor African Americans tend to live a "stress-primed" state of existence.

Myers goes on to show how certain internal and external factors either increase or decrease (mediate) the subjective experience of stress and, as a result, the risk of stress-related diseases:

- Externally, current economic conditions set the stage for whether race- and social-class–related experiences will be sources of greater or lesser stress.
- Internally, individual temperament, problem-solving skills, a sense of internal control, and self-esteem reduce the likelihood that an event or situation is experienced as stressful.

With these factors as a baseline, two additional conditions seem to mediate the individual's response when a stressful situation is actually presented:

- The actual episodic stressful event that occurs.
- The coping and adaptation of which the individual is capable.

Myers contends that for poor African Americans, episodic crises are more frequent, and because of their higher basal stress levels, such crises are more likely to be damaging and disruptive.

> Thus, for example, the death of a spouse or relative or the loss of a job due to economic downturns is likely to be more psychologically and economically devastating to the person who is struggling to find enough money to eat, to pay the rent, and to support three or four children than it would to someone without those basic day to day concerns. (1982, pp. 133–134)

Myers has identified substantial differences among group members in their ability to cope and in the type of coping strategies used. Street youth, for example, resort to "cappin', rappin', conning, and fighting" as coping mechanisms for survival in the streets. For others, the "ability to remain calm, cool, and collected in the face of a crisis" is primary. Still others may turn to alcohol and drugs or religion as a means of gaining some distance. Myers believes that for African Americans as a group, stress-related illness risks are higher than for the general population. But he does point out that there are effective ways to reduce the risk:

> To the extent that ethnic cultural identity can be developed and stably integrated into the personality structure, to the extent that skills and competencies necessary to meet the varied demands can be obtained, to the extent that flexible, contingent response strategies can be developed, and to the extent that support systems can be maintained and strengthened, then resistances can be developed that will enhance

stress tolerance and reduce individual and collective risk for disorders and disabilities. (Myers, 1982, p. 138)

Daly, Jennings, Beckett, and Leashore (1995) amplify on Myers's findings by describing specific coping mechanisms within the family, at the community level, and within organizations.

■ Psychological Trauma

Stress reactions, which Myers (1982) sees as having particular impact on People of Color, serve to deplete psychic resources and ultimately lead to some kind of breakdown in functioning or illness. There are, however, stress experiences that are so extreme that they not only deplete personal resources but actually shut down an individual's basic psychic adaptation systems. Clinically, we call these traumas or traumatic events. According to Herman (1997), "traumatic events overwhelm the ordinary systems of care that give people a sense of control, connection, and meaning . . . Unlike commonplace misfortunes, traumatic events generally involve threats to life or bodily integrity, or a close encounter with violence and death" (p. 33). Intense trauma, which has been diagnostically labeled *post traumatic stress disorder* (PTSD), involves a loss of basic safety, intense fear, helplessness, loss of control, and threat of annihilation. Herman (1997) distinguishes four major symptom-groups associated with trauma:

- *hyperarousal*, in which the internal biology of self-preservation goes on permanent alert
- *intrusion*, in which traumatized people relive the event as if it were recurring in the present
- *constriction* and *numbing*, which involve a psychic deadening or dissociation from reality
- *disconnection*, which involves a shattering of the self, its attachment to others, and the meaning of human experience

Much of the research on trauma has involved victims of genocide, torture, ethnic conflict, and racism as well as women, children, and gay people. Too often racial and ethnic animosities end in violence and hate crimes which target People of Color and other minorities. It has been argued by certain authors (Brave Heart, 2005; Duran & Duran, 1995) that in some ethnic populations PTSD is a derivative of racism and colonization. The topic of social trauma (and I refer to it and other forms of mass violence as social because it tends to involve identifiable ethnic populations and is fueled not only by personal but also by social, cultural, and political motives) is more fully explored in chapter 8, "Addressing Ethnic Conflict, Genocide, and Mass Violence."

There are five important points to be made in relation to psychological trauma.

- The source and type of trauma dictate its impact and magnitude. Trauma resulting from natural disasters such as floods and earthquakes tends to be less debilitating than that caused by other human beings. "Acts of God" tend to be less personally destructive and easier to recover from psychologically than those carried out in an interpersonal context. One possible explanation is that trauma by human hand is experienced as more personal and purposeful and, as a result, is more likely to destroy a victim's basic sense of attachment to others and safety in the world. Similarly, repeated and long-term abuse, as in the case of torture, captivity, and repeated child abuse, is generally more destructive and debilitating than single, isolated incidents.

- It is important to understand that although the trauma experience happened in the past, it can best be understood, Gobodo-Madikizela (2000) suggests, as "lived memory." The victim has been reliving it, over and over again, in great detail as if it is still happening. Gobodo-Madikizela relates the experience of listening to a South African mother describing the death of her 11-year-old son.

The death was so vivid to me that it was as if it were happening in the moment. Her use of tense defied the rules of grammar as she crossed and recrossed the boundaries of past and present in an illustration of the timelessness of traumatic pain . . ." He *ran* out. He *is* still chewing his bread . . . *Now* I am dazed. I *ran* . . ." And the final moment when she recalled seeing her son's lifeless body: "Here *is* my son." With a gesture of her hand she transformed the tragic scene from one that happened more than ten years earlier to one that we were witnessing right there on the floor of her front room."(pp. 88–89)

- Various researchers (Duran & Duran, 1995; Epstein, 1998; Fogelman, 1991) have suggested that social trauma can be passed on or transmitted intergenerationally within ethnic families. An individual growing up in such an environment internalizes the trauma of past generations and responds to present events and experiences in light of that traumatization. Brave Heart (2005) in fact argues for the creation of a new diagnostic designation, historic trauma, which emphasizes the massive cumulative trauma that can occur across generations and reflects a broader range of social consequences and dysfunction than is referred to by the more limited and ahistorical diagnosis of PTSD. By way of evidence, Yehuda (1999) points to studies which show that children of Jewish Holocaust survivors are more vulnerable than others to the development of PTSD, including a greater degree of cumulative lifetime stress. Brave Heart (2005) explains: "This finding implies that there is a propensity among offspring to perceive or experience events as more traumatic and stressful; children of Holocaust survivors with a parent having chronic PTSD were more likely to develop PTSD in response to their own lifespan traumatic events. The traumatic symptoms of the parents, rather than the trauma exposure per se, are the critical risk factors for offspring manifesting their own trauma response" (p. 12). Historic trauma is also often associated with the destruction of traditional cultural and spiritual rituals that might have ameliorated the effect of the trauma in the first place.
- Substance abuse and dependence often occur with trauma. Physical pain and the disruption of healthy bodily functioning are regular occurrences in

trauma. A first step in treatment involves regaining control of the body and often involves, as Herman (1997) suggests, restoring biological rhythms of eating and sleep and reducing the symptoms of hyperarousal and intrusion. The psychic pain is less easily or quickly controlled, and patients regularly self-medicate in order to reduce the on-going emotional pain.

■ Finally, it is important to acknowledge that therapeutic work with trauma survivors is particularly challenging for a number of reasons. First, the clinical material that the trauma victim must share is not only painful for her or him to relive, but it is also very difficult for the therapist to hear and assimilate. There is in each of us a strong, unconscious tendency to avoid such disturbing material. Victims are often fearful that others including the therapist will not believe them. Second, it is also quite natural for the client to project feelings about the perpetrator onto the therapist. As McWilliams (2004) points out: "Because the transferences of clients with histories of traumatic abuse tend initially to be intense and relatively undiluted by observing capacities, it is hard for such individuals to take in the possibility that the therapist sincerely has their best interests at heart" (p. 253). It has been suggested that working with trauma survivors can be "traumatic" in its own right. Such trauma is referred to as "vicarious traumatization." Third, trauma work is long-term, highly emotional and very draining, and it can involve frequent setbacks, re-traumatization, hospitalizations, and efforts at self-injury. Trauma in its most extreme form transforms one's physiology, sense of self and safety, attachment to others, and sense of meaning in life. As Herman (1997) emphasizes, "Because trauma affects every aspect of human functioning, from the biological to the social, treatment must be comprehensive and stage-appropriate. A form of therapy that may be useful for a patient at one stage may be of little use or even harmful to the same patient at another stage" (p. 156).

■ Drug and Alcohol Use

There are three important points to be made about substance use and ethnicity.

1. First, there are numerous myths about substance abuse among People of Color. Rather than reflect anything akin to empirical reality, they are based on distorted stereotypes of excessive use and abuse by People of Color, especially in comparison to beliefs about the consumption patterns of Whites. "All Mexicans use and sell drugs" is a typical stereotype. Recently, for example, a report was issued regarding profiles of suspected drug traffickers to be routinely stopped and searched by the Oregon State Highway Patrol. Included among the characteristics that were sufficient to initiate a search was "being Hispanic." In reality, research shows that, with a few notable exceptions (to be discussed shortly), People of Color tend to use drugs and alcohol much less frequently than do dominant-culture Americans.

2. Second, there are real cultural differences in consumption patterns, in the meaning of drinking and substance use, and in what is socially acceptable

across cultures. Like the interpretation of any cultural differences, it is dangerous to make clinical judgments about patterns of substance use by culturally different clients without knowledge of the norms that exist around drinking or drug use within their culture. The same consumption pattern in an Asian American male, for instance, may have very different meaning vis-à-vis possible excesses and pathology than it would for a similarly aged Native American male.

3. Third, the meaning of recovery and abstinence is very different for People of Color and dominant group members. Substance abuse among Whites tends to be understood as a personal issue; for People of Color, it is as much a social-cultural issue as a personal one.

A good place to begin is by citing research findings on substance use and abuse in Youth of Color. Drug research on youth is more plentiful than similar data on adults and, in general, tends to reflect similar patterns to those of adults within the same culture. The following data are drawn from and summarized in Bernard (1991):

- With the exception of Native American youth, other ethnic populations exhibit use patterns that are significantly less than young Whites. This fact challenges common beliefs and stereotypes about runaway abuse and addiction among minority youth. As ethnic group members acculturate, however (and this is true for youth as well as adults), research shows that use levels increase and begin to approximate those of White counterparts.
- The lower use rates among less acculturated African Americans, Latinos/as, and Asian Americans may reflect protective factors that exist in traditional ethnic cultures, including emphasis on cooperation, sharing, communality, group support, interdependence, and social responsibility. These values are believed to mitigate against social alienation, which has regularly been shown to be associated with high substance abuse. It is interesting to note that complementary values (i.e., competition, individualism, self-first, and nonsharing) are more closely aligned with Northern European dominant culture and are seen as risk factors implicated in the development of substance abuse problems.
- It has also been found that bicultural youth (i.e., those who can move effectively between the dominant culture and their culture of origin) tend to exhibit rather low levels of drug and alcohol use.
- Although Youth of Color generally show lower rates of substance use, their use tends to lead to more behavioral and health problems. This is because there is a cumulative effect of substance abuse with other risk factors such as poverty, unemployment, discrimination, poor health care, and general depression, which correlate highly with ethnicity. It is believed that prevention is of little use unless these other risk factors are addressed.

More specific information on use and abuse patterns of Youth of Color by community is summarized in Tables 6–3 through 6–6.

■ **TABLE 6–3**   Key Findings from *Prevention Research Update Number Three: Substance Abuse Among Latino/a Youth*

- ■ Hispanics are one of the largest, youngest, and fastest-growing of the nation's subgroups (half of the Hispanic population is now under age 18).
- ■ While Hispanics, in general, have no higher levels of use prevalence than Whites or other ethnic groups, some research has found that Hispanics have more drug-related problems and that drug abuse is a serious, chronic, and multigenerational problem in many Hispanic families and communities.
- ■ Hispanic youth consume heavier quantities and experience more drinking problems than do other adolescents.
- ■ Heavier use patterns beginning in late adolescence appear to result from a blending of the drinking patterns of the donor cultures with those common among U.S. youth and reflect the value that the right to drink is a rite-of-passage.
- ■ Differential acculturation can produce stress in family relationships and behavioral problems in immigrant children who may acculturate to the U.S. culture at a faster rate than their parents.
- ■ Prevention efforts must (1) encourage biculturalism and bilingualism, building on cultural strengths and pride while facilitating the development of skills necessary to succeed in U.S. society; (2) involve the community in community development efforts, especially the development of cultural arts centers; and (3) involve the community in public awareness campaigns to counter the efforts of the alcohol/tobacco industry in Hispanic communities.

Note. From *Moving toward a "just and vital culture": Multiculturalism in our schools* by B. Bernard, April, 1991. Reprinted by permission of Northwest Regional Educational Laboratory.

■ **TABLE 6–4**   Key Findings from *Prevention Research Update Number Five: Substance Abuse Among Asian American Youth*

- ■ Other than Native Hawaiians, whose drug and alcohol use is more similar to Whites, Asian Americans have low levels of use compared with other ethnic groups.
- ■ Consistent with their low levels of use, Asian Americans suffer less from substance-related problems than do other ethnic groups, and most of these problems are male-owned.
- ■ Drinking in Asian society is governed by social norms that condemn excessive use and encourage moderation.
- ■ The more acculturated Asian males are, the higher their levels of alcohol use become.
- ■ A concern among some researchers and practitioners is that Asian American substance use problems are underreported because of their "model minority" stereotype status and because they do not want to bring shame on their families.
- ■ Prevention efforts should focus on (1) encouraging biculturalism; (2) involving youth in community prevention; and (3) providing indigenously owned family counseling and support services.

Note. From *Moving toward a "just and vital culture": Multiculturalism in our schools* by B. Bernard, April, 1991. Reprinted by permission of Northwest Regional Educational Laboratory.

Comparing Latinos/as and Asian Americans

Differences in patterns of use and social attitudes and behaviors associated with drinking and drugs vary dramatically across cultures. To appreciate the enormity of these differences, it is useful to juxtapose the characteristics of two groups—Latinos/as and Asian Americans—by way of comparison. It should be

■ **TABLE 6–5** Key Findings from *Prevention Research Update Number Two: Substance Abuse Among Minority Youth: Native Americans*

- The rates of use for almost all drugs, but especially alcohol, marijuana, and inhalants, have been consistently higher among American Indian youth than non-Indian youth.
- The rate of alcoholism is two to three times the national average.
- Heavy drinking has been called the main reason that one in two Indian students never finish high school.
- Native American adolescents are profoundly alienated and depressed and experience high rates of delinquency, learning and behavior problems, and suicide.
- This situation is the result of persistent and deep sociocultural and economic exploitation, which has made them the most severely disadvantaged population in the United States.
- The main risk factors for Native American adolescent substance abuse are (1) a sense of cultural dislocation and lack of integration into either traditional Indian or modern American life; (2) community norms supporting use; (3) peer-group support for use; and (4) lack of hope for a bright future.
- Prevention efforts must focus on (1) community involvement in community development efforts with youth playing a major role and (2) educational interventions that allow Native American youth to develop bicultural competence (i.e., to develop the skills necessary to be successful in the dominant culture while retaining their identification with and respect for traditional Native American values).

Note. From *Moving toward a "just and vital culture": Multiculturalism in our schools* by B. Bernard, April, 1991. Reprinted by permission of Northwest Regional Educational Laboratory.

■ **TABLE 6–6** Key Findings from *Prevention Research Update Number Four: Substance Abuse Among Black Youth*

- Substance use is lower among Black adolescents than among Whites or any other ethnic group except Asian Americans.
- While Blacks are more likely to be abstainers and to have lower levels of alcohol use than Whites, they experience more drinking-related *problems*, especially binge drinking, health problems, symptoms of physical dependence, and symptoms of loss of control.
- Compared with Whites, adult Blacks are more likely to be victims of alcohol-related homicide, to be arrested for drunkenness, and to be sent to prison rather than to treatment for alcohol-related crimes.
- At even moderate levels of use, the adverse consequences of substance use are exacerbated by the conditions of poverty, unemployment, discrimination, poor health, and despair that many Black youth face.
- Drug trafficking adversely affects the ability of the entire Black community to function and deal with its other problems.
- Black communities are particularly exploited by the alcohol industry through excessive advertising and the number of sales outlets in these neighborhoods.
- Prevention efforts must (1) involve the community in community development efforts that include an active role for youth; (2) facilitate the development of racial consciousness and pride; (3) include public awareness campaigns that counter the alcohol/tobacco industry's advertising; (4) be broad-based (i.e., providing access to a range of social and economic services and opportunities); and (5) restructure schools to provide opportunities for academic success.

Note. From *Moving toward a "just and vital culture": Multiculturalism in our schools* by B. Bernard, April, 1991. Reprinted by permission of Northwest Regional Educational Laboratory.

remembered, however, that with acculturation these patterns move toward approximating dominant cultural norms or result in a kind of hybrid behavior.

For instance, the use of illicit drugs increases dramatically with acculturation among Latino/a youth. Drug use is much less prominent than alcohol use among more traditionally identified youth. Or by way of example of the interaction, Mexican men tend to drink less often but more per occasion than U.S. men. After arrival in the United States, however, they tend to retain their heavier consumption patterns and also begin to drink more frequently. Gender differences in substance use among traditional Latino/a youth are far more pronounced than among Whites. Traditional women have very low consumption rates. With acculturation, these rates increase dramatically, reducing the disparity between the genders. Young men's drinking patterns, on the other hand, do not change noticeably with acculturation because drinking is an acknowledged part of male role behavior within Latino culture; it is an aspect of male bonding. For women, American culture gives much more permission regarding drinking behavior than does Latina culture. In comparison to other Communities of Color, Latino/a youth are particularly susceptible to peer influence in drug and alcohol use. This is probably related to the high value placed on interpersonal relationships within the culture. In addition, consumption varies with the presence of parental and sibling role models of drinking in the home. The use of dangerous drugs by males also seems related to a need to both escape pain and present a macho image. Thus, cultural values such as "personalismo" (an emphasis on interpersonal connections as opposed to personal accomplishments), "machismo" (male role characteristics), and "carnalismo" (an emphasis on ethnic pride) play a major role in shaping the way substances are used.

Among Asian Americans, on the other hand, use is more culturally controlled. There is, first of all, evidence of innate biological reactions that discourage drinking. A "flushing" or reddening reaction, which is reported to be rather uncomfortable, is found among some Asian American subgroups. Similarly, there seems to be a physiologically based dislike for the taste of alcohol among some individuals. But these seem to discourage drinking only to the extent that traditional cultural prohibitions are still in place. According to Austin, Prendergast, and Lee (1989):

> In accordance with Asian cultural values, Asian drinking is social rather than solitary, occurs in prescribed situations, is usually accompanied by food, is used to enhance social interaction, and occurs within a context of modern drinking norms. (p. 8)

Women drink little or no alcohol. Aggressive and noisy behavior when intoxicated is looked down upon. Even when drunk, Chinese and Japanese men are seldom loud or disorderly. Asian philosophies emphasize moderation, order, and social harmony and tend to discourage practices that compromise these values. Thus, for Asian Americans, alcohol consumption is culturally contained. It occurs as an essential part of religious ceremonies and festive occasions but only in moderation, and excesses are seen as an embarrassment to the individual and the family.

The Cultural Meaning of Recovery

Substance abuse, though its addictive qualities make it a problem in its own right, is most usefully viewed as symptomatic of other underlying psychological and emotional conditions. From such a perspective, it is believed that individuals use substances to either medicate themselves or escape inner pain. For People of Color, however, substance abuse and recovery possess cultural and communal meanings as well. I will never forget a talk given by a Native American elder, who had for many years worked as a substance abuse counselor and was himself a recovering addict. "My problem was not alcohol," he emphasized. "It was not knowing who I was and where I belonged. The alcohol was just the way I killed the pain."

In chapter 8 you will learn more about unresolved historic grief, how its source can be located in a history of cumulative traumas as well as the destruction of cultural methods of grieving. According to Duran and Duran (1995), before colonization, alcohol use (as well as the use of substances such as peyote) was strictly controlled by tribal tradition and its use was primarily ceremonial. As Native American culture was systematically destroyed, these controls were eliminated, and with the widespread introduction of excessive drinking as a means of pacifying Native American males, heavy alcohol consumption itself became a tradition on the reservation.

Standard treatment methods, based on dominant cultural views of substance abuse, are totally ineffective with Native Americans because they do nothing to change the social and cultural roots of the problem. Only by retrieving what was culturally lost and simultaneously instilling a positive sense of ethnic identity is there any real hope for overcoming substance abuse among Native Peoples. As Duran and Duran pointed out earlier, to subject Native American clients to Western modes of treatment, substance abuse included, that have inherent in them the very processes that undermined Native American culture in the first place is merely to dig the hole deeper.

Duran and Duran argue for the adoption of indigenous views of alcohol abuse, coupled with traditional methods of healing. Traditionally, alcohol was viewed as a destructive spiritual entity that had to be addressed in the spiritual realm if healing was to occur. Healing, in turn, had to occur not only within the individual but also within the context of the community. More and more, even within the confines of some Western agencies, sweat lodge ceremonies and other spiritual rituals are being introduced as part of treatment.

At a more universal level, the idea is that true recovery for People of Color must involve an acknowledgment of the impact of racism as well as substantial clinical efforts to heal its destructive inner effects. In a group therapy session for older African American addicts, I once observed a clear consensus that getting "clean" was not enough. One could never get beyond the "inner prison of drinking or drugging" until the "spiritual ghosts" of racism had been laid to rest.

■ Summary

This chapter focuses on mental health issues that plague People of Color. We begin with a discussion of racial identification and group belonging in adults. (Similar issues related to the experience of children are explored in chapter 5.) Ethnic identity refers to the individual's subjective experience of ethnicity and group belonging, including related meanings attached to ethnicity, conscious and unconscious feelings, and behavioral manifestations. Klein (1989) and Diller (1991) refer to three states of ethnic identity: positive identification, ambivalent identification, and negative identification. An alternative method of conceptualization, that of models of racial identity development, as proposed by Helms (1990), Cross (1995), and others, hypothesizes that People of Color go through a series of predicable stages as they struggle to make sense out of their relationship to their own cultural group as well as to the oppression of mainstream White culture. Both approaches assume the possibility of difficulties in ethnic identification and suggest different implications for treatment.

Ethnic group members can differ greatly in the amount of assimilation and acculturation that they have experienced. Both involve ethnic individuals' taking on different cultural forms. Individual group members can vary from retaining intact traditional culture at one extreme to having totally acculturated into the mainstream at the other. One's location on this continuum is useful in determining the most appropriate mental health intervention.

Acculturation can also create serious emotional strain when contradictory cultural values have been internalized or vary within the family. Unidimensional, bicultural, and behavior-specific models of acculturation are contrasted. Acculturative stress is most pronounced during periods of transition, especially during migration and the adjustment to a new society.

Stress is suggested as the mechanism through which People of Color are put at greater risk for physical and mental health, that is, how social factors such as racism, acculturation, identity issues, and poverty translate into physical and mental distress. Myers (1992) offers a broad-based model of the internal and external risk, and coping factors related to stress in African Americans. For example, he contends that poor African Americans experience episodic crises more often, and because of higher basal stress levels, such crises are more likely to be damaging and disruptive. Positive ethnic identity is seen as an important resiliency factor.

Psychological trauma is an extreme and highly debilitating instance of stress; involves threats to life and body integrity or close contacts with violence and death; and causes a loss of basic safety, intense fear, helplessness, loss of control, and threats of annihilation. People of Color and other minorities are at higher risk for social trauma. Trauma resulting from interpersonal and prolonged and repeated violations tends to be most debilitating. Trauma is best understood as lived and repetitious memory; can be transmitted from generation to generation; often co-exists with substance abuse; and is particularly demanding to treat.

Drug and alcohol abuse among People of Color is explored. Various popular myths of excessive use by People of Color are unfounded. There do exist differences in consumption patterns and the meaning of substance use across cultures as well avenues toward recovery.

■ Activities

1. *Undertake a guided fantasy.* Seat yourself comfortably, close your eyes, take a few slow, deep breaths, and relax. Try to project yourself into the following situation (unrealistic as it may seem). You wake up one morning, get out of bed, see yourself in the mirror and discover that you, normally a White person, have become African American. Or you, normally a Person of Color, have become a White person. Envision yourself as such. Now fantasize your way through a typical day as a Person of Color or as a White person. What happens and how are your reactions and the reactions of those around you different? What kind of emotions and feelings are building up within you? How has the world changed for you? Stay with it for as long as you can. This exercise can be done by yourself, in a dyad, or in a small group. In the latter configurations take turns sharing your experiences, and then discuss and compare them.

2. *Carry out a community needs assessment.* You have been recently hired as director of a community mental health center located in a mixed-race, working-class neighborhood in a major urban area. You have become aware that there is in the community a small group of Cambodian refugees who do not avail themselves of your center's services. You know from your course in cultural diversity that probably the most culturally sensitive way to approach them is a community needs assessment, that is, approaching the community and in various ways gaining information from them on what kind of mental health needs they may have and how you might best provide those services. Design a plan for carrying out such a needs assessment. Be specific.

7 Bias in Service Delivery

The following case study of a Navajo male who was diagnosed psychotic, first described by Jewell (1965), is a classic example of cross-cultural misunderstanding and bias in the delivery of mental health services.

Case Study 1

Bill was a 26-year-old Navajo man who had been hospitalized as psychotic in a California state mental hospital for 18 months. Little was known about him on admission. He had been jailed for bothering a woman dressed in white (he had mistaken her for a nurse) on a street corner in Barstow. He was taken for Mexican and placed in the jail's psychopathic ward when he did not respond to the questions of a Spanish-speaking interpreter. He appeared "anguished," kept repeating the phrase "Me sick," was diagnosed as schizophrenic, catatonic type by the medical examiner, and was eventually sent to the state hospital. There, he was taken to be Filipino, but also did not respond to questions in that language. He appeared "confused, dull, and preoccupied," kept repeating the phrase "I don't know," seemed anguished, and was believed to be hallucinating. He was again diagnosed as schizophrenic, this time hebephrenic type, which was altered back to catatonic 2 months later when a psychiatrist tested him and found *cerea flexibilitas* (muscular rigidity and lack of movement characteristic of catatonia). He was very quiet, appeared withdrawn and sleepy (there is no mention of the medication that was probably administered), and would arouse himself only for eating and personal care.

He would periodically approach staff in broken English and, pointing at his chest repeat: "Me, no good in here." He would also at regular intervals ask: "Can I go home?" Eight months after admission, Jewell, a psychology intern at the hospital who had been testing Bill, managed to discover his true ethnicity and was able to find a professional Navajo interpreter. Bill talked freely with the interpreter and expressed appreciation for being able to converse in his Native tongue.

His answers to questions indicated that he was experiencing no hallucinations, delusions, or other manifestations of schizophrenic thinking, and according to the interpreter who had extensive experience interviewing young Navajos in strange environments, "Bill's behavior and attitudes were not unusual under the circumstances." He was subsequently released to a Native American boarding school where he adjusted well and later returned to the reservation.

The life journey that ultimately brought Bill to the hospital was not atypical for a young Navajo. He was born in a remote, very traditional, and poverty-stricken area of the Arizona reservation. He was born during an eclipse, which spiritually destined him to take part, at different points in his life, in a ceremony that he described as the "Breath of Life" sing. He had participated in it as an infant and at age 6 and was supposed to engage in it once again during the time of his hospitalization. At age 6, he went to live with and assist his grandfather as a sheepherder. He worked for him until the old man's death, when Bill was 17. He reported that his grandfather never talked to him.

Bill then got a job with the railroad, which was interrupted by an 8-month hospital stay for tuberculosis. He returned to his previous employment, which took him to several states. He was always part of a Navajo crew and, thus, never exposed to acculturative influences. After saving a good bit of money and a brief return home to his family, Bill traveled on his own to California in search of additional work. A White man offered to find him a job and, in the process, swindled him out of his savings. Bill returned home, sold some jewelry, borrowed money, and returned to California in search of the man who had tricked him out of his money. He ended up in jail for vagrancy. He traveled with some Navajos whom he met in jail in search of employment, picked up a few odd jobs, but his money quickly ran out, and eventually he decided to return home. He thought that if he could get to a hospital, they would send him back to the reservation. That was why he had approached the woman whom he had mistaken for a nurse.

What is most striking about Bill's misdiagnosis is the fact that it was made on the basis of external observation alone. The doctors had never talked with him and, until Jewell took an interest in Bill, did not even know his ethnic origin. He had, in fact, been twice misidentified: first as Mexican and then as Filipino. The doctors first assumed the existence of serious pathology (if he is here in a mental hospital, he must be crazy) and then proceeded to find evidence in Bill's observable behavior. Evidently, they had never felt the need to actually talk with him to make a diagnosis. Equally disturbing was their total disregard of culture and the possibility that cultural differences might have played a role in understanding Bill's behavior. I am reminded of research by Rosenhan (1975), who had himself and colleagues, all mentally fit, checked into a private mental hospital where they merely observed what happened to them and others and took careful notes. Their copious note taking received extensive comment in their respective clinical files: "Patient exhibits excessive writing behavior."

From the perspective of Navajo culture, Bill's behavior made perfect sense and was anything but indicative of the deep mental and emotional pathology that the label "schizophrenia, catatonic type" implies. Consider the various symptoms on which Bill's diagnosis rested. His "apathetic and withdrawn behavior" was characteristic of the way Navajos respond to situations of stress and crisis. Inactivity is their chosen mode of psychological defense. He must have been traumatized by his experiences with the mental health system, not to mention culture shock, and he was also being forced to reside in a hospital, which is a symbol of death in Navajo culture. His unwillingness to talk and his repeated statement: "Me no good in this place" (pointing to his chest) relate to his need to perform the "Breath of Life" ceremony and the belief that he must conserve vocal energy until the ritual is completed. This statement may also have referred to his earlier bout with tuberculosis. The *cerea flexibilitas* was demystified when Jewell learned from the interpreter that Bill held these grotesque positions because he thought that it was expected of him. The most significant symptom of schizophrenia—lack of contact with reality and massive ego disintegration—was never really assessed because that requires talking with the patient.

Bill's experience with the mental health system, though perhaps extreme in its absurdity, is not atypical. In a variety of ways, mental health professionals have repeatedly introduced bias and cultural insensitivity into their work with culturally different clients. Ethnic patients, in turn, have responded by avoiding such services whenever possible and resisting them when they are not voluntary. The result has been the systematic underutilization of services by Clients of Color. This chapter focuses on various sources of bias in cross-cultural helping. You will begin by looking at ways in which attitudes of the provider can shape treatment values and decisions as well as who the providers are and the kind of skills and preparation they bring with them to their work with cross-cultural clients. Next you will learn about the helping process itself and the cultural relevance of its various practices and the concepts that support it and their applicability to culturally diverse populations. A number of important questions will emerge. Do ideas such as "helping" and "mental health," especially as they have been traditionally conceived, make sense in all cultures? Has racism or stereotyping played any role in how helping professionals have conceptualized work with Clients of Color? Have standard methods of assessment and diagnosis been culture-free, or has their use tended to differentially affect Clients of Color? Are the various forms of mental disorder, as defined by DSM-IV, found in all cultures, and are their symptom patterns and etiology (i.e., how they develop) the same cross-culturally? For example, do all cultural groups experience emotional states similar to what Western psychology calls "clinical depression," and if so, do they manifest symptoms in the same way?

■ The Impact of Social, Political, and Racial Attitudes

There is a vast body of research in social psychology that shows how attitudes can unconsciously affect behavior.

- Rosenthal and Jacobson (1968), for example, looked at the relationship between teacher expectations and student performance. Teachers were told at the beginning of the school year that half of the students in their class were high performers and the other half were low. In actuality, there were no differences among the students. By the end of the year, however, there were significant differences in how the two groups performed. Those who were expected to do well did so and vice versa. In another experiment, Rosenthal (1976) assigned beginning psychology students rats to train. Some were told that their rats came from very bright strains; others were told that their rats were genetically low in intelligence. The rats were, in actuality, all from the same litter. By the end of the training period, each group of rats was performing as expected. In these two experiments, what the teachers and the psychology students believed and expected was translated into differential behavior, which in turn became what Rosenthal called a "self-fulfilling prophesy." In other words, what we believe (i.e., the attitudes we hold) about people shapes our treatment of them. Freud called this phenomenon countertransference when it occurred in the clinical setting.

- Similar dynamics have been demonstrated in relation to helping professionals.

- In another classic study, Broverman, Broverman, Clarkson, Rosenkrantz, and Vogel (1970) looked at gender stereotyping and definitions of mental health. They asked a group of psychiatrists, psychologists, and social workers to describe characteristics they would attribute to healthy adult men, healthy adult women, and healthy adults with sex not specified. There was high agreement among subjects, and there were no differences between male and female clinicians. As a group, the clinicians enunciated very different standards of health for women and men; that is, a healthy woman was described in very different terms than was a healthy man. The concept of a healthy adult man and that of a healthy adult of unspecified sex did not differ significantly; that of a healthy adult man and a healthy adult woman did. Compared to men, healthy adult women were seen as more submissive, less independent, less adventuresome, more easily influenced, less aggressive, less competitive, more excitable in minor crises, more easily hurt, more emotional, less objective, and more concerned with appearance. It is probably fair to say that such beliefs about gender differences cannot help but translate into the ways these clinicians work with their male and female clients.

- In yet another study, researchers looked at the effect of political attitudes on the diagnosis of mental disorders (Wechsler, Solomon, & Kramer, 1970).

Clinicians in the study were asked to rate clients on the severity of their symptoms, based on videotaped interviews. All clinicians were shown the same videotapes in which the clients described their symptoms. The only difference was what the clinicians were told about the political activities of the clients. Clients described as being more extreme politically were regularly rated as having more severe symptoms (i.e., as being "sicker" than those who were presented as more conservative). Similarly, when clinicians were told that some subjects advocated violent means of bringing about political change, they too were rated as having more severe symptoms, as were those who were described as having very critical attitudes toward the field of mental health. Again, it is a short step to suggesting that the political attitudes of providers can color their perception and treatment of politically different clients.

- Although there is less empirical data on the effect of racial attitudes on provider behavior (probably because of the desire to appear "politically correct" and, therefore, the difficulty in accurately measuring and identifying racist attitudes), some exemplary studies do exist. Jones and Seagull (1983), for example, asked African American and White clinicians to evaluate the level of adjustment of African American therapy clients. He found that White clinicians tended to rate African American clients as more disturbed than did the African American therapists, especially in relation to how seriously they viewed external symptoms and their assessment of the quality of family relations. Other studies show that counselors and trainees tend to think in terms of stereotypes when working with culturally different clients (Atkinson, Casas, & Wampold, 1981; Wampold, Casas, & Atkinson, 1982).

- In addition, there is much research that shows dramatic differences in the kinds of services that White and non-White clients receive. For example, African Americans are more likely to receive custodial care and medications and are less often offered psychotherapy than are Whites (Hollingshead & Redlich, 1958). When they are offered psychotherapy, it tends to be short-term or crisis intervention as opposed to long-term therapy (Turner, 1985). Similarly, African Americans are overrepresented in public psychiatric hospitals (Kramer, Rosen, & Willis, 1972), and African Americans, Latinos/as, and Asian Americans are all more likely to receive supportive versus intensive psychological treatment and to be discharged more rapidly than Whites (Yamamoto, James, & Palley, 1968).

In short, there is no reason to believe that racial attitudes are any less likely to affect the perception and treatment of clients than social or political ones.

■ Who Are the Providers?

Underrepresentation in the Professions

It is well documented that clients prefer helpers from their own ethnic group (Atkinson, 1983). The sense of familiarity and safety that this affords cannot be underestimated. Present statistics do not bode well, however, for potential

Clients of Color; the reality is that People of Color are sadly underrepresented among the ranks of helping professionals. This serious lack of non-White providers is often cited as one of the reasons for underutilization of mental health services by People of Color.

A study of membership in the American Psychological Association (APA) in 1979, for example, showed that only 3% of the members were non-White (Russo, Olmedo, Stapp, & Fulcher, 1981). Of more than 4,000 practitioners who claimed their specialty to be in counseling psychology, fewer than 100 were of Color. A more recent study showed little change, with Members of Color representing only 4% of the APA membership (Bernal & Castro, 1994).

Nor has the situation improved noticeably when one looks to enrollment figures for graduate training programs. As Atkinson, Brown, Casas, and Zane (1996) point out, "the key to achieving ethnic parity among practicing psychologists rests on the profession's ability to achieve equity in training programs" (p. 231). Statistics collected by Kohout and Wicherski (1993) show that African Americans make up only 5%, Latinos/as 5%, Asian Americans 4%, and Native Americans 1% of students enrolled in doctoral psychology programs. These figures represent a decrease for African American students and only a slight increase for the other three groups over the last 25 years (Kohout & Pion, 1990). Over the course of training, however, disproportionate dropout rates for Students of Color bring their number at graduation close to the 3% or 4% reported for APA membership.

While much lip service is paid to the need for recruiting more Students and Faculty of Color, the numbers say it all and remain consistently low over time. In addition to cost, a major deterrent keeping non-White students out of the university (or contributing to their dropout rate) is the Northern European cultural climate that predominates. It is not only difficult for Students of Color, especially those who are not highly acculturated, to navigate the complex application and entry procedures that training programs typically require but also difficult to feel comfortable, safe, and welcome in a monocultural environment that is not their own.

An equally critical factor is the number of Faculty of Color within these programs. These statistics also continue to be quite low. Atkinson et al. (1996) note that within doctoral training programs in clinical, counseling, and school psychology, African Americans make up 5% of the faculty, Latinos/as 2%, and Asian Americans and Native Americans 1% each. These authors succinctly summarize the current situation as follows: "Although ethnic minorities make up approximately 25% of the current U.S. population with dramatic increases ahead they constitute less than 15% of the student enrollment and less than 9% of the full-time faculty in applied psychology programs" (p. 231).

▪ Dissatisfaction Among Providers of Color

These numbers will not change until significant diversity is introduced in the helping professions as well as into their training facilities. At present, both remain overwhelmingly White. D'Andrea (1992) documents this fact by pointing to "some of the ways in which individual and institutional racism imbues the profession." He offers the following seven examples:

1. Less than 1% of the chairpersons of graduate counseling training programs in the United States come from non-White groups (89% of all chairpersons in counseling training programs are White males).
2. No Hispanic American, Asian American, or Native American person has ever been elected president of either the ACA (American Counseling Association) or APA (American Psychological Association).
3. Only one African American person has been elected president of APA.
4. None of the five most commonly used textbooks in counselor training programs in the United States lists "racism" as an area of attention in its table of contents or index.
5. A computerized literature review of journal articles found in social science periodicals over a 12-year period (1980–1992) indicated that only 6 of 308 articles published during this time period that examined the impact of racism on one's mental health and psychological development were published in the three leading professional counseling journals (*The Counseling Psychologist, Journal of Counseling and Development,* and *Journal of Counseling Psychology*).
6. All of the editors of the journals sponsored by ACA and APA (excluding one African American editor with the *Journal of Multicultural Counseling and Development*) are White.
7. Despite more than 15 years of efforts invested in designing a comprehensive set of multicultural counseling competencies and standards, the organizational governing bodies of both ACA and APA have consistently refused to adopt them formally as guidelines for professional training and development (p. 23).

It is not difficult to read between the lines of D'Andrea's examples and sense the enormous frustration of Providers of Color with the seeming slowness with which the professional counseling establishment has moved toward actively embracing and implementing its verbalized commitment to multiculturalism. D'Andrea and Daniels (1995) summarize these feelings as follows:

> Although persons from different racial/cultural/ethnic backgrounds must continue to lead the way in promoting the spirit and principles of multiculturalism in the profession, it is imperative that White counseling professionals take a more active stand in advocating for the removal of barriers that impede progress in this area. Together we can transform the profession, or together we will suffer the consequences of becoming an increasingly irrelevant entity in the national mental health care delivery system. (p. 32)

Similar sentiments are offered by Parham (1992):

> To make the types of changes that are necessary in order that the counseling profession will be able to meet the needs of an increasing number of clients from diverse cultural and racial backgrounds, the profession

in general and its two national associations—the American Psychological Association and the American Counseling Association—in particular, will have to learn to share more of its power and resources with persons who have traditionally been excluded from policy-making and training opportunities. (pp. 22–23)

The Use of Paraprofessionals

One strategy that held great promise for dramatically increasing the number of Providers of Color was the use of indigenous paraprofessionals. Stimulated by a visionary book by Art Pearl and Frank Reissman (1965) entitled *New Careers for the Poor,* the National Institute of Mental Health committed extensive resources to educating mental health facilities in the use of ethnic paraprofessionals.

The idea was a rather simple one. Individuals who were natural leaders within ethnic communities were given training in the rudiments of service delivery (basic assessment, interviewing skills, knowledge of psychopathology) and then hired to act both as liaisons and outreach workers to the community and as adjunct providers working under the direction of professional staff. Often, special satellite centers were established in ethnic communities and staffed by local paraprofessionals. The concept worked exceptionally well for over 10 years. Community members were more willing to bring their problems to paraprofessionals who were already known, respected, and able to understand their culture and lifestyle.

Paraprofessional involvement in mainstream agencies, in turn, gave them a certain credibility that was not afforded when the staff was all White. The strategy also served to inject a large number of entry-level ethnic paraprofessionals into the system. Many, in fact, chose to return to school and became professionals. Ironically, this strategy was ultimately undermined by the development of a number of academic paraprofessional training programs. Viewing the paraprofessional role not so much as a means of creating more indigenous providers, but rather as a new entry point into mental health jobs, these programs attracted primarily White middle- to upper-middle-class students. Agencies, in turn, received increasing pressure to hire these "professional nonprofessionals. The ultimate result was that indigenous providers were slowly, but systematically, replaced by trained paraprofessionals, and a very functional approach to infusing ethnic community members into the mental health delivery system was undermined.

The Use of Traditional Healers

Another potentially useful strategy for overcoming the lack of ethnic helping professionals is the involvement of traditional healers, that is, indigenous practitioners from within traditional ethnic cultures, as part of a mental health organization's treatment team, either on staff or in a consultative role. This is not only a mark of cultural respect, but it is also an invitation to less acculturated community members who would not normally avail themselves of mainstream services to view mental health services (thus more broadly defined) as a resource for them as well. Barriers to including traditional healers usually come from Western professionals who see the use of shamanic healers as unscientific, superstitious, and regressive. Their hesitancies come from conflicting worldviews, although Torrey (1986), for one, has argued that Western mental health approaches work structurally in much the same way as do indigenous healing systems. Both, for example, are afforded high status and power and also depend on clients' sharing the same worldview. Torrey suggests that both be incorporated under the broad multicultural rubric of healer.

Lee and Armstrong (1995), however, enumerate a number of content differences:

- Traditional healing views human capacities holistically, whereas Western providers typically distinguish among physical, spiritual, and mental well-being.
- Western healing stresses cause and effect; traditional approaches emphasize circularity and multidimensional sources in etiology.
- In Western psychology, helping occurs through cognitive and emotional change. In traditional healing, there is a spiritual basis to health and well-being as well.
- In Western psychology, helpers tend to be passive in their interventions; indigenous healers are more active and take a major role and responsibility in the healing process itself.

In spite of such differences, the only reason for not pursuing cooperation and consultation is ethnocentrism. Such narrow thinking typically goes hand in hand with cultural insensitivity in Western providers because the very spirituality and religiosity of which they are generally critical play a central role in the worldview of most culturally different clients.

One last point needs to be made regarding increasing the number of ethnic helpers. Just because providers have certain racial or cultural roots does not guarantee their cultural competence or ability to work effectively with clients from their group of origin. Making an extra effort to hire Providers of Color sends an important social and political message. But to do so without careful consideration of a candidate's experience, skills, training, and cultural competence is merely racism in reverse. No agency would think of randomly selecting White candidates irrespective of their credentials and assume that they will be competent to work successfully with a broad spectrum of White clients. Agencies do, however, on a much more frequent basis, assume that hiring a Person of Color will automatically resolve problems of racism and cross-cultural service delivery.

As has been continually stressed throughout this book, ethnic groups encompass enormous diversity, and it is dangerous to make assumptions about the characteristics a given individual possesses merely on the basis of group membership. For example, an agency has within its service jurisdiction a small but growing Latino/a population and wishes to hire someone of Latino/a descent to help provide services. Some of the following questions may prove useful in making informed and culturally sensitive choices among possible candidates:

- Are they bilingual, fluent in both English and Spanish, written and verbal?
- Are they bicultural; that is, familiar with the traditional as well as the dominant culture?
- With what specific ethnic subgroups within the broad category of Latino/a culture are they familiar and knowledgeable?
- What is their knowledge of class, gender, and regional differences in the Latino/a community?
- Where were they born, and how acculturated was their family of origin?
- Do they have firsthand experience with the migration process?
- What is the nature of their own ethnic identity?
- With what other ethnic populations have they worked?
- How culturally competent are they?

■ Cultural Aspects of Mental Health Service Delivery

The chapter has so far looked into sources of bias related to the provider. There are, in addition, aspects of the helping process per se that limit its relevance to Clients of Color. In general, these relate to the fact that current mental health theory and practice are defined in terms of dominant Northern European cultural values and norms and therefore limit the ability of providers to adequately address and serve the needs of non-White populations. Chapter 4 includes a description of four characteristics of the helping process (as it is currently constituted) that directly conflict with the worldview of Communities of Color.

Here we explore additional sources of this cultural mismatch as well as describe ways in which the current helping model portrays Clients of Color in a negative light, highlights their "weaknesses," and assumes pathology even when it does not necessarily exist. The case study of Bill, a supposedly psychotic Navajo with which this chapter opens, is an extreme example. His behavior, when viewed through the lens of Navajo culture, looked quite normal, but from the perspective of Western psychology, it reflected deep disturbance and psychopathology.

Bias in Conceptualizing Ethnic Populations

There is a long history in Western science of portraying ethnic populations as biologically inferior:

- Beginning with the work of luminaries such as Charles Darwin, Sir Francis Galton, and G. Stanley Hall, one can trace what Sue and Sue (1990) call the "genetic deficiency model" of racial minorities into the present carried on by research psychologists such as Jensen (1972).

- Similarly, Jews have been vilified under the guise of psychological analysis.
- Jung (1934), for example, wrote the following comparison of Jewish and Aryan psychologies: "Jews have this peculiarity in common with women, being physically weaker, they have to aim at the chinks in the armor of their adversary, and thanks to this technique . . . the Jews themselves are best protected where others are most vulnerable" (pp. 165–166). Jung, who also wrote disparagingly of the African American psyche, found his ideas on national and racial character warmly received by the Nazi regime.
- McDougall (1977), an early American psychologist, offers similar sentiments against Jews in his analysis of Freud's work: "It looks as though this theory which to me and to most men of my sort seems to be strange, bizarre and fantastic, may be approximately true of the Jewish race" (p. 127).

As biological theories of genetic inferiority lost intellectual credibility, they were quickly replaced in social science circles by notions of cultural inferiority or *deficit theories*. While political correctness would not allow practitioners with negative racial attitudes to continue to embrace the idea of genetic inferiority, they could easily attach themselves to theories that assumed "that a community subject to poverty and oppression is a disorganized community, and this disorganization expresses itself in various forms of psychological deficit ranging from intellectual performance . . . to personality functioning . . . and psychopathology" (Jones & Korchin, 1982, p. 19). These new models took two forms: cultural deprivation and cultural disadvantage. In relation to the former, non-Whites were seen as deprived (i.e., lacking substantive culture).

Disadvantaged, on the other hand, a supposed improvement over the term *deprived*, implies that although ethnic group members do possess culture, it is a culture that has grown deficient and distorted by the ravages of racism. More recent and acceptable are the terms *culturally different* and *culturally distinct*. But as Atkinson, Morten, and Sue (1993) point out, even these can "carry negative connotations when they are used to imply that a person's culture is at variance (out of step) with the dominant (accepted) culture" (p. 9).

Psychological research on ethnic populations has also tended to be skewed in the direction of finding and focusing on deficits and shortcomings. This body of research, which Jones and Korchin (1982) refer to as part of a "psychology of race differences tradition," has been widely criticized for faulty methodology. They explain:

> Studies typically involved the comparison of ethnic and white groups on measures standardized on white, middle-class samples, administered by examiners of like background, intended to assess variables conceptualized on the basic U.S. population. (p. 19)

But even more insidious have been two additional tendencies:

1. Researchers have chosen to study and compare Whites and People of Color on characteristics that culturally favor dominant group members. Thus,

intelligence is assessed by measuring verbal reasoning, or schoolchildren are compared on their ability to compete or take personal initiative. In other words, research variables portray White subjects in a more favorable light and simultaneously create a negative impression of the abilities and resources of minority ethnic subjects.

2. Where differences have been found between Whites and People of Color, they tend to be interpreted as reflecting weaknesses or pathology in ethnic culture or character. Looking at such studies, various researchers have asked why alternative interpretations stressing the creative adaptiveness or strengths inherent in ethnic personality or culture might not just as easily have been sought. Hampden-Turner (1974), for example, writes the following about the "Moynihan Report," which attributes various African American social problems to deterioration of the Black family and has been soundly criticized both for blaming the victim and pathologizing to the exclusion of other possible explanations: "Moynihan's accusation of 'pathology' . . . is an excellent illustration of the mental health paradigm in political use. . . . If we regard the social oppression of blacks by whites as a total dynamic, why is the black end of this dynamic more pathological than the white end? . . . And how does one distinguish a 'pathology' from an 'heroic adaptation to overwhelming pressures?'" (p. 83). Inherent in Hampden-Turner's critique is a very important point: These negative portrayals and stereotypes of People of Color serve as justification for the status quo of oppression and unfair treatment and, thus, serve political as well as psychological purposes.

An interesting and provocative example of the psychological mystification of ethnic culture and cultural traits is offered by Tong (1981). Tong argues that the psychological representation of Chinese Americans as the model minority—that is, "passive, ingratiating, reticent, non-complaining and self-denying" (p. 3)—is more a survival reaction to American racism than a true reflection of traditional Chinese character. He goes on to suggest that there is within traditional culture a "heroic tradition" that portrays the Chinese in a manner very different from the uncomplaining model minority: "Coexistent with the Conventional Tradition was the 'heroic,' which exalted a time-honored Cantonese sense of self: the fierce, arrogant, independent individual beholden to no one and loyal only to those deemed worthy of undying respect, on that individual's terms" (1981, p. 15). Tong calls to task fellow Chinese American psychologists for perpetuating the myth through their research and writings and thus for confusing psychopathology with culture:

> Timid and docile behavior *is* indicative of emotional disorder. If Chinese Americans seem to be that way by virtue of cultural "background," it is the case *only* to the extent that white racism, in combination with our heritage of Confusion [*sic*] repression, made it so. The early Chinamans [*sic*] consistently shaped themselves and justified their acts according to the fundamental vision of the Heroic Tradition. Their stupendous feats of daring and courage, however,

remain buried beneath a gargantuan mound of white movies, popular fiction, newspaper cartoons, dissertations, political tracts, religious meeting minutes, and now psychological studies that teach us to look upon ourselves as perpetual aliens living only for white acceptance. (p. 20)

Tong calls this mystification of the Chinese American psyche "iatrogenic." *Iatrogenesis* is a medical term that means sickness or pathology that results from medical or psychological intervention and treatment.

A final difficulty with contemporary psychology's model of helping is its theoretical narrowness and inability to acknowledge different cultural ways of looking at and conceptualizing mental health as valid. I once worked as part of a team whose task was to create a mental health service delivery system for recent Southeast Asian refugees. This is an at-risk population that has suffered serious emotional trauma as a result of war, migration, and rapid acculturation in the United States. The first problem we encountered was that there was no concept within their culture for mental health per se, nor was there a distinction between physical and mental health. Problems were not dichotomized, and as we were to learn later, what we considered mental health problems were generally presented in the form of physical symptoms.

In time, however, it was possible to discern certain patterns of physical complaints that seemed to indicate emotional difficulties (e.g., depression and PTSD). But the symptom patterns for these disorders within Southeast Asian populations looked very different from those presented in the DSM-IV, which is normed primarily on Northern European clients. In addition, the Western concept of helping (i.e., seeking advice, help, or support from a professional stranger) made no sense to our Southeast Asian clients. In most Asian cultures, one does not go outside of the family, let alone to strangers, for help. The acknowledgment of emotional difficulties brings shame on the family. It is expected that individuals accept their conditions quietly. From a Western perspective, this is denial or avoidance.

As a general strategy for intervention, we decided to train paraprofessionals from the community to serve as outreach and referral workers. Not only did our paraprofessionals (who were young adults and among the most acculturated individuals in the community) have great difficulty grasping, understanding, and using the mental health concepts and simple diagnostic procedures we tried to teach them, but there was also a problem in their being accepted by older community members as legitimate resources for health providers. This was largely because of age. As long as we approached the community from a Northern European perspective, we were destined to fail. We had pushed the model of training with which we were familiar as far as it could be stretched and were still unable to accommodate major aspects of Southeast Asian culture.

What does one do when the very concept of mental health makes little sense within a culture? Or when the very notion of helping as conceived in Western terms is irrelevant because it is considered shameful to share one's problems with complete strangers? I came away from that experience realizing that if we were to continue, we would have to start from scratch and create a new helping model that was not merely an adaptation of mainstream helping practices, but rather was specifically tailored to the cultural needs of Southeast Asians. (You might want to review chapter 4 and its discussion of conflicting strategies of cross-cultural service delivery.)

Bias in Assessment

In no other area of clinical work has there been more concern raised about the possibility of cultural bias than in relation to psychological assessment and testing.

This is because People of Color have for many years watched their children being placed in remedial classrooms or tracked as retarded on the basis of IQ testing and seen loved ones diagnosed as suffering from serious mental disorders because of their performance on various personality tests. Serious life decisions are regularly made on the basis of these tests, and it is reasonable to expect that they be "culture-free"; that is, they should be scored based on what is being measured and not differentially affected by the cultural background of the test taker. In reality, there probably is no such thing as a culture-free test, and it has been suggested, and supported by some research, that ethnic group members tend to be overpathologized by personality measures and have their abilities underestimated by intelligence tests (Snowden & Todman, 1982; Suzuki & Kugler, 1995).

Reynolds and Kaiser (1990) list several factors that can contribute to cultural bias in testing:

- Test items and procedures may reflect dominant cultural values.
- A test may not have been standardized on Populations of Color, only on middle-class Whites.
- Language differences and unfamiliarity or discomfort with the client's culture can cause a tester to misjudge them or have difficulty establishing rapport.
- The experience of racism and oppression may lead to groupwide deficits in performance on tests that have nothing to do with native ability.
- A test may measure different characteristics when administered to members of different cultural groups.
- Culturally unfair criteria, such as level of education and grade point average, may be used to validate tests expected to predict differences between Whites and People of Color.
- Differences in experience taking tests may put non-White clients at a disadvantage in testing situations.

In short, it is very difficult to ensure fairness in psychological testing across cultures, and practitioners should exert real care in drawing conclusions based exclusively on test scores. They should, as a matter of validation, gain as much nontesting collaborative data as possible, especially when the outcome of the assessment may have real-life consequences for the future of the client. They should also be willing not to test a client if it is believed that the procedure will not give useful and fair data.

Having raised all of these cautions, the fact remains that a great deal of culturally questionable testing still takes place. Clinicians tend to be overattached to psychological tests as a means of gaining client information. When they do try to take into account cultural differences, it is done not by creating new instruments, but rather by modifying existing ones—adjusting scores, rewriting items, or translating them into a second language. In general, this merely creates new problems in the place of old ones. The MMPI and TAT, probably the two most widely used personality assessment techniques, provide excellent examples.

The Minnesota Multiphasic Personality Inventory (MMPI) is by far the most widely used instrument to measure psychopathology. Historically, it has been administered without reservation to racial and ethnic minorities:

- Concerns about cultural bias were first raised because it had been normed (i.e., standardized as far as cutoff scores reflecting normal vs. psychopathological behavior) exclusively on White subjects and second because it was being used extensively to make decisions about hospitalizing patients, a disproportionate percentage of whom were People of Color.
- Cultural differences and the possibility of bias are most evident in differential scoring patterns. African American test takers (from normal, psychiatric, and inmate populations alike), for example, consistently score higher than Whites on three scales: F (a measure of validity), 8 (a measure of schizophrenia), and 9 (a measure of mania).
- In addition, 39% of the items are answered differently by African American than by White subjects. Of these, a third are not clinical scale items, which implies that differences are related to culture as opposed to pathology.
- There is also evidence that MMPI items are neither conceptually nor functionally equivalent for African Americans and Whites; this suggests that they neither mean the same thing nor fulfill a similar psychological purpose for the two groups.

As a means of dealing with these problems, Costello (1977) developed a Black–White Scale that adjusted African American scores so that they might be interpreted similarly to White scores. But Snowden and Todman (1982) are critical of this procedure:

The Black–White Scale may be useful in the short term for making interpretive adjustments to allow for known differences, however it must be seen as a stopgap measure. In the long run, it leaves unanswered all the pertinent questions raised by both cross-cultural and environmental psychologists alike. . . . The Costello Black–White Scale does not ask these questions; it merely corrects for them. The logical extension of this scale could very well be the following: If one subtracts a factor of x from the score of a black male, his profile is then "as good" as if it were of a white. One can conclude with confidence that the MMPI has never established its validity as a diagnostic or assessment instrument with blacks. (pp. 210–211)

The MMPI-2, a revision of its predecessor, was tested initially on both African American and Native American sample populations. The resulting research has been so confusing, however, that Dana (1988) and Graham (1987) both conclude that it is best not to use the test with ethnic group members.

The Thematic Apperception Test (TAT) and the Rorschach are the most widely used projective tests for assessing personality and psychopathology. The TAT involves showing clients drawings of people in various situations and asking them to tell a story about the picture. Scoring involves both the kinds of themes that are generated and the style of responding:

- Questions about its use with non-White populations were raised early because the stimulus figures on the cards were White, and there was the obvious question of whether African American clients, for example, could identity with these figures or would instead inhibit self-disclosure because of them. To test this, Thompson (1949) developed the same cards redrawn with African American figures and used them with African American clients. Though he showed that his cards generated more responses than did the original White cards, all the questions about cultural comparability raised by Reynolds and Kaiser (1990) still remain unanswered.
- TAT scoring generates impressions about unmet needs within the client. Who is to say that such needs or motivations are equivalent across cultural groups or that the stimulus pictures, irrespective of the race of the figures, have equivalent cultural meanings?
- Finally, there is a question about the use of projection with non-White groups. Generally, it has been found that Blacks are less responsive, less willing to self-disclose, and more guarded about their participation in the TAT testing situation than members of other groups. Snowden and Todman (1982) suggest that this guardedness may be culturally determined and the result of a long history of dealing with racist institutions.

In spite of all of these questions about the cultural validity of the TAT, it continues to be used cross-culturally. There is, in fact, now a Latino/a version as well as one specifically designed for children, which has cards showing animal characters instead of people.

Bias in Diagnosis

According to Gaw (1993), culture shapes and affects the very essence of how clinical work is done. It colors the following areas:

- How problems are reported and how help is sought
- The nature and configuration of symptoms
- How problems are traditionally solved

- How the origin of presenting problems is understood
- What appropriate interventions involve

Each culture, in short, has it own paradigm of how these processes occur, and there is enormous variation. Difficulties emerge, however, when practitioners superimpose their cultural worldviews onto the life experience of culturally different clients and then make clinical assumptions or judgments from that perspective. This is where things stand today vis-à-vis Western mental health service delivery and the desire to serve other cultural groups. Most practitioners tend to be far too narrow and ethnocentric in their thinking to acknowledge and accept other versions of clinical reality. Rather than try to redesign the "puzzle" and broadening their perspective, providers keep trying to force the "round piece" into the "square hole," and the "hole" keeps objecting.

Cultural Variations in Psychopathology

Nowhere is the limited thinking of Western psychology more challenged by cultural variation than around the question of what psychopathology is and how it is diagnosed. This is also where misdiagnosis of those who are culturally different most regularly occurs. Jones and Korchin (1982) summarize the issue as follows:

> Most mental health workers proceed on the assumption of the pancultural (i.e., etic) generality of categories, criteria, and theories of psychopathology originated in Western cultures. Minority clinicians have long objected that standard psychiatric nomenclature does not recognize cultural variation in symptomology.
>
> This position is quite consistent with a growing view among crosscultural psychologists that problems of identifying cases of psychopathology in clients from different cultures, and comparing incidence and forms of psychopathology across cultures, need to be reconsidered. (pp. 26–27)

Cultural Attitudes Toward Mental Health

Cultures differ dramatically in their orientation and attitude toward mental disorders as well as in their understanding of personality dynamics, what is considered therapeutic, and how help is to be sought. Cultural responses to these issues are shaped by certain key themes that contribute a distinctive Gestalt to how each culture relates to the problem of mental illness. By way of example, I will summarize R. G. Lum's (1982) early research on mental health attitudes among Chinese Americans, whose clinical worldview differs substantially from that of Western psychology. Within Chinese American culture, mental health and mental illness are two sides of the same coin.

- According to Lum, individuals are considered mentally healthy if they possess the capacity for self-discipline and the willpower to resist conducting oneself or thinking in ways that are not socially or culturally sanctioned;

a sense of security and self-assurance stemming from support and guidance from significant others; relative freedom from unpleasant, morbid thoughts, emotional conflicts, and personality disorders; and the absence of organic dysfunctions, such as epilepsy or other neurological disorders. (1982, p. 183)

- Similarly, mental illness involves the opposite: a loss of discipline, preoccupation with morbid thoughts, insecurity because of the absence of social support, and distress stemming from external factors.

- Consistent with this, Chinese Americans tend to externalize blame for mental illness, thus setting the stage for avoidance of unwanted thoughts and feelings. Traditional Chinese wisdom sees value in learning to inhibit and control one's emotions. Defensively, according to Hsu (1949), Chinese tend to use suppression as opposed to repression, which is more common among European Americans. Suppression tends to have an obsessional quality because to use it effectively one must rationalize, justify, or use other intellectual strategies to blunt the anxiety. Using it, in turn, tends to encourage obsessive-compulsive qualities including extreme conscientiousness, meticulousness, acquiescence, rigidity, and a preference for thinking over feeling.

- As patients, Chinese Americans prefer helpers who are authoritarian, directive, and fatherly in their approach. In turn, they expect to be taught how to occupy their minds to avoid unwanted thoughts and feelings. Insight approaches tend to have limited meaning, and generally, therapy does not seem to affect Chinese Americans characterologically.

- Finally, help-seeking is limited because within the Chinese community there is a stigma and shame around mental illness. Shame often leads to minimizing the seriousness and frequency of a problem. Patients often feel "ashamed and ambivalent about their illness" and are reluctant to tell others about their emotional difficulties. In sum, the threads that run through the Chinese American worldview of mental health and illness are the importance of controlling emotions and thoughts and their avoidance when they become too intrusive or distracting, the necessity of social support as a precondition for healthy mental functioning, the submerging of the self as a means of deferring to family and authority, and mental illness as a stigma that requires the individual to tolerate disturbing symptoms rather than bring shame on the family. These themes translate basic cultural values into behavioral prescriptions for living that, in turn, reinforce basic cultural values.

Cultural Differences in Symptoms, Disorders, and Pathology

Cultures also differ as to what disorders are most typically observed, how symptom pictures are construed, and even what is considered pathological.

- Some disorders (e.g., schizophrenia and substance abuse) appear to be universal, although the exact content is culture specific. Hallucinations, for example, tend to contain familiar cultural material such as voices speaking to the person in his or her native language or visions infused with cultural symbols and motifs. Other disorders (e.g., depression) can be observed across cultures, but they vary dramatically in relation to specific symptoms. In Western clients, for example, depression is diagnosed on the basis of a combination of psychological and physical symptoms, whereas among Southeast Asian clients physical symptoms such as headaches and fatigue are more prevalent indicators.

- There are also culture-specific syndromes or disorders that appear only among members of a single cultural group. Jones and Korchin (1982) point to two—ataque, found only among Puerto Ricans, is a hysterical seizure reaction in which patients fall to the ground, scream, and flail their limbs. Largely unfamiliar to majority practitioners, it tends to be misdiagnosed as a more serious seizure disorder. A similar disorder, called "falling out" disease, is found only among rural, Southern African Americans and West Indian refugees and is regularly misdiagnosed as epilepsy or a transient psychotic episode.

- The same symptom can have very different meanings depending on the cultural context in which it appears. Mexican Americans, for instance, view hallucinations as far less pathological and more within the realm of everyday (normal) experience than do Whites. Hearing voices is, thus, more culturally sanctioned and often associated with deep religious experiences. Meadow (1982) shows that hospitalized Mexican American patients report significantly more hallucinations, both visual and auditory, than do Whites. The question all of this raises is exactly where culture ends and psychopathology begins. Meadow (1982) attempts to sort it out as follows:

Some Mexican-American hallucinatory experiences may simply reflect a cultural belief and occur in persons completely free of psychopathology. In other cases Mexican-American hallucinations may have the same significance as those reported by Anglo-American patients. There exists an intermediate group of Mexican-American patients in which the hallucination may be interpreted as a symbolic expression of a wish fulfillment or as a sign of a warded-off superego criticism. For these patients the hallucination is a symptom of psychopathology, but it does not signify the serious break with reality that would be implied if it occurred in an Anglo-American case. (p. 333)

The Case of Suicide

The same mental health problem can be configured very differently as far as both its sources (etiology) and frequency (incidence) across cultures. A classic example is suicide. According to the Group for the Advancement of Psychiatry's Committee on Cultural Psychiatry (1989), suicide rates differ substantially across ethnic groups in the United States:

- By far, the highest aggregate suicide rate (i.e., for all ages and genders combined) is found among Native Americans.
- The next highest is among European Americans followed by Chinese Americans and Japanese Americans.

- The lowest aggregate rates are found among African Americans and Latinos/as.

Practitioners are often surprised by the relatively low rates of suicide among People of Color. Why? Because stereotypically, many equate non-Whites with violence. It is also useful to note, as pointed out previously, that as ethnic groups assimilate, their relative position in the hierarchy increasingly comes to approximate that of European Americans. Thus, with acculturation, it is expected that African Americans, Latinos/as, and Asian Americans will increase their aggregate suicide rates.

Looking at peak rates across ethnic groups provides even further insights, especially since it is reasonable to assume that suicide rates reflect periods of optimal stress in a group's life cycle:

- For European Americans, suicides tend to occur three times as often for men as for women. In addition, peak rates tend to increase with age. For men, the highest rates are in those over 65, and for women, rates are highest in the early fifties.
- The picture is very different for the Communities of Color. First, suicide occurs most frequently among young males in African American, Native American, and Latino cultures. Japanese Americans show a similar trend, but less pronounced. Chinese American young males are a notable exception (Group for Advancement, 1989).These high rates most likely result from the fact that young non-White males are usually "the point men" for acculturative stress. They tend to be the ones who have the closest, most sustained contact and least positive interactions with White institutions, usually through schools and then work. High rates of unemployment and underemployment are certainly contributing factors. Research has also shown that young Men of Color who have consolidated a positive ethnic identity and attachment to tradition are less likely to be at risk for suicide than those who have become marginalized from their culture. The same is true for other self-destructive behaviors such as substance abuse and violence.
- A second major finding of the 1989 study is the extremely low suicide rates among African American, Native American, and Latina women when compared with ethnic males and majority group members combined. The one exception was Chinese American women, who showed a peak incidence in later life. There seem to be two reasons for these low rates. First, because of traditional sex roles, ethnic women have less exposure to the stressful effects of acculturation. In addition, they tend to experience much lower rates of unemployment and underemployment and can also derive personal satisfaction from alternative roles in the home. The higher suicide rate among older Chinese women is probably due to the interaction of several factors. They tend to remain closer to their cultural tradition and, as such, separatist in their orientation toward majority culture. As they lose their nurturing role in the family with age and as their children acculturate, they tend to grow even more isolated and lack support for their traditional orientation. In addition, many experience poverty without support from their family, and they are unable or unwilling to seek help from majority social agencies.

■ Finally, there are especially low rates of suicide among older African Americans, Native Americans, and Latinos/as in comparison to younger ethnic group members and majority group members combined (Group for Advancement, 1989). It is likely that these individuals have learned to cope with the acculturative stress. They tend to be revered in their communities and supported by strong community institutions that they likely helped found. The fact that older Asian Americans were not included in this statistic may reflect the effects of greater acculturation, which would lead to greater isolation of the elderly as is more common in mainstream culture.

Given such cultural relativity in defining mental health and psychopathology, an interesting question arises as to the appropriate criteria to be used in assessing psychopathology. From what cultural perspective should deviant behavior be judged? And within any particular cultural perspective, what makes a behavior deviant or psychopathological? The problem is made difficult by the fact that ethnic group cultures exist within a broader framework than is usually identified and are defined culturally as Northern European. From a clinical standpoint, individuals' behavior must be judged in accordance with the values and criteria of their own group's culture. Thus, "to justify an interpretation of behavior as an instance of psychopathology, it must be established that there is intersubjective agreement among members of the culture that the behavior in question represents an exaggeration or distortion of a culturally acceptable behavior or belief" (Jones & Korchin, 1982, p. 27). If one applies this maxim to the case of Bill, the institutionalized Navajo with which this chapter begins, it is clear that he was acting within the bounds of culturally acceptable Navajo behavior and that his diagnosis as catatonic, his assessment as psychopathological from a Western psychological perspective, and his institutionalization were all inappropriate.

■ Summary

In various ways mental health professionals have introduced bias and cultural insensitivity into their work with culturally different clients. In turn, ethnic patients have responded by avoiding such services in general whenever possible and resisting them when they were not voluntary. The result has been systematic underutilization of services by Clients of Color. This chapter focuses on sources of such bias in the field.

First, attitudes including prejudices and stereotypes can shape treatment values and decisions. Exemplary research show that experimenter and teacher expectations affect performance of subjects and students (an effect that has come to be known as a "self-fulfilling prophesy"), that social and positical attitudes affect the assessment of the mental health of clients by therapists; clinicians differentially diagnose patients on the basis of race; and White and non-White clients regularly receive different treatment options.

Bias is also introduced because of who the providers are. People of Color are sadly underrepresented among the ranks of helping professionals, and it has been regularly shown that clients prefer and feel most comfortable with therapists from their own ethnic background. People of Color are underrepresented in professional group memberships, as students in training programs (and they drop out more frequently than White students), and as faculty in those training programs. Providers of Color are frustrated by the slow pace in which the profession and its training facilities have moved toward addressing these numbers and committing themselves to multiculturalism. Neither the use of People of Color as paraprofessionals in their communities nor the use of traditional healers has served to increase the number of available Practitioners of Color.

A third source of bias exists because of cultural differences and cultural insensitivity among providers. Ethnic populations have been regularly viewed pathologically and cultural differences interpreted so as to favor White "characteristics" and portray People of Color in a less favorable manner. Because of culturally biased instruments and interview protocols People of Color have been harmed and had their opportunities limited through psychological assessment and diagnosis. The tracking of Children of Color in special education programs is a particularly disturbing example. Underutilization has also been attributed to cultural difference. This includes: negative and nonexistent attitudes toward the concepts of mental health as well as ignorance about cultural variation in symptomology, characteristics that define a disorder, and what behaviors are considered pathological. The example of suicide shows how the etiology and frequency of psychological disorders can look very different across cultures. It has been found, for example, that People of Color tend to have lower suicide rates than Whites.

■ Activities

1. *Assess community needs, part 2.* Return to Activity 2 at the end of chapter 6. Reread it to familiarize yourself with what it asks you to do, which is develop a procedure for a needs assessment of a small, Cambodian refugee enclave in your agency's service area. Using the ideas of this chapter on how bias is introduced into clinical work with culturally different clients and communities, generate a list of ways in which a needs assessment can be done insensitively and without attending to cultural differences, thereby turning off members of the Cambodian community. Be specific and creative.

2. *Rewrite Bill's case.* Refamiliarize yourself with the specifics of Bill's case at the beginning of this chapter and review our critique of it. Now try your hand at rewriting the case, but this time as it would unfold if Bill found his way into a mental hospital whose staff, procedures, and system were highly, culturally competent, or as Cross et al. (1989) would have called it "culturally proficient." Describe in detail this new scenario.

8 Working with Culturally Different Clients

So far, in the earlier chapters of this book, you have been exposed to a variety of conceptual issues related to working with culturally different clients. You have learned about cultural competence, explored the meaning of racism (especially as it impacts clients and providers), and come to understand culture and worldview as well as the cultural limits of the helping models that have shaped most providers' thinking. In addition, you have learned about a number of factors unique to the experience of ethnically diverse clients. These include child development and parenting issues, differences in family structure, biracial/bicultural families, potential areas of psychological difficulty for Clients of Color (conflicts in identity development, assimilation and acculturation, stress, trauma and unresolved historic grief, and alcohol and drug problems), and sources of bias in cross-cultural service delivery.

It is now time to shift focus to the the process of actually working with culturally different clients. You will begin chapter 8 by exploring how cross-cultural service delivery differs from monocultural work and then proceed to develop an understanding of the psychological dynamics that play themselves out in situations where the therapist and client are ethnically different. The work of Elaine Pinderhughes (1989) will be especially useful here. Next, you will learn how to assess culturally different clients, receive tips on establishing rapport and how to maximize productivity in your initial contact with cross-cultural clients, and, finally, be given suggestions on how to avoid stereotyping clients. At the end of the chapter you will be given an opportunity to analyze case studies of two hypothetical Clients of Color. In chapter 9 you will be exposed to a critically important and emerging area of cross-cultural work—the treatment of social trauma and victims of ethnic conflict, genocide, and mass violence. Through the interviews of chapters 10–14 you will begin to develop cultural specific knowledge. In each an expert human service provider offers cultural background as well as detailed information about how best to work with clients from their respective communities: Latinos/as, Native Americans, African Americans, Asian Americans, and White ethnics.

■ How Is Cross-Cultural Helping Different?

There is general agreement among practitioners that cross-cultural helping is more demanding, challenging, and energy-draining than work with same-culture clients. According to Draguns (1981), for example, it tends to be more

158

"experiential, freewheeling, and bilateral" (p. 17).

- By "experiential," he means that it is more likely to directly and emotionally impact the provider. Draguns likens it to culture shock, where providers are immersed in a foreign culture in which familiar patterns of behavior are no longer useful and new means of acting and relating must be discovered. It has also been described as more labor intensive and more likely to result in fatigue.
- "Freewheeling" refers to the fact that the helping process must be continually adapted to the specific cultural needs of differing clients. As suggested earlier, the only constant is the shared humanity. Standard approaches are overwhelmingly culture-bound and Northern European in nature, and even efforts to catalog cultural similarities among racially related ethnic groups must be tentative and ever mindful of enormous intragroup diversity. To this end, Draguns suggests:

Be prepared to adapt your techniques (e.g., general activity level, mode of verbal intervention, content of remarks, tone of voice) to the cultural background of the client; communicate acceptance of and respect for the client in terms that make sense within his or her cultural frame of reference; and be open to the possibility of more direct intervention in the life of the client than the traditional ethos of the counseling profession would dictate or permit. (p. 16)

- Finally, "bilateral" implies collaboration. By the very nature of cross-cultural work, the provider is more dependent on the client for help in defining the process itself. Though it is common practice, for example, for providers to collaborate with clients in setting treatment goals, in cross-cultural work it is even more imperative. Providers need direct and continuing client input on what is culturally valued so that goals are culturally appropriate, useful, and minimize ethnocentric projection. Since provider and client begin at very different cultural places, it is reasonable to expect some mutual movement in the direction of the other. Culturally competent professionals adapt and adjust their efforts to the cultural milieu of the client. At the same time, by entering into the helping process, culturally different clients cannot help but gain some knowledge and insight into the workings of mainstream culture and its worldview.

■ Conceptualizing Cross-Cultural Work

Cross-cultural work is challenging in yet another respect, and that has to do with the complexity of emotional and psychological dynamics at work in the lives of ethnic individuals. As pointed out earlier, for example, ethnic children must negotiate not only the same developmental challenges that all other children face, but also a series of issues resulting from race, ethnicity, and minority status. Keeping track of these various psychological phenomena, sorting them out, and addressing them is our job as human services providers. One might say that this is yet another aspect of cultural competence.

Pinderhughes (1989) suggests four different systems of psychological dynamics that especially define cross-cultural work and the relationship between client and practitioner. Included are the psychologies of difference, ethnicity, race, and power. The task of the practitioner is twofold: first to understand how these four systems shape the behavior and experience of the client and second, to understand how they play themselves out in the way the practitioner perceives and relates to the culturally different client. As stressed throughout this text, self-awareness is a critical aspect of cultural competence.

Pinderhughes describes ethnicity as follows:

> Involving individual psychological dynamics and socially inherited definitions of self, ethnicity is connected to processes, both conscious and unconscious, that satisfy a fundamental need for historical connection and security. . . . It thus embraces notions of both the group and the self that are, in turn, influenced by the value society places on the group. Societal definition and assigned value, among other factors, help determine whether ethnic meaning for a given group or individual becomes positive, or negative, which then has great significance for how they behave. (p. 39)

Race, in turn, refers to an acquired social meaning in which

> biological differences, via the mechanism of stereotyping, have become markers for status assignment within the social system. The status assignment based on skin color identity has evolved into complex social structures that promote a power differential between Whites and various people-of-color. These power-assigning social structures in the form of institutional racism affect the life opportunities, life-styles, and quality of life for both Whites and people-of-color. In so doing they compound, exaggerate and distort biological and behavioral differences and reinforce misconceptions, myths, and distortions on the part of both groups about one another and themselves. (p. 71)

The psychologies of difference and power, not having been introduced before, deserve additional attention.

Understanding Difference

According to Pinderhughes:

> How one responds to being different from others and what it means are issues that are rarely given attention in preparing people for cross-cultural work. Yet the experience of the self as different from another is important . . . And the feelings, attitudes, perceptions, and behaviors that are mobilized can play a prominent part in the work they do. Because these responses are more frequently than not negative and driven by anxiety, they can interfere with successful therapeutic outcome . . . Unconscious distancing and defensive maneuvers are only a few of the unhelpful responses practitioners as well as clients may manifest in relation to perceptions of themselves as different from one another. (p. 21)

Feelings generated by the experience of being different tend to be negative and can include the reactions of confusion, hurt, pain, anger, and fear as well as envy, guilt, pity, sympathy, and privilege. Interpersonally these reactions can lead to a sense of distancing from others, loneliness, isolation, rejection, and abandonment. All of these reactions influence the helping situation. As Pinderhughes points out by way of example:

> A client may seek to ease his [*sic*] discomfort over differences by resisting involvement in treatment. A practitioner may react to similar discomfort by devaluing, ignoring, or misperceiving the cultural identity and values of the client. And these responses may be compounded when the source of discomfort lies in early developmental struggles. (p. 39)

Understanding Power

Power is the "capacity to produce desired effects on others." Powerlessness, in turn, is the inability to influence the other. The helping relationship is by nature a power imbalance in favor of the practitioner; therefore, the client is in a potentially vulnerable situation in which practitioners may seek to use their power to meet personal needs. According to Pinderhughes:

> In the cross-cultural helping relationship the compounding of the power differential that exists between helper and client due to their respective cultural identities and group connections can mean that helpers may be doubling vulnerable to invoking the power inherent in the role for their own needs. (1989, p. 110)

This is especially likely when the helper is unaware or uncomfortable with her or his ethnic or racial identity or unaware or uncomfortable with those aspects of the cross-cultural client. Pinderhughes suggests that there are two very important ways that power and powerlessness can be valuably explored and used in treatment.

First, powerlessness can be an unpleasant and painful psychological experience, and people respond to it "in ways that will neutralize their pain with strategies that enable them to turn that powerlessness into a sense of power" (p. 124). Such responses can be very positive and productive, as in the case of those who gain power through self-development, achievement, and personal mastery. Alternatively, a false sense of power can be gained by putting down others, "powering over them," inspiring fear, manipulating them. Even accommodation and dependency can be seen as strategies for overcoming powerlessness. Often such maladaptive practices are related to problems in clients' lives, and exploring them in treatment and developing alternative behavioral reactions can be very freeing and empowering. A second strategy offered by Pinderhughes is to introduce practices within the therapeutic structure that equalize or reverse the power relationship between a practitioner and culturally different client. She refers to the latter as "taking a one down" position. For example, the client may take on the role of cultural expert, teaching the practitioner, who is ignorant in the ways of the client's culture. Through such strategies, clients can learn to become more comfortable in this new role and empowered by the acquisition of new behaviors in relation to it. Pinderhughes seems to be suggesting that a basic component of working with clients whose life experience is defined by powerlessness is reducing the power relationship between herself or himself and the client.

■ Preparing for Cross-Cultural Work

To be perfectly honest, no amount of preparation can totally allay the anxiety that is typical of providers-in-training when they first contemplate working with culturally diverse clients. Students regularly ask: "But what do I do when I find myself sitting across the desk from someone who is culturally different from me? I'm afraid I will panic or draw a blank and not know what to say." My usual answer is: "Just do the same thing you do with any other client— begin your work." The anxiety and hesitancy reflect a basic discomfort with cultural differences and the fact that most providers have grown up in a racist society separated from those who are different from them. They are afraid, because of their ignorance about a client's culture, of making a cultural faux pas or of missing something very obvious. They are, in addition, often anxious and uncomfortable due to feelings of guilt over the existence of racism or embarrassed because of past indifference, the racist behavior of family and friends, or feelings of personal privilege or entitlement. It feels like very dangerous territory, and after reading chapter after chapter about the complexity of issues in working with diversity and how easily cross-cultural communication can break down, the prospect of facing people from a different culture and providing them with useful help can be rather daunting. At such moments of doubt, it is important to remember several things:

- First, as a provider, one is already, or is in the process of becoming, a skilled professional. Becoming culturally competent does not mean starting from scratch or learning everything anew. Rather, it means honing skills one already has, broadening clinical concepts that are too narrow in their application in the first place, and gaining new cultural knowledge about clients with whom one will be working. Culturally competent providers are, in general, more competent professionals because they must remain more conscious about what they are doing to be vigilant as to the cultural appropriateness of tasks, methods, and perspectives that others may routinely overlook. In a certain sense, one might say that every client carries his or her own unique culture, and it is the professional helper's task to discover how to respectfully gain entry into that culture and offer services that are sensitive to its rules and inner dynamics.
- Second, the clients with whom one will be working are, above all, human beings, and this is the ultimate basis for connection. They, too, are anxious about coming to see someone new, especially if that person is culturally different. More than likely, they have had experiences that make them mistrust

the kind of system in which the provider works. The initial task, then, is to set clients at ease in a manner that has meaning for them. Helping is, above all, a human process. It is bound to fail, however (with all clients, not just culturally different ones), when this awareness is lost.

■ Unfortunately, in the process of teaching people about cultural differences, there is a tendency (that must always be guarded against) to objectify and stereotype clients by seeing them only in terms of their differences. By attending to these too fully, one can easily lose sight of the person sitting across from the provider.

■ Focusing too heavily on differences, and thereby overlooking basic human similarities, can turn cross-cultural work into a mechanical process. For example, with Asian Americans, you must do this, be aware of this, assume this, and so forth. Nothing could be further from the truth. Cross-cultural interaction must be based on the shared humanity that exists between client and provider. That is the one place where both are similar and can most easily join. Kroeber (1948), an early anthropologist, pointed out three kinds of human characteristics: those that one shares with all other human beings, those that one shares with some other human beings, and those that are unique to each individual. It is in relation to the first that cross-cultural communication and helping are made possible. A sensitivity to the second and third allows for the defining of human differences and uniqueness once a basic connection has formed. Again, it is through the very human capacities of caring, having sympathy and empathy for others, and identifying with the basic joys and predicaments of being human that differences can best be bridged.

■ Assessing Culturally Different Clients

A good, culturally sensitive assessment provides valuable information about how to proceed with treatment. It can give insight into the problem as conceived by the client and a sense of barriers that might stand in the way of seeking help. It can suggest what clients expect to receive from the helping process and their notions of what the process will involve. It can also provide a reading of how acculturated they are, how comfortable they would be with a more mainstream approach, how much the process needs to be adjusted, and whether any special preparation of clients is necessary prior to treatment. On the basis of answers to these questions and impressions gained during early contact, reasonable and informed decisions about how to proceed can be made. Collecting data about the client's cultural history and lifestyle is an excellent place to start. The following list of specific items can serve as a starting point:

■ Place of birth
■ Number of generations in the United States
■ Family roles and structure
■ Language spoken at home
■ English fluency

- Economic situation and status
- Amount and type of education
- Amount of acculturation
- Traditions still practiced in the home
- Familiarity and comfort with Northern European lifestyle
- Religious affiliation
- Community and friendship patterns

Together, these items provide a good initial basis for understanding the client ethnically and culturally.

Grieger and Ponterotto (1995) suggest six additional areas of assessment that should be useful in deciding how the helping process must be adjusted in relation to the cultural needs of the client. These include:

- Client's level of psychological mindedness
- Family's level of psychological mindedness
- Client's and the family's attitudes toward helping
- Client's level of acculturation
- Family's level of acculturation
- Family's attitude toward acculturation

If a client's or family's worldview precludes "conceptualizing one's problems from a psychological point of view and having the construct of emotional disturbance as a part of one's interpretive lens" (Grieger & Ponterotto, 1995, p. 363) and their levels of acculturation are low, several alternatives to insight approaches are possible. One is to work with the problem as defined by the client (irrespective of whether the provider sees underlying psychological issues). For example, Grieger and Ponterotto describe a case where a Chinese student presents with academic problems and an underlying depressive disorder. In such a situation, it is possible for the helper to work directly with the academic problems, perhaps via improving study skills, time management, and so on, without raising the issue of the depression. Behavioral types of intervention for depression (that don't require psychological insight) offer a second alternative. A third possibility involves trying to educate the client vis-à-vis psychological mindedness. The choice between the three approaches is, however, an ethical, not a clinical, one. Similarly, low acculturation and negative attitudes toward it tend to mitigate against general insight work. It is also likely in such a situation for the family to serve as a force against the client seeking help.

Pinderhughes (1989) offers the following series of questions that further pinpoint and define the cultural dimensions of the problem being presented. All are worth exploring in depth:

- To what extent is the problem related to issues of transition such as migration and immigration?
- To what extent is the client's understanding of the problem based on a cultural explanation, for example, "evil curse," "mal ojo," and so forth?
- Is the behavior that is a problem considered normal within the culture or is it considered dysfunctional?

- To what extent is the problem a manifestation of environmental lack of access to resources and supports?
- To what extent is the problem related to culture conflict in identity, values, or relationships?
- To what extent is the behavior a consequence of psychological conflict or characterological problems?
- What are the cultural strengths and assets available to the client such as cultural values and practices, social networks, and support systems? (p. 149)

Combining all three sources of information—that is, the basic demographics and the more specific questions raised by Grieger and Ponterotto (1995) and Pinderhughes (1989)—provides a good beginning for understanding the life situation and presenting problem of the culturally different client.

A somewhat different approach to cultural assessment and diagnosis is offered in the "Outline for Cultural Formulation," which can be found in the DSM-IV (American Psychiatric Association, 1994). Based on the work of Lu, Lim, and Mazzich (1995), the Outline was developed to help clinicians identify cultural factors in individual cases that may dictate special attention or alternative approaches or conceptions to diagnosis and treatment. The Outline comprises five general components: the cultural identity of the individual (aspects of self-definition), cultural explanations and expressions of the individual's illness (a description of the illness from within the individual's culture), cultural factors (stresses and supports) related to the psychosocial environment and levels of functioning, cultural elements of the relationship between the individual and the clinician, and the culture's effect on diagnosis (how cultural considerations specifically affect diagnosis and treatment activities and interpretations). The construction of the Outline was an attempt to address some of the diagnostic and treatment biases described in chapter 7. A more detailed version of the Outline appears in Table 8-1.

■ Establishing Rapport and the First Session

In working with culturally different clients, the first session is especially critical. Research has shown that up to 50% of all Clients of Color do not return for a second session (Sue & McKinney, 1975; Sue, McKinney, Allen, & Hall, 1974). This suggests that clients either do not feel safe with the provider or conclude, based on what had transpired during the first session, that their needs are not going to be met. Sue and Zane (1987) argue that culturally different clients must come away from early sessions with a sense that their problems are understood from their own perspective and that they will receive concrete benefits from their work with the provider. Thus, goals for the first session should include:

- Establishing good rapport
- Gaining an understanding of the client's problem
- Gaining an understanding of what he or she expects from the helping relationship
- Communicating clearly what the provider can reasonably offer

■ **TABLE 8–1**   DSM-IV Outline for Cultural Formulation

A. Cultural Identity of the Individual
- Ethnic or cultural reference group
- Degree of involvement with both culture of origin and host culture
- Language ability, use, and preference
- Other aspects of identity: age, gender, sexual orientation, religion/spirituality, disability, class, etc.

B. Cultural Explanations and Expressions of the Individual's Illness
- Predominant idioms of distress
- Meaning and perceived severity of the individual's symptoms in relation to the norms of their cultural reference group
- Local illness categories used by the individual's family and community to identity the condition (See Glossary of Culture-Bound Syndromes)
- Perceived cause or explanatory models
- Current preferences for and past experiences with professional and popular sources of care

C. Cultural Factors Related to Psychosocial Environment and Levels of Care
- Culturally relevant interpretations of social stressors, available social support, levels of functioning and disability
- Stresses in the social environment
- Role of religion and kin networks

D. Cultural Elements of the Relationship between the Individual and the Clinician
- Differences in culture and social status between the individual and the clinician
- Problems that their differences might cause in diagnosis and treatment
- Negotiating an appropriate level of intimacy
- Rapport
- Respect
- Communication (verbal and nonverbal)
- Using interpreters

E. Overall Cultural Assessment for Diagnosis and Care
- Differential diagnosis and treatment:
- Effects on treatment planning: biological outcomes, psychotherapy outcomes, social cultural outcomes, spiritual outcomes.

Note. Adapted from Outline for cultural formulation, Appendix. *In Diagnostic and Statistical Manual of Mental Disorders* (4th ed. rev.) by American Psychiatric Association, 1994. Washington, D.C.: American Psychiatric Association. Copyright © by American Psychiatric Association.

- Providing the client with the experience of being heard and understood and (if possible and appropriate) hope that the process into which he or she has entered can offer some immediate help

The following general suggestions will contribute to approaching these goals:

- Be warm, sincere, and respectful in your manner. Introduce yourself by the title and name you wish the client to use. Mutual introductions are very important. Northern European American culture is unusual in its desire to "get down to business." Other cultures are more personal in preceding business matters with introductions and inquiries as to health, family, and the like. Refer to adult clients as Mr. or Miss or Mrs. initially. (It is usually most appropriate to address the oldest family member present if it is a family session.) Be sure to inquire as to whether you are pronouncing their name correctly and how they wish to be addressed. Also ask by what name or names they wish you to refer to their ethnic group. If you are comfortable doing so, share with them some personal information (e.g., family data, where you reside, etc.) along with your professional credentials. Most cultures do not view others in terms of their social roles to the extent that European Americans do in regard to professional behavior.

- If you are anxious about your lack of knowledge about your clients' culture, do something about it by way of research prior to meeting with them. At the same time, it is not realistic to expect that you can become an expert on their culture and all of its diverse aspects. Exhibiting such a position about another person's culture is, in fact, likely to be taken very negatively—as haughty, presumptuous, or even demeaning. It is far better to be open about one's lack of knowledge and ask questions. For example, "I have not worked with many clients from your community and feel I do not know as much about your culture as I would like. I would appreciate your help in explaining certain things I may not understand as you refer to them." Your sincere openness and desire to learn is not a hindrance but rather a matter of respect for them and their culture. At the same time, it is necessary to point out that many People of Color (e.g., African Americans) may react negatively to being expected to educate Whites about their culture. "If you want to learn about me, read a book." Anger at such expectations reflects a historical experience of People of Color, which involves both an attitude on the part of Whites that it is the responsibility of People of Color to deal with racism and injustice and the feeling that the desire to "learn about us" is not really sincere. I would suggest asking the client if he or she is comfortable playing such a role.

- Give a brief and nontechnical description of the helping process, its purpose, and the specifics of how often you would like to meet, for how long, when, where, and so forth as well as any other relevant information such as where and how to contact you. Describe what is expected of them and what they can expect from you. Be sure to discuss confidentiality and what happens to the information they share with you. Remember, this may be their first experience with a professional helper and such roles may not formally exist in their culture.

- Have clients describe in their own words the problem(s) for which they are seeking help. Feel free to ask questions and get as much clarification as necessary. Then, summarize for them what you heard and ask if your summary is accurate. It is critical that you truly understand what they are communicating and similarly that they are aware that you understand. Also ask what kind of help they need most immediately, how other family members view them and the problem, and whether family members or significant others are willing to participate in future sessions. Throughout this phase of the process, try to determine what the client expects vis-à-vis gaining help with the problem.

- On the basis of the information you now have, share with them what you believe can be accomplished in terms of both more immediate and long-range needs. It is important that you describe possible goals in collaborative terms (but at the same time do so in a manner that continues to emphasize your skills and knowledge) and indicate that if they choose to proceed, the specific goal setting will be done jointly. Also discuss what might be some of the consequences of successfully achieving the goals.

■ Ask clients if there are any aspects of the helping process, as it has been described and experienced so far, that may be difficult for them. Similarly, if you notice anything that already seems problematic, it would be good to raise your concerns at this point.

■ The session should end with a formal good-bye and concrete plans for what will transpire next: another appointment, a referral, or a call to the client with some additional information at which time you will discuss continuing.

Remember, these general suggestions must be altered and adjusted in relation to the individual circumstances and personal characteristics of each client.

■ Two Case Studies

The following two case studies, borrowed from Aaron Rochlen's (2007) excellent text *Applying Counseling Theories*, will give you an opportunity to apply some of what you've learned so far to actual case material. Read through the whole case carefully. Then reread it more slowly, making note of thoughts about the cultural and racial dimensions of the case. Can you see any of the patterns, dynamics, issues, processes that have been discussed in the book? How have the dynamics of difference, race, ethnicity, and power affected the client? How are the behaviors and problems for which they are seeking help related to ethnicity and racism? Give yourself some time to ponder each case. When you feel that you have exhausted all possibilities, turn to the cultural analysis at the end of the chapter and see how you did. Which dynamics did you miss? Which did you identify? Did you find any that the author missed? You might want to read the interviews with cultural experts in chapters 10 and 12 about working with clients from their respective cultures, before reading the author's analysis, which can be found in Appendices A and B, respectively, see if the culture-specific material in the interview provides you with further clues to what might be going on with each client.

Case Study 1

The Case of Elena

Reason for Referral

Elena was strongly encouraged to seek counseling by her parents out of concern of her shifts in mood during the past 2–3 months. Her parents also recently found a bottle of vodka in her room and wanted her to be evaluated.

Behavioral Observations

Elena is a 17-year-old second generation Mexican American female. She is currently in her junior year at a local Catholic high school. She arrived on time for her appointment and was casually dressed. She made periodic eye contact with the counselor, but frequently cast her eyes downward. Her posture throughout the session was somewhat slumped. Elena appeared a bit anxious, as evidenced by frequently fidgeting with her hands. Her tone, body language, and content suggested she was tense and frustrated throughout the session. Elena responded appropriately to questions and became increasingly willing to talk as the session progressed. Insight and level of psychological mindedness seemed age appropriate.

Presenting Concerns

Elena's most pressing concern is feeling conflicted about her decision to apply to college next fall; although she wants to go to college, her mother is terminally ill and expects Elena to stay with and attend to her. Elena expressed feeling "down" and "pressured" regarding this decision. She feels guilty that she may fail to measure up to what a "good daughter" "should" be (i.e., devoted to family) and as a result may lose her parents' acceptance and approval. Elena explained that her family is extremely important to her and she believes she has an "obligation" to her parents. Yet she also desires the opportunity to meet new people and to have new experiences; she expressed concern that, "If I stay with my family my whole life, I'll be a failure . . . I'll have wasted all my potential." Elena reported trying to explain her perspective to her parents, but said she felt they were unable to understand her because "they hear what they want to hear." She also stated that she is receiving conflicting sources of pressure about the college decision and does not want to disappoint anyone. While her parents want her to stay home, her boyfriend and friends, whose parents tend to be very supportive of their applications to college, believe Elena should leave. Elena described feeling pulled in two different directions and said she is, "stuck in the middle . . . If I make the wrong decision I'll regret it forever."

Elena also worries about "bombing in school" because her schoolwork no longer seems important, she has difficulty concentrating, and her various sources of worry (i.e., mom, college, grades) feel like "too much" to handle. Elena further described feeling "blah" toward working on the school newspaper, of which she once served as editor. Elena admitted that she sometimes thinks it would be easier "if I wasn't here," but noted she would not hurt herself by stating," I wouldn't do that to my family, especially my mom." She admitted drinking vodka by herself one night in the hopes it might make her feel better, but insisted that her parents "freaked out" over nothing when they found the bottle; she swore that drugs and alcohol are "not the kind of thing I do; I'm not really into that."

Family Background

Elena's parents are both Mexican; they immigrated from Mexico 30 years ago. Most of her extended family still lives in Mexico. Elena's family currently enjoys middle-class standing; her father owns a small business and her mother worked part-time as a secretary before her illness prohibited her from working outside the home. Elena is the youngest of three children. Her older brother is in his first year of college, aspiring to be a dentist. Elena said she is proud of and close to her brother, yet she feels resentful that "he got away (from the family), while I have to stay here." She described "hating" her older sister who has a history of

(continued)

drug usage and infrequently visits the family. Elena reported that her sister "ruined everything for me," explaining that their parents unfairly compare Elena to her sister and "if I make one wrong move . . . (they think) I'm going to end up just like her; I'm going to be a total failure and a bad daughter."

Elena said she has always been "really close" to her parents, especially her mother. She expressed gratitude for the sacrifices they made on her behalf. While she noted feeling they can be unfairly strict with her, Elena qualified her concern by saying that, "They are strict because they care." Elena described the customs—i.e., cooking Mexican food and visiting Mexico—and the qualities—i.e., rigidly Catholic and close knit—that she believes makes them a "traditional" Mexican American family. She noted that although her father is the primary breadwinner, her mother has the "real power" in the family with regard to making decisions.

Elena does not speak Spanish; her parents had a "hard time" when they came to the United State and, not wanting their children to experience similar anti-immigrant discrimination, refused to speak Spanish to them. Elena said that although her parents have learned English, she sometimes wonders whether not communicating in a shared native language hinders their ability to understand one another. She recalled an incident when she was younger: she asked her mother to pick her up from a friend's home at a certain hour; her mother misunderstood her directions and arrived 6 hours late. Elena recalled feeling abandoned by, angry at, and ashamed of her mother. Elena reported also feeling that her parents don't "get" that American youths are traditionally afforded more independence and freedom than Mexican youths.

Elena's mother's illness has greatly impacted the family. Although her mother may live 10–15 years, her imminent death and compromised physical state have cast a shadow upon the family. Elena states that her mother needs a good deal of help. She apparently feels conflicted in that she wants to provide help yet is angry in being the only child expected to care for her.

Relational and Interpersonal History

Elena reported a supportive circle of friends, but admitted feeling that her friends "don't listen to me." She explained that her friends, like most students in her high school, are White European Americans and she feels they "don't want to hear about how my family works" differently from theirs. She noted that some friends have recently expressed concern that she has started acting "like I don't care anymore." However, Elena doesn't feel she can really talk to her friends about her problems. She experiences their concern that she be allowed to go to college as yet another source of pressure. Elena's boyfriend of 5 months is also White. Elena said their relationship has recently been strained by her indecision over college. She described him as "inconsiderate" and as unfairly judging her parents to be "stupid and ignorant" regarding their stance on Elena's future, rather than considering that they simply "think differently."

Coping Strategies

Elena has no history of previous treatment for an emotional problem. She generally perceives her friends and family as supportive, yet expressed disbelief that anyone really understands her. When probed for coping strategies, she noted that writing in her journal, taking walks, and spending time alone some-times helps to ease her feeling that "people are always on my back." She denied regular use of alcohol, but admitted that her recent experimentation with vodka somewhat helped her to relax. To cope with her mother's illness, Elena said that her family relied largely on religion and family solidarity.

Career Progress

Academically, Elena reported she has traditionally done well, particularly in English. She expressed interest in studying journalism because she is intrigued by people's stories and unique cultural experiences. Elena said she thinks her parents are supportive of her education, but believe "family comes first."

Note. Rochlen, Aaron B., *Applying Counseling Theories: An Online, Case-Based Approach,* First Edition, © 2007. Electronically reproduced by permission of Pearson Education, Inc., Upper Saddle River, New Jersey.

Case Study 2

The Case of Theo

Reason for Referral

Theo came to the university counseling center after being told by his girlfriend that if he did not seek help, she would end their three-year relationship.

Behavioral Observations

Theo is a 22-year-old, tall, African American male. He is currently in his final year of college at a large university with a major in Math and Computer Science with plans to enter the military after graduation. He was appropriately dressed and had a cooperative attitude. Although he presented himself with a very calm and even-tempered mood, Theo indicated that he felt as if he "was going to explode." At times he seemed noticeably uncomfortable, but he kept good eye contact throughout the session. As the session progressed, he seemed increasingly more comfortable and relaxed.

Presenting Concerns

Although encouraged to seek help from his girlfriend, Tamia, Theo seemed open to discussing several concerns he wanted to address in counseling. The most pressing was to better understand his problems controlling his anger and how it was related to various feelings and behaviors. Most recently, Theo became angry with Tamia after she failed to return his phone call and stayed out "partying" all night. He indicated that Tamia claimed she had told him of her plans and that his anger felt controlling and threatening. Theo also

(continued)

expressed concern about his inability to control his anger when dealing with his family and professional relationships.

Theo first noticed his problems with anger when dealing with a middle-school teacher who falsely accused him of cheating on a test. He remembers this being the first time he felt what he described as "the rage." During such instances, he describes feeling "helpless" and reported it being the only way to communicate his frustrations. In high school, he also frequently felt angry toward girls. Theo noted he initially thought they wanted to be friends but later realized they were "all using him" to get rides or gifts and were "not interested" in being friends or having a romantic relationship.

Theo also noted having difficulty being understood and making friends, at one point comparing himself to "The Incredible Hulk" because he was feeling as if he was "losing control." He also reported that "people just don't get him." He reported few "real friends" in high school and only a few since starting college. He reports feeling increasingly misunderstood, ignored, and isolated. He stated, "I wish people would really try to get to know me." He discussed that as a tall, Black man, he has also frequently perceived that others find him intimidating and imposing.

Since beginning college Theo has tried to be more sociable, but he expressed feeling anxious toward people and believes he cannot trust them. These problems of anxiety and trust have surfaced both with other college students and professors. Theo reported that he often has troubling dreams of being at parties where people who he does not know ignore and walk away from him when he attempts to be sociable.

After discussing these issues and becoming more comfortable in the session, Theo disclosed that his girlfriend is also unhappy with his viewing pornography on the Internet. When his girlfriend learned that he had been engaging in this, she told him that if she caught him doing it again, she would break off the relationship. He was reluctant to discuss the details of this behavior, but indicated that it began after receiving an ex-rated "pop-up ad." Recently, it has progressed to the point that he sometimes spends several hours a day viewing pornographic material on the Internet. He noted his frustration with his lack of intimacy with his girlfriend and control issues as possible sources leading to these behaviors.

Family Background

Theo was raised in a rural Texas town and is the middle child of three boys. At age ten, his parents divorced and his mother relocated Theo and his siblings to a larger metropolitan area. After residing in this area for 2 years, his parents reconciled and remarried. Theo reported that he did not want his parents to remarry and still believes they should not be together because of the regular arguments about financial issues. He also cited the degree to which Theo's father travels as a sales representative as a source of stress in their relationship. In commenting on his parents' relationship, he noted "his parents did lots of yelling and throwing objects at one another." He noted that his older brother was frequently the one to take care of him and his younger brother and to try to maintain peace in the house.

Theo described growing up in a lower-class background as a child and progressing toward middle-class standing when his parents remarried and moved into their first house. Both parents completed college at historical Black colleges. Although supportive of Theo going to college, they would have preferred that he went to a historical Black college, especially because most of Theo's primary and secondary school education took place in primarily White schools. Theo said that even though he chose to go to a different college, he still identified with his background and being African American. He chose to attend a predominantly White college because he did not want to follow in his parents' footsteps, getting away from them and what they represented, namely, "a lot of fighting and yelling." Theo maintains monthly contact with his brothers who decided not to attend college. Instead, both joined the military after high school. One brother currently resides in Japan while the other lives in Germany. He sees him and his brothers as the "three musketeers" and said that no matter what, "nothing could tear us apart." Although Theo indicated that he loves his parents, he also stated that he does not have much respect for them returning to a marriage that "wasn't good in the first place." Theo did not comment on his personal relationship with his father however, indicated that most of his memories about his father have not been positive.

Relational and Interpersonal History

Theo has been seeing Tamia for 3 years. They met at the campus multicultural center and first noticed her at a church they both attended. He said he was initially drawn to her because she seemed to be equally invested in the same types of campus and national issues as himself. He expressed frustration, however, that they had not been sexually intimate for the majority of their relationship. After dating for about 2 years, he indicated that they were intimate on one occasion, the first sexual experience for both of them. Afterwards, Tamia talked with Theo about her feelings of extreme guilt, sadness, disappointment, and regret due to fears of becoming pregnant and how premarital sex was prohibited due to her religious (African Methodist Episcopal) values. He feels conflicted about premarital sex because he feels ready to become sexually active on a regular basis, although he also believes that premarital sex is a sin. Theo also seems to resent that she was the one to make the final decision on the issue and felt he was not heard and his feelings were not considered.

Coping Strategies

Theo reported that he has tried to find ways to reduce his anger and attempted to be more sociable by working out on a more regular basis. He often plays sports, but he reports that this provides him little relief. He admits to being at a loss for how to cope with his feelings of anger, particularly when he feels "the rage." Theo denied drinking frequently as it makes him "lose control" and get into fights.

Career Progress

Theo's career goal is to join the military after graduation and hopefully join his brothers at one of the locations at which they are stationed. He said he has

(continued)

thought about asking Tamia to marry him, but is concerned that he is not ready given the problems they are currently having. Theo expressed concern about the ways in which his inability to control his anger effectively could influence both his relationship with Tamia and his career goals in the military.

Note. Rochlen, Aaron B., *Applying Counseling Theories: An Online, Case-Based Approach,* First Edition, © 2007. Electronically reproduced by permission of Pearson Education, Inc., Upper Saddle River, New Jersey.

■ Summary

This chapter speaks more specifically about concrete issues in working with culturally different clients. There is general agreement among practitioners that cross-cultural helping is more demanding, challenging, and energy-draining than work with same-culture clients. Draguns (1981), for instance, describes it as more "experiential, freewheeling, and bilateral." It is also more complex conceptually in that it involves, according to Pinderhughes (1989), an understanding of four separate but interrelated psychologies: the dynamics of race, ethnicity, difference, and power. It is critical for the practitioner to understand these both as they operate in the lives of clients and also within themselves as they work with culturally different clients. The first two have been discussed extensively in earlier chapters. The psychology of difference refers to the experience of oneself as different from others and the feelings it generates. Feelings created by the experience of being different tend to be negative and can include reactions of confusion, hurt, pain, anger, and fear as well as envy, guilt, pity, sympathy and privilege. These emotions can lead to a distancing from others, loneliness, isolation, rejection, and abandonment. The psychology of power refers to the amount of influence one has on the behavior of others. Having power means one can influence the actions of others. Powerlessness is the lack of such influence. Cross-cultural helping can represent a particularly imbalanced power situation. The traditional therapeutic dyad represents a power imbalance in favor of the practitioner; in cross-cultural helping, this differential is tipped even further by differences in respective cultural group identities and connections. Therapeutically, power is important, first, because powerlessness often forces individuals to adopt behaviors that allow them to feel more powerful, and these strategies are often counterproductive and need to be addressed in treatment. Second, empowerment may be best dealt with in the therapeutic situation by the practitioner's consciously choosing to "take a down position," to borrow Pinderhughes's term.

Various suggestions are offered by way of allaying some of the anxiety that is a natural part of beginning to do cross-cultural work. For example, it is useful to focus on human similarities as well as differences and begin by just trying to make human contact with the client. A good cultural assessment is critical in defining the kinds of help a culturally different client needs as well as how the client may be viewing the problem from his or her cultural perspective. Several strategies for collecting such information are described including the DSM's "Cultural Outline for Case Formulation," a guide developed to sensitize users of the DSM to cultural issues in clients.

Next, guidelines for developing rapport with culturally different clients during the first and early sessions are offered. For example, Sue and Zane's (1987) work suggests that clients should come away from the first session feeling that they have been understood from their own perspective and that they have received something concrete from their work with the provider.

The chapter ends with two detailed case studies, which you are invited to analyze for cultural issues and dynamics. The authors' cultural formulation of each is included in Appendices A and B.

■ Activities

1. *Explore the psychological experience of being different.* Although you can do these by yourself, it works well to pair off with a partner and take turns answering the following questions:

   ■ What is your earliest memory of encountering someone who was different from you? See if you can briefly go back to it. Who was there? What was happening? What were you feeling? Stay with it for a moment.
   ■ What is your earliest memory of feeling yourself as different? See if you can briefly go back there. Who was there? What was happening? What were you feeling? Stay with it for a moment.
   ■ In growing up, in what ways did you feel different?
   ■ In what ways do you feel different today?
   ■ In what ways do you feel challenged as a helping professional by the racial/ethnic differences of a client, the personal experience of "being different" that clients report as part of their life experience, or your clients' voicing feelings that they experience you as different from them.

2. *Explore power in the therapeutic relationship.* Pair off with a partner or gather in a small group and take turns answering and discussing the following questions:

   ■ Do you believe that there is a significant power difference between the helper and the client? Why or why not?
   ■ Do you experience yourself as having more power and control in the helping relationship than those with whom you are working? How so? Describe your emotional reactions to that experience.
   ■ Are there things you do in session or might do in session to change the power balance in the room? If so, describe them.
   ■ Have you ever worked with someone and felt you were not in control or in charge? Describe the situation and how you felt and handled it.
   ■ What might you envision to be some of the differences and difficulties that White and Of-Color therapists face vis-à-vis their reactions to power in their role as helpers?

Addressing Ethnic Conflict, Genocide, and Mass Violence

In the following excerpt from a *New York Times* op-ed piece, psychologist Pumla Gobodo-Madikizela (2003) describes the complexity of healing in her native South Africa after apartheid.

The Roots of Afrikaner Rage

"There were places black people were forbidden to go," my mother says as we near the restaurant in an upmarket Cape Town shopping mall. "And now we can come to the same places as whites, walk into a café, and pay the same money—just like that."

For some white South Africans, mingling with blacks in urban malls is a welcome change from the racial isolation of the past. Some are simply resigned to this post-apartheid reality . . . But for others, the appearance of black faces in spaces that were previously reserved for whites is seen as an invasion of what belongs to them—things they worked so hard to build, their pride, their vaderland. This has evoked bitterness and unleashed their wrath and violent outrage.

Having been a child and an adult under apartheid, and having grown up in a family and community of dispossessed and disenfranchised adults, I can understand their anger. For the sake of the nation's future peace and unity, I hope that everyone concerned will consider its sources . . .

Some see the rising tide of discontent among Afrikaners as evidence of racist attitudes that won't go away. This may be so. But we also must consider the bitter memories that have been unleashed by the transfer of power to a black government. Most Afrikaners carry in their consciousness the spirit of survival; there is always an "other" from whom the volk must be protected. They suffered serious loss and humiliation in their war with the British, the Boer War. In that conflict . . . British troops destroyed thousands of Boer farms, blew up homesteads . . . Thousands of Afrikaner women, children, and elderly men were sent to internment camps . . . homeless and humiliated, the Afrikaners lost their fight against British domination.

After the British, there was another enemy. Mr. deKlerk apologized to South Africans who were oppressed by apartheid laws, "in the spirit of true repentance." Yet the ghosts of the past have yet been laid to rest . . . The dialogue that was begun by the truth and reconciliation commission must continue . . . Acknowledging the loss that Afrikaners feel would be a start."

The task of picking up the pieces of a society shattered by violence is not easy. My mother, who grew up in rural KwaZulu-Natal Provence, remembers the loss of her family's land and witnesses the humiliation of a father who had to seek work in the faraway place that black people call "Gauteng," "the place of gold": Johannesburg. She and my father were married in Cape Town in 1951, the year in which more than 70 oppressive laws were passed by the apartheid government.

She, like many black people I know, has every reason to remember with bitterness and to harbor a desire for revenge. But she prefers to live without that burden.

Note. From *New York Times*, January 10, 2003, p. A 23.

In chapter 7 you were introduced to the concept of trauma. It will be remembered that a *trauma* is an extraordinary psychological experience—caused by threats to life and bodily safety or personal encounters with violence and death—that overwhelms ordinary human functioning. When the source of trauma is natural such as a hurricane or flooding, we speak of disasters. When traumatic events are caused by other human beings, they are referred to as atrocities. In the pages that follow you will learn about violence and atrocities caused by ethnic and racial hatred as well as efforts to heal the survivors of such experiences. Herman (1989) describes a basic dilemma that confounds the treatment of such trauma.

The ordinary response to atrocities is to banish them from consciousness. Certain violations of the social compact are too terrible to utter aloud: this is the meaning of the word *unspeakable*. Atrocities, however, refuse to be buried. Equally as powerful as the desire to deny atrocities is the conviction that denial does not work. Folk wisdom is filled with ghosts who refuse to rest in their graves until their stories are told . . . Remembering and telling the truth about terrible events are prerequisites both for the restoration of the social order and for the healing of individual victims. The conflict between the will to deny horrible events and the will to proclaim them aloud is the central dialectic of psychological trauma . . . When the truth is recognized, survivors can begin their recovery. But far too often secrecy prevails, and the story of the traumatic event surfaces not as a verbal narrative but as a symptom. (p. 1)

Violence and atrocities are typically directed toward the weak and the powerless. Victims of individual crimes of violence tend to be women, children, gays, the disabled, the poor, ethnic minorities, the elderly. The same populations tend to be the targets for mass violence as well: war, genocide, ethnic conflict, torture, enslavement, ethnic cleansing, colonialism, and racism. Both are crimes of power and hatred. When the diagnosis of post/traumatic stress disorder (PTSD) was first introduced in 1980, it was described as "out of the range of usual human experience." Clinical, social, and historical reality has since shown just how naïve such an idea is. If one considers the actual frequency of rape and other sexual crimes, battery, child abuse, domestic violence, hate crimes, war, ethnic conflict, terrorism, what is "out of the range of usual human experience" is our tendencies to remain silent in the face of trauma, to not get involved, and to avoid actively responding both in our roles as ordinary human beings and as helping and healing professionals.

Herman (1989) points to an interesting parallel between the dilemma of silence and truth-telling in treatment and the history of research on trauma. "The study of psychological trauma has a curious history—one of episodic amnesia. Periods of active investigation have alternated with periods of oblivion" (p. 7). She refers, for example, to Freud's early findings of sexual abuse in all children and his subsequent denial or recanting of it as fantasy, to research on shell-shock after World War I and PTSD after Vietnam and its subsequent suppression, and the emergence of concern over domestic violence in the 1960s stimulated by a new feminism and the continuing efforts to silence its voice. Once again, we find ourselves entering a new period of enlivened concern over trauma, this time in relation to mass ethnic violence. According to Minow (2000):

> The mass atrocities of the twentieth century, sadly, do not make it distinctive. More distinctive than the facts of genocides and regimes of torture marking this era are the search for and invention of collective forms of response . . . The novel experiment of the Nuremberg and Tokyo tribunals following World War II reached for a vision of world order and international justice, characterizing mass violence as crimes of war and crimes against humanity. (p. 235)

In this chapter we will identify some of the processes by which individuals and societies heal after the trauma of ethnic conflict, genocide, and mass violence and begin to provide answers to the following questions:

- What steps can be taken after mass violence to heal and restore its victims to ordinary living?
- Can societies, as well as individuals, heal from their own traumatic histories? In this regard, what is the distinction between retributive and restorative justice?
- Is it possible for enemies and perpetrators and victims to reconcile and have meaningful dialogue about what happened?
- What are the meanings and conditions of justice and forgiveness?

There is an important "given" fueling all trauma work, and that is the seemingly inconvertible evidence that if victims of violence are not healed, they will eventually perpetuate violence against others. We know this from research on child abuse, intergenerational trauma literature, and the clinical value of such theoretical notions as Freud's idea of identification with the aggressor and his prediction of the "return of the repressed." We also know that ethnic violence calls forth vengeance and some form of retribution unless there is some intervention and that history is bound to repeat itself if it is not remembered.

In the pages that follow you will learn about three examples of efforts at healing and social restoration after the trauma of ethnic conflict, genocide, and mass violence. Specifically, we will discuss the plight of the Lakota Sioux in the United States and the efforts of Brave Heart (1995) to heal the historic trauma and unresolved grief in this Native American population; South Africa's national response to apartheid and its Truth and Reconciliation process; and research on the treatment of Jewish Holocaust survivors, Nazis, and their children, and efforts at reconciliation between the two groups.

■ Historic Trauma and Unresolved Grief among Native Americans

The Lakota Sioux, like many Native American groups, are beset by serious and widespread social problems. Their rate of death by alcoholism is 7 times the national average and 2.5 times that of other Native American People. Suicide rates are 3.2 times that of Whites. Historically, they have been plagued by high rates of coronary heart disease and hypertension. Unemployment rates on the Lakota reservation average from 50% to 90% and about 50% of the group live below the poverty level. Brave Heart (1995) contends that these depressing statistics are the result of generations of chronic, *historical trauma and unresolved grief,* "a repercussion from the loss of lives, land, and aspects of culture rendered by the European conquest of the Americas" (p. 2). This unresolved grief has dual sources: massive trauma that has endured from generation to generation and the systematic destruction of traditional Lakota ways of grieving for both individuals and the community as a whole. In other words, not only have the Lakota been devastated by an ongoing series of traumatic events, but they have also been robbed of the traditional rituals that would have allowed them to adequately mourn and thereby resolve their grief. The result, according to Brave Heart, is frozen, unresolved grief, passed on across generations, which is the underlying cause of the community's out-of-control alcoholism and mental and physical health problems.

Legters (1988) believes that the treatment of Native Americans in the United States meets the United Nations' definition of genocide. Nowhere is this fact more evident than in the traumatic history of the Lakota Sioux. The mid-1800s saw the loss of traditional hunting grounds; the spread of smallpox and cholera; the killing, imprisonment, and relocation of hundreds of innocent tribal members; a bounty on Lakota scalps; and the death of hundreds by starvation and exposure. In 1871, President Grant asserted that the government would no longer consider Indians to be nations with whom treaties would be negotiated. Instead, they were wards of the state. This declaration set the stage for increased persecution and widespread invasion of Lakota territories. An army attack in 1868 on a peaceful encampment led ultimately to the Lakota victory at Little Big Horn.

This, however, only intensified government efforts to steal land and break the spirit of the People. In 1877, Lakota spiritual leader Crazy Horse was arrested and killed. The rise of Sitting Bull temporarily reunited and gave some encouragement to the People. By then, however, he alone remained a symbol of resistance to the White man and ensured the practice of traditional Native ways.

His eventual assassination, the suppression of the spiritual Ghost Dance cult, and the massacre at Wounded Knee left the surviving Lakota totally traumatized.

A series of more recent experiences have only intensified the cumulative effect of the historic past. These include:

- The experience of Indian boarding schools with their forced separations of children from parents, physical and sexual abuses, and destruction of traditional cultural knowledge among the children
- Death by tuberculosis
- The introduction of widespread alcohol use
- Continued land loss, relocation, and government termination policies of Native rights

Paralleling this massive trauma and contributing to the difficulty in grieving was the systematic destruction of traditional beliefs, ceremonies, and rituals of grief. Boarding schools made many strangers to their own cultural heritage. Traditional ways were disenfranchised by government control of reservations, the prohibition of ceremonies, and the intrusion of White attitudes toward grieving. In other words, the massive trauma was accentuated by a lack of functional cultural methods of mourning the losses. The grief could not go away; it could only accumulate and be passed on from generation to generation.

Brave Heart's Cultural Intervention

To intervene in this process and see if it was possible to reintroduce traditional means of grieving to her people, Brave Heart designed an experimental healing intervention to be given first to a group of Lakota human service providers, healers, and community leaders. If successful, they, in turn, would take the experience back to their respective communities and lead similar workshops for community members. Brave Heart drew many of her ideas for treating trauma from research on Jewish Holocaust survivors and their children. She saw strong parallels in intergenerational transmission of grief and difficulties in accessing cultural and communal forms of grieving between the Lakota People and the Jewish survivors who remained in Europe. Survivors who immigrated to Israel and the United States had significantly more opportunities for collective mourning than those who remained in Europe, living "among the perpetrators and murderers of their families" (Fogelman, 1991, p. 67) as did the Lakota Sioux. Similarly, both groups had also survived the loss of relatives to the anonymity of mass graves and had placed great import on collective grieving, community rituals, and memorials.

The Lakota intervention, spanning 4 days, entailed a series of experiential exercises and presentations of Lakota history, the process of trauma and grief, and traditional spiritual practices and ceremonies. It was designed for "stimulating mourning resolution of historical grief" among the provider participants, all of whom were Lakota. All were tested before and after the intervention on a variety of assessment instruments. Brave Heart (1995) found the following significant effects:

- Education about historical trauma led to an increased awareness of personal trauma and the experience of grief and related effects.

- Sharing grief and related effects within a traditional Lakota context led to a cathartic sense of relief.
- A grief resolution process was initiated with an eventual reduction in grief-related effects.
- Positive group identification increased.
- Positive commitment to community healing increased. (p. 126)

Subsequently, Brave Heart has expanded her work by creating a network of "survivors," who are carrying out trainings, therapy, and the creation of memorial ceremonies and grieving rituals in their respective Lakota communities.

PTSD in Native American Males

Duran and Duran (1995) argue similarly that the psychological consequences of communal traumatization and colonization have led to PTSD in Native American men. "Once the warrior is defeated and his ability to protect the community destroyed, a deep psychological trauma of identity loss occurs" (p. 36). He will unconsciously turn against his loved ones and become abusive as his ego splits, one aspect in touch with the enormous pain and the other identifying with the aggressor. The rage that he feels and would like to turn on the destroyer of his culture is ultimately turned inward. The only way he can contain the rage and self-medicate the PTSD is through the use of alcohol. In discussing treatment, Duran and Duran (1995) warn against unintentionally retraumatizing the Native American patient.

> Without the awareness of some of these dynamics . . . most practitioners continue to invalidate the experience of trauma in Native American people, which in its own right becomes an ongoing infliction of trauma on the patient. The Native American patient already feels decades of horrendous unresolved grief and rage, and the practitioner adds to this through the insensitivity of blaming the victim by pathologizing clients, as is so common in Western psychotherapy. Such iatrogenics perpetuate the suffering. (p. 42)

The work of Brave Heart and Duran and Duran on resolving historical grief and trauma holds relevance not only for Native Americans but also for other ethnic groups with collective histories of trauma and oppression. Such wholesale loss and disenfranchisement have certainly been the experience of People of Color in the United States: African Americans with the lingering effects of slavery and the ongoing trauma of racism; Latinos/as with the trauma of migration north, expatriation of lands in the Southwest and, for some, escape from political genocide in South and Central America; and Asian Americans with their oppression as an immigrant labor force, internment of the Japanese during World War II, and the traumatic experiences of refugees from war in Southeast Asia. Similarly, there are groups within the United States (e.g., Jews, Irish, Armenians, and Gypsies [Rom]) with long histories as victims of political and social oppression in their native lands. It is possible that members of these various communities, like the Lakota Sioux, suffer from undiagnosed historic traumatic response and unresolved, frozen grief, and they might benefit from grief work, both individual and communal, similar to that developed by Brave Heart.

■ South Africa and Its Truth and Reconciliation Commission

Hayner (2000) succinctly summarizes the history of South Africa that set the stage for the Truth and Reconciliation Commission (TRC):

> After 45 years of apartheid in South Africa, and thirty-odd years of some level of armed resistance against the apartheid state by the armed wing of the African National Congress (ANC) and others, the country had suffered massacres, killings, torture, lengthy imprisonment of activists, and severe economic and social discrimination against its majority black, coloured and Indian population. As the transition out of apartheid began to unfold in the early 1990s, many insisted that this horrific past must be addressed. (p. 10)

Nelson Mandela, then leader of the ANC, who became South Africa's first Black president, favored a truth commission to make public all human rights abuses and atrocities committed on both sides during the years of the apartheid government. The ANC had already carried out its own internal inquiries into human rights abuses committed by its members during its military struggle against apartheid and hoped to do the same in relation to the activities of the outgoing apartheid government. Its intention was to send a strong message that things would be different in the new South African regime with strong human rights guarantees for all of its citizens. The National Party (the outgoing government), not surprisingly, argued for a reconciliation process that would grant amnesty for all activities carried out in the name of the apartheid regime. A compromise of a conditional amnesty clause was struck, and on April 27, 1994, South Africa held its first-ever democratic elections.

The TRC was unique and unprecedented in world history. There had been truth commissions in other countries, but none had been so far-reaching nor had offered amnesty in exchange for telling the truth. The agreed-upon conditions for amnesty were that perpetrators had to apply in person and fully disclose the facts of their crimes, and those crimes had to be political rather than personal. The goal of the process was national reconciliation, not retribution. Never before had a nation so fully pursued the idea of restorative justice, that is, set a course toward healing rather than punishment. Restorative justice, according to Minow (1998),

> emphasizes the humanity of both offenders and victims. It seeks repair of social connections and peace rather than retribution against the offenders. Building connections and enhancing communication between perpetrators and those they victimize, and forging ties across the community, takes precedence over punishment or law enforcement. (p. 92).

Goals for the TRC were as follows:

- To document the human rights abuses that had taken place during apartheid
- To publicly acknowledge the experience and fate of victims
- To restore their dignity, allowing them to bear witness to what had happened to them
- To grant reparations, that is, some type of compensation (though it must be understood that compensation can only be symbolic)
- To produce a final report that is a detailed and frank history of what took place over the half century of apartheid, a document that would become a shared, societal narrative

The essence of its philosophy was summarized by the then Minister of Justice Dullah Omar (1996) as "the need for understanding, not vengeance; the need for reparation, not retaliation; and the need for 'ubuntu' (fellowship and interconnection), not victimization."

The undertaking was enormous. The TRC comprised three committees: Human Rights Violations, Amnesty, and Reparations and Rehabilitation. The staff numbered three hundred; the budge amounted to $18 million per year; and four large offices located throughout South Africa coordinated activities. In 4 years testimonies were taken from more than 23,000 witnesses and victims, 2000 of whom appeared in public hearings throughout South Africa. All meetings were very well attended. Coverage of the hearings by the media was extensive: newspapers, radio, and television, international and local. The overriding intent was to make the findings and testimonies public in the broadest possible ways and to write and disseminate a new narrative history.

Impact on Victims

Gillian Straker (1999), a White, South African psychoanalyst, offers an insightful analysis of what happened psychologically as a result of the TRC. She divides her analysis into three parts: its impact on victims, bystanders, and actual perpetrators. In relation to the victims who gave testimony, Straker identified four important outcomes:

- Many victims described the experience of *breaking the silence* around their testimony as "amazingly liberating." To quote Straker: "What the TRC is doing is allowing the unspoken to be spoken, and in trying to locate perpetrators, it is both in a symbolic and in a real way putting a name to the nameless . . . and by affirming the reality of the victims and freeing them from the power of the secret, is serving a liberatory function" (p. 257). But it was a silence that had existed on many levels. Blacks in South Africa had to keep the daily horrors of apartheid contained within themselves for several reasons. First, there was the necessity of not "discomforting" Whites and the White world around them with the truth of their existence. Also, for many active in the struggle for freedom, remaining silent was a matter of life and death. And internally, what many people had experienced was so horrific that it was "almost impossible to conceptualize and . . . in the realm of the unthinkable and the unspeakable" (p. 257).

- The actual experience of *telling one's story* was enormously therapeutic as well as liberating. Increasingly, research on PTSD has shown that sharing the trauma narrative is a first step toward healing and a sign that healing has begun. Until then the actual details of the story are frozen in time, locked away in "body and iconic memories," to use Cardinal's (1984) terminology, disconnected from both the narrative and the "words to say it." The TRC supported the process of giving voice to these words.
- "Telling the story in a public forum contributes to the documentation and rewriting of history . . . it allows the victims to exercise an *altruistic function*" (p. 258). By their very acts, victims are reconstructing the past for others, creating a shared societal narrative, giving to others, and playing an active role in the healing of society. In a similar vein, Herman (1989) points to the importance of finding a "survivor mission," that is, a personally meaningful source of social action in the world that is reparative and at the same time transcends their particular trauma situation, as a further source of healing.
- Last, Straker emphasizes the importance of the TRC in reconnecting the survivor to her or his geographic and social community as well as humanity in general. Trauma at its most basic level involves disconnection from one's community and all that is human. It disrupts the "basic assumptions about one's own vulnerability and the notion of a just world. It interferes with the individual's internalized object relations and their containing functions" (p. 258).

One criticism of the TRC's healing function, as suggested by Straker, is that although giving testimony "stimulated catharsis and outpouring of emotion," it lacked a "forum for working these through" and for learning to contain such feelings upon returning to the ordinary demands of life. For example, some individuals who reported feelings of elation after testifying later experienced being overwhelmed by what they had revealed and needed support and ongoing help. This is a point where human services professionals can make significant contributions toward supporting processes such as the TRC by providing continuing services to survivors. Many South African mental health workers did involve themselves with the TRC by "preparing briefers and debriefers who were assigned to individuals who spoke before the TRC and who followed them up after they had given evidence" (p. 259).

Impact on Bystanders

The impact of the TRC is less clear in relation to bystanders, that is, among Whites, who had not been directly involved in perpetrating crimes but had remained silent and benefited from the apartheid regime, and active perpetrators. In relation to the former, the TRC seemed to have stimulated within many White South Africans an awareness, for the first time, of the scope of atrocities that had been carried out in their names as well as an appreciation of the need for giving reparations to those who had suffered. Many were deeply shocked and moved by the testimonies that were given. But what remains unclear is how so many were able to deny what was going on in the first place and to continue to not fully own their complicity in what happened. The majority of the White population had after all remained silent about the "evils of apartheid" and actively supported the Nationalist regime. Probably the best explanation of such behavior can be found in the idea of dissociation.

> The very existence of apartheid depended on the ability of white South Africans to dissociate and to compartmentalize aspects of the horror-filled reality of apartheid and racism to which they were exposed on a daily basis. Underpinning the ability to disassociate . . . is the mechanism of projective identification. It allows all good to be invested in one object . . . and all bad to be vested in another object. (p. 253)

This splitting is supported by another internal mechanism, projective identification, which allows bystanders to project their own unwanted, negative identifications onto out-group members and thereby justify their negative treatment of them. What this does psychologically is block the experiencing of empathy and concern in the bystander. Promoting empathy through TRC testimony may lessen the tendencies toward dissociation, splitting, and projective identification in bystanders, and thus allow the creation of natural empathy. Klein (1937) sees such dynamics as being at the psychic roots of racism.

Impact on Perpetrators

"The impact of the TRC on perpetrators is probably most variable because testimony may be given solely for the reason of gaining amnesty rather than seeking forgiveness; that is, "confession is not being solely made to obtain freedom from a sense of wrongdoing or from a sense of being chained to and haunted by the one whom one has wronged" (p. 265). Sincere regret may be avoided in two ways: through shame and humiliation stimulated by feeling that one has been coerced into taking responsibility for a crime that one does not truly believe is wrong or by experiencing "superiority" or "triumph" by secretly retaining an "unshifting internal position" and denigrating the work of the TRC. Impact on perpetrators seems to be most likely to occur when they experience true remorse and when the victim feels that forgiveness is justified.

A final point that is quite important to understand is the profound, psychic interdependency of the victim and the perpetrator; each really holds the key to the other's healing process. Gobodo-Madikezela (2000) describes the reciprocity with a clarity that is worth quoting at length.

> People who come to the point of forgiveness have lived with and know pain . . . All these emotions connect them with their departed love ones . . . Paradoxically, these emotions also tie them to the one who caused the traumatic wounds. On the one hand, the perpetrator is the hated one responsible for the family's anguish; on the other hand, the

family members . . . look to the perpetrator to get a glimpse of the final living moments of the loved one. The perpetrator is the bearer of the secrets, the only one who observed that important moment when the loved one breathed their last. (p. 19)

By providing loved ones with specific details the perpetrator can allow them to finish their incomplete narrative and move on toward healing. Often, the unknown facts of how one's father or son or brother died freeze and interrupt the grieving process. Gobodo-Madikezela continues,

When the perpetrator shows remorse, which is to say when that person knows the pain of the victim with a heartfelt "I'm sorry," the moment becomes his own turning point. When he committed the horrible deed, he denied not only the humanity of his victim . . . he denied his own humanity as well. His genuine apology is his way of reclaiming a humanity that was lost in a life of violence, and a crying out to be re-admitted in the circle of humanity. (p. 19)

Institute for the Healing of Memories

The healing work accomplished by the TRC was extensive, but it was only the beginning of a process of societal change. In addition to an ongoing reparations program, it was intended that those who had testified would receive follow-up therapy and support and that additional South Africans would also need to be brought into this process. The establishment of the Institute for the Healing of Memories is an example of the kind of organizations that have come forth to fill this void. The Institute's mission statement (2006) speaks directly to the import of such continuity.

At the time when the Truth and Reconciliation Commission was set up, it was obvious that only a minority of South Africans would have the opportunity to tell their story before the Truth Commission. It was argued that platforms needed to be provided for all South Africans to tell their stories, and it was in this context that the Healing of Memories workshops were developed as a parallel process to the forthcoming Truth Commission. (http://www.learningtoforgive.com, History, p. 1).

The founder and director of the Institute, Father Michael Lapsley, is an Anglican priest and trauma specialist. He is an internationally know anti-apartheid activist and although White, served as a chaplain and spiritual advisor to the ANC, the African party that formed South Africa's first Black government. According to Nelson Mandela, "Michael Lapsley's life is part of the tapestry of the many long journeys and struggles of our people." Michael actively challenged the hierarchy of the church for its silence about apartheid, was exiled from South Africa because of his politics during the closing years of apartheid, and finally became a direct victim of the terror in April of 1990, when he was the target of a letter bomb and lost both hands and one eye. His long and painful healing process served as inspiration for his trauma work with other victims around the world. In this regard, Lapsley speaks of the "journey" of healing as movement from being a victim, to a survivor, to "a victor over evil, hatred, and death." He argues that if an individual or a nation does not follow such a model of action and healing, the only alternative psychically is for survivors, both individually and as a society, to becomes victims and then victimizers.

The Institute for Healing of Memories runs workshops, typically 3 days long, which bring together former enemies, victims, by-standers, and perpetrators in a context of mutual sharing and self-exploration.

> Emotional scars are often carried for very long, hindering the individual's emotional, psychological and spiritual development . . . The power of the workshops lie in their experiential, interactive nature, and their emphasis on the emotional and spiritual, rather than intellectual, understanding and interpretation of the past. Through an exploration of their personal histories, participants find emotional release and as a group gain insight into and empathy for the experiences of others. These processes prepare the ground for forgiveness and reconciliation between people of diverse backgrounds, races, cultures and religions. (http://www.healingofmemories.com.za, Workshop)

The workshops are highly eclectic, based to a large extent on narrative therapy, the use of expressive arts and rituals, and group process. But their center is the sharing of personal narratives empowered by Lapsley's "journey" metaphor of healing. This idea is particularly well captured in the following excerpt from the Journey to Healing and Wholeness (2004) sponsored by the Institute and held on Robben Island, the site of Nelson Mandela's 27 years of captivity, and now a South African National Monument.

> At all times, the gathering was constructed around the metaphor of a journey. By constructing a process of "healing" as a journey, this implied movement, changes of territory, and attention to differences of experience over time. When people were interviewed in front of the group, the interviewers took care to ask about the differences in experiences of the past in comparison to the present. They also took care to elicit the different stages of a person's journey, including the most difficult periods as well as the passages of relief . . . In these ways we were all invited to consider ourselves to be on a journey, one that would continue into our futures. This orientation captured participants' imagination and encouraged us to revisit territories we have passed through in our lives, the ground we are currently standing on, and the directions we wish to explore in the future. (p. 16)

Forgiveness

At this point it is important to say something about the meaning of forgiveness within such models of healing as well as within the broader context of restorative justice. Forgiveness does not mean condoning or excusing what happened in the past. Nor does it mean forgetting, accepting the behavior of the other, reconciling with the other, suppressing feelings of hurt, or losing one's moral compass or outrage at injustice. Rather, it points to a process of healing within the victim whereby she or he is able to disconnect from destructive defenses and reactions, such as anger and guilt, brought to bear intrapsychically in reaction to a traumatic experience and which keeps the person locked within its parameters. Luskin (2002) suggests a similar perspective for working with anyone who is self-destructively attached to grievances of the past. According to him, "Forgiveness is the feeling of peace that emerges as you take your hurt less personally, take responsibility for how you feel, and become a hero instead of a victim in the story you tell. Forgiveness is the experience of peacefulness in the present moment. Forgiveness does not change the past, but it changes the present" (pp. 68–69).

Luskin's (1999) cognitive-behavioral intervention strategy includes attention to all of the following:

- Learning to view the offending event less personally
- Learning to take responsibility for one's own emotional experience, rather than blaming the source of the frustration for those feelings
- Changing one's grievance story (the narrative about the event that supports a person's negative attachment to the grievance) to an alternative conception which focuses on a choice to grow and prosper instead of suffering
- Identifying and altering the "unenforceable rules" which underpin the grievance story, that is, internal rules that we have for our own and other people's behavior that one really has no control over. (http://www.learningtoforgive.com/)

Reparations

The South African effort at implementing a system of restorative justice involved three components: truth-telling, public acknowledgement, and reparations. The final leg of the process, that is, the specifics of reparations, is only now being worked out by the South African government in consultation with various community groups. Minow (1998) speaks to the possible forms that reparation might take. "The TRC includes a committee devoted to proposing economic and symbolic acts of reparation for survivors and for devastated communities. Monetary payments to the victimized, health and social services, memorials, and other acts of symbolic commemoration would become governmental policies in an effort to restore victims and social relationships breached by violence and atrocity" (p. 91).

Reparations are, thus, acts of compensation offered to victims in an effort to restore what has been lost. They can include financial compensation, the offering of services, and symbolic acts of acknowledgement like community art or the construction of memorials, or something as seemly small and individualistic as providing a mother who has lost a son with a copy of the death certificate. Two additional forms of reparation are restitution and apologies. *Restitution* is the return of property, things, and even human remains to their rightful owners. Apologies are formal statements of regret that include all of the following:

- An acknowledgement of the facts of what occurred
- An acceptance of responsibility

- An expression of sincere regret
- A promise to not repeat the offense

Like compensations, each of these has its potential value, but also its difficulties. Restoration, for example, is impossible in situations where innocent individuals are now living in the former residences of victims or entire communities have been totally destroyed. Or in relation to apologies, who is the appropriate person to give an apology, and to whom should it be addressed? What good is an apology if no real changes have occurred in the material situation that created the atrocities in the first place?

As Joseph Singer so concisely suggests: "Compensation can never compensate." How can a dead child, a traumatized life, a lost past or way of life be truly compensated for or restored? The bottom line is, they can't. Reparations can only be symbolic and at their most effective communicate a society's formal and public acknowledgement of the violations that occurred within it and an acceptance of responsibility for trying to set things right, including a societal pledge of "never again." The ultimate value of reparations as restorative depends, according to Minow (1998), on several related factors:

- First, do reparations serve a role in the continued healing of the victim? Minow (1998) discusses such possibilities.

  The process of seeking reparations, and of building communities of support while spreading knowledge of the violations and their meaning in peoples' lives, may be more valuable, than any specific . . . remedy. Being involved in a struggle for reparations may give survivors a chance to speak and to tell their stories. If heard and acknowledged, they may obtain a renewed sense of dignity. (p. 93)

- Second, how are reparations perceived by the victim and have the specifics of the reparative act been sensitively thought through? If not, such tokens may end up causing more harm than good. Minow gives the example of a Japanese offer of reparations to 500 sex slaves exploited by the Imperial Army during World War II. Most refused the payments offered because they came from private funding sources rather than from the government. Many would have preferred some form of gesture of prosecution of specific perpetrators by the government, such as when the United States put 16 Japanese individuals directly involved in enslaving them on a watch list that barred them from entry into the United States. Others suggest including treatment of their plight during the war in school textbooks as an act of reparation through memory. Similarly, many Jewish Holocaust survivors have refused reparation payments from Germany after the war because they found them demeaning and insulting.
- Third, are they offered with the implication, no matter how subtle, that accepting them in any way minimizes, undoes, or diminishes the harm that has occurred? Minow speaks to this point as follows:

  Nothing in this discussion should imply that money payments, returned property, restored religious sites, or apologies seal the wounds, make victims whole, or clean the slate. The aspiration of repair . . . will be defeated by any hint or hope that then it will be as if the violations never occurred. For that very suggestion defeats the required acknowledgement of the enormity of what was done. (p. 117)

There have been efforts within U.S. history to make reparations to groups that have been harmed by actions of the government. Most notable is the apology and payment of reparations to Japanese Americans for their internment in U.S. concentration camps during World War II. But it should be pointed out that this gesture of reparation did not issue forth on its own; rather, it was the result of 48 years of intense legal wrangling, politicizing, and lobbying by the Japanese American community. The eventual result was the signing of a letter of apology by President Reagan and checks in the amount of $20,000 sent to all survivors. Observers who have reflected on this lengthy process suggest that its most valuable consequence was the return of honor to members of the Japanese American community, which in fact grew more out of their own actions than any governmental perception or acknowledgement of culpability. Efforts for reparations have also been partially successful in relation to Native Hawaiians seeking redress for the overthrow of the Hawaiian monarchy by the U.S. government. Sadly, a variety of efforts by the African American community at seeking redress and reparations for slavery have failed, in spite of Congressman John Conyers's yearly introduction of a bill to establish a commission to determine if reparations for slavery are appropriate, which always lacks sufficient support from other congressmen to pass. Note that in the few successful efforts at redress, the victims, not the government, were the driving force behind efforts to gain reparations. Similarly, none of these efforts was supported by processes of truthtelling or public acknowledgment of facts and responsibility, thus undermining their effectiveness as authentic gestures toward repair and healing. In fact, the opposite might be true. To once again quote Minow (1998): "Here and elsewhere, the process of seeking reparations and facing rejection can create new wounds for individuals affiliated with victimized groups" (p. 101).

■ Holocaust Survivors, Nazis, Their Children, and Reconciliation

Research

No event in history has generated more psychological research on the effects of trauma, its treatment, and its intergenerational impact than the Nazi Holocaust of Jews and other "undesirables."

- There is, first of all, an extensive literature regarding the psychological impact of the concentration camp experience on survivors. One sees in these studies an array of serious reactions that would today be diagnosed as PTSD, including the full range of trauma reactions described by Herman (1989) as symptoms of hyperarousal, intrusion, constriction, and disconnection.

- In relation to the continuing effects transmitted to children, and children of children, terms such as *vicarious* and *secondary traumatization* are used. Research on the children points to high incidents of anxiety, depression, personality disorders, dependence, immaturity, and inability to cope as well as emotional fragility, vulnerability to stress, fearfulness, and lack of trust.
- A second literature, though much more limited, involves the effects of the Holocaust on Nazi perpetrators and their offspring. Research on the Nazi generation itself focuses primarily on identifying internal psychological mechanisms that allowed individual perpetrators to carry out their heinous acts. Explanations of compartmentalization, splitting, dissociation, psychic numbing, and most popularly Lifton's (1986) concept of "doubling" have been offered. Doubling, for example, involves "the division of the self into functioning wholes, so that a part-self acts as an entire self" (p. 418). Thus, in a sense, two different autonomous sides of the individual are created, whereby a Nazi doctor could perform killings during the day, and without guilt or remorse, become the perfect, loving father and husband to his family in the evening. Studies such as those of Milgrim (1974) on conformity, the authoritarian personality complex of perpetrators (Adorno, Frenkel-Brunswik, Levinson, & Sanford, 1950), and Arendt (1964) on the Eichmann trial have focused on processes of obedience to authority to explain the compliance of ordinary German citizens with orders to harm and kill others. Perhaps most shocking about such human possibility is Arendt's notion of the "banality of evil," that is, the idea that what fueled the Holocaust and its killing of 6 million Jews was not a world gone insane or sadistic, but rather the obedience and compliance of ordinary citizens to genocidal plans without protest.
- In turning to the literature on the children of Nazis and other Germans and their intergenerational psychic legacies, one can identify two general reactions: individuals who have split off negative feelings about their parents and the German past or those who are haunted by them. The latter tend to exhibit feelings of guilt, anger at their parents, an inability to mourn what happened and their parents' complicity, ambivalence about the past, and general emotional upset and turbulence.

Little is known, however, about the relationship that exists between children of survivors and children of Nazis, and the possibility of reconciliation between the two groups, or about each group's relationship with their own parents. The work of Mona Weissmark (2004) is exemplary in this regard. According to Weissmark (2004):

> psychological studies have traditionally overlooked how stories about past injustices are transmitted from parent to child, how the offspring of both sides make sense of the stories, the way it influences their identities, and the way in which they rebalance an injustice in their lives. In short, there is practically no research relating to the actual experiences of offspring whose parents inflicted injustice or of those whose parents suffered injustice. There is little research on the quality of emotions or cognitive processes that follow perception of a past injustice. (p. 54)

Central to understanding the psychology of all survivors and their offspring is the difficulty experienced in letting go of perceived or real unjust harm done in the past. Such feelings, in spite of the emotional harm that carrying them causes to the self, are regularly passed on across generations, blocking and negating the possibility of returning to a more psychologically healthful state, or of forgiving and reconciling with former enemies. Such dynamics can be regularly observed generations after the fact of the original trauma.

Seeking Justice

Thus, central to any discussion of healing after mass violence and reconciliation is the question of seeking justice. Most victims and children of victims continue to struggle with a desire for revenge and justice. When someone is harmed in what is perceived as an unjust manner, an inner process is set into motion whereby there is a compulsion to even the score and gain some form of moral and psychic balance. Such balance may require:

- "An eye for an eye," that is, some form of physical or psychic retribution
- A sense that the perpetrator has suffered for his or her acts
- A setting right of the moral wrong, that is, the perception that the perpetrator has learned a moral lesson and now repudiates the belief that once justified the harm that was done

According to Weissmark (2004), ethnic identity and the dynamics of interethnic conflict play a vital role in perpetuating this sense of injustice and the need for revenge and retribution. She points to five processes that exacerbate and fuel interethnic hatred:

- Each side experiences past grievances, injustices, and harm as contemporary; that is, they have been passed down intergenerationally, internalized, and experienced as current threat directed toward the self.
- The worldview of group members becomes one-dimensional, that is, narrows in perspective so that it becomes impossible for the wronged person to empathize with members of the enemy group or to adopt the other's perspective on his or her grievances.
- Only the crimes and injustices of the other side can be acknowledged; one's own acts of violence and harm cannot be judged in a morally balanced way; they are not perceived in a similar light.
- Each side sees itself as the legitimate victim. Weissmark calls this "double victimization."
- The "tunnel vision" just described is also supported by a need to protect one's own group and its values. To do otherwise is often experienced as "letting down one's people and ancestors" or as "being a traitor to the past."

Weissmark (2004) elaborates on these dynamics:

> An individual's sense of justice is never simply a matter of rationality. It is first a matter of feelings in defense of one's self, one's group, and inherent in this is the unwillingness of both sides to face the others'

passions and viewpoints . . . From one generation to the other, each is told stories of unjust acts perpetrated by others, and of the loyal acts in defense of one's own ethnic group and its honorable values . . . We can see that the experience of injustice leaves a powerful imprint upon both sides that continues to be transmitted through the generations. (p. 50)

In reference to the question of reconciliation, is it possible for members of long-standing ethnic conflicts to transcend such dynamics and change perceptions and stereotypes of the other as well as rid themselves of the desire for retribution and the sense of injustice? In her research, Weissmark (2004) addresses these questions directly by bringing together children of Jewish survivors of the Holocaust and children of Nazis. She first studied group members from each side individually, inquiring into four areas of information:

- Developmental histories with a focus on how they learned about the war, the Holocaust, and theirs parents' involvement
- Their reactions to this information and its influence on them
- Their ideas about justice
- Their views of descendants from the other side

Next, she brought the two groups together, 22 Jews and Germans, for 4 days of dialogue and discussion, facilitated by her husband, Daniel Giacomo, a psychiatrist who is ethnically neither Jewish nor German. It is important to acknowledge that in certain circles the idea of bringing these two populations together is viewed as dangerous and as taboo. According to Weissmark, "Many people feared that my study would be interpreted as a justification of Nazism or as a challenge to the Holocaust's status as the symbol of absolute evil. Or as a voice of moral obtuseness" (p. 13). She responds to such charges as follows:

There is a difference between 'understand' and 'condone.' Hearing the other side, seeing another view, only means we use thinking in an open manner, in contrast to a closed biased manner. It means we consider conflicting viewpoints . . . It does not mean we forgive or excuse, or approve their viewpoints or that "anything goes." (pp. 13–14)

Weissmark carefully observed the interaction of the two groups and identified six stages in the transformation of how the children of Holocaust survivors and the children of Nazis perceived and interacted with each other over the 4-day period:

- *Stage 1. Generalizing.* Survivors' children saw Nazis' children not as individuals but as nonhuman stereotypes and symbols of anti-Semitic Germany. Nazis' children tried to explain and justify their parents' attitudes and behavior. Survivors' children refused to believe them and reacted with rage, indignation, incredulity at the possibility that they would ever view the past in a different way. "What was the point of being here?" they asked.
- *Stage 2. Revealing.* The Nazis' children began to reveal personal views about what happened in Germany, condemned the perpetrators, and expressed

negative feelings about their parents. The survivors' children in turn began to question some of their own anger at the Nazis' children present.

- *Stage 3. Distinguishing.* Survivors' children began to distinguish their desire to hurt and make Germans suffer from the emotions and reactions of their parents. They also began to experience the German participants as "good people" as opposed to their perception of the Nazis' children's parents. Both groups began to realize that they shared the experience of being imprisoned by their respective parents' pasts.
- *Stage 4. Discussing the here and now.* Both groups increasingly focused on themselves interacting in the present, in the "here and now," and explored the effects that the other group's words and actions have on them, for example, how it felt to be categorized and labeled by the other side.
- *Stage 5. Sharing of hurts.* Both groups talked in greater personal detail about the difficulties of growing up with their parents and how the experience of the Holocaust affected them. Both began to realize that what they shared was a sense of being victims of the past and that they have paid dearly for it emotionally.
- *Stage 6. Transformation.* As the group moved toward completion, both sides expressed how the group had affected them, the difference it could make in their lives, and how it had transformed their feelings, images, and attitudes toward the other. They also expressed hope about the possibility of working together in the future.

Although these results do not reflect the experience of all group members, they are substantial enough to reflect the possible value of such efforts at dialogue and reconciliation. By way of summing up her findings, Weissmark (2004) concludes: "These statements suggest that despite past injustices and the tendencies to revenge and one-dimensional views, when people experience a measure of compassion for one another person's well-being, a transformation occurs" (p. 162).

When one looks across such group experiences, one begins to discern certain critical dimensions that seem necessary for reconciliation between former enemies so that each can move ahead emotionally:

- Members of ethnic groups in conflict seldom are given an opportunity to interact as equal individuals in safe settings. Segregation or isolation from the other breeds suspicion and creates distorted and dehumanizing perceptions of the other. Interactions that allow one to see the other as well-rounded human beings, not very different from themselves, is critical.
- Perceptions of the other tend to be based on stereotypes and distorted images that engender fear and a desire to avoid contact. Members of the other group, through real human interaction and sharing, can slowly be transformed into individual persons instead of faceless stereotypes.
- Intimate sharing of one's personal narrative allows for the humanization of the other as well as the development of mutual empathy, a critical ingredient necessary for mutual understanding and a hedge against psychic splitting of the world into good and bad.

- Learning to listen to the other is a very important process, as opposed to debating or arguing over the facts of the conflict, which actually serves as a defense against letting in contrary information about the other. By focusing on and expressing feelings instead of thoughts, the sharing of significant and impactful information is more likely.
- Safety and emotional comfort for all members of the group must be considered carefully and guaranteed. When individuals are threatened or feel unsafe in the group, they become defensive, cannot take in information, and may feel the need to blame and attack, rather than remain open to the processes that are occurring.
- In the case of groups with offspring of victims and perpetrators, as in Weissmark's research, it is imperative that the group process serve to help children perceptually detach from their internalization of the parents' experience and attitude and learn to relate to the other as individuals rather than as sons and daughters of victims.
- It is, in addition, very useful to encourage members to speak in the here and now about their perceptions and reactions to others in the group.
- Finally, to the extent that members can develop perceptions of similarities between themselves and the other, empathy is more likely to occur.

■ Summary

Trauma is an extraordinary psychological experience that overwhelms ordinary human functioning. Herman points out that in working with trauma there are always conflicting tendencies to seek the truth and to obliterate it. One sees this within the victim, within the helper, and within the history of trauma research and treatment. Violence and atrocities are typically directed toward the weak and the powerless, and victims will become perpetrators if no healing or intervention occurs. Three examples of efforts to heal victims of mass violence are offered.

The Lakota Sioux are typical of Native Americans who are beset by serious and widespread social problems. Brave Heart contends that her people suffer from historical trauma and unresolved grief passed on from generation to generation. Its source is both massive trauma caused by violence against them by the U.S. government and the systematic destruction of traditional Lakota ways and rituals of grieving. Based on research on Jewish Holocaust survivors Brave Heart created an intervention that included education about Lakota history and personal trauma, introduction and experience of Lakota grieving rituals, and development of positive group identification. The four-day workshops were given to professional helpers and community leaders who would then return to their communities and facilitate similar experiences with their members. Significant positive changes were found among workshop participants. Taking a similar perspective, Duran and Duran argue that Native American men routinely suffer PTSD as a result of their treatment by White society and that improper professional intervention can retraumatize this population.

The South African Truth and Reconciliation Commission (TRC) represents a unique and unprecedented effort at pubic healing through a process of restorative justice. Its goal was national reconciliation after 50 years of apartheid, not retribution. The TRC involved three processes: truth-telling, public acknowledgement, and reparations. In 4 years testimonies were taken from more than 23,000 witnesses and victims, 2000 of them in public hearings. Victims seemed to benefit from telling their stories publicly through a process of breaking the silence, sharing their narrative, experiencing its altruistic function, and reconnecting to others and the world. Mental health professionals aided victims in this process. The testimonies gave bystanders a new awareness of the atrocities that had occurred in South Africa in their names and with their support. Bystander behavior can best be understood as a result of internal mechanisms of disassociation, splitting, and projective identification. Perpetrators' behavior toward the TRC was variable. The intimate link between perpetrator and victim and their interdependency for healing is stressed. The work of the Institute for the Healing of Memories and its founder Michael Lapsley is an example of efforts to continue the work of the TRC. Forgiveness is viewed as an internal process of healing whereby one disconnects from destructive defenses and reactions. The need for reparations including restitution and apology is discussed and the relative merits and difficulties of each is described. Efforts at reparation in U.S. history are assessed.

No event has generated more research on the effects of trauma than the Nazi Holocaust, including its impact on victims, perpetrators, and the children of both. Little information, however, exists on the relationship between these parents and their children as well as how the children of each relate to each other. The role of the perception of justice in perpetuating mass violence is explored as well as its implications for reconciliation. Weissmark's study of the interaction of children of Jewish Holocaust survivors and children of Nazis in face-to-face encounters is summarized. Five stages in the interaction were noted, and suggestions for productive aspects of reconciliation efforts are given.

■ Activities

1. *Explore a personal grievance.* You can do this exercise either individually, in a dyad, or in a small group. Think of a personal experience when you felt treated unfairly or unjustly by another person, one which you found particularly difficult to deal with. What exactly happened? Can you specify the aspects of the experience that were particularly painful for you? What specifically about the experience feels unjust and unfair to you? Were you ever able to forgive the other person or let go of your negative feelings about what had happened? If so, how did the resolution occur? If not, what

is still in the way of moving on and what acts or changes would it take (perhaps from the person) for you to feel you could forgive?

2. *Explore personal experiences of trauma.* Have you or anyone you know ever experienced or exhibited symptoms of trauma, that is, PTSD? Describe the precipitating situation. What happened? How did you or they react? What specific symptoms did you or the other person experience? Was there any treatment for the symptoms or intervention to address what had happened? How did recovery and healing proceed and are there still residues of the experience? How did it affect and change you or the other person?

■ Introduction to Chapters 10 through 14

Avoiding the Stereotyping of Individual Group Members

The chapters that follow are organized according to ethnicity—that is, each focuses on working with a different ethnic community. Chapters 10 through 13 deal with Clients of Color: Latinos/as, Native Americans, African Americans, Asian Americans; and chapter 14 looks at White ethnics. Although adopting such a general "cookbook" approach (i.e., the enumeration of stock formulas or "recipes" for understanding and dealing with a certain group of people) is a convenient way of summarizing a good deal of culturally specific information, it does present certain pitfalls. To begin with, the division of America's non-White populations into four broad racial categories, although a common practice within majority culture, is artificial and serves to mask enormous diversity. For example, Americans who have immigrated from Asian countries do not generally identify or call themselves Asian Americans. They may self-identify as Chinese Americans, Chinese, of Chinese descent, or even according to more regional or tribal groupings. Some may find being called Asian American offensive. The term is, in fact, bureaucratic in origin, developed by the U.S. Census Bureau. It is used here, as elsewhere, for convenience but should not be assumed to imply sameness. In actuality, as Atkinson, Morten, and Sue (1993) point out, the term *Asian American* refers to "some twenty-nine distinct subgroups that differ in language, religion, and values" (p. 195). The important point here is that such broad categories subsume many ethnic groups, each with its unique culture, and to lump them together on the basis of certain common geographic, physical, or cultural features merely encourages an underestimation of their diversity and uniqueness.

Thinking about People of Color through such categories also serves to encourage stereotyping. Such thinking tends to be most common among inexperienced providers who find the prospect of cross-cultural work, at least initially, anxiety-producing. Stereotyping, in turn, is an effective means of reducing what might be experienced as unpredictability in the behavior of culturally different clients. Thus, less experienced providers often project the same cultural characteristics onto all individuals they identify as belonging to a specific group. The thinking might be as follows: "If I can be sure that all clients will act similarly, I can more easily develop a general strategy of how to deal with them in session and, therefore, feel more in control. If I believe, for example, that all Native American clients are reticent, I can prepare myself to be more active in seeking information, or if I know that all Asian Americans are taught early to suppress emotions, I can be on the lookout for more subtle forms of emotionality in their presentation."

Similarly, descriptions of what approaches have been most successful with a given client population can be misread by those who wish to limit complexity as the only approaches to be adopted. In sum, then, taking the material that appears in the following chapters too literally (i.e., as some sort of gospel) limits provider creativity and adaptability and at the same time suppresses sensitivity to intragroup differences.

Instead of assuming unanimity among clients from the same group, a far better way to proceed is to treat all guesses about what is going on with a culturally different client as hypotheses to be verified clinically. "I may know, for example, that alcohol abuse is a very common problem in Native American communities. If I inquire about it and the client says he is not abusing alcohol, I must consider the possibility that his statement is true rather than suspect massive denial. Or in contemplating work with a recent immigrant Latina, I should not assume that she is experiencing serious conflict with her culture's traditional role for women, even though that often occurs. Perhaps she is, but then again, maybe she is not." It is clearly best to hold off making such judgments until one has carried out a thorough cultural assessment to check the hypotheses that the following chapters can help generate.

The Interviews

These chapters contain five in-depth interviews, four focused on working with clients from one of the four Communities of Color and the fifth on working with White ethnic clients. Each is written in conjunction with a member of that community who is a human service professional with extensive experience working with clients from his or her respective group. All were asked to answer the following general question: "What do you think is important, or even critical, for a culturally different provider to know in relation to working with a client from your community?" Their responses are presented according to a number of distinct topics that provide the structure for the interviews including the following:

- Professional and ethnic autobiographical material
- Demographics and shared characteristics of their community
- Group names
- Group history and story in a nutshell
- Help-seeking behavior
- Family and community characteristics
- Cultural style, values, and worldview
- Common presenting problems
- Socioeconomic issues

- Important assessment questions
- Subpopulations at risk or experiencing transition
- Tips for developing rapport
- Optimal therapeutic styles
- A short case study

The text of each chapter was generated through an interview format in which the provider summarizes his or her thinking about the general characteristics that community members share. This is not an easy task given the fact that each racial category in essence represents an array of ethnic groups that are quite diverse. Each interviewee tried to speak broadly enough to fairly represent the cultural and psychological characteristics shared by the majority of the ethnic group he or she is representing. At the same time, they tried to make distinctions among subgroups where necessary. Since no single provider can claim expert knowledge or experience working with all of the subgroups or divisions within any racial category, the interviewees were asked to discuss specifically and draw examples from subpopulations with which they are most familiar. Answers to the various questions in each interview have been left close to verbatim to retain their personal and cultural flavor.

10 Working with Latino/a Clients: An Interview with Roberto Almanzan

■ Demographics

With the 2000 Census, Latinos/as became the largest racial minority in the United States, numbering 35,305,818, or 12.5% of the U.S. population. These figures represent an increase of 58% over the last decade and are in actuality an underestimation because they do not reflect the influx of undocumented and illegal migrants who are continually entering the United States. Garcia (1995) estimates illegal immigration at approximately 200,000 per year. Projections into the future suggest that by the year 2100 Latinos/as will make up one third of the U.S. population. This dramatic growth is attributed to high birth and fertility rates, immigration patterns, and the average young age of the population. As a collective, Latinos/as are quite diverse, including individuals whose roots are in Mexico, Cuba, Puerto Rico, and South and Central America. Those of Mexican descent, now numbering 20 million, make up 64% of the Hispanic population, Puerto Ricans at 3.4 million and 10%, Cubans at 1.2 million and 4%, and Central and South Americans at 3.1 million and 10%.

For the purpose of census data, the government considers race and Hispanic origins as "two separate and distinct concepts." The term *Hispanic* is used to denote a common Spanish-speaking background. A notable exception, however, are Latinos/as of Brazilian descent whose native language is Portuguese. Racially, individuals of Mexican descent identify their roots as "mestizo" (i.e., a mixture of Spanish and Indian backgrounds). Puerto Ricans consider themselves of Spanish descent, Cubans of Spanish and Black descent, and Latin Americans consider themselves as having varying mixtures of Spanish, Japanese, Italian, and Black heritage. In the 2000 Census, 48% of Hispanics identified themselves as White alone and 42% as White and one other race.

Geographically, Latino/a populations are largely urban and concentrated in the Southwest, Northeast, and in the State of Florida, according to country of origin: Mexican Americans in Texas, California, Arizona, New Mexico, and Illinois where they make up a significant proportion of each state's population; Puerto Ricans in large northeastern urban areas; and Cubans in the Miami area.

The vast majority of Latinos/as are Spanish-speaking, are Roman Catholic, and share a set of cultural characteristics that are described later. One must be careful, however, to not underemphasize the differences among groups; there are as many differences as there are similarities. Klor de Alva (1988), for example, points out that "different Hispanic groups, generally concentrated in different regions of the country, have little knowledge of each other and are often as surprised as non-Hispanics to discover the cultural gulfs that separate them" (p. 107).

Compared to non-Hispanics (again, a census term rather than an identity of choice among most group members), Latinos/as tend to be younger—on average younger than 30 years old and 9 years younger than the average White American; poorer—40% of Hispanic children live below the poverty line; less educated—approximately 30% leave high school before graduation (the highest rate of all minorities); and more consistently unemployed or relegated to unskilled and semiskilled jobs.

A unique set of factors related to their entry and circumstances in the United States puts Latinos/as at high risk for physical and psychological difficulties. Included are pressures around bilingualism, immigration and rapid acculturation, adjustment to American society, intergenerational and cultural conflict, poverty, racism, and the loss of cultural identity.

As our expert guest, Roberto Almanzan, indicates a central factor in understanding the psychological situation of most Latino/a clients is their individual experience as well as the experience of their family units in migrating to the United States.

■ Family and Cultural Values

As a collective, Latino/a subgroups share a language, Spanish; a religion, Roman Catholicism; and a series of cultural values that define and structure group life.

Carrasquillo (1991) lists the following shared values:

- Importance of the family, both nuclear and extended, or "familialismo"
- Emphasis on interdependence and cooperation, or "simpatico"
- Emphasis on the worth and dignity of the individual, or "personalismo"
- Valuing of the spiritual side of life
- Acceptance of life as it exists

Garcia-Preto (1996) offers an excellent description of the nature of Latino/a families:

> Perhaps the most significant value they share is the importance placed on family unity, welfare and honor. The emphasis is on the group rather than on the individual. There is a deep sense of family commitment, obligation, and responsibility. The family guarantees protection and caretaking for life as long as the person stays in the system. . . . The expectation is that when a person is having problems, others will help, especially those in stable positions. The family is usually an extended system that encompasses not only those related by blood and marriage, but also "compadres" (godparents) and "hijos de crianza" (adopted children, whose adoption is not necessarily legal). "Compadrazco" (godparenthood) is a system of ritual kinship with binding, mutual obligations for economic assistance, encouragement, and even personal correction.

"Hijos de crianza" refers to the practice of transferring children from one nuclear family to another within the extended family in times of crisis. The others assume responsibility, as if children were their own, and do not view the practice as neglectful. (p. 151)

Family roles and duties are highly structured and traditional, as are sex roles, which are referred to as "machismo" and "marianismo." Males, the elderly, and parents are afforded special respect, and children are expected to be obedient and deferential, contribute to family finances, care for younger siblings, and act as parent surrogates. Males are expected to exhibit strength, virility, dominance, and provide for the family; females are expected to be nurturing, submit to the males, and self-sacrifice (Sue & Sue, 1999). Both boys and girls are socialized into these roles early. Boys are given far more freedom, encouraged to be aggressive and act manly, and discouraged from playing with girls and engaging in female activities. Girls are trained early in household activities and are severely sheltered and restricted as they grow older.

The authoritative structure of the family also reflects a broader characteristic of Latino/a culture, which Marin and Marin (1991) describe as the valuing of conformity, obedience, deference to authority, and subservience to the autocratic attitudes of external organizations and institutions. Individuals from what Marin and Marin call "high power distant" cultures are most comfortable in hierarchical structures where there is an obvious power differential and expectations are clearly defined. Professionals and helpers who disrespect this power distance—by deemphasizing their authority, trying to make the interaction more democratic, communicating indirectly, or using subtle forms of control such as sarcasm and causing an individual to lose face—tend to confuse, alienate, and disrespect Latino/a clients. Respect for authority can also have its shadow side by forcing individuals from high power distant cultures to adapt to the status quo as well as restraining them from asserting their rights. Garcia-Preto (1996) offers the example of illegal migrants whose cultural hesitancy is exacerbated only by the fear of being caught and sent back to more oppressive and dangerous circumstances.

"Personalismo," an interpersonal attitude that acknowledges the basic worth and dignity of all individuals and attributes to them a sense of self-worth, serves as a powerful social lubricant in Latino/a culture. Unlike mainstream American culture where respect is garnered through achievement, status, and wealth, the individual in Latino/a culture merits respect by the very fact of his or her humanity. "Simpatico," or valuing of cooperation and interdependence, is a natural outgrowth of "personalismo." Competing, undermining the efforts of another, asserting one's individuality, and working to inflate one's ego are all viewed negatively in Latino/a culture. In cultures where the needs of the individual are suppressed to serve the interests of the group—the dimension of culture Brown and Landrum-Brown (1995) call "the individual vs. the extended self" (see chapter 3)—the individual ego must be contained, and this is done through "Simpatico," which serves to promote cooperation, noncompetition, and the avoidance of conflict between individuals.

A final series of values in Latino/a culture relate to beliefs fostered by the Roman Catholic church. These include:

- Focus on spirituality and the life of the spirit
- Fatalistic acceptance of life as it exists
- Time orientation toward the present

Latino/a culture places as much emphasis on nonrational experience as it does on the material world. Belief in visions, omens, spirits, and spiritual healers is commonplace, and such phenomena are viewed from within the culture as normative rather than pathological. Latinos/as are also willing to forgo and even sacrifice material comfort in the pursuit of spiritual goals. Yamamoto and Acosta (1982), for example, suggest that the Latino/a church emphasizes that sacrifice in this world promotes salvation, that one must be charitable, and that wrongs against the person should be endured. Sue and Sue (1999) assert that because of such beliefs "many Hispanics have difficulty behaving assertively. They feel that problems or events are meant to be and cannot be changed" (p. 290). This relates in turn to a time orientation to the present that is shared by most Latinos/as. Focus tends to be on the here and now, not on what has happened in the past or what will happen in the future. Present-oriented cultures, according to Marin and Marin (1991), place special value on the nature and quality of interpersonal relationships as opposed to their history or functionality. Such an orientation is psychologically related to a kind of fatalism and particularly common in peoples who suffer economic deprivation and powerlessness and find themselves at the whim and mercy of those with more power.

■ Our Interviewee

Roberto Almanzan, M. S., is a counselor, teacher, trainer, and consultant on diversity and multicultural issues in the San Francisco Bay Area. He has worked with schools, corporations, mental health agencies, and various nonprofit organizations. He also teaches in the multicultural program at the Wright Institute, Berkeley. He has trained with StirFry Seminars in Berkeley, is a key participant in the film *The Color of Fear,* produced in 1994, probably the most widely used film in training and education on racism, and participated in the production of *The Color of Fear 2* and *The Color of Fear 3* as well as a number of other documentaries on racism, privilege, and social justice.

■ The Interview

Question: First, could you begin by talking about your ethnic background and how it has impacted your work?

Almanzan: I am Mexican, and this ethnic and cultural identity has been an influential factor in most facets of my life. It was my experiences as a Mexican American in a White-dominated society that really motivated me to do the kind of work that I do, much of which involves healing in the lives of People of Color, and in the relationships between them and with people of European descent.

I'm the second generation born in the United States. My grandparents on my father's side migrated from Chihuahua in the north of Mexico to El Paso, Texas, on the border. My grandfather was a carpenter. He married my grandmother in Parral, Chihuahua, and in the early 1900s in search of work he went to El Paso, Texas, where he found employment. Shortly he brought his wife and first child to El Paso. My father and other children were born there and in gradual steps over 10 years the family moved to Los Angeles where my father grew up.

My mother's family came from Sonora, a northern state on the western edge of Mexico and settled in Douglas, Arizona, another border town. I don't know much about my maternal grandparents. They both died before I was born. I do know that my mother's father was a successful businessman. My mother's family was large, like many Mexican families. My maternal grandfather owned a large general store and stables in Douglas. All the children including my mother were born in Douglas, so the family was settled there. My grandfather was able to send his eldest son, José, to Stanford University in 1915. However, when the United States entered World War I in 1917, my grandfather feared that his son was going to end up in the U.S. military fighting in the war. He did not want his son to go to war in Europe, so he pulled him out of the university and brought him home. He sold everything in Douglas, moved his family back to Mexico and settled in Mexicali, a city on the border with California.

In the 1920s in Los Angeles, my father was the first of his family to graduate from high school. Some of his classmates from Polytechnic High School went to Stanford University. After hearing about Stanford from his friends, he set his mind on joining them. He was accepted at Stanford and although he had to drop out for a while due to lack of finances, he graduated from Stanford as a civil engineer in 1933. Racism and the Depression made it very difficult for my father to land an engineering job. He finally ended up working for an American company that was doing some surveying in the agricultural area around Mexicali. My mother was living there with her eldest brother, José, and his family. By a miraculous coincidence, the kind that only happens in real life, my father was placed on a survey crew led by my mother's brother, José. It wasn't long before José introduced my father to his eligible sister, Bella. My father met my mother, courted her, and they married. I was their first child, born in Calexico, again on the border in California.

This was the history of my family, a border existence, back and forth, living on both sides. I grew up in Los Angeles but with family in Ensenada, Mexicali, and as far south as Mexico City. We visited our relatives in Ensenada and Mexicali often and occasionally our relatives in Mexico City. They visited us, sometimes staying for extended periods of time. I always thought of all of us as Mexicans. I was a Mexican that lived in the United States (*en este lado*—on this side) and they were Mexicans that lived in Mexico (*al otro lado*—on the other side). I was not aware of the differences between us and the privilege that I had growing up within the United States. So I was shocked the first time my Mexican cousins called me a *pocho*, which is a derogatory term for Mexicans who have become Americanized by living in the United States. They could easily see and hear a difference in me and my life, but I couldn't, not for a long time. I thought I was Mexican. I didn't want to think of myself as different and therefore separate from them. But I was and am a *pocho*. I realized that I was culturally different from my relatives in Mexico.

I grew up in a Mexican barrio in East Los Angeles. We started out in Boyle Heights and moved eastward as I grew older. All the teachers, counselors, principals, police officers, anyone in authority in East Los Angeles then was White. Although there was racism present and a White power structure, I felt fairly protected and supported in my identity as most of the people in my environment were Mexican and I was enveloped in my extended family. It was a White world but in some way I did not really see that until I graduated from Garfield High School and, following my father's footsteps, went to Stanford University. That was 50 years ago. There was no diversity on the Stanford campus then. The need to include American Students of Color in universities or the benefits of a racially integrated student environment did not exist and were not known. The only ones I could see who were non-White on campus were the international students from Asia, Africa, and Latin America. I ended up hanging out at the International House because in a way I felt more at home there and more included.

Question: What led you to become a human service provider and involved in the kind of diversity training you do?

Almanzan: It's kind of a jagged history. When I graduated from Stanford with a degree in international relations, my first job was working for the State Department of Employment (now EDD) in one of its newly created Youth Opportunity Centers. There were at the time various efforts to locate satellite offices in minority communities in San Francisco and other cities and target Youth of Color for intensive counseling and support services in finding employment or vocational training. I worked in these programs for several years, at first excited by what seemed to be a shift in attitude and a desire to do more for people in minority communities. In time, however, I grew discouraged with things that were going on around me. Many of the people we had trained were coming back through for another vocational training program. It seemed like the programs were not working, and we were just going through the motions.

My disenchantment led me in another direction. It seemed to me that what we needed was to build our own economic institutions, engage in economic development for the community, start businesses and employ people from our communities and train them in business practices and leadership. I started a business importing handcrafted sterling silver jewelry from Mexico and wholesaling to retailers. I managed to sell to retailers from the

East Coast to Hawaii but the business never became the multimillion-dollar enterprise that I had envisioned. I worked in this business for 20 years and it supported me and my family but in a way it was not deeply fulfilling. Yet I did not know what other work I could do or how I could transition.

In the mid-eighties I was drawn to the men's movement and attended several men's groups and conferences. I liked that men were encouraged to talk openly to each other about their inner lives in ways that men don't usually do. It was referred to as "men's work," although almost all of the men who participated were middle class, White, and heterosexual. I thought if we are really doing "men's work," where were the Black men, the Latinos, the Asians, or the Native Americans? I met other Men of Color and gay men who wanted more diversity. Together, several of us went to the organizers of a large up-coming conference and challenged them to change it in ways that made it more accessible and attractive to Men of Color and gay men. After a bit of resistance, they agreed, and we created the most diverse men's conference I had ever seen.

My interest in these diversity issues led to a career change. I applied to CSU East Bay (Hayward) to enter their master's program in counseling. Shortly after I was accepted and before classes started, I was asked to participate in a documentary film about a racially diverse group of men talking about race and ethnicity. That documentary film was *The Color of Fear*. After earning my master's, I worked with immigrants, particularly Latinos, at The Center for New Americans in Contra Costa County. I kept getting requests to facilitate dialogue based on *The Color of Fear* and these increased to the point that I had to make a choice between continuing my work with immigrants or to focus on dealing more directly with diversity issues. Although working with Latino immigrants and their families was very satisfying, I decided to focus on the diversity work because it connected me deeply with issues I had been dealing with all my life.

Question: Who are the Latinos and Latinas, and what characteristics do they share as a group?

Almanzan: *Latinos* refers to people whose ancestry lies in the nations to the south, who were originally conquered by Spain in the early 16th century, with the exception of Brazil, which was occupied by Portugal. Except for Brazil, where Portuguese is spoken, and a few other countries with historical connections to other European nations, all share Spanish as a common language. Although many Latinos in the United States today are immigrants or children of immigrants, some Latinos have lived in the United States for many generations. Some families have lived in the Southwestern part of the United States since before it was taken from Mexico in 1848 in the U.S.–Mexican War. Even though many of these Latinos have lost their Spanish language skills, they still share many cultural traits with recent immigrants.

Latinos, first of all, share a deep belief in and connection to their extended families, a sense of family loyalty and honor that's very powerful.

Often, extended family members live in close proximity to each other and family members visit with each other often. When I was young, we visited my grandparents every weekend and sometimes during the week. Other members of our extended family would visit at the same time so that we spent a lot of time with our uncles, aunts, and cousins. This is different from what we see today in the dominant U.S. culture where the nuclear family and individualism are most valued. Among Latinos, the family is often more important than the individual. Extended family members often help each other in whatever way is needed. Sometimes, for economic or other reasons, children may live with an uncle and aunt for a while. In my family, we had different cousins and an aunt live with us at different times.

Latinos also share a sense of basic respect for the person, a sense that everyone merits respect and dignity whatever their status socially or economically. Elders especially merit respect and honor. Elders live within the family, are looked after and consulted, and treated with great dignity. My paternal grandmother, who survived my grandfather, was definitely the head of the family while she was alive. Interactions with Latinos need to convey a sense of respect in order to communicate effectively.

There is also a personal warmth that is expressed between people that often includes physical expression and connection. Latinos are much more likely to embrace, to touch, to kiss on the cheek, to connect with each other physically. There is also a certain generosity and willingness to share what one has with others. Often this is expressed through food. When someone comes to the home, they are always offered something to eat, no matter who it is. In fact, if you are working with Latinos as a provider, it would not be unusual to be brought some kind of food during the relationship, and it has no meaning other than an act of kindness, gratitude, and respect.

Latino culture is hierarchical. Latinos hold authority and those with it in high esteem: doctors, priests, lawyers, therapists, counselors, and any other providers of services. Their authority is respected and listened to because it is assumed that they hold special knowledge that can be beneficial. They are likely to pay close attention to and follow the directions of such authority figures as long as those don't conflict with their values and traditions.

Latinos also tend to be religious, the majority of them Catholic. I remember that my mother always had an altar somewhere in the house where she lit candles and prayed, perhaps with an image of *la Virgen* (the Virgin Mary), a crucifix, and a rosary. Evangelical Christians are not uncommon, and one also sees in some areas, elements of the Catholic religion with native Indian traditions, practices, and beliefs. In Cuba, Dominican Republic, Brazil, and elsewhere Catholicism is mixed with African religions. Santería is the most common and is a melding of Catholic and Yoruba beliefs.

Time also takes on a different flavor than in dominant White culture. Latinos tend to be more flexible about it and tend to experience the precision and narrowness of the White definition of time as overly rigid and often problematic. They don't think of time in such rigid concepts, and this can be a source of conflict. Latinos may not show up for appointments at the exact time specified. Punctuality does not have the same importance and value for Latinos or often for other People of Color as it does for the dominant culture. Time does not take precedence over other matters such as greeting others or attending to personal relationships.

A final difference has to do with gender roles and the concepts of *machismo* and *marianismo*. For men the concept of machismo has been very much distorted and corrupted in the popular media in United States. In its purest form it refers to the sense of responsibility the male feels to care for and protect his family and those around him. Especially in the United States, it has come to mean a sense of bravado, being loud, aggressive, and tough. This is really its shadow side. Latin America itself has been influenced by this distorted image through the media and has come to increasingly see machismo in this way. I remember growing up with this image of Mexican men from the movies I saw and was shocked when I asked my mother, and she told me this was not machismo. She said that machismo means that "you must make sure that your wife and children are safe and cared for and that you always show respect to your elders." Similarly, *marianismo*, the role of women in Latino culture, has come to be wrongly defined by its extremes. It is the tendency in women toward self-sacrifice and a focusing on the needs of others for the benefit of the family as well as to acquiesce to their husband's role as the head of the family.

Question: Could you now talk a bit more about the various names that different Latino and Latina subgroups use to describe and identify themselves?

Almanzan: The two most commonly used names today are Hispanics and Latinos/ Latinas. *Hispanic* is a term that was adopted by the federal government in the early seventies for census and administrative purposes, in order to create a single category for all the people whose origins are in Latin America. It seems to have been adopted more by people in Texas and on the East Coast. It is less popular in California. I prefer the term *Latino*. *Hispanic* doesn't acknowledge our indigenous past, and that's an important part of who I am. I identify more with the indigenous part than the Spanish. My family comes from Mexico, as do the majority of Latinos in the United States. I call myself Mexican American. Many people from Latin America are *mestizos*, that is, of mixed race that may include indigenous, African, Spanish, Portuguese, Jewish (Jews who converted to survive), Asians, and other Europeans. Identification as a *mestizo* is less common in parts of South America, where there is more of a tendency to identity with Spanish roots and with other Europeans. Some immigrants from these countries do not connect with the concept of being Latino or being a Person of Color.

A final term is *Chicano* or *Chicana*. Its origins probably go back to the 1920s and was developed by Mexican Americans who found themselves no longer from Mexico but also not clearly from the United States. It tended to be taken on by the young, coming out of the streets, and spoken with a sense of pride and assertiveness. I am Chicano. I am this hybrid. Those of the middle and upper classes tended to look down on them. They didn't want to be associated with being called Chicano. In the '60s and early '70s, there was a real sense of pride when Mexican Americans called themselves Chicanos. The term was associated with a struggle for civil rights and social justice. It is not widely used by Latinos whose origins are not in Mexico.

The majority of Latinos today, if asked how they identify, would probably refer to their country of origin—I'm Mexican or Guatemalan or Peruvian or Colombian—or where their parents or ancestors came from. There is so much variety that one needs to ask a Latino or Latina how he or she identifies.

Question: Could you describe some of the shared history that Latinos and Latinas bring with them to the United States?

Almanzan: An important piece of our shared history is the fact that we were all colonized. We come from countries that were colonized and did not gain their independence until the nineteenth century. Historically, that's not very long ago. Along with this, there is a sense, that many immigrants carry with them, of having been bullied and oppressed by the United States. There is a long political history of the United States running roughshod over the interests and the peoples of Latin American. One third of Mexico was in fact taken as a result of the War of 1848. This represents the whole of the U.S. Southwest: Texas, New Mexico, Arizona, California, Nevada, Utah, and parts of Colorado and Wyoming.

Even though this may seem like ancient history to many in the United States, it is still very much alive for Mexicans in Mexico. I remember growing up and being aware of a statue in one of the main parks in Mexico City of the cadets who were the last holdouts when the Americans invaded Mexico City. They all committed suicide, jumping from the highest tower of the national military institute, one wrapped in a Mexican flag, rather than surrender. This sense of pride in their history and connection to the past is something that is important to many. For some Latinos— those from Mexico, Guatemala, Honduras, and Peru—this sense of history stretches back thousands of years to indigenous civilizations that predated the invasions of the Europeans.

Many Central American immigrants—who have come more recently— share a history of war, repression, imprisonment, and torture at the hands of regimes that were supported by the United States. Many fled for their lives from their Central American countries and carry emotionally stressful memories of what happened to themselves, their families, or neighbors.

Another shared experience, which we will be talking about at greater length later, is the process of migration.

Question: Let's switch our focus and begin to look at issues related to providing services to the Latino community. Could you talk about factors that
influence how Latinos and Latinas go about seeking help when they have
problems?

Almanzan: First, it is important to keep in mind the great diversity within Latino
culture. When I talk about aspects of service delivery, how members of the
Latino community go about looking for help, for example, I will be making
generalizations that cover many but not all Latinos. What I will be sharing
are general guidelines, but these may vary from case to case.

The Latinos most likely to be looking for help or finding themselves
with problems are recent immigrants and first-generation born in this
country. Latinos will turn to their own extended families for help first.
After that, they will usually go to their church for help. The church plays
a powerful role in their lives, so when they encounter problems, it is often
the first place they turn to outside the family. As much as possible, they
will first try to solve their problems within the family. If there is a
respected elder available, they might speak to him or her. If the problem
revolves around issues of physical or mental health, and the family
believes in folk healers, they might consult a *curandera* or *curandero*. But
in general, they are more likely to first approach their priest or clergyman.

If they are willing to approach an agency, it is usually one that exists
in their community and one with which someone they know and trust has
had some experience. They have seen the agency and know of its existence
in the community. They may know some of the people who work there or
people who know people who work there. They may have family members, neighbors, or friends that have received services there. In some way
there needs to be a personal connection and credibility, often through
word of mouth. They are less likely to seek services outside their community or speak to people who are strangers and not of their community.
Referrals to unfamiliar agencies are most likely to be successful if they are
made by someone familiar to the client's family.

In relation to mental health services, the less acculturated the individual or family, the less likely they are to look for mental health treatment. For many Latinos mental health problems are manifested through
physical symptoms. More obvious emotional problems—anxiety, depression, paranoia—are understood as having had the evil eye put on them
(*mal ojo*), been cursed by a witch (*bruja*), or a case of irritated nerves
(*ataque de nervios, susto*). They don't usually look for therapy and to do so
is often considered shameful.

I have sought therapeutic help at various times in my own life. My
mother was scandalized when I told her that I had gone to see a therapist
when I was at Stanford. She was perplexed and really outraged. "How can
you do this? What are you talking to them about? You're going to talk to
somebody outside the family? What do you think I'm here for? What do you
think your father's here for?" It was scandalous and even offensive to conceive that someone outside the family would know about any problems
within the family. In her declining years, before her death, my mother was

living alone, having a hard time, but refusing to move. She would not leave her house, and we could only visit her every few days. We had a social worker come to see her once every week to listen, converse, and offer help. My mother wanted to believe that she was a friend coming by to talk, which meant she could then talk personally with her. My mother would put out coffee and some food and have a social visit with her. It took her about a year to realize that this was in fact counseling, and she immediately cut it off. Many Latinos—depending on class, education, and acculturation—are just not open to mental health approaches, especially nondirective therapy. If they do find themselves seeing a therapist or counselor, what they expect is good advice, not a free-flowing dialogue or therapeutic reflections. They want to be told what they need to do, what they should do, or where they can access resources.

Question: What are some of the common problems that Latino clients might bring to you as a counselor?

Almanzan: Many problems have to do with the process of immigration, coming to this country and not knowing how the system works. How do I do this? I got this letter from immigration, where do I go? Where can I get some legal assistance? What to do about food stamps? Very much related are the difficulties of learning and understanding English and, as a result, being taken advantage of, for example, by landlords. Being ripped off for their deposits or having their rent raised or given short notice to vacate. Not getting plumbing or roofs or other repairs taken care of. Then there are problems related to dealing with the government and its bureaucracy: driver's licenses, taxes, social security, etc. All of these are issues that have to do with a lack of familiarity with American culture and how to operate within it. Also employment and the fact that new immigrants can only get menial jobs that don't pay a lot and don't have benefits, and that they often have to hold two or three jobs at once and require all family members to work in order to survive.

Many of the clients I have seen are here illegally and are incredibly fearful that they will be picked up and deported by Immigration and Naturalization Service (INS). But even those who are here legally can have continuing difficulties with INS. They get bureaucratic letters concerning actions they must take. Many of them can't read them, let alone understand them. Most of the time when they try to follow through by calling INS or going there, they can't get any resolution. The phone lines are always busy. The lines at the offices are blocks long. They can't afford to spend all day waiting. Most don't have leave of any kind. If they miss work, they don't get paid.

There are also social problems. With migration, children tend to acculturate more quickly than their parents. They are in school, exposed more extensively to an acculturated environment, learn English more rapidly, are attracted to the ways and values of the nonimmigrant children. This inevitably creates separation and conflicts with parents, especially when the values and behaviors that the children are adopting are in conflict with family values. And there are often relationship issues between husbands and wives due to changing gender roles and women having to work outside of the home and children getting involved in delinquent activities, antisocial behavior, maybe even gangs and drugs. All of these social and migration issues are translated into stress, culture shock, self-esteem issues, depression, anxiety, etc.

Question: How do socioeconomic and class issues affect the psychological lives of Latinos?

Almanzan: I have already talked about those who are poor and from lower socioeconomic classes. Often, Latinos who were professionals in their country of origin migrate to the United States but cannot work in their professions here. I have met lawyers and medical doctors who have menial jobs in the United States as janitors and warehousemen because they can't get anything else. For such middle-class people, the experience of such loss, of being reduced in status and income can be very debilitating. They are more likely to seek help, including mental health treatment, because they tend to be more sophisticated about modern culture, having already acculturated in Latin America. They are also in a better position to assimilate because they tend to be more steeped in modern ways and knowledgeable about bureaucracies. Generally, with each generation here and the more education, economic stability, and acculturation they gain, Latinos tend to avail themselves of mental health services when they are needed.

Question: Could you talk about issues of identity and belonging in different generations of Latinos in America?

Almanzan: The majority of immigrants I have worked with say that they are here only temporarily, and have come only to make some money, and will then be returning permanently to Mexico or Guatemala or wherever. Often several family members come together and send money back to the rest of the family. They truly believe they will be doing this for only a few years and then going back. But many of them never go back. I've talked to Latinos who have been living and working here 8, 10, 12 years and contend that they are not here permanently, but there's no evidence of any planning or intention to go back. One consequence of this dynamic is that it keeps them from putting down roots, really learning English, improving their education, and establishing a presence and identity here. For those who do not have the legal paperwork, it makes some sense; they could be deported at any time. For the others it may have to do with a hesitancy to give up their cultural identities or acknowledge the emotional loss and separation that is involved. There are two things that can tip the scales. The first has to do with those who have children that are born here or have spent several formative years here. Their children do not want to go back. They were raised here, identify as Americans, and are used to the lifestyle. To propose a return to the country of origin creates an enormous conflict in the family. People who have been here for a while also get used to the higher standard of living and know that they will have to give this up if they return. Single men who have worked here for a long time often become attached to the new lifestyle and in time separate emotionally from their family back home. They may go home to visit but always seem to return. This conflict in going and coming, in never really separating or attaching, often is never resolved until the next generation.

Question: Next, let's talk about some of the factors that you see as important in assessing a Latino client. What kind of things would you look for, what kind of information do you need?

Almanzan: First, I'd notice if they spoke to me in Spanish or English. My Spanish is not completely fluent, but it's good enough to make myself understood. I would speak Spanish with them if they spoke Spanish. I'd try to find out whether they were born here or immigrated. Each represents a very different type of experience. I would assess their degree of acculturation.

What country did they come from? What is their immigration story? Did they come alone? If they joined family members that are already here, I would know that they are more secure and settled. If they are alone and their family is in Latin America, I would ask how long they have been away. If from Central America I would try to ascertain if they immigrated because of the conflicts in their country. If they have fled a conflict, I would look for evidence of emotional distress.

If they are here with family and settled with children in school, I would expect that more acculturation has occurred. As the relationship develops, I can become more personal. I can find out what kind of home life they have, whether they observe more traditional relationships within the home between men and women, the value placed on education and who is to become educated. I also ask about religion. Are they religious? Most Latinos say they're Catholic, but do they actually go to church and follow the precepts of the church, and how big a role does it actually play in their daily lives?

Question: What suggestions might you have for providers about developing rapport with Latino clients?

Almanzan: When Latinos come to see a provider, they expect to see someone with authority, someone who is knowledgeable and appears professional. They want to see someone who is well dressed, not wearing casual clothes. A male provider should wear a dress shirt, tie, and jacket; for a woman, a dress or blouse and skirt. They want to be treated warmly, respectfully, greeted, and made to feel welcome. It would be good to inquire about the well-being of their family and to engage in social conversation before addressing the issues that bring them into the office. They don't want to be made to feel anonymous, or invisible, a nameless person in the system. They don't want to feel that they are being rushed. They want to see someone who will look them straight in the eyes, introduce themselves, shake hands, and make inquiries about their family.

It helps if they feel listened to empathically. At the same time they expect to be provided with some concrete assistance. It is very useful to develop a list of referrals and resources of services specifically tailored for Latinos, for instance, to help with legal and immigration issues, rent, even food. If you can provide some immediate concrete help with their situation, they are more likely to come back and trust that you will be able to help them next time. It is preferable if you can address them in Spanish, in a formal attitude, but with warmth. At the end of the session I would walk them to the door and offer regards and greetings to their family even though I hadn't met them.

I would be prepared for the person who is coming in with the problem to not come alone, but to bring other relatives, a husband or a wife, an uncle, even children. Again, conveying warmth and genuine interest is critical. It is also helpful to self-disclose. I would say things about myself and my own experience with some of the issues being discussed, even though it may not be done traditionally in therapy. Two last points. If you aren't bilingual, use a translator, but someone who is truly familiar with Latino culture rather than a European American who has learned Spanish. Also, be very aware of appropriate sex role customs. And if you see a couple with a wife with the presenting problems, make sure you spend adequate time giving the husband a chance to speak and a place in the counseling if possible.

Question: Do you feel that there are any therapeutic approaches that are better matched with certain Latino subgroups?

Almanzan: I think that any approach can work well with someone who is acculturated. With more traditionally oriented people I would use a more directive style and would take my lead from them. It is very important to be able to understand their problem from their own perspective, not that of the counselor, and communicate that understanding. Also, be very careful to not unintentionally pathologize them or their behavior. Try to get a sense of why it is problematic for them from their cultural perspective and normalize it.

When I first began therapy in my 20s at Stanford, I was still living at home with my parents. The counselor questioned my living situation and his questioning made me feel that there was something wrong about that. I came to feel very bad about myself and that this reflected my thwarted development. In retrospect I am aware that there was nothing wrong with the fact that I was living with my family at that time. It is a very normal behavior in my culture, and I had been pathologized because of his cultural ignorance.

Question: Are there any subgroups within the Latino/Latina community that are at particular risk for mental health problems?

Almanzan: Research has documented that the closer one is to the immigrant experience, the less mental health issues one has. The longer one has been living in the United States, the more likely that mental health issues will crop up. I find that very interesting. I have already talked about the stress of the immigration experience, but there is also the daily stress of living as a Latino, an immigrant, and a Person of Color in this country and experiencing the impact of racism and discrimination. Together, they wear on one's self-esteem and sense of who one is and what one's values are. But there is more. When people come from Latin America, they have coherent worldviews and coherent cultural values. Living here, these cultural identities and worldviews are taken apart, picked at, and strained. In time they lose this coherent sense of who they are. They try to assimilate to improve their situation. They are pressured to adopt some of the cultural values and perspectives of the dominant culture, and this sets up a lot of conflicts within them and adds to their stress and internal confusion.

As far as specific groups at risk, I think first of the teenage children of immigrants. They are probably experiencing continuing language problems. They may well be doing poorly in school and getting a lot of negative feedback. They are prime candidates for getting involved in gang activity, drugs and alcohol, illegal behavior, and dropping out of school. The dropout rate among Mexican Americans is over 50%. One of every two young persons will not finish high school, even fewer will go on to college. This is an incredibly high rate and a damning statistic when it is known that education is such a key to an individual succeeding in this culture.

Question: Last question. You've shared a lot of rich information with us. Could you finish by presenting a case that shows how it comes together in work with a client?

Almanzan: I would like to talk about a Latino woman I saw for depression whose husband eventually joined her in the treatment. I remember seeing this female client for depression, and it soon came out that there were serious relationship issues between her and her husband. At first she came by herself for two afternoon sessions. She was in her mid-30s, Mexican. They had been in the United States for less than 10 years, probably around 8. They were lower socioeconomic class, with limited education, and had three children: one girl and two boys. The girl was 16, the boys 12 and 10. She came in complaining of depression, of hopelessness. Much of it revolved around surviving financially. She was desperately looking for work without success. Then she found some work and I didn't see her for a while.

After several weeks she called and made an appointment to see me in the early evening because she was working in the day. Her husband came with her but sat in the waiting room as if he was only there to give her a ride in the evening. I was very conscious to attend to him with a sense of respect and to acknowledge that this was his wife that I was working with. There can be a lot of fear and jealousy in such a situation, and I wanted him to know that I respected him and his family.

She complained that her husband often spoke of going back to Mexico, that they were here just temporarily. Even after 8 years in the United States, this was an ongoing conversation in the household. The children said they wouldn't go back. The girl, the oldest, had become rebellious and was staying out late and ignoring their rules. The daughter and what to do about her out-of-control behavior became a central issue in the parents' escalating conflict. The daughter worked at stimulating the conflict between her parents. The mother, though very worried about where her daughter's out-of-control behavior was heading, sided with her daughter because the husband was being increasingly violent with the kids.

She and I talked about what other resources that she might have available to her, about problems with her daughter, about speaking to school authorities about her two boys, and making sure they continued in school. Finally, she asked her husband to join us, and he did. He seemed quite scared initially but he talked tough in the session. He said he was going to straighten out all of the kids and then was openly abusive toward his wife. I intervened, telling him that his behavior was not acceptable. I talked to him about his abusive behavior at home and how that was the source of many of the problems they were having. I tried to help him connect the abusive behavior with his own feelings about his work situation, which was sparse, and his inability to support his family. This was delicate because it was touching on his identity as a macho male who could provide for and protect his family. This was very hard for him to face. He didn't really want to go back to Mexico because there was nothing waiting for him, but he wasn't making it here for his family. I had him talk about the different perspectives on staying and leaving.

The process we went through helped them communicate a little better and lessened the tension in the household. But it did not totally change everything. He still had outbursts of violence, and she eventually decided to leave the relationship. I had given her information on an organization helping battered women earlier and she had contacted them. She left him while he was at work and took the children with her. She spent some time in a battered women's shelter, then some transitional housing, before going on her own.

I saw him alone for two sessions afterwards, and we talked about what had happened, why she left, and how he was going to carry on. I can't say this therapy was totally successful. They were able to communicate better; she found the courage to move out and hopefully become helpful to her teenage daughter. I felt particularly proud that he was willing to meet with me and open to understanding why she had left, for it would have been very easy to blame others, me included, and not return. It was his style to externalize his anger, disappointment, and helplessness, all of which were made worse by his lack of work, the increasing loss of control at home, and his related migration experiences. I did feel he was able to relate his wife's leaving to his own behavior, and that was a big step in understanding what had happened. He left after the last two sessions and I didn't hear from him again. I would have liked to see both of them longer, but in this kind of work clients are often transitory, and it is important to appreciate the small successes and little victories in such difficult situations.

Working with Native American Clients: An Interview with Jack Lawson

11

■ Demographics

The only word that adequately captures the horrors that befell the Native Peoples of this continent at the hands of the White majority is *genocide*. According to Churchill (1994), the population of Native Peoples in the United States fell from 12 million to 237,000 during the first 400 years of this country's history. During that period, the U.S. government expropriated (a fancy word for legal theft) 98% of Native lands. Today, 2.5 million survive, but many are riddled by debilitating alcoholism, high suicide rates, unresolved historic grief, economic hardships, and loss of cultural ways. They represent a true American tragedy.

According to the 2000 U.S. Census, American Indians and Alaska Natives (the U.S. Census category) number 2,475,956 individuals, or 0.9% of the population. If one includes those who identify themselves as multiracial with Native American as one of the components, the number increases by 1.6 million. Over the past four decades, the Native American population has been on the rise. Between 1960 and 1990, for example, their numbers increased 255%, and since the last census count (1990–2000) the population increased by 516,722, or another 26%. Adding multiracial individuals, the numbers leap to an increase of 2.2 million in the last 10 years, or 110%. Pollard and O'Hare (1999) offer a number of reasons for this upward trend:

- Census counting has improved.
- Birthrates are high.
- Mortality rates have gone down.
- Reclaiming of Native American heritage and identity among those who have been passing as White, Black, or another race as well as those with partial ancestry.

As a collective, Native Americans represent almost 500 tribes and 314 reservations. Seventy-nine percent of the population report tribal enrollment. Tribes with the largest populations are the Cherokee (281,069), Navaho (269,202), and Latin American Indian (104,940), followed by the Choctaw, Sioux, and Chippewa. The largest Alaskan Native tribe is the Eskimo (45,919). Geographically, Native American populations cluster in certain regions. Forty-nine percent live in the West, 31% in the South, 17% in the Midwest, and 9% in the Northeast. More than half of the total population reside in nine states: California, Oklahoma, Arizona, Texas, New Mexico, Washington, North

Carolina, Michigan, and Alaska. California has the largest total population with 627,562, followed by Oklahoma at 391,949. The State of Alaska has the largest proportion of Native residents at 19%, followed by Oklahoma (11%) and New Mexico (10%). About half of the Native population is located in urban centers and half on rural reservations. There is, however, extensive mobility between the two locations: city dwellers returning to the reservation for ritual and family business; Indians traveling from the reservation to the cities for work, advanced education, and so forth.

■ Family and Cultural Values

Sue and Sue (1999) identify five values that typify Native American cultures:

1. Sharing and cooperation
2. Noninterference
3. A cyclical orientation to time
4. The importance of extended families
5. Harmony with nature

Sharing and Cooperation

Sutton and Broken Nose (1996) quote an Oglala Lakota elder regarding the Native American attitude toward sharing: "When I was little, I learned that what's yours is mine and what's mine is everybody's" (p. 40). Status and honor are earned not by accumulating wealth but rather by sharing and giving it away. Gifts are profusely given, especially during life cycle events, as a means of thanking others and acknowledging their achievement. Material possessions are freely shared and expected to be shared. Similarly, great importance is placed on hospitality and caring for the needs of strangers. Working for wages is purely instrumental. A native person, for example, may stop working once enough money has been earned to meet immediate needs. Of course, such a selfless attitude toward material wealth and possessions may prove counter-productive in the mainstream economy. Sutton and Broken Nose (1996) describe the traditional owners of a restaurant on the Navaho reservation who were hard put financially because they felt obliged to serve free food to rela-tives, and most people on the reservation were relatives. Related to sharing is cooperation. As in Latino/a culture, competition and egotism are anathema to Native ways. The family and tribe take precedence over the individual, and it is expected that one will set aside personal activities and striving in order to help others. Interpersonal harmony is always sought and discord avoided.

Noninterference

It is considered inappropriate in Native American culture to intrude or inter-fere in the affairs of others. Boundaries and the natural order of things are to be respected. Similarly, stoicism and nonreactivity are highly valued. In regard to communication, a premium is placed on listening. Sutton and Broken Nose (1996) suggest that "silence may connote respect, that the client is forming thoughts, or that the client is waiting for signs that it is the right time to speak" and that the "non-Indian therapist may treat silence, embellished metaphors, and indirectness as signs of resistance, when actually they represent forms of communication" (p. 37).

Time Orientation

"Indian Time" is cyclical, rhythmic, and imprecise. People are orientated toward the present, the here and now, not to future events and deadlines. Activities take as long as they take and have a natural logic and rhythm of their own. "Lateness" and defining time by external clocks and circumstances are Western concepts, the product of a linear time frame. Long-term goal setting is viewed as egotism, and life events are experienced as processes that unfold in their own time and way. As Sutton and Broken Nose (1996) suggest: "the focus is placed on one's current place, knowing that the succeeding changes will inevitably come" (p. 39). Such a notion of time, which has a tendency to frustrate mainstream providers who work on a "tight schedule," interfaces perfectly with the previous value of noninterference in the natural order of things.

Extended Families

Although the specifics of power distribution, roles, and kinship definitions vary from tribe to tribe, the vast majority of Native Peoples live in an extended family system that is conceptually different from the Western notion of family. Some tribes are matrilineal, which means that property and status are passed down through the women of the tribe. When a Hopi man marries, for example, he moves in with his wife's family, and it is the wife's brothers, not the father, who have primary responsibility for educating the sons. Family ties define existence, and the very definition of being a Navaho or a Sioux resides not within the individual's personality, but rather in the intricacies of family and tribal responsibilities. When strangers meet, they identify themselves, not by occupation or residence but by who their relatives are. Individual family members feel a close and binding connection with a broad network of relatives (often including some who are not related by blood) that can extend as far as second cousins. The very naming of relationships, in fact, reflects the unusual closeness that exists between relatives. The term *grandparent*, for instance, applies not only to the parents of one's biological parents but also to their brothers and sisters. Similarly, the concept of "in-law" has no meaning within Native culture because after entry into the family system no distinctions are made between natural and inducted individuals (Sutton & Broken Nose, 1996). Thus, the person one would call mother-in-law in mainstream culture is referred to simply as mother in Native culture. The responsibility for the parenting of children is communal and shared throughout the extended family. Sue and Sue

(1999) point out that it is not unusual for children to live in various households of the extended family while growing up.

Harmony with Nature

Native American cultures emphasize the interconnectedness and harmony of all living things and natural objects. This spiritual holism affirms the value and interdependence of all life forms. Nature is held in reverence, and Native Peoples believe that it is their responsibility to live in harmony and safeguard the valuable resources we have been given. Sutton and Broken Nose (1996) quote the following sentiment from Chief Seattle:

> My mother told me, every part of this earth is sacred to our people.
> Every pine needle. Every sandy shore. Every mist in the dark woods.
> Every meadow and humming insect. The Earth is our mother. (p. 40)

This message, which implies the importance of noninterference in the natural order and stewardship over the environment, stands in stark opposition to the mainstream value of mastering, controlling, and taking what we want from the earth. The idea of spiritual harmony with the natural order also underlies Native beliefs about health and illness. Illness, both physical and emotional, reflects disharmony between the person or the collective and the natural world. Only by bringing the system back into harmony with itself can healing be achieved.

Unlike other Peoples of Color, Native Americans have found it impossible to assimilate upward into American society. While the other Communities of Color struggle to increase their underrepresentation in the ranks of the middle class, in professional and white-collar job categories, in higher education, and so on, Native representation in these groups is all but nonexistent. Why these great disparities?

- First, if one were to construct a continuum of cultural differences with White Northern Europeans at one end and plot other cultural groups in America along that line, Native culture would most appropriately be placed at the far extreme. The radical differences between their ways and those of mainstream White culture set the stage for what was to occur. Their notions of stewardship of the land, fair play, honor, and dignity paled in comparison to mainstream values of capitalism and "might makes right" and made them easy victims in a clash of cultural systems.
- Second, so horrendous were the actions against Native Peoples that the victims needed to be silenced. To accomplish this, Native People were turned into stereotypes: savages of the frontier, drunken Indians, Pocahontas, mascots for sports teams, and emblems for automobiles. Regarding the latter, Kivel (1996) suggests various mechanisms of denial such as minimizing estimates of the number of Native Americans who lived here, questioning the vitality and stability of their culture, picturing the genocide as a natural process with a life of its own, and attributing their demise to biological inferiority.

■ Third, for generations, the government systematically destroyed Native culture and alienated individuals from their traditions and customs. Our guest expert, Jack Lawson, describes this loss of identity and disconnection from tradition as the source of all contemporary Native woes.

■ Our Interviewee

Jack Lawson has worked in the field of alcohol and drug treatment, primarily with Native People, for over 22 years. Currently, he is the Native American Coordinator for the State of Oregon Youth Authority. In this position, he is responsible for establishing relations with the nine federally recognized tribes in Oregon, developing and implementing culturally relevant treatment services, and helping to oversee the Oregon Youth Authority's mission of implementing cultural competency and community development in juvenile crime prevention plans. He has also provided treatment services to Native inmates in the Oregon State Prison System, was lead trainer for the Oregon State Alcohol and Drug Office's cultural diversity training program, and worked as a counselor in a wilderness treatment program for the Siletz tribe in central Oregon. Ethnically, he is a member of the Creek Nation.

■ The Interview

Question: Could you first talk about your own ethnic background and how it has led to your work in alcohol and drug treatment?

Lawson: I am a Creek. My family is originally from Oklahoma. I was born in California and moved to Oklahoma when I was about 6 years old, and then moved back to California when I was 10 years old, where we continued to live. While in Oklahoma, I remember attending ceremonies and gatherings. Feasts, singing, and dancing are part of my memories of that time. After returning to California, I lost contact with my relatives in Oklahoma. As a consequence of moving back to California, I was separated from my Native culture and traditions. I attended public schools all my life, and for the most part, the information I received about Native Americans has been negative and based on stereotypes. Most western movies portrayed us as drunks, heathens, violent, and dirty, which supported the information I received in the schools. I knew I was a Native American, but I didn't have any way of accessing positive information about who I was racially and culturally. Growing up in a situation where I was not exposed to my own culture and traditions left me lost as to who I was and open to accepting what others said about Native people. One of the first signs of oppression is when you start believing other people's version of history about yourself. I seemed to have only numb feelings about my Native identity back then.

Both my mother and stepfather were alcohol dependent. After their separation, my stepfather died in a fire. My mother remarried when I was about 16 and has quit drinking. During high school, I developed an alcohol addiction. I took to alcohol like birds to flight. In retrospect, I realized what I was struggling with was issues of internalized racism and, as a result of it, a variety of self-destructive behaviors. I received my first message about recovery from a couple of Native Americans who were active in Alcoholics Anonymous (AA) while serving in a military jail. After a couple of false attempts at sobriety, I was able to catch onto the program. My first 2 years of recovery were made possible by strict attendance at AA meetings. Several years later, I had the opportunity to attend my first sweat lodge ceremony. Experiencing it seemed to make all the difference in the world for me. It directed my recovery in a way that would not have been possible without access to my culture and identity as a Native person. It was through exposure to the traditions of my People that allowed me for the first time to develop long-term relationships with others and good connections with my community. As a result of this experience, I began to understand the influence of culture and identity in the recovery process and the influence of people who can teach these cultural ways and traditions to us. My own recovery experience taught me what has to happen for other Native People. It has been a real blessing to be exposed to people knowledgeable in the ways of our culture and traditions, who could and did teach me about myself, about who I am, and where I came from.

Having those mentors in my life, with their understanding of Native ways and identity issues, has allowed me to access areas of my life that otherwise would have remained invisible to me. I would have been left with a substantial void inside. Learning how I, as well as my People, reacted to being oppressed by oppressing others and losing ourselves in destructive behavior and thinking has made it possible for me to bring that understanding to the treatment process and to others who are still suffering from mental health and addiction problems so that they, too, can transcend those barriers for themselves.

Question: How would you define Native Americans or Native People as a group, and what characteristics do they share?

Lawson: Native People comprise over 350 different tribes and languages that are unique to this continent. We are both very different and very similar. There is not, for example, one monolithic religion that belongs to all Native People. We have many languages, cultures, and many religions. We understand these differences, as we always have. But today, we are focusing more on our commonalities, on those things that pull us together. Paramount among these are historical experiences. As a group, we have all been systematically subjected to colonization, to the effects of losing our language and our culture, and to governmental policies that have been destructive to our People and eventually led us to a variety of social and health problems. These, in turn, have divided us in relation to ourselves and into differences in levels of acculturation. There are people that range from very traditional to fully assimilated and differ enormously in how they relate to their culture and identity.

Differences among Native Peoples are small in comparison to those things that set us apart from members of the dominant culture. I think we stand apart both because of a value system that is qualitatively different and a set of historic experiences that cannot really be understood by dominant culture. When I take a look at the behavior of Native People, the first thing that strikes me is that we keep to ourselves, are very insular and private, especially in comparison to members of the dominant culture. Some of this is certainly dictated by culture. But for Native Peoples it is also a matter of self-protection. This is because of a shared sense of historical oppression and victimhood. The historical experiences of genocide and culturicide have left a deep mark upon our thinking and feelings, which is all the more tragic because our only "crime" was being on this land first. Everyone else that is in America today has come from somewhere else, but as Native People, this is the land from which we originated. We believe that we were created here. This is where our People have come from. It is an intricate part of who we are: how we define our communities and our mental health. When we view many of the problems that have arisen in our communities, we know they arise because of the loss of our land and our way of life that is so tied to the land. And of all the peoples in America today, we have been the least welcome.

The process of becoming an "American" for most citizens involved willingly giving up one's cultural heritage or identity in order to assimilate into the dominant culture and its values. This has been a very damaging process for Native People. We did not ask to be part of this process; it was forced upon us. Native People experienced enormous and long-standing traumas in their lives as a result of the assimilation process. And it is not an experience that many dominant culture people can really identify with: having your religion outlawed, having your language outlawed, and living in a world that has devalued your very existence. And that brings about feelings of justified anger that are present in our Native communities. Anger is everywhere, and it plays itself out in different ways as our People respond to both historical and ongoing oppression. It comes out in the form of self-destructive behavior, alcoholism and drug addiction, suicide, and homicide. We have become very different as a result of our historical experiences in "America," and these differences have to be paid attention to in the counseling setting. Our mental health issues involve the forced imposition of the dominant culture's value system over our indigenous value system and have resulted in vast conflicts and misunderstandings as well as much resentment and mistrust that exist in our community.

Culturally, Native People tend to be nonintrusive and nondirective. They let people make up their own minds. If people come and seek advice, it will be given, but not offered. Life is experienced as an interconnected entity. Nature, the People, the community all intertwine and depend upon each other for meaning and existence. We also tend to be very spiritual in our orientation, and the underlying force of our spiritual beliefs comes from the geology of the area from which we come. That spirituality infuses the community and becomes its base. It is central to the identity of each person and gets expressed through various religious and cultural practices. The creation stories of each People, for example, are set in the geographic area from which they came. The Navajo and the Hopi believe that they came up through the center of the world, and that center is located in their sacred places. For the Modoc people of central Oregon, their creation story is built around the lava beds of northern California, and they believe that humanity enters the world through the creation center, which is located there. All things come from our ties to the land, and all Native People are joined in their commonality with the Turtle Island, as we refer to the continent.

Question: Could you describe some of the names that have been used historically to describe and identify Native Peoples and the general process of naming within the culture?

Lawson: In regard to names, there are the names that we call ourselves, and then there are the names that other people have given us. Most familiar to dominant culture is the term *Indian*. It is actually a misnomer. It comes from the time that Europeans first landed on this continent. Christopher Columbus mistakenly believed he had landed on the coast of India, and hence, we got tagged with the name Indian, which has over time taken on a pejorative meaning for us. In spite of the fact that the term has been prevalent in describing us, it carries no significance in our world. At some point, we as a People decided to take control of how we identify ourselves.

The process began with the term *Native American,* which signifies that we come from this continent. But then, because we predate the naming of this continent and the Americas, we have begun to look at ourselves as the Indigenous People or First People of this land.

Outside of these more political distinctions, we also have names which we prefer to use and with which we more closely identify ourselves. There are tribal names and affiliations, such as Creeks, Choctaw, Crow, and so on. There are often clan names within the tribes, and then there are individual names: how we identify ourselves personally. Many of us have a Christian name that was given to us. But we also have personal names that are received through ceremony, a spiritual name that is often kept secret and used only for special occasions. It is important to realize that Native Peoples vary greatly in which of the various terms they prefer, and to some extent, our choices say something about where we stand politically and culturally. Some of us still refer to ourselves as Native American, and others prefer Indigenous People. Sadly, there are still many who do not care or feel anything about who they are.

When first making contact with a Native client, it is perfectly appropriate to ask where they are from, what their tribal affiliation is, and how they prefer to identify themselves. I think we get into trouble when we don't do that and start making assumptions or just randomly use a term without being respectful enough to ask.

Asking about this information is probably a good way to begin contact. In mainstream America, people are identified primarily by what kind of work they do. We don't ask people what they do for a living. Instead, we ask each other, "Where are you from?" or "Who are your people?" This is because we come from a relationship-based culture, and our relationships are defined by our communities, our relatives, and our tribal affiliations. We socially locate ourselves by our human connections, not by our activities or jobs. Two last points. Spiritual names are sacred and private, and used only during ceremonies. It is considered inappropriate to inquire about these names unless they are spontaneously offered. In addition to Christian names, nicknames are very commonly used in Native communities. One might go an entire lifetime calling someone by a nickname and never know their given name.

Question: We have already talked some about history. Could you give us a nutshell version of historical events of which a provider should be aware?

Lawson: Historically speaking, Native People have suffered greatly at the hands of governmental policies and the actions of various religious groups. The experience of colonization is not just historical, but is still happening in our communities today. Loss of our culture, loss of religion, loss of community, and loss of family cohesion are contemporary realities. And these patterns, which are the consequences of oppression, continue to play themselves out emotionally and psychologically in the lives of our people. They are major issues that concern us deeply because they involve nothing less than the loss of our identities and integrity.

The boarding school experience is a particularly destructive example. Until the mid-1980s, many Native children were taken from their natural families and communities and forced to reside in boarding schools, where they were isolated from Native culture and ways and then immersed in the dominant culture and Christian values. In these institutions, children were punished for speaking their Native tongue or practicing traditional ways. The motto of the time was, "Kill the Indian, but save the man," and its purpose was to eradicate all traces of Native culture and identity. Once accomplished, the child could be molded as desired, which meant shaping them into White Christians with mainstream values and attitudes. To make the task easier, the government outlawed our religion.

Perhaps most insidious about this practice was its effect on the Native family and its cohesion. When the children were taken out of their families, they were separated from their grandparents, parents, extended family, aunts, uncles, community, and so on. For generations, many Native American children were robbed of the nurturing of their families, deprived of the opportunity to learn parenting skills and other cultural lessons that would have enabled them to raise healthy families of their own. These children were forced to reside in institutions that were harsh and brutal. Some of our elders believe that our many social problems stem from the boarding school experience. Many of the children, as adults, remained isolated from families, no longer able to communicate because their language had been beaten out of them. They felt no comfort returning to their communities and were generally left alone to deal with the many internal issues that had been created as a result of growing up in the schools: low self-esteem, negative feelings about being Native, and a deep self-hatred. We can now see very clearly how generations of such experiences have impacted our communities and made them into what they are today.

We have begun to look at the consequences of the loss of our culture and realize that some Native People have come to internalize the stereotypes Whites hold about them. As a result, they have become those stereotypes: the subtle ones and the not-so-subtle ones, the "drunken Indian," the "lazy Indian." How can all those negative stereotypes not affect us? I am thinking of one of my uncles. He once told me that during high school, he very much wanted to go on to college. He went to see a school counselor and was strongly discouraged from going on. "Native People tend to be better with their hands," he was told and encouraged to pursue a trade. And so, with that advice, he didn't go to college, but went on to a trade school. He also went on to become alcoholic and drug dependent and has since been in recovery. He attributes a lot of his problems to that stereotype and how believing in it changed his life. So for some of us, it is all too easy to live down to the stereotypes and to begin thinking about ourselves in self-deprecating terms—that we are not very smart or that we are only good with our hands and that we are destined to become alcoholic. These issues—residual effects of the boarding schools and stereotypes—are still being played out in our present-day experience. But fortunately, there has been a growing movement among many Native Peoples to regain our self-identity, to regain cultural pride, to regain our self-respect, and to learn about the traditions of our families, tribe, and People.

Question: Let's switch focus and begin to look at issues related to help giving and treatment. What factors influence how Native People go about seeking help?

Lawson: When Native People become involved in treatment programs, it's usually because of some external motivating force. That is, they are mandated either because of trouble with the law, family problems, child protective services, or the like. Generally speaking, that's how most people will come to be involved with outside agencies. Sometimes the tremendous anger and mistrust that Native People feel prevent them from seeking help outside of their community. Sometimes it is discrimination against them that serves as a barrier to accessing treatment. When you do find Native People coming into your agencies by themselves seeking help or assistance, they often are assimilated or bicultural—those who are more familiar and comfortable with White institutions and practices.

As a result of these patterns, there is a movement among various tribes to develop mental health and addiction services within our own communities so that people no longer have to choose between White services or no services at all. The hallmark of this trend is the creation of culturally relevant services. "Culturally relevant" means that the treatment process is infused with Native cultural values, that treatment goals make sense to Native sensibilities, that the need and value of developing positive ethnic identity are acknowledged, and that services are relevant to the lives and daily existence of the people being served. It also means that services are provided in a manner that is culturally comfortable to Native People. This trend is extremely important because the fact is that Native People usually experience less success in programs designed for mainstream White clients. Cultural barriers are a major obstacle to successful treatment in any program.

Question: Are there any other things you would like to say about the nature of family, community, and culture among Native People that have relevance for human service providers?

Lawson: Family structure in Native communities is very different from the nuclear family that predominates in dominant culture. Among Native Peoples, extended families are more typical, where an aunt may also act in the role of the mother or the grandparents raise the children or an uncle is the primary teacher for a youth or cousins are treated as brothers and sisters. Traditionally, responsibility for child care is communal. Also included in the family structure are clans, which are determined by kinship, and bands, which are people living in the same locale.

There are and have been many obstacles for the Native American family. As mentioned previously, the boarding school experience left many people devastated. Many of our social problems stem from them. Having been forced into these institutions, children were separated from an environment where they would have been socialized and reared culturally by parents, grandparents, aunts, and uncles and placed in an often harsh environment which did not recognize Native American beliefs as having any value. Today, alcoholism is our number one health problem with 100% of all Native Americans affected, either directly or indirectly. In the age group of 16 to 21, we lead the nation per capita in suicides and higher than national rates of diabetes. Currently, our average life span is 45. These statistics attest to the problems faced in the Native American community and more privately by family members, and most of these are linked to the destruction of the cultural family.

Other disruptions for the family come from state children services agencies that routinely adopt our Native children out to non-Native homes. Often in conjunction with religious organizations or acting on stereotypical beliefs about Native American families, these agencies disregard the critical importance of Native culture for these children. There are many horror stories from the past of White people coming into Native American communities and removing children. Fortunately, this is a practice that has been stopped by implementation of the Indian Child Welfare Act of 1978, which reestablished tribal authority over the adoption of Native children. Even though our rights have been reinforced, we are constantly struggling with agencies who are working to undermine the law. By these few examples, it is obvious how there has been a basis for the development of mistrust of social service agencies, a feeling that continues today.

Oppression has had a significant effect on our family structure. Some Native People have decided not to teach their children about the culture, language, or traditions because they do not want their children to experience the same treatment of degradation and rejection from the outside world. Others have successfully made the transition into dominant society, taking on mainstream values and religious beliefs and living happily. There are also many who have managed to hang onto and practice cultural traditions and beliefs, learning from elders who have been able to share their wisdom with a younger generation. Some families mix traditional and dominant cultural ways. Clearly, we are a community in transition, adjusting to significant changes in social structure and identity, with much from the past to set right. But in spite of the historical and contemporary obstacles, our Native community is healing itself. We have weaknesses and strengths within the Native families. We have oppression and discrimination to overcome. We have social problems with addiction and abuse. But our People are making a comeback in pride and dignity by reclaiming indigenous family values and recovery.

Question: What are the kinds of problems with which a Native client might present?

Lawson: One hundred percent of Native People are affected either directly or indirectly by alcoholism. Underlying this are a host of complex problems related to the loss of culture, identity, and disruption of the family unit, all symptomatic of a long history of genocide and oppression. There are also a lot of anger and anger-related issues, depression and hopelessness, health problems, and unusually high rates of suicide and homicide, especially among the young. There has also been a serious increase in the diagnosis of HIV in our community, mostly related to IV drug use. Among Native People who are incarcerated, alcohol and drugs are a major contributor to their incarceration.

Question: Do class or other socioeconomic issues play any role in these various problems?

Lawson: Definitely. Unemployment rates can be astronomical on a reservation, and the same is true for Native Peoples living in urban areas. The Relocation Act of the 1940s was one in a series of efforts by the government to encourage Native Peoples to leave the reservation, move to cities where jobs are more plentiful, and become part of the American mainstream. That was the ultimate goal. However, the reality was not quite as simple as that. Although some did relocate successfully, many found the experience traumatic. In the move from reservation to city, many traditional ties were lost. Kinship ties weakened with distance, and some people became disassociated from their relatives and community. Many ended up living marginal existences in the skid row areas of cities, and those who followed them from the reservations would tend to migrate toward these same enclaves. What the logic of the Relocation Act did not envision was the reality that most of these people, familiar with a very different kind of existence, did not have the dominant cultural tools to survive successfully, let alone prosper in such a foreign environment where they were met with substantial discrimination and rejection.

The move to the city was also instrumental in cutting off many from traditional cultural ties to their People. In addition, certain patterns of connection between the reservation and urban settings began to emerge. First, it was not uncommon for individuals to move back and forth between the two, and for many, this became a lifelong pattern. Second, animosities and various conflicts developed between people from these increasingly divergent lifestyles, with each looking down on the other. In general, some people in the urban centers may tend to view those on the reservation as backward, their ways antiquated, rustic. Those on the reservation in turn tend to see the urban dwellers as having lost their way, as suffering from the same malaise as the White man. Today, increasing numbers of Native People are returning to their traditions and culture in both locations and striving for unity.

There is an important cultural point here as well. In mainstream culture, success is measured in economic terms, and socioeconomic success implies a certain lifestyle that depends on having sufficient monetary resources, accumulating wealth, regular employment, living according to a certain style, and so forth. Our traditional cultural values are very different from this. Our wealth is located in the richness of our culture, tradition, ceremonies, and in the richness of our lifestyle. Difficulties arise when a person tries to live by a cultural value system that is not based on material economic gain within a broader culture that is so absolutely dedicated to it. These are not value systems that are easily integrated. Such clashes set the stage for Native Peoples losing our lands and having our language and culture outlawed in the first place. Today, we struggle with a similar conflict around remaining attached to our traditional way of life that cares little about accumulating economic wealth. It comes down to the question of divergent value systems. Those who are bicultural know what they would need to do to be successful, and that would be to eliminate their culture and perform accordingly, but that would go against their beliefs, which are based in indigenous culture and tradition. The integration of two such diverse value systems is difficult, to say the least.

Question: In making an initial assessment, what kinds of information do you feel it is important to collect from a Native client?

Lawson: Before getting too specific, I want to say something about cultural perspective and worldview. During any assessment process, it is *vital*—I can't emphasize this enough—that counselors and other human service providers be aware of their own cultural values, biases, and barriers, and understand clearly how they themselves have been influenced by culture. All behavior is derived from a cultural context, as are treatment programs. If one is going to assess a client whose worldview is culturally different from one's own, then it is likely that if the client displays culturally relevant behavior, it may well be labeled as "deviant" or "abnormal." For example, in dominant culture, a firm handshake is seen as a sign of honesty, sincerity, and straightforwardness, whereas if one encounters a person of traditional Native beliefs, a firm handshake is avoided because in our culture it is sometimes seen as being intrusive, rude, overbearing, and impolite. However, someone assessing that behavior from a dominant cultural perspective might construe it as reflecting dishonesty, nonassertion, withdrawal, and evasiveness. When working with people from different cultures, it's always important to validate their experience and existence in terms of their own cultural perspective. In order to do this, we as service providers must be aware of our own culture and how that culture affects our lives.

Assessments must be carried out within the framework of the client's own culture. It is important, however, to not let the client be your only source of information about their culture. This information needs to be balanced with information from their community as well. It's necessary that you reach out to our communities and listen to the people. It has been my experience that the more you learn about another's culture, the more open they are to you. Learn as much as you can. You get that information from the community through developing relationships. Go to the communities and events and develop relationships. This doesn't mean that you have to give up your own cultural values or beliefs. It does mean that you should be able to understand and respect beliefs of others and evaluate their behavior from within their cultural context.

Perhaps the most important piece of information to gain about Native clients is where they fall on a continuum from assimilated to traditional. People that are assimilated will often feel uncomfortable around their own People, not knowing the behaviors and what is expected of them. They appear to be Native and possess all the physical features of being Native, but internally they're different. They may feel uneasy because of their lack of knowledge of traditional ways and may feel unaccepted because of it. Assimilated individuals tend to act differently than those who live by traditional values and possess a traditional belief system. The assimilated person may appear more talkative and open, even though there might be distrust. They will be the ones who know the rules of the program and of society in general. In short, they will have learned what one needs to do within dominant culture to survive. Traditional Native People present themselves as more reserved and quiet. But rather than being indicative of withdrawal, it comes from a cultural value of respect, nonintrusiveness, and honor.

What kind of information should you seek from a client? There is all the standard assessment material. Who was a person raised by? Family structure? Religion? But with Native People, what is important is to interpret this information through the filter of how they see themselves culturally.

This would include identity development, involvement with the community, involvement with family, how family views its situation, whether or not traditional beliefs are practiced. Again, the distinction between assimilated and traditional is important because treatment methods may differ according to where a person falls on that continuum. By way of example, there was a doctor in Seattle who noticed that Native People weren't recovering as fast in the hospitals as he felt they should. They regularly spent longer periods in the hospital. One of the things he did was go to the elders of the Native community and started incorporating medicine people and traditional healers as part of the treatment process in the hospital. And recovery times shortened dramatically.

Question: Are there subgroups within the Native community that are particularly at risk?

Lawson: I believe that all Native People, especially children, are at risk for developing alcoholism or some other form of dependency. There are physiological issues—social, economic, and emotional ones as well. They have been passed down from generation to generation and together create a "lump sum" of a risk for us as Native People. At one time, it was prevalent in our communities to accept alcoholism as a way of life. That is how we tended to cope with oppression and the discrimination in our lives. It became part of our continual grieving process. Although in many places this is still the norm, there are many of us who are beginning to take more control over our lives and find recovery.

Question: What suggestions can you give regarding developing rapport with Native clients?

Lawson: I believe we have to be aware of our own prejudices and biases and the way we regard people who are culturally and racially different from us. It is not a matter of learning to say or do the right things. Instead, we have to be aware of ourselves and the underlying issues that affect our clients. It's not about having to learn all the ins and outs. We are dealing with a very diverse population. It's impossible for me to say: "Well, this is the one thing you will need to say, or this is the one thing that you do in order to develop rapport." I would be merely creating a new stereotype.

We are all going to make mistakes, and mistakes are a common thing in working with diverse cultures. But if one really comes from a place of acceptance and respect as a care provider, then that is going to translate into developing rapport with clients. As helpers, we all have a goal in mind: helping to develop a therapeutic relationship so that clients can heal themselves. But there is more than one road we can travel to get to the same place.

In order to develop rapport with Native clients, one has to learn to not be afraid of their anger. You can be sure that there is going to be mistrust and anger that may very well be directed toward you personally as a White provider. But if you can tolerate it, not be frightened by it, and just allow it to be expressed as honest communication, you will be on the road to making a connection. There is the possibility the client will see you as part of the White establishment and, as such, unlikely to be of any real help. Remember: Historically, Native Peoples have had their feelings discounted, been patronized and demeaned, and chronically abused by the system. You may be witnessing justified anger running rampant. In short, you may be stereotyped and lumped into this category of the enemy. The only way to get beyond this is to acknowledge your Whiteness and the feelings they are likely to project onto you as well as your general understanding of what they have experienced as a people. But be clear, the walls are not going to come down overnight, but only with time and patience. In addition, becoming aware of the effects oppression has on a people will aid in understanding self-destructive behavior, such as addiction being systemic to oppression.

Question: What else is important to know about working therapeutically with Native clients?

Lawson: I have provided services to both White and Native clients, and there are clearly some important differences. In the White groups, traditional counseling methods are effective. I am more direct and confrontational here, and the clients tend to respond positively. I use a very different approach with Native clients. We sit in a talking circle, but it is the issues we talk about that are important. The issues have to do with Native culture, identity, how they see themselves as Native People, the effects of stereotyping, justified anger, positive identity development, and ceremony. And we use ritual objects and ceremonies as part of the process: eagle feathers and pipes, smudging, sweat lodges, and so on, introducing our culture into the treatment process and acknowledging what they are going through ritually and with ceremonies. Such a process fits naturally with our cultural understanding of health and sickness. We also discuss the effects of oppression, while at the same time addressing the issues around denial, relapse prevention planning, and recovery maintenance.

As far as therapeutic styles with Native People, you will most likely be working with those who either know nothing of their culture or are bicultural. In both cases, I find that traditional counseling methods generally prove effective, but with the incorporation of cultural material. My approach with Native Americans is to use culture as an avenue to recovery because loss of culture and identity is the most basic problem that Native People face. In this regard, I assist clients in identifying their culture, how it has influenced them, how they came to lose touch with it, and how they may become reconnected to their culture. I also have them identify where they stand along the continuum between traditional and assimilated. At times, I come across clients who hide their issues behind culture or try to use it to get something for themselves. They use it as a "front," as a means of not dealing with treatment issues. The value of culture and community is not about what it can get you, but who you can become because of it. The challenge for non-Native service providers is to know the difference between clients using culture as a defense and when the Native culture is genuine.

I provided culturally relevant treatment services for the Native Americans incarcerated within the Oregon Department of Corrections who are dealing with their addictions. As a part of those services, I conducted a weeklong alcohol and drug workshop and ongoing treatment groups that focus on Native American spirituality, ceremony, and recovery. As a part of the workshop, we utilized the talking circle, drumming and singing, sweat lodge ceremony, smudging with sweet grass or sage, use of eagle feathers and other sacred objects, and discussed issues that are relevant to their recovery. Through this service, many Native inmates have been given their first positive encounter with Native American culture and tradition. I believe this is an important thing to offer them: to be able to get in touch with their culture and to be able to have some experience with their traditions. Again, I see that as critical to recovery for Native American clients. But there are some diverse opinions about this within our communities. Some of our elders say, "They never sought out the culture while they were in the community. Why should we go to the institutions to provide them with anything cultural? When they get out of the institution, let them come to us." That's a valid point. But at the same time, I feel that it's important for a person's recovery to develop some cultural awareness. The issue of them learning it in the institutional setting is that often much of the learning comes from other inmates. So, information can get contaminated inside institutions.

Similar dynamics can occur in treatment in general, and that's why it's important for non-Native providers to have connections and resources in the Native community. It is clearly not productive for providers to exclusively learn about Native culture from their clients. Contact with the community will also give you a certain credibility. In working with our People on a regular basis, you just have to get out of your office and make contacts. We are a relationship-based culture.

Question: Finally, could you present a case that brings together the different issues and dynamics about which you have been talking?

Lawson: I am thinking of a client I'll call Joe. Joe came to a program that I once worked called Sweathouse Lodge. It was an inpatient alcohol and drug treatment program that focused heavily on traditional Native modes of healing. We used sweat lodges, brought in traditional people to speak, brought in medicine people, hosted spiritual gatherings, took clients to powwows, and did a lot of resocialization work. When Joe entered the program, he was 25 and very angry and mistrustful, not only toward the system, but toward the program as well. He had developed a severe alcohol and drug problem by the age of 17. His family had a long history of alcoholism. His parents knew nothing about their culture and traditions, and although he had a grandfather who was very traditional, he had only limited contact with him. Joe was mandated to the program by court order and was initially very resistant to treatment. While in the program, he experienced his first sweat lodge ceremony. It was a very positive experience for him, and he reported that during the ceremony, he felt for the first time some connection with his Native heritage and the value it might have for him. This motivated him to seek out further information about his own culture and traditions. In group therapy, he revealed harboring prejudicial and destructive thoughts about being Native. As a result of growing up in an alcoholic home, he had learned to equate being Native with being drunk and violent, as these were the only role models he had.

Through continuing positive contact with Native culture, both in the form of ceremonies and positive role models, he was able to begin to distinguish between what was truly cultural and what was internalized from negative stereotypes of Native People and culture. This in turn enabled him to develop a more positive cultural self-image, something which was totally lacking before coming to the program. He increasingly took pleasure in attending sweat lodge ceremonies, learned to drum and sing, learned more about Native values, and in time began to work at incorporating these values in his treatment plan. He became more open to attending Alcoholics Anonymous (AA) and Narcotics Anonymous (NA) meetings and eventually involved himself more and more in the Native community. As part of treatment, he received a lot of very direct feedback from other Native clients and staff. He found it very helpful to hear others who had gone down a similar path of alcoholism and dysfunction "call him" on his self-destructive behavior, attitudes, thinking patterns, and lifestyle.

The eventual result was better feelings about himself, an emerging ethnic identity, and a positive sense of belonging to the Native community. During group therapy, he was able to make the connection between his own self-destructive ways and the lack of culture and traditions in his life. In short, participation in the program forced him to experience a powerful identity crisis and reformation, and it gave him an outlet and place to experience feelings that he thought were unique to him. After completion of the program, Joe continued to seek out sweat lodges and remained actively involved in community events. He has begun to take on some communal leadership roles and actively strives to encourage others to find recovery through their culture and traditions.

12

Working with African American Clients: An Interview with Veronique Thompson

■ Demographics

The term *African American* subsumes a diverse array of peoples including African Americans born in this country, Africans, and individuals from the West Indies and Central and South America. The 2000 Census numbers African Americans in the United States at 34,658,190, or 12.3% of the population. Since the time of slavery, they have been this country's largest minority until the 2000 Census when they were passed by Latinos/as with 12.5% of the population. Projections show African Americans increasing to 13% by 2010 and leveling off at 13% into mid-century. They are the most widely dispersed ethnic group in the United States, both geographically and economically. In 1997, for example, 55% lived in the South, 36% in the Northeast and Midwest, and 9% in the West. Although most African Americans are descendents of families who have been in the United States since the time of slavery, immigration has been slowly increasing over the last two decades, leading to increasing levels of linguistic and cultural diversity. Immigrants from former British Caribbean colonies bring with them a mixture of African and British customs, and those from former Spanish, French, and Dutch colonies do the same. In 1980, only 3% were foreign-born. By 1998, the figure had risen to 5% with most of the increase coming from immigration from the Caribbean. Projections predict increasing immigration from sub-Saharan Africa. Previous immigration from Africa has come primarily from Nigeria, Ethiopia, Ghana, Kenya, and Morocco (Pollard & O'Hare, 1999). Such diversity leads Hines and Boyd-Franklin (1982) to warn providers against assuming the existence of a "typical" African American family.

■ Family and Cultural Values

Black (1996) points to four factors that have shaped African American experience and culture:

- African Legacy, rich in culture, custom, and achievement
- History of slavery and deliberate attempt to destroy the core and soul of the people
- Racism and discrimination and ongoing efforts to continue the psychological and economic subjugation started during slavery

- Victim system and process by which individuals and communities are denied access to the instruments of development and advancement (p. 59)

Black slaves brought with them a rich amalgam of cultures from West Africa, and according to Hilliard (1995), rather than eradicate African culture and consciousness, slavery actually served to preserve it. Aspects of an African worldview still infuse African American life: a deep religiosity and spirituality, cooperation and interdependence, and a oneness with Nature. According to Marshall (2002), enslavement added a complex of core values and attitudes: emphases on resistance, freedom, self-determination, and education. African culture also contributed a tradition of strong family structure in which extended families and close-knit kinship systems were the basis for larger tribal groupings.

According to researchers who have worked to adapt family therapy practices to the cultural realities of African American families, three strategies are critical:

- Understand the cultural context of the family
- View differences in family dynamics as adaptive mechanisms and strengths
- Develop practices that take into account the needs, cultural dynamics, and style of African American culture

Further, these researchers favor interventions that mobilize existing family structures and are opposed to creating new forms similar to those found in White families. Hill (1972) identifies the following three factors as positive strengths to be built upon.

Kinship Bonds

Most African American families are embedded in complex kinship networks of blood and nonrelated individuals. Stack (1975) found patterns of "coresidence, kinship-based exchange networks linking multiple domestic units, elastic household boundaries, and a lifelong bond to three-generation households" as typical (p. 124). White (1980) points to a series of "uncles, aunts, big mamas, boyfriends, older brothers and sisters, deacons, preachers, and others who operate in and out of the Black home" (p. 45). Such extended patterns and the multiple resources they provide must be acknowledged and worked with by family therapists as a legitimate locus of intervention. Key family members must be identified and included in the treatment planning, even if they do not fit traditional definitions of the family. It is critical that they play significant roles in the family system. One is reminded of Elena's godfather in the case study of the Martinez family in chapter 4.

Hines and Boyd-Franklin (1982) and Boyd (1982) suggest the use of genograms or family trees to map out the roles of family actors and their relationships and conflicts. Caution, however, should be exercised in the collection of such data because African American families are often suspicious of "prying" professionals. These authors suggest delaying data collection until adequate trust has been developed and that information be sought in a natural as opposed to a forced manner. Extended kinship bonds also suggest the usefulness of working with subgroups of the extended family and including only those who are directly relevant to a particular issue. It may also be necessary to schedule family sessions in the home to include key figures who cannot or will not visit clinics. Again, entering the home, like seeking information, should be done with sensitivity in light of past abuses of the welfare system against poor families.

Role Flexibility

Role flexibility within the African American family, like extended kinship bonds, is highly adaptive for coping with the stresses of oppression and socioeconomic ills. It is most evident in the greater role diversity found among African American men and women as well as in the existence of unique familial roles such as the *parental child*. African American males traditionally have been seen by social scientists as "peripheral" to family functioning (Moynihan, 1965). Hill (1972), among others, has challenged this notion. He argues that the father's frequent absence from the home reflects a lack of neither parenting skill nor interest, but rather the time and energy required to provide basic necessities for the family. The father's precarious economic position coupled with the need for African American females to work outside the home often lead to extensive role reversals and flexibility in childrearing and household responsibilities. These circumstances have led White (1972) to suggest that, as a result, African American children may not learn as rigid distinctions between male and female roles as their White counterparts. In approaching therapy, Hines and Boyd-Franklin (1982) caution against routinely excluding the father, as has frequently been the case with those who subscribe to the myth of peripheralness. Instead, they suggest doing everything possible to include him, even if for only a single session. They encourage the therapist to regularly keep him abreast of events and developments in therapy when he is unable to attend. They also caution against assuming the absence of a male role model when the father has abandoned the family. Given the variety of extended family figures, someone often emerges to fill this role.

While the African American male has been viewed as peripheral, the African American female, often forced to assume responsibilities well beyond those typically taken on by White women, has frequently been mislabeled as overly dominant. African American couples are, in fact, often more egalitarian than their White counterparts. Scanzoni (1971), for example, found that, more often than Whites, Black males and females grow up with the expectation that both will work. Minuchin, Montalvo, Guerney, Rosman, and Schumer (1967) offer some interesting insights into the dynamics between African American males and females. Discord tends to be dealt with indirectly and not through direct confrontation. Solutions to long-term disharmony are typically informal, and long periods of separation may occur without the thought of divorce.

African American couples tend to remain together for life, often for the sake of the children, and typically seek therapy for child-focused issues rather than for marital dissatisfaction. In spite of ill treatment by a husband, African American women tend to resist the dissolution of a relationship. Hines and Boyd-Franklin (1982) suggest that this may result from three factors:

- Greater empathy for the husband's frustration in a racist society
- Awareness of the extent to which they outnumber Black males
- Strong religious orientation that teaches tolerance for suffering

Economic demands and oppressive forces have, in addition, created unique roles in the African American family. Included are the parental child, which involves parental responsibilities allocated to an older child when there are many younger children to attend to or when both parents are absent from the home for considerable amounts of time, and the extended generational system of parenting, in which the parent role is shared and distributed across several generations living in the home. It is important to emphasize that such adaptive strategies within the African American family, while clearly a potential positive force, can in themselves become sources of problems that require intervention. This occurs when their intended function becomes distorted, overused, or rigidified. According to Pinderhughes (1982), "if the mother's role is overemphasized . . . it can become the pathway for all interactions within the family. This requires children to relate primarily to her moods and wishes rather than to their own needs. The result is emotional fusion of the children with the mother . . ." (p. 113). Or parental children can be forced to take on responsibilities well beyond those of which they are capable and at the expense of necessary peer group interactions (Minuchin, 1974). Or shared parenting in the multigenerational family can become highly chaotic or a source of open conflict and dispute. In each of these cases, the goal of therapy should not be to eliminate or "repair" the adaptive pattern (i.e., to move the family closer to White middle-class norms). Such patterns may, in fact, be necessary for family survival. Rather, the goal should be to set it back on its purposeful course so that it can once again function as intended.

Religion

Religion is an extremely important factor in the life of the African American community and provides a valuable source of social connection as well as self-esteem and succor in times of stress. According to Boyd (1977), however, it is frequently overlooked by clinicians in therapy. Specifically, religious issues are seldom discussed; African American families seeking help from mental health agencies may be unconnected to church networks; and clients may dichotomize problems as appropriate for discussion either with ministers or with mental health professionals. For clients with elaborate church connections, such networks can represent valuable resources. This might include seeking necessary information from religious leaders, calling on the network for help and resources during times of crisis, or including ministers as "significant others" in therapy or as cotherapists. In addition, religiosity is not infrequently related to a family's presenting problem. For example, Larsen (1976) reports the case of a highly religious family dealing with the rejection of religion and traditional values by a rebellious preadolescent. An understanding of its impact on behavior (e.g., strict adherence to harsh physical punishment and discipline of children based on religious maxims such as "spare the rod and spoil the child") is critical to any potentially successful therapeutic intervention.

The trauma of slavery and a long history of racism have shaped and defined the African American experience in the United States. It is impossible to understand the African American psyche without keeping these two events clearly in mind. Kivel (1996) states the facts of slavery quite succinctly: "From 1619 until slavery ended officially in 1865, 10–15 million Africans were brought here, and another 30–35 million died in transport" (p. 121). The magnitude is staggering and even difficult to conceive. But that is not even the full story; there was also the systematic destruction of African culture and identity by the slavers and slave masters, the tearing apart of families, the creation of myths of inferiority and subhuman status to justify what was being done, and an entire nation that benefited greatly, economically and socially, from this cruel institution.

Racism replaced slavery as a vehicle for the continued exploitation of African Americans as well as a justification for continuing to deny them the equality guaranteed by the U.S. Constitution. As a people, they survived, grew strong, and fashioned a new culture in America but continue to this day to pay an awesome price for the color of their skin. Hacker (1992) argues that the United States is functionally "two nations," Black and White, and that there is an enormous disparity in the access that these two groups have to the resources and benefits of this rich nation. The long list of statistical inequities—from average salaries to unemployment, from incarceration figures to education levels, from teenage pregnancies to poverty statistics—is staggering. For example, poverty rates among African Americans is almost three times that of Whites; life expectancy is 6 years shorter; and infant mortality rates are twice those of Whites, Asians, and Latinos/as. African American households receive the lowest annual median income at $25,100 and African American men experience the highest rate of unemployment among ethnic minorities. African Americans have, in turn, been the "point men" for the struggle that has been waged against the inequality and social injustice that continues to exist in this country. Through the Civil Rights and various other social movements, they have been the voice of conscience in America, not allowing it to forget the grave injustices that are still very much alive. As Kivel (1996) suggests, they have been the "center of racial attention," and all other oppressed groups have learned from and modeled their fights after that of African Americans. But it is little wonder, as our guest expert Veronique Thompson points out, that African Americans mistrust and avoid seeking help from established White agencies and institutions. Their motives and agendas, throughout history and into this day, have just not proved to be trustworthy.

■ Our Interviewee

Veronique Thompson, Ph.D., received her training at Spelman College and the University of California, Berkeley, where she held several distinguished minority fellowships. She is a licensed clinical psychologist and a tenured faculty member at the Wright Institute in Berkeley, California. She is the Director of Clinical Training at the Center for Family Counseling in East Oakland, where she conducts training for the counseling staff that provides family therapy and community-based prevention programs in the Oakland Public Schools. She also maintains a small private practice. Dr. Thompson has special expertise in narrative theory and social justice therapy and has received training in the Dulwich Center, Australia, and the Family Center, New Zealand.

■ The Interview

Question: Can you begin by talking about your own ethnic background and how it's impacted your work?

Thompson: I identify as African American, although I use the words *Black* and *African American* interchangeably. My racial identity impacts and shapes my life—who I am—and has a heavy, heavy influence in my work. Racism, in fact, makes it impossible for me to forget about the color of my skin. In some ways, sexism does the same thing. Both are at the forefront of my thinking and so cannot help but affect me as a professional. African American culture focuses my attention on certain aspects of experience. It teaches me about what's important, like spirituality and respect, education, family relationships, political unity, and fighting for the oppressed, freedom fighting. My culture has me paying attention to these things, and it shows up in my practice. It forms the metaphors and language I use and shapes and defines the way I think about psychological problems. Take respect, for instance. Because I come from a group that's been very disrespected, respect is a real important thing to me and other African Americans. There's a slang term that the young people use called "dis," to "dis" somebody, and it means to disrespect them. My style of therapy is very connected, intimate. The humor that I use is very cultural. My language, the intonations that I use, how I speak, all come from being African American.

Being African American has also sensitized me to spirituality. I didn't grow up in the black church the way a lot of people did and so am not terribly religious, though being in church is quite comfortable for me. Yet I have a strong sense of spirituality that runs very deep and affects my work in terms of values such as humility, obligation, respect, being thankful, being grateful, not putting myself at the center of things. I also feel a strong sense of responsibility as an African American, both personally and in my work, to understand the African American perspective and what the psychological effects of living in this country and this culture are. What kind of problems does that pose for us and how the negative effects can be best treated. But it is important to not define these effects only as pathology, for I feel a responsibility to focus on the strength it brings out, to observe and promote these strengths.

The thing that really got me interested in psychology was a book called *I Never Promised You a Rose Garden* that I read as a teenager. It was about mental illness, and I was fascinated by the realization that everybody had different minds, different inner worlds, different personalities. I have a sibling who struggles with depression, and it made me curious about such differences. As African Americans, we also occupy a certain reality that is different than other peoples' reality. Things like sexism and racism are really up close and personal. They're not merely interesting intellectual constructs. As a result of the denigration and oppression, there is often rage and anger, and you have to do something with that. I use it to inform my work, turn it into something constructive. It fuels my commitment for working with my own people.

Lastly, I have a lot of passion and try to be creative with it in my work. That part of me feels very African American. My mother always mentions a paradox she sees in our culture, that there is so much joy among us in spite of all the hardship. There's really a lot of exuberance, joy, and zest for life that shows up in things like the arts and all the many ways that African American people contribute to American culture. It comes from a deep place of both spirituality and joy.

Question: How would you define African Americans as a comprehensive group? What characteristics do they share?

Thompson: The term *African American* refers to people of Black, African descent, who can be distinguished from people of White African descent as well as from Black Africans who are currently immigrants to this country. There are Caribbean Blacks who have a very similar history to African Americans but who reside or have resided in the Caribbean Islands, and Black people from South America and other places in the larger African diaspora. African Americans have a particular common history of being the descendants of those people who survived the Middle Passage and went through post–Civil War Reconstruction, the period of Jim Crow law, the period of cultural revolution, really from the '30s up into the 1950s and '60s.

The characteristics that African American people share are residuals of African culture that have sometimes been reshaped and adapted because of our current circumstances in North America. I like the way James Jones talks about those cultural residuals. He calls them TRIOS, which stands for time, rhythm, improvisation, oral, and spiritual.

Time. Every group has their own time frame. We refer to ours as CP time, that is, Colored People time. African Americans tend to be more informal around social time. For example, when I have a party and am inviting both my African American and White friends, I often tell them two different times because I know that the African American people are going to come later and they're going to stay later. Work time, like for everyone else, is on the clock. Rhythm is pretty self-evident. African Americans seem attracted to certain rhythmic patterns and cadence that infuse all that we do and how we communicate and express ourselves. It has in fact become part of a stereotype of us, that all African American people can dance. But God forbid, if you can't dance, it can be a bit hard on you. Improvisation refers to our attraction, as African Americans to novelty, creativity, spontaneous creation. Jazz music, for instance, which grew out of African American culture, is about improvisation, always evolving and changing. Or look at the slam dunk in basketball. It is about style over function. You have to get the ball in the hoop, that's function, but how you do it is style. African American culture is very vocal and expressive, very oral. Speaking well and having good verbal communication and persuasive skills are highly prized among African Americans. Look at rap music, the high value placed on people being ministers and preachers. In my generation it was called "capping," a contest to see who could verbally outdo the other person. Spirituality, even if it's not religious, there's great respect there. You almost never see African American people, if they win some kind of award on TV, I don't care what it is, you know, the Academy Awards, the Tony Awards, the music awards, they thank God. That reverence is always there.

As African Americans, we also have a shared history here in America that has been organized around oppression and its consequences. Included are the experiences of economic disenfranchisement, second-class citizenship, racial discrimination, healthy paranoia, social vigilance. Not every African American person reacts to these factors in the same way, and some may be well off right now, or second- or third-generation middle-class, but at some point economic disenfranchisement was a shared and common experience, even if it is not currently in a person's life. It remains a generation or two away from you. A last thing related to all of this is a shared concern for the importance of respect. Parents being respected by their children; men being respected in a certain way. Self-respect is shown in how we dress, grooming, the very fancy clothes. Dressing down, not wearing shoes or going barefoot are not valued because such activities are associated with being poor and economically disenfranchised. I remember being at an agency picnic and noticing that all of my White colleagues were sitting on the ground to eat and my African American colleagues were all standing. They all agreed that if you have on your professional clothes, you just never sit on the ground.

Question: What names or terms do individuals within the African American community use to describe and identify themselves?

Thompson: I think the most current and contemporary term is *African American*. Whether one prefers Black or African *American* seems to depend on the era in which one was raised. *Black* was more typical of the 1960s and '70s. What I think is interesting about the list of names we have called ourselves—Negro, colored, Black, African American—is that the earlier names all focused on skin color. *Negro*, though nonderogatory in its meaning, comes from the Spanish word *negre* which means "black." But it focused on skin color. *Colored* brought us further away from the word *black* and it tends to be kinder and more polite. My mother's generation referred to themselves as *Colored*. *Black* was a reaction of pride and solidarity. "Let's not water it down anymore. Let's say Black! I'm Black and I'm proud, say it loud." That whole thing. It was an affirming of African identities in both skin color and hair style. The afro was really a fascinating thing. It was like we're going to take our hair and let it stand up on our heads very proudly. Though it was about pride, it was still about appearance and skin color.

The term *African American* is my preference. First, it focuses on culture, both our connection to Africa, where we came from, and America where we reside now. It also distinguishes us from other peoples with black skin. East Indians can be very dark in their complexion. The aboriginals in Australia have very dark skin. But what makes us African American is having a cultural connection to Africa and to others who have come from there. It is also the only term that we've truly chosen for ourselves. It puts us on the same status as other groups in America. It describes the kind of American you are. Like, a person is an Italian American or Jewish American or African American. It both gives us status and places culture in a very salient position in defining who we are. Finally, it tends to be more inclusive. I have not found it useful to distinguish people who are recently mixed racially from African Americans, who have always been a mixed people. From the time we came to this country, there was extensive mixing with Whites and Native peoples. By "recently mixed," I mean a person who has a parent from another race and an African American parent. I see these children as part of the African American group. They are welcome within our community, and the term *African American* is more inclusive and makes room for them. Jane Lazar wrote a book entitled *Beyond the Whiteness of White: White Mother Raising Black Sons*. In it she argues for the importance of giving her "mixed-race" sons a powerful and accurate identity as part of the African American community.

Question: What historical experiences should providers be aware of in relation to the African American community and African American clients?

Thompson: I would divide our history into four segments: pre-enslavement, the Middle Passage, enslavement, and post-enslavement. You'll notice I'm using the term *enslavement*. I do that because it is more socially responsible and accurate as far as providing a context for understanding. It focuses on what has been done to our people, as opposed to labeling them as just slaves, as if that is a part of their character and who they are.

I begin with the period of pre-enslavement because it is important for providers as well as African Americans themselves to be aware that we were not always slaves, but rather descended from many different cultural groups across the continent of Africa. We existed prior to enslavement. The Middle Passage describes the ways in which African Americans were physically brought to America. It was the brutal transition from pre-enslavement to being enslaved, from being free and autonomous to becoming slaves. It was a journey by ships, human beings packed like sardines, during which more people died than were actually delivered to the United States. It is important to know about the brutality of the process as well as the fact that the enslaved Africans resisted from the very beginning, many choosing to jump ship, end their lives rather than be enslaved.

The enslavement period, the institution of slavery, was about economics. Skin color, race, and supposed inferiority were all concepts used to justify slavery, which was at its core economic. The money that was made from slavery allowed this country to become what it is. Providers need to know that this person in front of them belonged to a group that was enslaved and helped create the wealth of this country. What is particularly ironic are the stereotypes that paint African American people as lazy. It's so crazy. Here's a group of people that worked for over 300 years for free, doing back-breaking and servile work, to be described as lazy. What an incredible reaction formation. But it is important to also realize that the institution of slavery challenged us with a lot of psychological residuals that still exist today. For example, Ken Hardy talks about silence and rage: how during slavery African Americans were going through a dehumanizing process in which they had to be silent and witness their own abuse, and how this has turned into rage and then violence. There is a lot of anger in the African American community, and anger is always a reaction to something. It comes from injustice, brutality, and abuse. So when you see a lot of violence in the African American community, and you might be tempted as a provider to say, "Why are these people so violent?" If you understood what the process of enslavement did to turn rage directed toward the self, directed toward one's community as violence, it would give you a different way of understanding.

How can one deal with that rage without pathologizing the person and making their anger the only issue to be addressed? I actually like to talk about turning rage into outrage. Typically, we say, if a person is full of rage and anger, they need treatment. They have an "anger" problem, and we give them a diagnosis, medication, perhaps an anger management group. When a person is outraged, they're outraged for a reason, and the reason is injustice. So the period of enslavement is important because it shows us where the anger came from. And there are a lot of residuals from our history, having to do with anger, trust, suspicion, which really should be renamed healthy paranoia.

Post-enslavement. There was the whole post–Civil War Reconstruction period. It was quite short-lived, however. The period of Reconstruction was important because it showed our talents, our forgiving spirit, and our intelligence. The newly freed Africans were ready to pitch in and become part of American culture and to contribute with businesses and industry.

Many black businesses and communities thrived after slavery. And amazingly there was not a strong spirit of retaliation. I think African American people have an incredibly forgiving spirit. It's something I try to draw upon in therapy. I think spirituality has a lot to do with forgiveness. Here were a people ready to participate in healthy, positive, forgiving ways. Film director Spike Lee has named his film company 40 Acres and a Mule. With the end of slavery, each slave was promised 40 acres and a mule, and as Lee suggests, he is still waiting for those 40 acres and a mule. This broken promise was only the beginning of a process of re-enslavement through a system of legislation known as Jim Crow laws, segregation, and unequal treatment. The psychological residual of Reconstruction followed by Jim Crow for African Americans was a widespread mistrust of the governmental systems as well as of Whites in general. The people I know and clients I see freely state that: "I don't trust White folks." The distrust is immediate and general, and Whites must prove themselves as safe and okay. Until proven otherwise, they're not. So it's important for practitioners to know that this is a group of people that were lied to in this country; if you see mistrust, that may be its roots.

Post-enslavement also includes a number of revolutions within the African American community, continuing the long-standing spirit of resistance within our history. There was a cultural revolution in the '30s with the Harlem Renaissance led by authors such as Langston Hughes and Zora Neale Hurston. It was the beginning of social commentary, of great creativity and intelligence, and again, the forgiving spirit of African American people as expressed through the work of these writers. They fought with the pen rather than with arms. We all know the Civil Rights Movement of the late 1950s and '60s with Martin Luther King and Malcolm X. They all show how we have resisted our mistreatment. We've not been docile or turned over on our backs. It's really important for young people to know that, and practitioners as well. In growing up I knew about slavery, but I didn't know about the uprisings. And having the opportunity to have Black scholars focus our attention on resistance to slavery, the uprisings, and the incredibly creative ways that Africans tried to resist their inhumane treatment leads to a very different kind of self-understanding. But at the same time it is necessary to realize that though resilient, creative, and strong, we are not indomitable. Many people fail to see the soft side of African Americans, the fragility, the need for human kindness and connection like anyone else. There are many negative statistics and problems in our communities that bear this out: poverty, drug addiction. We're not infallible, but we are strong. So holding both of these ideas at the same time is critical for practitioners.

Question: Can you next discuss some of the factors that influence the ways African Americans seek mental health services?

Thompson: Trust, as I said before, is a very big influence. African Americans tend not to seek help from professionals. We have learned not to trust them, and our reasons are legitimate and sound, not a reflection of some sort of pathology. Really bad things have happened to us in the name of professional treatment, like the Tuskegee Syphilis Study. African American men participated in research without their knowledge and consent; they had treatment withheld so that the researchers could watch the course of development of syphilis. Psychological testing has been used against us, and many in our community just don't feel that psychology has much to offer us as a system of care. Cost and access are also factors. Many of the fees are just too high, and it is difficult to get to where therapists are located. There aren't tons of people with private practices located in East Oakland. Cultural competence is also a big issue. Will my life experience be understood and valued by the counselor? I would say that most practitioners are not culturally competent. I've also talked about respect. I think many African Americans expect that if they go to a practitioner, they will be blamed, misunderstood, and pathologized. We feel we're going to be seen as somebody who has a problem with anger, as opposed to somebody who's outraged at unjust treatment.

So we don't go. Instead we find other help-seeking opportunities, find other institutions for help. We rely heavily on the church, on Black social organizations, and there are many of these. And we rely upon our leaders in the community and our ministers. We seek out people that we can relate to, identify with, who understand us. So it's about how we relate, our accessibility, and how we enter the community. I recently spoke to a women's group that meets at a local church. I was asked to come and talk about psychotherapy: what it can offer, what I do. This group of African American women was incredibly receptive, and we had a wonderful time. But it came through the church. Someone that they trusted invited me, and this was a group of African American parishioners. Of course, my being African American helped, but not just because of my skin color. I think it was how I related to them that was key. Because for African American people, it's all about how you relate to them—how it feels, if they can identify with you, if there is respect and comfort. I could be African American and still put them off by a certain kind of professional distance or behavior that seems too "White," for instance. So my being Black is not the issue; it's how I relate. I use a more interactive and personal way of relating and that was what allowed them to hear what I was saying. Most people wouldn't go or continue with therapy if they feel like they cannot relate to, identify with, or connect with their therapist. Nancy Boyd-Franklin talks about this when she describes the concept of "vibes."

Question: What do providers of service need to know about family and community issues among African Americans?

Thompson: As I have been saying all along, practitioners need to know the present-day ramifications of our history: to really understand what it is like for an African American client to live life in their community today, to focus on and appreciate the strengths and creativity that it takes to survive and live a full life, and to understand and acknowledge the privileges they hold in the world because they are White and how their African American client might feel about those privileges.

Let's begin with privilege. It is important to know that African Americans see White privilege as problematic for them as is racism. And I want to acknowledge that this is hard stuff for White providers to sit with. So I appreciate that. But unless you understand this and bring it into the room with you, you are not going to be accepted and trusted. The fact is that not only are there the acts of direct discrimination and racial injustice that African Americans experience on a daily basis, but also we see that White people are by and large still benefiting from a system that gives them advantage and at the same time treats us unfairly. We just want a fair and equitable system, and the privilege Whites hold is a constant reminder of what we as African Americans don't have. When White practitioners are able to cop to the fact that White privilege exists, to acknowledge it and the effects of racism, they're more likely to be trusted and thus helpful.

Let me switch to what life experience is like for many African Americans today, especially those living in the urban, inner city who are primarily working and of the lower and middle class. We see that there is still modern-day slavery, as in the prison system and industry, and that our people are disproportionately represented in jails. We see that drugs that devastate us are allowed into our community. In fact, we are systematically targeted for alcohol and tobacco sales. But there are a lot of current forms of modern-day slavery, like the prison industry. It's an industry, a money-making venture. And that's modern-day slavery to people in African American communities. We know this, and it's important that practitioners know that this is how many of us think about it. That drugs are allowed into our community. It is not surprising that African American people feel abandoned, uncared for, disenfranchised by the social institutions that are "supposed" to help them. When you have a poor school, and you have unequal protection under the law, when you have a lack of basic services, like you don't have any banks in your neighborhood or groceries that have good prices, and you have more alcohol stores than grocery stores, and you have media that portrays you negatively, and only fast foods that are available to you, and unaffordable brand names that are targeted specifically toward your group. When all of this continues to happen, your relationship to these larger social institutions is going to be one of mistrust. You feel uncared for, unprotected at a basic level. For example, you know that if you call the police right now, and live in Berkeley, they will probably come within a half hour. If you live in Oakland, they will come in four hours.

So here comes the psychologist: well-meaning, a professional, who's part of a social institution, a school or maybe the client is court-mandated. You're not going to be necessarily trusted. Practitioners need to know that. It has not to do with you as an individual; you're connected to a larger social institution that does not have a track record of building trust.

Our families feel disrespected by contact with the system, intruded upon by institutions that are largely staffed by White people that don't understand or care for us. That's how many people in the community think. Here's an agency whose staff is all White, and all the kids getting treatment in the program are Black. And then they're calling CPS (Children's Protective Services). If an African American client is testing you or untrusting, you might see that as a natural and healthy thing because these folks come from a group that has not been cared for. Providers of service also need to know that there's a real lack of safety in our communities, and that lack of safety is stressful for those of us who live there. You may feel some fear coming to that community. Imagine what it's like to live in a community where you're continually afraid. But it's more complex than that because you also have really good relationships with many of the people there (your neighbors) and there are times when the fear is not present. You have to be strong, creative, and adaptive to survive here.

Question: What kinds of problems are most commonly brought by African Americans into treatment?

Thompson: All the problems that other Americans have, African Americans have too. Depression. Anxiety. We all live in American society and that can create stress and problems: too much time at work, not enough help and support. People get tired and cranky, drink, abuse their partners, etc. It is the same for African Americans, but on top of that we have to deal with the effects of modern-day discrimination and racism. It's much more subtle. Nobody's riding down the street burning a cross on your front lawn. That subtlety in some ways is harder to understand for the person who's experiencing it. Sometimes a client doesn't realize it (the experience of racism, for example) until you ask the question, and then they can put it together. But it subtly makes it extremely stressful to African Americans. They bring it (stress) into therapy and they don't bring it in saying that's what it is. Some people call it extreme mundane environmental stress. It comes out as self-doubt, self-criticism; that's how it comes into the office. But it is really the effects of social and economic disenfranchisement. People come in with the problems that are most obvious to them: self-doubt, family problems, drug, alcohol, tobacco-related addictions (our community is targeted for these), and issues of group identity and belonging. A bit more about the last one. When you belong to a group that's really put down, it poses quite a challenge for you because you have a human need to belong, yet who wants to belong to a group that's seen so negatively? That's what you see with the early doll studies (Clark & Clark, 1947) with African American children, when they were choosing the White doll. The kids got, really early on, that there is something about that Black group nobody seems to like. Children may say: "I think I'd rather belong to the group that people like." The only thing that can really buffer and save us from this brutality of discrimination is to belong to our own group and to have pride and a healthy sense that the people that you come from are good people. This is a dilemma that every African American person faces and can get addressed in therapy with a practitioner who is aware of it.

Question: What factors do you see as important in assessing African American clients?

Thompson: Formal testing and assessment of clients is not something I practice these days. African American clients have good reason to be suspicious of psychological testing. Historically, it has been used to track our children into special education classes and to justify stereotypes of lower intelligence. The instruments that have been traditionally used have not been culturally sensitive and, therefore, put our children at a disadvantage. There is also the issue of trust once again. Everyone who is assessed by a psychologist feels somewhat vulnerable. When you assess someone, you're in the position of judging them. If you are from a group of people who are incredibly vulnerable to rejection, who are incredibly sensitive to being misunderstood, trust is enormously important, and you must develop it before conducting an assessment

Question: Are their subpopulations in the community that you feel are particularly at risk?

Thompson: I think there are subpopulations that we need to pay particular attention to. Black men, for example. There have been books written about the Black male as endangered, and understanding their position is a complex task having to do with the intersection of racism and sexism. In some ways they are accorded some amount of privilege for being male, but at the same time are devalued because White society fears them, and fears them even more than Black women. So their maleness both hurts and helps them, and this can be very confusing both for them and for practitioners. Understanding the situation of African American women is important because there is the double burden of being both female and African American. Yet at the same time, African American woman are elevated over Black men, and you can imagine the conflicts that that causes in relationships and families. African American women are seen as less threatening (by the general society) and therefore viewed as objects of oppression in the same way White women are. So we are subjected to the same things that make it harder for all women—the focus on beauty, lowered expectations around intelligence, etc. —but also higher mountains to climb as African Americans.

And then there is the gay/lesbian/bisexual/transgendered community. First, you're outcast in the wider culture and then you're outcast in your own African American culture. I get so angry about that and even tearful, that the GLBT community would be doubly rejected from within their own group, which should be more sensitive to such issues of exclusion. There needs to be more attention paid to what it is like being Black and gay.

Finally, there are the children, who are the most voiceless. A significant number of African American children are born below the poverty line, and for generations have remained impoverished, born into poverty and most likely to stay in poverty. There is this overgeneralization that all African American people are poor, and as a result, both the very poor and those who are economically higher up remain invisible. Another issue that impacts African American children greatly, as it does White children, is addiction to drugs among their parents. Addicted parents are unable to properly raise children because drugs rob you of your mind, your sense of social connection, and your ability to be responsible. Families with rampant addiction tend to be chaotic environments, difficult places to grow up, and addicted parents are incapable of passing on cultural knowledge and identity, a very significant loss for African American children.

Question: What suggestions do you have for developing rapport with African American clients, and is there a therapeutic style with which African American clients are most comfortable?

Thompson: Being direct is very well received by African Americans. I don't mean doing away with social niceties or being blunt, rude or crude, but not beating around the bush. Directness is often appreciated. There is this culture of politeness that shows up among practitioners that is mistrusted by African American people. Being too nice, or too open, or too solicitous, before you know somebody is perceived as inauthentic. Remember, we are as a people very sensitive to inauthenticity and dishonesty. Many therapists claim to create a safe environment for all clients. But therapists really don't have the power to do that, and having such an attitude is likely to raise the suspicion of African American people. Saying "I'd like this to be a safe place, and I'll do my best to do that, but I don't know if I can do that for you" would be much more authentic and therefore more trust-inducing.

So directness, authenticity, and honesty are vital because people who have been lied to have special antennae in relation to: "This doesn't sound right. Why are you being so nice to me when you don't even know me?" We have feelers. Nancy Boyd-Franklin talked about it as a vibe. African American people get your vibe, and it's really hard to hide. Being passionate and interactive are also important because our cultural style is to be both. We're a very passionate, exuberant, excitable people. So if your style as a practitioner is flat in its affect or distant, passive, or minimally reactive with frequent silences, it is likely to be interpreted as something negative. And it is critical to be respectful of people's spiritual beliefs. Not all African Americans are religious. In fact, awful things have happened to many of us in the name of religion. But African Americans are still spiritual and that is a powerful issue around which to connect.

I have found that the use of (what I have termed) "socially conscious self-disclosure" is very effective with African American people. Non-disclosure can be problematic with people who are from oppressed groups. If you don't disclose personal information, there is no way to place you in a context and, therefore, to know if you can be trusted. The therapist must be sure that the self-disclosure is done in the service of the client—that is, it is an attempt to create safety, connection, empathy—not because the therapist is insecure, needs to vent, or needs to be heard. If the therapist shares personal information in that spirit, to do so in a socially conscious way, it will be helpful with African American clients.

The African American people I work with, they know I'm African American by looking at me, but again, it's not just a skin color thing. They have to know how "Black" I am. They really want to know where my consciousness is located. They don't come out and ask me. But I know it is important that I make disclosures to them so that they know that we share a worldview, that I know what they are talking about. For example, I have an African American client who's raising boys. It was very important for her to know that I too have a boy, and we are both attempting to raise Black boys in a culture that is very brutal on Black males. I didn't go on and talk about my son, but that little bit of information changed things. Most people feel greatly held by such connections. There's something very healing and soothing about knowing that somebody shares a problem with you. Another therapeutic tool I use with African American clients is something I call "deep cultural knowledge." By that I mean knowledge about my group that I have gotten from living in and being a part of the culture. For example, I use humor. There are certain things that I could probably say in a humorous way with African Americans that would be shared, that if someone else did it, it would be insulting. All of the folk knowledge that I've picked up as part of my culture I refer to and ask questions about as a way of connecting with my clients in small but mutually meaningful ways. These things come up in talking about people's lives, so I may refer to them or ask where you heard or were taught that. Using cultural metaphors is also helpful. I use a lot of them. Metaphors about freedom, escape, liberation, our ancestors, spirit and spirituality. African American people love these metaphors because they just make sense to us in a very deep place. And, of course, my language style. I use Black English to flavor my speech. There are just certain things that have to be said in a particular way.

I would encourage other African American practitioners to consider some of these approaches. Now, if you're not African American, you obviously can't use deep cultural knowledge, and that's a limit. I don't think that means you can't work with African American clients, but I think it's important to acknowledge the limits of what your experience is. And don't try to join with African American clients by acting Black. When White people try to do the "slap me five, brotha" thing, it's a turn-off. It's likely to be experienced as inauthentic and phony. I've met a few White people who grew up in African American culture and for them such behavior is natural, so that's fine. But for most Whites, such appropriation of our culture is considered an insult.

Finally, it's not a good idea to ask too many questions initially. Such questioning without sufficient trust and rapport will be viewed as interrogation. Too many questions too soon. We're talking about people with a history where trust and giving out information about oneself has been repeatedly violated. When I was a teenager, the census person came to the house. My mother said, "Don't tell them anything," and my mother is a very warm, welcoming person. She's not particularly suspicious or paranoid. We, as African Americans, are raised not to tell strangers, especially White ones, anything about ourselves. The census, for example, was just seen as White people coming in and trying to find out about us. But as therapists, we're taught to ask questions. So how do you do that? The timing and pace of when you ask questions is critical. I would suggest that one wait before asking too many direct questions. Give the client time for them to tell you their story, time to check you out and time to develop rapport. That's a style I think works better with African Americans.

Question: By way of ending and putting together some of the ideas you've shared, could you present a case?

Thompson: OK. Let me give you a shorter and then a longer example. I had an African American graduate student who doubted herself so much, doubted her intellectual capacities in spite of the fact that she was a teaching assistant in her graduate program, in a statistics course. If you are a TA for a statistics class, you're probably very good at math, right? She just couldn't shake the idea that she really wasn't good at math and had a nagging worry about her intelligence. But when you are viewed and portrayed as being from a group where you are "less than" others, "bad," or "lacking intelligence," it's no wonder that you show up in my office with: "I don't feel good about myself, and I can't figure out why." For this particular woman, who's African American, I believe both sexism and racism had her doubting her intelligence, yet she was the TA for one of the classes that everyone else is really anxious about. I think this is one of the subtle ways that racism affects our people. She would never have named that as racism, and I asked her quite frankly, "Do you think racism has anything to do with this?" which is one of my favorite questions. Most clients' immediate response is no. But after a few minutes they reconsider and come back to the question. Eventually, they begin telling you all the ways that racism has affected them. Why was it so initially hard to identify? Because it is quite painful to think about and easier to push it out of consciousness. And you don't want to think that so much of your life is defined by it (racism).

I was working with a second woman who had a lot of social anxiety and came into therapy quite well versed in the language of social phobia. She said she knew they had medicine for it and could she get some of that? I don't prescribe medication but told her she could pursue that if she liked. In her work with me I was particularly interested in how she came to think of herself as a social phobic. Using narrative therapy, I helped her deconstruct the messages she had gotten in life about who she was and how she had gotten to think of herself. So, we developed a metaphor for how she was feeling, using the language of escape, liberation, and freedom. We externalized her fear as imprisoning her. She had become a prisoner of it. Though it is normal for most people to feel a little awkward in new social situations, she was terrified of meeting people, especially about going back to school.

She wanted to go back to school but felt quite strongly that she didn't belong. Part of it was the fact she would be going to a largely White institution where she was going to be an ethnic minority. This scared her and stimulated a sense of not belonging. As we sorted out what this was about, we found hidden messages about poor black girls not going on for higher education, about her not having important things to contribute, and that no one would listen to her. This is another subtle way that racism shows itself in people's lives, and therapists can ask questions that can help uncover racism in this way.

So, we externalized the fear as the experience of feeling imprisoned, of living in a prison of fear. Before looking into how to escape from that prison, it was necessary for her to understand the interior of that prison, what it told her, how it spoke to her, how it kept her locked away. In terms of her breaking out, I asked, "Who might know about escaping to freedom?" In response she said: "I wonder if our ancestors might know, since they tried to escape slavery." Then she wondered how she might ask her ancestors. Would it be in a prayer, a meditation, or a reflective moment? I encouraged her to pursue the thought. She said, "I think I'll go to the ocean because we came from the other side of the ocean, and we were dropped off here" and added, "I like the ocean; I have this affinity to it. When I have a burden, I often go to the ocean and it helps me think, clear my mind." In her next session she told me she had gone to the ocean and asked the ancestors about escaping.

And I asked, "What did they say?" sitting on the edge of my seat. She said that the answer came to her in the form of a poem. She shared the poem, and it was eloquent. It was about breaking free, cutting the shackles of fear, liberating her from social anxiety and fear. The poem connected her culturally, and gave her both pride and courage.

Here's a young woman who came in talking about social phobia and medication, disconnected from the social context of her fears. She was able to connect the fear to a cultural background, and through that connection deepen her own connection with who she is culturally.

Working with Asian American Clients: An Interview with Dan Hocoy

13

■ Demographics

Asian Americans were the fastest growing racial group in the United States from 1980 to 2000, their population nearly doubling (179%) during that period. The 2000 Census (which now divides the larger group into two subgroups) reported an Asian population of 10.2 million, or 3.6% of the general population, and a Native Hawaiian and other Pacific Islander population of 400,000, or 0.1%. Projections into the future estimate a population increase from 5% of the United States total in 2010 to 9% by the year 2050.

Like the Latinos/as, Asians represent a diverse collection of ethnic groups with very different languages, cultures, and in some cases a long history of intergroup conflict and hostilities. Included in this collective are 43 ethnic groups, 28 in the "Asian" category and 15 in the "Pacific Islander" category. Included in the former are individuals who identify themselves as Asian Indians, Chinese, Filipino, Korean, Japanese, and Vietnamese and in the latter are individuals from Hawaii, Guam, and Samoa. With changes in the Immigration Act of 1965 and large-scale immigration from Southeast Asia and other parts of the Asian continent, relative percentages of Asian American subgroup size changed dramatically. According to the 1970 Census, Japanese were the most populous, followed by Chinese and Filipinos. By 1980, however, Japanese were in third place, Chinese moving to first, and Filipinos to second. As of 2000, Chinese represent the largest Asian subgroup with 2.3 million, Filipinos at 1.9 million, Asian Indians at 1.7 million, Vietnamese at 1.1 million, Korean also at 1.1 million, and Japanese at .8 million. Native Hawaiians and Pacific Islanders make up only 5% of the Asian population in the United States.

Most Asian Americans come from recent immigrant families. During the 1990s, immigrants were in fact responsible for two thirds of the growth of the overall Asian population. In 1998, for instance, 59% were foreign-born, with 74% arriving since 1980. Many Chinese and Japanese Americans, however, have been here for three or more generations, originally a source of cheap labor in the economic development of the Western United States. Their history was one of extensive suffering and racial discrimination. According to Pollard and O'Hare (1999):

> Legislation enacted in 1790 excluded Asians and other non-Whites gaining citizenship by limiting citizenship to "free White residents."

254

Because most Asians were foreign-born and not citizens, they could be legally kept from owning land or businesses, attending schools with Whites, or living in White neighborhoods. Asian immigrants were not eligible for U.S. citizenship until 1952. The 1879 California constitution barred the hiring of Chinese workers, and the federal Chinese Exclusion Act of 1882 halted the entry of most Chinese until 1943. The 1907 Gentlemen's Agreement and a 1917 law restricted immigration from Japan and a "barred zone" known as the Asian-Pacific Triangle. During World War II Americans of Japanese ancestry were interned in camps by Executive Order signed by Franklin D. Roosevelt. (pp. 5–6)

Recent Asian and Pacific Islander immigration has followed two streams. One came from countries such as China and Korea where there were already large populations in the United States. The majority of these were college-educated and entered under special employment provisions. The second stream came from Southeast Asia—Vietnam, Laos, and Cambodia—arriving after the Vietnam War to escape persecution in their home countries. Most were poor and uneducated.

As a group, Asian Americans and Pacific Islanders, 49% of the U.S. population, are concentrated in the Western United States, with the largest urban populations located in Los Angeles and New York City. Sixty percent of the Chinese population reside in California and New York; two thirds of the Filipinos and Japanese live in California and Hawaii. Koreans and Asian Indians tend to be more dispersed, with the largest concentrations in California, New York, Illinois, New Jersey, and Texas. Southeast Asians, on the other hand, can be found in unexpected pockets of population as a result of governmental resettlement policies. Forty percent of the Hmong population in 1990, for example, resided in Minnesota and Wisconsin (Pollard & O'Hare, 1999).

Unlike African Americans, Latinos/as, and Native Americans, Asian Americans have been quite successful economically and educationally, even in comparison with the White population. In 1998, the median income in an Asian household was $46,637 when it was $42,439 for White households and $25,351 for African Americans. Asian Americans, in addition, account for 30% of minority businesses, although they account for only 13% of the non-White population. They also score high on business ownership rates (BOR) (businesses per 1,000 population) with Koreans and Asian Indians surpassing White BOR rates. Asians and Whites graduate from high school at the same rate as do Whites, approximately 90%, but the former are more likely to complete 2 or more years of college. In 1990, 13% of the Asian and Pacific Islander population earned graduate and professional degrees in comparison to 9% of Whites, and three to four times the rate of other minorities.

Because of such statistics and a cultural tendency to defer and not compete openly with White Americans, Asian Americans have been described as a "model minority," a veritable success story. Sue and Sue (1999), however, see this image as a myth based on incomplete data that serves to validate the erroneous belief that any ethnic group can succeed if they only work hard enough, stimulate intergroup conflict, and shortchange Asian communities from needed resources. According to Sue and Sue (1999), the following facts need to be understood. High median income doesn't take into consideration the number of wage earners, the level of poverty among certain Asian subgroups, or the discrepancy between education and income for Asian workers. Education in the Asian community is bimodal; that is, there are both highly educated and uneducated subpopulations. Asian towns in large urban areas represent ghettos with high unemployment, poverty, and widespread social problems. Underutilization of services does not necessarily mean a lack of problems, but it may in fact have alternative explanations such as face saving, shame, or the family's cultural tendency to keep personal information hidden from the outside world. In short, the belief in Asian success does not mean that there is any less racism or discrimination directed toward Asian Americas or that there are not serious problems within crowded urban enclaves. At a psychological level, "model minority" status refers to the lack of threat Whites experience in relation to Asian Americans. Such an attitude has eroded somewhat, however, with increased economic competition from Japan and other Pacific Rim countries and a growing number of Asian American students competing successfully for college and university slots.

■ Family and Cultural Values

Lee (1996) offers the following description of traditional Asian families:

> . . . in traditional Asian families, the family unit—rather than the individual—is highly valued. The individual is seen as the product of all the generations of his or her family. The concept is reinforced by rituals and customs such as ancestor worship, family celebrations, funeral rites, and genealogy records. Because of this continuum, individuals' personal action reflects not only on themselves but also on their extended family and ancestors. . . . Obligations and shame are mechanisms that traditionally help reinforce societal expectations and proper behavior. An individual is expected to function in his or her clearly defined roles and positions in the family hierarchy, based on age, gender, and social class. There is an emphasis on harmonious interpersonal relationships, interdependence, and mutual obligations or loyalty for achieving a state of psychological homeostasis or peaceful coexistence with family or other fellow beings. (pp. 230–230)

Family and gender roles and expectations are highly structured. Fathers are the breadwinners, protectors, and ultimate authorities. Mothers oversee the home, bear and care for children, and are under the authority of their fathers, husbands, in-laws, and at times even sons. Male children are highly prized, and the strongest bond within the family is between mother and son. Children are expected to be respectful and obedient and are usually raised by an extended family. Older daughters are expected to play a caretaking function with younger siblings.

Traditional Asian values differ dramatically from those of White, middle-class American culture. Immigration brings the strong possibility of cultural conflict within the family. Lee (1996) differentiates five Asian American family types that differ in relation to cultural conflict:

- "Traditional" families are largely untouched by assimilation and acculturation, retain cultural ways, limit their contact with the White world, and tend to live in ethnic enclaves.
- "Culture conflict" families are typified by traditional parents and acculturated, Americanized children who experience intergenerational conflict over appropriate behavior and values, exhibit major role confusion, and lack agreed-upon family structures.
- "Bicultural" families tend to include acculturated parents, born either in the United States or in Asia, and exposed to Western ways. They are professional, middle-class, bilingual, and bicultural. Family structures tend to be a blending of family styles but with regular contact with traditional family members.
- "Americanized" families have taken on the ways of the majority culture with ties to traditional Asian culture fading and little interest in connection to ethnic identity.
- "Interracial" families represent marriage with a non-Asian partner where family styles from the two cultures have been successfully integrated or there is significant value and style conflict.

Sue and Sue (1999) similarly identify five potential value conflicts that may arise between Asian American clients and Western trained counselors:

- Asian clients value a collective and group focus that emphasizes interdependence, and Western counselors adopt a focus on individualism and independent action.
- Asians tend to be most comfortable with hierarchical relationships in comparison with a Western emphasis on equality in relationships.
- Asian cultures see the restraint of emotion as a sign of human maturity and the Western counselor is likely to see emotional expressiveness as healthy.
- Traditional Asian clients will expect the counselor to provide solutions but the Western counselor will encourage finding one's own solutions through introspection.
- Mental illness and emotional problems are seen within the Asian context as shameful and indicative of family failure in contrast with Western counseling, which views mental and physical illness similarly.

As we shall learn from our guest expert, Dan Hocoy, Asian Americans, when they do seek professional helping services outside of their community, tend to present with a variety of problems including value conflicts with parents and family, difficulties regarding identity issues, acculturation, extreme work ethics, and familial obligations.

■ Our Interviewee

Dan Hocoy, Ph.D., received his degree in clinical psychology from Queen's University, Kingston, Ontario, Canada. His dissertation focused on the effects of apartheid and racism on Black mental health in South Africa. He has also carried out research on racial identity and other cross-cultural topics throughout the world, including Chinese racial identity and the psychological impact of racism on Chinese in Canada. He is a member of the core faculty of the Psychology Department of the Pacific Graduate Institute, Carpinteria, California, and previously served as assistant professor in the PsyD (Doctor of Psychology) Program at John F. Kennedy University, Orinda, California.

■ The Interview

Question: One of your areas of expertise is racial identity. Could you talk about some of your own experiences growing up Chinese?

Hocoy: Being Chinese has always been very central to my life, although I haven't always been conscious of it. That is to say, I didn't always recognize its influence. I went through various phases of racial identity development. At first, I felt embarrassed about being Chinese. My family was the only Chinese family on the block, and because we were struggling immigrants, I always associated being Chinese with being poor. There was a lot of ethnic self-hate in me at that time. There was also external discrimination. For instance, I was always picked on in school for being Chinese; kids would tease me about the way my eyes, hair, nose looked. I got into a few fights in the school yard as a result. During this stage of my racial identity development, I always wanted to be White. This continued into high school. I wanted wavy, more combable hair. I wanted to be taller. I wanted a sharper nose. I always felt inferior. Chinese people were always ugly to me. At the time, I wasn't aware of the influences of having internalized Euro-American standards of beauty. I didn't think I was very attractive. At the height of my racial self-hate, my looks actually disgusted me. Not accepting my ethnicity pushed me toward greater degrees of conformity and assimilation. Yet I never felt I fit into the dominant culture either. Not feeling comfortable in either culture, I found myself marginalized and caught in the middle.

In university, I moved into another phase of racial identity development. Initially, I still didn't like the fact that I was Chinese, but I began to challenge my negative self-feelings and attitudes toward my people. Fortunately, at this time, I had an opportunity to visit other cultures through international development work. It was in Africa that I observed the psychological effects of colonialism and Western domination. Witnessing Black self-hatred helped me come to terms with my own racial self-hatred. This began a process of reclaiming my ethnicity, and eventually, I would study the impact of racism on Black South Africans for my doctoral dissertation. I was attending a very Anglo-dominated graduate school, and it was an especially fertile environment in which to come to terms with my race. I realized that much of my perception of the world was based on a lack of acceptance of who I was. I grew increasingly uncomfortable with the feelings of self-hatred and was in time able to come to terms with them. I wrote my master's thesis on the topic of racism against the Chinese in Canada, and this was obviously motivated by a struggle for racial self-acceptance. In time, I developed a great interest in my heritage and started buying and reading books about the Chinese and, in a variety of ways, immersed myself in Chinese culture.

My training in psychology helped me process what was going on inside me, both in realizing the effects of my experiences as a Person of Color and in coming to terms with the self-hate. Today, I regard my Chinese identity as an asset both personally and professionally. As I became clearer about my own ethnic heritage, I also became aware of the cultural bias in psychology and the need to redress the systematic neglect of minorities in both research and therapy. That in turn spawned an interest in multicultural counseling. But the process of racial self-acceptance is an ongoing one, and I have yet to completely free myself from what Bob Marley called "the chains of mental slavery."

Question: Let's begin with some definitions. Who are the Asian Americans and what characteristics do they share as a group?

Hocoy: First, I think it is important to understand that there is a large degree of diversity among Asian Americans and that they do not conveniently fit into one categorization or description. There are many shades of yellow, so to speak, and it is difficult to make global generalizations. Having said that, individual and subgroup differences are significant, and there do exist commonalities that Asian cultures share. When I talk about Asian Americans, I am referring to people with Mongolian and early Chinese ancestry. This includes the mainland Chinese, Japanese, Koreans, the Vietnamese, people from Hong Kong, Taiwan, Singapore, Malaysia, the Philippines, Laos, Thailand, and others from that region. I know this is not inclusive of all Asians, as it omits East Indians and others, for instance, but these are the groups with which I am most familiar.

With regard to Asian Americans, it is useful to realize that there are a number of factors—historical, psychological, and otherwise—that set them apart as a group in America. First of all, unlike any other minority group, there is a history of warfare between the United States and many of these Asian countries. You have the Japanese in World War II, the Korean War (in which the Chinese and North Koreans were both involved), the Vietnam War, and so on. So for many Americans, there is a visceral resentment and distrust of all things Asian. This is reflected in U.S. culture

and media, where Asians were and at times still are portrayed as the pro-
totypical villains.

I think the lack of acceptance of Asians in U.S. culture at least partially stems from the fact that Asians possess such a different worldview.
For instance, "East versus West" is a common dimension of comparison
and dichotomy. Individuals who have been socialized into traditional
Asian cultures are likely to possess completely different worldviews with
philosophies, values, and beliefs that are very disparate from Western
ones. This major difference, I think, engenders much of the fear and misunderstanding about Asians. Another important factor is that much of
Asian culture and society is based on the value of collectivism, which in
recent years has been associated with Communism. Such ideas go against
the familiar values and traditions of individualism and capitalism that are
so basic to American culture and thus threaten many Americans.

The history and treatment of Asians in the United States have caused
them to be very closed in terms of their interactions with other Americans. Asians have generally kept to themselves in very small enclaves. For
instance, to this day, there are Chinatowns in most large urban areas,
which from early times served as ghettos that ensured survival in the
economic and political structure of the United States. Another trait
Asians generally possess is a tendency to be less overtly militant and
politically active than other racial groups. As a result, they have been an
easy and frequent target for abuse and discrimination. (Although it
should be acknowledged that Asians have historically made significant
challenges to the status quo through equity legislation; this has primarily been through the judicial system.) Generally, Asians have been less
likely than other ethnic groups to engage in activism toward redress of
public policy. Characteristically, this is very reflective of the Asian attitude of not wanting to disturb things. There's a saying among the Chinese: "If you don't know what to do, at least don't do anything." This is
very different from the American maxim: "If you don't know what to do,
at least do something." This tendency is probably also related to the cultural norm of not showing certain emotions in public. It is very important in many Asian cultures that certain social protocols are followed
and that one conforms to the cultural script of not displaying emotions
in public.

Recent research findings show that Asians as a collective group are
more accepted in America than other ethnic minorities. This, too, seems
to be culturally based, with Asians generally perceived as less threatening
to the status quo or dominant culture. The Chinese, for example, have
survived in America by not having competed economically with Whites.
Historically, they have always offered services that were lacking. For
instance, when the Chinese were first brought to California, it was to provide services typically offered by women. California society at that time
was predominantly male. Pioneer men had crossed the flatlands and over
the Rockies looking for land and gold. Their womenfolk had in general

remained behind. So, when the Chinese came to America, they took on what at that time was considered women's work. They cooked, cleaned, and did laundry for these pioneers. The Chinese also provided valuable labor for the expanding railway and picked grapes for the wine industry. These were services that were needed and desired by the dominant culture but were not in direct competition with those offered by Whites. This tendency has generally held true to this day. Thus, in America, Asians have taken jobs that other Americans have just not wanted, especially those which are tedious and long in hours. Even now, many corner stores and restaurants are owned by Koreans, Chinese, and Japanese. These businesses involve excessive work and meager wages, but offer a means of developing marketable skills and services without displacing and incurring the wrath of others in the economy.

Question: Could you next talk about the various names that Asian American subgroups use to describe and identify themselves as well as protocols in addressing various individuals within Asian culture?

Hocoy: Again, I can speak most confidently about the Chinese. In terms of racial self-labeling, I think most Chinese regard themselves as Chinese, Chinese American, or just American. The name or self-reference that one uses is a useful source of information. Clinically, by asking clients what they consider themselves or what they would like to be called, you can get a sense of where they fall in terms of acculturation; namely, assimilation, integration, marginalization, or separation. If they identify themselves as Chinese, this says something very different about their cultural attachment, as opposed to referring to themselves as American. An integrationist would be more likely to say, "I'm Chinese American," whereas a separationist is more likely to self-label as Chinese. An assimilationist would typically use the term *American*, while someone marginalized would probably have difficulty identifying with any of these labels. It is thus quite useful for a provider to ask this question early on and to use it as an entree into these issues.

Personal names also vary somewhat from person to person. More recent immigrants and more traditional individuals use their Chinese name as their legal name. You have the person's family name, preceded by their Chinese first name. Both would be phonetically translated into English for purposes of pronunciation. Again, this kind of information is suggestive of a person's cultural background and degree to which they had been acculturated. On the other hand, a fifth-generation Chinese American family would probably have an Anglicized or transliterated family name, with a Christian first name in addition to a more familiar Chinese first name that is used only in the home. This is my experience. I was given a Chinese first name at birth which is known to and used only by family members. The Chinese practice of naming is similar to the Native tradition. A person is named according to their character at birth, and it is believed that this quality will define them throughout life. My

Chinese name is Siao Kee, which translates into "small wonder" to reflect my early curiosity about the world. Many Asians are also given a European name for the sake of convenience in interacting with the non-Asian world.

There are other aspects of naming that are important to know. Within Asian cultures, great honor is given to authority and age, and this is manifest in a general respect for people who are older than you. So, if there is someone in the room of similar age or older than the therapist, it is important to address them formally and with deference, as Mr. or Ms. or whatever is appropriate. If there were several people present, the therapist should address the older person first. Conversely, an Asian client may feel uncomfortable calling a therapist, especially an older one, anything other than "Doctor," even if invited to do so. I, for instance, didn't call my supervisor by his first name until the 6th year of graduate school, when I was about to defend my dissertation. I didn't feel comfortable referring to him in such a familiar manner until I was of similar academic status. It is also important to be aware that older Asian clients, as a result of their traditional Asian worldview, expect to be treated with a great deal of tolerance and patience by the therapist. Asian culture dictates that elders be treated with an obvious tone of respect and deference, and such an attitude is a necessity for facilitating rapport with older clients.

Question: These sound like some very useful and important suggestions. Let's go back to a topic you alluded to earlier, the history of Asians in the United States. Could you give a nutshell version of this history?

Hocoy: Of the Asians, the Chinese were the first immigrants in the United States. Unlike other People of Color who were either brought here forcibly, such as African Americans, or already here and physically displaced, such as Native Americans and some Latinos/as, they came voluntarily, as did the other Asians. The history of Chinese in the United States dates back to the 1840s. Many Chinese American families have roots in California that go back many generations to the time of the Gold Rush. They came mainly for a better life and to escape harsh economic circumstances and a variety of social problems in their native lands. Again, the early presence of Chinese made up for a lack of people willing to do what was considered women's work in California. They found work in areas which were sanctioned by the dominant culture. From these vocations came the core of the stereotypes of the Chinese laundry, the Chinese restaurant, hiring a Chinese cook, and so forth. They also were instrumental in building a national railroad system through both the United States and Canada. As I said, the Chinese were willing to take the jobs most Americans would not do. They were usually very dirty or involved high risk. There is a saying "not having a Chinaman's chance," which comes from this period. In the building of railroads, it was often necessary to dynamite the sides of a mountain. Chinese workers would be sent to set the dynamite, and often it would go off prematurely or the mountain would collapse on them. Many Chinese died this way, and as a result, the phrase "a Chinaman's chance" was coined. I have also heard the phrase used to describe the already exhausted mine areas which were the only sites in which the Chinese were allowed to look for gold during the Rush.

There is a long history of racial discrimination against Asians in both legislation and public policy. In 1882, Congress passed the Chinese Exclusion Act, which prohibited Chinese immigration for 10 years. It was renewed in 1892 and became permanent law in 1902. This resulted in great difficulties for the Chinese men already here. They were forbidden to bring their wives over, but what they could do was go back and father children, and these offspring were allowed to enter. The result was a very lonely existence: a culture of lonely, hardworking men, isolated from the dominant culture, who kept largely to themselves and lived lives of great hardship and misery. By 1943, immigration restrictions were loosened, and women were allowed to enter. They worked as dressmakers and in sweatshops in the growing Chinatowns, while men opened laundries and restaurants and, as had become typical, took jobs that were of interest to no one else.

And then there are the more recent reminders of discrimination against Asian Americans in the United States: the internment of Japanese during World War II; reactions to the influx of Southeast Asian refugees; reactions to Asian economic success in the United States; reactions to the emergence of Japan and the other "four tigers" as global economic forces; and in the 1990s, talk of quotas limiting the enrollment of Asian American students in U.S. colleges, universities, and specialized professional programs.

There is anti-Asian sentiment intertwined throughout the history of this country, permeating all aspects of U.S. society, some more subtle than others. For instance, with the growing interest in Asian martial arts in the late 1960s, American television producers conceived of a story line about a Chinese Shaolin priest set in the Old West. Chinese martial arts expert and actor Bruce Lee was initially chosen for the role of Cain in the television series *Kung Fu*. When the show was pilot tested, the White audience felt quite strongly that Lee was just too Chinese for the part. A White actor, David Carradine, was chosen instead. Bruce Lee was a hero to many Asians in North America at the time, myself included. One can only imagine the racial affirmation that Lee could have provided for Asians if he had been chosen for the TV series.

Question: Let's change our focus somewhat and begin to look at issues related to help-seeking and treatment. First, could you talk about issues that influence the ways in which Asian Americans go about seeking help?

Hocoy: In general, we are talking about very closed and tightly knit communities. They are very insular and cohesive and distrustful of outsiders. Their survival has depended on it being this way. These enclaves or ghettos—the Koreatowns, Chinatowns, Japantowns—have learned to live on the fringes and construct for themselves self-sufficient alternative social and economic systems outside the dominant culture. As a result of this mentality, Asians can be very distrustful of White people. The Chinese call Whites "ghost people" and consider their ways of life to be strange and sometimes inferior. There is clearly a sense of arrogance here. Both Japanese and Chinese mythologies contain beliefs that view themselves as highly advanced in terms of human evolution. My grandmother described it to me as there being a racial hierarchy according to color. White people reside below the Chinese because they are "pasty and ill looking" in appearance, whereas the Chinese have a touch of gold in their skin. Another example comes from the name China itself, which literally means Middle Kingdom; the early Chinese were pompous enough to believe that the world revolved around them. The Chinese do bring with them a rich cultural tradition outside of the United States and a long history of inventing everything from gunpowder to eyeglasses, from ice cream to the printing press. When these events were playing themselves out in the East, Europeans were still barbarians. This history engenders much pride among Chinese as well as arrogance and serves to support and justify their isolation.

In times of need, Asian Americans are more likely to turn to their immediate and extended family for assistance rather than to an outsider.

There are, however, exceptions, like the family doctor, who may not be Chinese, but who is someone the family has known for years and has learned to trust. With regard to psychological problems, Asian families may just live with the problem, preferring to work it out themselves, rather than going outside for help. Psychological counseling, as a profession, is clearly not an integral part of Asian culture. So, if a client is Asian American, the therapist may have to initially describe and explain the purpose of therapy, the role of the counselor and client, and so on. It should not be assumed that the client understands the nature of therapy. Therapy is a foreign concept in Asian culture. Meditation and self-reflection are traditional ways to self-knowledge, while the writings and sayings of Confucius, Lao Tse, and other philosophers act as guides for human behavior. In addition, one finds extensive informal networks of support within the family and community which provide counseling and advice.

Another thing to be aware of regarding help-seeking is the fact that there may be a great degree of shame and stigma associated with someone leaving the community and seeking professional help. The airing and telling of private affairs to strangers are virtually unheard of; it is a concept foreign to the Asian worldview. Part of this has to do with a fear of not being understood culturally by Western counselors. So, building rapport is an important first step to therapy. It is important for therapists to convey, both explicitly and implicitly, a knowledge of Asian culture or at least a respect for it and an openness to learning more. It is also helpful to understand that, given this general taboo, those who do seek out therapy are either very acculturated or desperate and have probably exhausted what resources they had within the culture and feel compelled to go outside.

Question: The discussion of help-seeking has led naturally to aspects of the Asian family and community. Could you talk more about family and community and how these shape what happens in therapy with an Asian American client?

Hocoy: To understand Asian culture, it's important to grasp the philosophical traditions and religious influences on the culture. One needs, for instance, to understand the role of Confucian ethics and the Buddhist "middle path" of moderation in life. Asians, in general, come from strong, interdependent family and community bonds; both are very self-contained and self-sufficient. Chinatown, for example, is a microcosm of the greater society in that it contains everything that is needed for life and sustenance. In terms of the family, an important value is the obedience of children. The flip side is respect for elders and their wisdom. These are Confucian values. In the home, there are many token gestures manifesting these attitudes. For instance, in my own family, my grandmother would always sit at the head of the table, even though she was demented in her later years. If there was a big decision to be made, her opinion would always be sought. It was obviously a token gesture, but what was more important was that it was a sign of respect. It's considered taboo to send relatives off to old-age homes once they get old as is common among Anglo Americans. Doing so is almost unheard of and looked upon with disdain in Asian cultures.

Asian culture is heavily based on interdependence; thus, dependence is not necessarily regarded as a bad thing as it is in Western culture, which places prime value on independence. This interdependence is reflected in the Asian attitude toward family relationships. It is understood that children will be dependent upon their parents for caretaking and that these same parents will eventually become dependent upon their adult children in old age. Since the therapeutic situation is a relationship, this value will likely manifest itself in therapy in terms of the client's dependence on the therapist and in terms of the client's goals for life and treatment. It is particularly important to realize that these priorities may not have to do with achieving relational independence.

Much communication in the Asian family is indirect, wherein messages are not directly stated, but instead must be inferred. There's a reticence to talk about personal issues openly. I think the fear is that someone may be embarrassed by what is said. In my own family, certain things are understood. For example, my mother says something without referring directly to it, but everyone knows what she's referring to. The therapist may see some of this reticence in therapy, especially in regard to subjects that are taboo or that the client finds sensitive. Sex might be such a topic.

The therapist may not initially get a very explicit account of the problem. Much may be implied, and clinicians must be attuned to subtle meanings and innuendoes. This is especially true with clients who are less acculturated. Again, this indirectness has to do with avoiding embarrassment. Clinicians need to be tactful and equally subtle in identifying the client's problems, being careful to validate the client's experiences, avoiding judgment or confrontation, and gradually honing in on the problem. In treatment, it may initially come down to talking in metaphors and indirectly about a topic in order to make the client feel comfortable enough to name and address it directly. This cultural tendency to imply meaning rather than to speak of it explicitly is very foreign to most Western therapists and counselors, whose training has focused on the spoken word and direct verbal communication. The therapist needs to recognize this difference as a cultural artifact rather than be frustrated by it.

Another Asian value that may result in different therapeutic goals for clients is tolerance for ambiguity and inconsistency in life. In Western psychotherapy, psychological integration is promoted through the achievement of clarity about one's life, consistency in various aspects of one's life, and the resulting decrease of cognitive dissonance. Among Asians, however, the ability to tolerate the ambiguities and contradictions in one's life is considered an aspect of maturity. Thus, striving for complete consistency in or understanding of one's life may not be considered as important, nor a goal of therapy. In general, it is essential for Western counselors to realize that the paradigms and models upon which Western psychology is based are infused with Euro-American middle-class values and may have little application to other cultural groups.

A sense of balance and reciprocity is also very important in Asian cultures. Because the family is such a cohesive unit, individuals are brought up to think of family over self. This basic aspect of the Asian worldview is diametrically opposed to the Western emphasis on self-realization. For instance, research has shown that the concept of "self-esteem" does not exist in Japanese culture. This value difference between the two cultures often becomes a major problem for young Asian Americans who become caught in a conflict of values between generations. The older generation demands obedience and respect; the younger one has been more socialized to the American values of independence and individualism. The result is a conflict of cultures and the need for reconciling two very disparate cultural views and sorting out the confusion as to how to live in both worlds.

Another aspect of therapy with Asians relates to the tendency of Asian cultures to de-emphasize the self and a prescription against self-promotion. For instance, one is not supposed to accept a compliment without resistance. If I compliment my mother on her cooking and the preparation of a certain dish, she would never acknowledge that it was deserved. She would probably say instead, "Oh, no. There's not enough salt, and this is actually the worst I've ever made." The implication of this for the clinical setting is that affirmation of the client's self, which goes against cultural norms, may be difficult for him or her to model. A corollary to the lack of emphasis on the self is the avoidance of personal embarrassment. Consequently, direct confrontations and demands on the client to accept personal responsibility for personal difficulties or specific behavior may be problematic for the therapeutic relationship.

Question: What are some of the common problems that might bring Asian Americans into treatment?

Hocoy: Again, I want to emphasize the fact that many Asians in the United States today still retain traditional norms and values; most of the Asian population in America are immigrants. So, only a limited segment of the Asian American community will ever find their way into a therapist's office. Those who do are generally more acculturated and bicultural, often students, as well as those who are particularly desperate for help and have not been able to find it in the family or community. For students, intergenerational and cultural differences are commonly a source of difficulty. Young people who have grown up with Western norms often find themselves at odds with parents who have very different values and expectations of them. One such issue revolves around strong parental pressures on the young person to excel. This can become especially problematic when the parents of their non-Asian peers are saying to their children, "Just relax. Do what you want." In traditional Asian homes, discipline is strongly emphasized, as is the demand to be successful academically and otherwise. One symptom that may emerge is depression, resulting from feelings of failure and inadequacy, engendered by internalized, unrealistic family expectations. Also common is a conflict between independence needs and loyalty to family. Excessive guilt can also result from not completely conforming to family demands, as obedience to parents and loyalty are cardinal Confucian rules. In general, holding Western values as offspring of traditional Asian parents is inherently problematic.

A related problem has to do with identity confusion resulting from minority status and the impact of discrimination on personality development. Some young people have a hard time identifying with their Asian heritage because this identity is often disparaged in their non-Asian peer group. Strong pressures to assimilate to Western ways are also likely to be communicated, either explicitly or implicitly. A client might experience "a tyranny of shoulds," pulling in opposite directions. They should be doing this according to the peer group; they should be doing that according to their family. In addition, people may not possess a strong sense of themselves, of who they are, or of what they really want to do. Instead, they may feel caught between two worlds: one side saying, "You should be studying or practicing violin; you shouldn't be going out drinking," and the other countering, "No, no, man. Come on out; you should be getting stoned and having lots of sex in college." It's a very difficult thing to bridge these different worlds. Feelings of being different because of one's ethnicity and not completely fitting in are often accompanied by feelings of alienation and loneliness as well as those of being misunderstood. It is a short psychological step from feeling different to feeling inferior—that there's something wrong with me; that I'm not worthy of love. And there's the depression that comes from wanting to be someone I'm not and will never be.

Many of these characteristics are subsumed in the literature under the title "mismatch syndrome," which speaks to the disparity in values between one's culture of origin and the dominant culture. Common symptoms of this mismatch are self-rejection and low self-esteem, depression, an emphasis on negativity, rigidity in thinking and problem solving, and even attempts to escape reality via addiction and suicide. Also inherent in the mismatch syndrome is active value conflict: traditional versus modern gender role definition, an emphasis on family and community versus self-interest, age status versus youth emphasis, obedience and conformity versus questioning authority and individualism. Self-restraint and formality may lead to a lack of social experience. People brought up in a culture that suppresses the open sharing of emotions may find themselves alienated and unable to make contact with their non-Asian peers, who depend on sharing emotions in order to move toward intimacy. Lack of emotional expression can also lead to the somatization of various ills. Insomnia is a particularly common way in which such problems are manifest.

Other typical problems for which Asian Americans may seek help include compulsive gambling, cross-cultural dating and marriage, overbearing parents, caring for aged parents and other family members, immigrant poverty, extreme work ethics, racial identity issues, and posttraumatic stress in those escaping war-torn countries of origin.

Question: In carrying out an assessment of a new Asian American client, what factors do you think are most important to attend to?

Hocoy: In working with Asian Americans, the first thing I would assess is where a client stands on the continuum of acculturation. It is useful to think of four modes of acculturation. Integration implies that the person equally embraces ethnic as well as dominant culture. An assimilationist tends to neglect his or her own culture in favor of fully adopting the ways of dominant society. A separatist chooses to maintain ethnic ties and traditions, at the same time refusing to take on Western values/culture. Those who are marginalized are caught between cultures, unable to identify as Asian, yet at the same time uncomfortable in the Anglo world. It's vital to make an assessment of where each client stands in relation to these four possibilities and to then identify the social demands that are impinging on them. In my own work, I tend to promote and encourage the integration mode. Research strongly indicates that integration, or biculturalism as it is sometimes called, brings with it the greatest likelihood of psychological well-being, with maximum flexibility, integration, and wholeness. Assimilation, with its rejection of cultural roots, is likely to bring up problems related to self-denial. Separation brings with it difficulties in navigating the dominant culture and can lead to isolation. Marginalization results in a lack of connection to any group and the possibility of serious mental health problems.

Equally important is assessing the nature of current demands upon the client, particularly from family. There may be serious difficulties both in the situation where (a) a family tends toward separation and is putting substantial pressure on one of its members to be more Asian, while the member has chosen a more assimilationist direction and (b) a client wants to remain traditionally Asian and must function in an environment that demands conformity to mainstream values. It is the disparity between where a person chooses to be on the continuum and what the environment demands of them that is critical.

Other dimensions that I would assess include language dominance, degree of adaptive behavior, degree of identification with cultural heritage, attitudes toward that heritage and themselves (self-esteem), life history (particularly with regard to events of intercultural significance, like racism), and attitudes toward the dominant culture.

Question: You talked earlier about cultural differences and therapeutic style. What other suggestions might you have regarding establishing rapport and working therapeutically with Asian Americans?

Hocoy: I think something that is essential for non-Asian counselors to do prior to working with an Asian client is a thorough self-assessment of their own competence to work with this cultural group. They must possess sufficient understanding and knowledge about the culture as well as an awareness of what they are bringing to the therapeutic relationship, namely, the assumptions and values of Western psychotherapy, their own worldview, and personal experiences with biases and attitudes toward Asians. This is a critical first step.

As alluded to earlier, it may help to remember that the concept of counseling is foreign to traditional Asians. It's the counselor's responsibility to introduce them to the roles of the counselor and client and explain the process of therapy before any kind of rapport can be established. Counselors have to be perceived as knowledgeable about that client's cultural group right off. That's particularly important for Asians because they may be apprehensive about therapy. Fear of shame and distrust of non-Asians act as potential obstacles to building rapport. Thus, it is critical that the therapist demonstrates clearly that he or she respects and understands the cultural differences that exist and that these differences are not obstacles. At the same time, therapists must be very careful of stereotyping and of recognizing the kind of expectations they hold about Asian clients.

When treating Asian clients, it may be important for Western therapists to be more directive than they normally are with non-Asian clients and to be prepared when an Asian client exhibits what might be considered more than normal dependency in the therapeutic relationship.

Western conceptions of psychological health emphasize client responsibility, openness, and personal exploration as well as self-reliance and self-determination in the therapeutic process. Clinical research, however, has found Asians to prefer a more directed and authoritative therapeutic style and to expect a certain degree of caretaking and direction. It is also important for the therapist to be nurturing and to have the therapeutic interaction reflect a familiar family atmosphere: directive regarding instructions, deferential to authority, but also nurturing.

For Asian Americans, few emotions are allowed, and there is generally difficulty with public displays of feelings. Emotionally laden content may not be easily discussed or easily identified by the therapist. The therapist must realize that there may be substantial difficulty with trusting and establishing rapport, given the taboos related to going to non-Asians for help and expressing emotions in public. Similarly, interventions should reflect or be consistent with Asian norms. The alternatives offered should be equally subtle, indirect, and nonconfrontational. There's a risk of Asian clients dropping out early, so it's especially important to build rapport and trust and to intuit any problems and check them out early on. As the client can be rather nonverbal, the therapist may have to ask if there are problems or identify them rather than waiting for them to be reported.

Asians also tend to have a very different nonverbal communication system. Providers need to be aware of this, because unlike the Western therapeutic focus on speaking, much of the communication in Asian cultures is nonverbal. The meanings of facial expressions, gestures, eye contact, and various cultural symbols or metaphors are usually completely different from Western ones. Research has found Asians to be a "low-contact" culture; that is, more comfortable with little physical contact and larger interpersonal distances. Studies also indicate that clients from various cultural backgrounds feel most comfortable with therapists that show similar nonverbal behavior. This mirroring of the client's nonverbal communication happens on three levels: proxemics, which refers to physical distance and touch; kinesics, which refers to body and facial movement, gestures, and eye contact; and paralinguistics, which refers to the extraverbal elements of speech, such as rate, tone, pauses, and so forth. It is absolutely essential that therapists pay special attention to the nonverbal dimension of therapy. Research has shown that appropriate nonverbal behavior conveys respect, honesty, interest, and genuineness.

With Asian Americans, the therapist may notice very subtle body gesturing and facial expressions. Large displays of emotion will rarely be seen, even if much is being felt and experienced. In many cultures, emotional states are rather transparent, easily read in the faces and body language of clients. With Asians (traditionally socialized), nonverbal communication is much more subtle. Sometimes all one can discern is a very slight head nod as a sign of affirmation if a question is asked. There may also be a general reticence. Asians are brought up to be indirect and to avoid emotional expressiveness. You probably won't see much gregariousness or strong displays of emotion. Also, as suggested above, nonverbal cues may have different meanings than for non-Asians. For instance, giggling often means embarrassment rather than a sign of humor. This is particularly true for the Japanese. Irrespective of the particular message, it is vital not to assume a commonality between Asian and Western "nonverbals."

The therapist should not challenge or confront avoidance or resistance immediately or in any way single out the client for what might be experienced as criticism. One may eventually be able to address relevant issues through more indirect communication. It is, however, important to lead with regard to the direction of therapy and spell out expectations the clinician has of the client. This is different than being confrontational, which is likely to induce shame and guilt. Again, it's related to "saving face." The therapist can subtly bring up deficits and shortcomings in the person, but not directly. Asians do tend to be familiar with very direct advice giving, but as to how or where they might go or what they might do as opposed to direct commentary on their personality, faults, or shortcomings.

For example, if the therapist wants to tell the client the reason he or she doesn't have a very active social life is because of excessive negativity, it must be stated in a way that the Asian client can hear. With Westerners, a therapist can generally be more direct, "I've noticed something and want to give you feedback on it; it seems you're very critical of other people." With an Asian client, it is preferable to be more subtle. For example, the therapist might gently ask, "Do you think there is anything you contribute to the fact that your social life is not so good?" When the concern involves aspects of the client's personality or interpersonal style, it might be shameful, so it's important to be more subtle, indirect, implicit about it. At the same time, Asians tend to be quicker to listen to implicit messages than non-Asians. That's because of Asian cultural emphases on subtleties in meaning.

Finally, it is important to remember that Asian Americans often experience a sense of guilt or selfishness in pursuing their own interests in therapy as opposed to thinking of the family first. The whole act or exercise of going to therapy is an individualistic pursuit. A client may feel some guilt around it. There is also a sense of collective embarrassment to have to go outside the community. It is a capitulation saying, "My community cannot serve me." It may, in addition, be considered a sign of weakness to go outside the community. These are all issues Asian clients might bring with them to therapy.

Question: Could you finally share with us a case that shows how these various themes that you have defined all come together?

Hocoy: When I worked as a university counselor, I'd very often work with Asian students feeling a lot of pressure to excel in school and having difficulty living in two cultures. Terrence is a good example. He was an engineering student who came to counseling because he was getting B's, and there was a strong demand both from his family and from himself to get better, and even perfect, grades. Terrence revealed other difficulties as well. Because he focused almost exclusively on academics, he had developed few social skills and didn't have many friends. During his 2nd year of university, these various factors came together to cause a depression. He found it difficult to concentrate in school and was increasingly losing interest because he was coming to the realization that there was more to life than just school. When his marks deteriorated, pressures from home increased. At the same time, he had difficulty forming the friendships he desired with non-Asians (his primary peer group).

It was obvious from his presentation that he wasn't clear what therapy was about. Nor was Terrence very psychologically minded. He had a low awareness of his own emotions and had difficulty identifying them. He experienced an amorphous bundle of vague, uncomfortable feelings, and he couldn't dissect, label, or identify their source. He initially came in because of slumping marks, saying that he wanted to be able to get A's and that he had problems with concentration. Through joint exploration, we discovered that he wanted to partake in more extracurricular activities. He also wanted to establish relationships with his non-Asian peers and had a romantic interest in a particular young woman (who was non-Asian). However, he knew his parents would not approve of his having a non-Asian girlfriend nor the time he spent away from studying. It was the family's position that school was a time for study and that relationships and hobbies could come afterwards.

It became clear very early that much of his conflict was cultural in nature. He was caught between two worlds: unable to negotiate socially and establish relationships with non-Asians and, at the same time, unable to motivate himself to focus on his schoolwork. He also questioned the expectation that he had to date another Asian. Ultimately, what was at conflict were Asian values regarding the paramount importance of study and maintaining Asian cultural separation versus the value of making friendships with non-Asian peers, and spending more time in nonacademic pursuits. He did not feel a part of his non-Asian peers and was increasingly feeling unaccepted by his family because of his "failing" grades. In short, he was increasingly becoming marginalized.

We spent the initial sessions helping him discern his emotions; often, I had to make suggestions as to what he might be feeling. With time and effort, a bit more clarity emerged in what he was feeling. He had great difficulty separating his feelings from those of other people, whether it be his peers or his parents. His emotional boundaries were very blurred, not uncommon in individuals from collectivist cultures. He was eventually able to report feeling pressured by his family to pursue good grades at the expense of social activities and to date and marry someone Asian. These were accompanied by simultaneous feelings of guilt and resentment. He was eventually able to understand that he had internalized the pressure his family had placed on him vis-à-vis academic performance and began to sense that there could be a difference between the demands his family placed on him and what he wanted for himself. It became clearer to him why his studying had become difficult and why he was internally caught between the values of two cultures. He also came to recognize the disparity between the Asian values of academic success and cultural isolation and his desire for relationships with those in the dominant culture and activities outside of school.

I encouraged him to pursue an integrationist path, one that allowed him to maintain his cultural traditions and, at the same time, establish relations outside the Asian community. By this point, he had developed clarity that this is what he wanted to do but felt uncertain as to how to proceed.

I assured him that he could participate in the non-Asian world without compromising his heritage and that, in fact, he could have the best of both worlds. The issue with his parents actually worked itself out as his marks improved because he was able for the first time to pursue the things he wanted to do, including spending more time enjoying himself and establishing friendships with non-Asians.

14 Working with White Ethnic Clients: An Interview with the Author

■ Demographics and Cultural Similarities

Who are the *White ethnics*? Put simply, they are national immigrant groups of Eastern and Southern European descent who share a common experience of immigration to the United States. They include Italians, Poles, Greeks, Armenians, Jews, and various ethnic groups making up the Russian Republic (Czech, Lithuanian, Russian, Slovak, and Ukrainian). Because of historical similarities, the Irish are also included in this category. All brought with them long histories of oppression and racial hatred in their native lands, were met with suspicion and rejection as newly arrived immigrants, and for a generation or two were exploited as cheap labor.

The United States has experienced two major waves of immigration from Europe. The first, which occurred in the early nineteenth century, was made up of Northern and Western Europeans: Germans, English, Scandinavians, and French. According to Healey (1995), these groups shared characteristics with the dominant culture already in the United States. They were Protestants, came from developing and industrialized countries, shared certain cultural values—such as the Protestant ethic of "hard work, success, and individualism," a belief in democratic governance, and levels of education and "occupational skill" that allowed them to compete in a modernized nation such as the United States. The second wave of Europeans, coming between the 1880s and 1920s, immigrated from Southern and Eastern Europe. These were the White ethnics. They were mainly Catholic and Jewish, came from rural, village-based cultures where the importance of family took precedence over individualism. As Healey (1995) suggests, they "came from backgrounds less consistent with the industrializing, capitalistic, individualistic Anglo-American culture" and, as a result, "faced more barriers and greater rejection than the Protestant immigrants from Northern and Western Europe" (p. 458).

In U.S. Census data, White ethnics are counted racially as "Non-Hispanic Whites." Respondents to the census are allowed to self-identify as to "ancestry" (defined as national origin) but may choose to defer. Because of inexact interviewing methods coupled with high levels of acculturation into "White" America, current White ethnic populations can only be estimated, not reported in exact numbers. The U.S. Bureau of Census (2000), for example, reports the following estimates for certain White ethnic groups: Czech, 1,248,159; Greek, 1,179,064; Irish, 33,067,131; Italian, 15,942,683; Lithuanian, 714,097;

Polish, 9,053,606; Russian, 2,980,776; Slovak, 821,325; Ukrainian, 862,762. The census does not report demographics for American Jews. They are considered a religious rather than an ethnic group and included in the census by national ancestry. Other sources, for example Singer and Seldin (1994), estimate the number of Jews in America at 5.5 million.

Today, there remain strong pockets of intact traditional culture within each of the White ethnic communities, although many descendants, as suggested previously, have taken the path of complete and irreversible assimilation. Because of their darker physical features and appearance, White ethnics were often viewed as non-White by Western Europeans and thus doubly rejected: both religiously and racially. In the United States, however, their skin color and physical features "paled" in comparison to the non-Whites who were already here. As the economic and social circumstances of White ethnics improved, they increasingly identified themselves as "White" in order to distinguish themselves from the People of Color with whom they competed for jobs and other economic resources. This dynamic is well described by both Ignatiev (1995) in his book *How the Irish Became White* and Brodkin (1998) in her book *How Jews Became White Folks*.

This newfound identification with "Whiteness" in turn allowed White ethnic group members to assimilate more easily. As they did so, they took on the racial attitudes and prejudices of the dominant culture to which they aspired. Thus, White ethnics exist in a kind of psychological "demilitarized zone." Being White in America, they share the privilege of Whiteness. But concurrently, as ethnic group members from cultures who have experienced long histories of oppression, they carry within them many of the internal dynamics that are similar to those of People of Color. Human service providers working with these groups face the task of helping them integrate and deal with these two very different psychological realities—that of the oppressor and the oppressed.

As clients, White ethnics, especially those who have been in the United States for several generations, feel comfortable with European American providers. Some have assimilated so fully into majority culture, in fact, that they are culturally indistinguishable from other White clients. Most, however, still retain some cultural connection to the past, and in approaching these individuals, helping professionals should be aware of four important points.

- Although White ethnics may be seen and treated as White by society at large, they do not necessarily perceive or identify themselves as members of the majority. More typically, there is the sense that "I am not White; I am Irish (or Italian or Jewish)." Nor may they identify culturally with the dominant Northern European worldview. Thus, it is important to be able to assess what a client's connection is to traditional ethnic culture and what traditional beliefs, values, and behaviors remain intact. If White ethnic clients do retain significant elements of traditional culture, providers must become familiar with the content of their culture.
- Such assessments should not be made merely on external characteristics. Like People of Color, White ethnics differ widely on assimilation and acculturation. As suggested earlier, some have so fully assimilated and

intermarried that there is little if any cultural material remaining beyond surface artifacts like family names, food preferences, and the like. Others are still very traditional, although they may have for convenience taken on some of the outward trappings of majority culture. Only through careful interviewing can an accurate assessment be made. In this regard, it is important to realize that external markers of culture disappear more quickly than internal ones. Thus, cultural artifacts such as values and worldview, psychological temperament, and family dynamics are more resistant to change and disappear more slowly.

- The cultural identity of White ethnics may be conflicted in much the same manner as it is for People of Color. This is true even for those who at first glance may appear highly assimilated. On a similar note, it is important to realize that even if an individual has been spared the direct experience of racial hatred and discrimination, its emotional consequences can be passed on from previous generations through family dynamics.
- The fact that White ethnics can so easily assimilate into American culture, thus seemingly escaping their collective past, creates a somewhat different identity picture. In comparison to People of Color, who are reminded constantly of their ethnicity, White ethnics can bury their conflicts much deeper and further out of awareness. But again, as in the case of People of Color, the rejection of such an important part of identity as one's ethnicity cannot help but cause deep inner conflicts that eventually affect behavior. Thus, it is not uncommon to find instances of identity rejection and self-hatred among White ethnics.

In the pages that follow, I "interview" myself about working with American Jewish clients as an in-depth example of clinical interventions with White ethnic clients. The interview is structured according to the question-and-answer format used in chapters 9 through 12. Unfortunately, space does not allow an extensive treatment of each White ethnic group in the United States. I hope that this interview will give you a rich sense of the kind of clinical and cultural issues faced by White ethnics in general.

■ Our Interviewee

Jerry Diller, Ph.D, is a licensed psychologist and member of the Faculty of the Wright Institute. He has also taught at the California School of Professional Psychology, Wilson College, and Thomas Jefferson College. He has worked clinically with American Jews and done original research on Jewish identity for more than 25 years. He is the author of two books on the subject: *Ancient Roots and Modern Meanings* (1978) and *Freud's Jewish Identity* (1991).

■ The Interview

Question: Could you talk about your own ethnic background and how it has impacted you and your work?

Diller: As an American Jew, I am quite familiar with the personal struggles and conflicts around ethnic identity that many White ethnics face. I just have to go back into my own personal history. I remember my grandfather, a tailor and immigrant to America, arguing with his old cronies about Jewish politics and the future of the Jewish people. And I remember him ending those discussions with a deep sigh and the words: "Nu, what can I say, it's not easy being a Jew." My grandmother, for her part, was always pouring over the "English" newspapers, and asking aloud to no one in particular whether this person in the headlines was a Jew or whether that event was "good for the Jewish people." For them, being Jewish was dangerous.

As a boy, I remember trying to tune out those comments. They made me uneasy, and I quickly learned to deflect them as nothing more than "Old World paranoia." I also remember my mother reassuring me that things were different in America and that this was a new start for the Jews. But that hopeful note was contradicted by other more subtle messages. It was the closing years of World War II. My father was fighting in France and, as I would later learn, the majority of my grandmother's family was being killed in Poland.

Although I didn't realize it at the time, I internalized my family's fears. In response, I did whatever I could to assimilate and become a good American. In the process I unconsciously rejected my Jewishness. As I grew into adolescence and young adulthood my sense of identity as a Jew continued to recede, eventually becoming, or so I thought, totally irrelevant.

It was not until well into my thirties, a college professor with a family, that I began to gain a sense of just how alienated I had grown from my ethnic heritage. The discovery of how I truly felt about being Jewish, that is, what really lurked beneath my conscious sense of indifference, came quite unexpectedly. One morning, while walking across campus, I looked down at the bundle of books I was carrying for a course on ethnicity and saw on top a book entitled *The American Jew*. Without thinking, I reached down and turned it over so that the word *Jew* could not be seen. Seconds later, the gravity of what I had done hit me. My first reaction was utter shock, profound surprise that being Jewish was still an issue in my life, let alone the source of such negative feelings. The shock was followed by waves of anxiety and the haunting realization that being Jewish had always felt very dangerous to me. Finally, feelings of anger began to surface: anger at myself and anger at a world that would make a child hate who he was. The simple truth was that I was fearful, embarrassed, and ashamed of being Jewish and had learned to minimize, degrade, and discount it through indifference. This experience propelled me into therapy to heal the inner rifts I had discovered. And I became so utterly fascinated by the process I was going through and what I found inside myself that I have been doing clinical work and research with Jews and Jewish identity ever since.

Question: Who are the Jews, and what characteristics do they share as a group?
Diller: Traditionally, Jews have been viewed as members of a religious community, sharing spiritual origins as well as a sense of peoplehood. But in fact they have become very diverse, and American Jewry is a microcosm

of that diversity. All Jews share common roots in a religious tradition and lifestyle and a long history of anti-Semitism and oppression. But differences in geographic location over the last 2000 years, acculturation into various host countries, modernization, and the extent of religious observance have created enormous diversity within the group. Jews range from ultrareligious to secular and atheistic. They reside everywhere, with the largest concentrations located in the U.S. and Israel. There are Jews who identify only on the basis of culture or politics or food preference. There are Jewish Buddhists, Jews by conversion, Jews of Color, children of Jewish intermarriage, Jews who believe in Jesus Christ, Jews who were raised not knowing they were Jewish, and Jews who have not an inkling of what it means to be Jewish. It is probably most accurate to define Jews as an ethnic group made up of various ethnic subgroups. Some people hold that the only thing that has kept Jews together as a people is anti-Semitism.

Jean Paul Sartre, for instance, once wrote: "If the Jews didn't exist, they would be created by anti-Semites." More traditionally based Jews see the commonality as spiritual and based in religious roots and observance. A traditional religious teaching in fact holds that all Jewish souls were formed during creation and were present at Mount Sinai for the giving of the Torah. As a psychologist, I see Jews as possessing a shared inner psychology and style which in general transcends all of the differences I have just described. Freud, himself a Jew, talked about the existence of an "inner identity" and a shared "psychological structure." I believe that each ethnic group has its own shared psychology. It is passed on within the family, like other cultural material such as language and communication patterns, through socialization and shared historical experience. Much of it also remains at the level of the unconscious as I described earlier regarding my own experience as a Jew.

First, like all oppressed peoples, most Jews have experienced a long history of trauma and grief, which shapes family dynamics and individual behavior. Clients often exhibit repressed fears, anxieties, and traumas associated with being Jewish. Second, I see certain consistencies in psychological structure: for example, a highly developed conscience or superego, the use of rationalization and intellectualization as defenses, and a propensity toward sadness and pessimism. Third, most Jews possess, I believe, a strong sense of morality, a strong utopian vision, that is, a desire to make the world a better place, and a spiritual urge toward wholeness and merging. Fourth, there is a shared worldview and style of thinking, one might call it "Talmudic," that involves a careful consideration of alternatives, emphasis on rationality, rule following, and creative problem solving. Fifth, there are a shared family structure and dynamics that I will describe later.

Question: Could you give us a nutshell version of Jewish history, especially as it has played itself out in the United States?

Diller: Jewish history is defined primarily by radical dislocations. A largely singular and insular ethnic people through Biblical times, the destruction of the

Second Temple drove Jews from their homeland and dispersed them throughout the world. The resulting geographically splintered subgroups experienced repeated migrations and resettlements. They existed at the whim of various host societies as anti-Semitism, based primarily on religious differences, ebbed and flowed in recurrent cycles. During their wanderings each took on an identity of its own, accumulating a unique history, assimilating aspects of the cultures with whom it came into contact, and adapting traditional customs as necessary. Surprisingly, there remained substantial contact between various geographic subgroups. Two general population groups evolved: the Ashkenazim and the Sephardim. The former were Jews who were dispersed throughout Europe and shared a common tongue: Yiddish. The latter were Jews who originated in Spain and Portugal and were forced to migrate to Arab lands, Italy, Greece, and Turkey after the Spanish Inquisition of 1472.

A second watershed in Jewish history, of more recent vintage, occurred in relation to the European emancipation of the nineteenth century. This democratization of European society set the stage for widespread Jewish assimilation into gentile society as well as a disruption in traditional Jewish religiosity. Emancipation provided Jews an opportunity to escape the traditional lifestyle and to take on non-Jewish ways and habits. Newly modernized Jews also took this occasion to "reform" traditional religious beliefs and practices so that these would be more in keeping with their new lifestyles. The result was the creation of a variety of new Jewish subgroups (most notably Reform, Conservative, and Orthodox) differing both on the extent of assimilation and modernization and the nature of the religious practices they adopted. These in turn existed side by side and often in tense conflict with those Jews who chose to ignore the lure of emancipation and stubbornly held to traditional lifestyle and religious observance. Many Jews rejected religion totally and became fully secular. The Holocaust and the establishment of the modern State of Israel represent two additional dislocations for the Jewish people.

Like the majority of American Jews, my own descent is Eastern and Central European in origin. My parents' families came from smaller villages in Galacia, located between Poland and the Ukraine. Most came to America to escape growing anti-Semitism and constricting economic conditions. Most wanted to forget the past and immerse themselves in American society and culture. Jewish identity became highly fragmented in America. With the exception of a relatively small group of Orthodox Jews who continue to practice a traditional Jewish lifestyle, most Jews have actively transformed themselves to better fit into American society.

Many have adjusted their religious practices to more closely parallel Christianity, attending services only once a week and on certain special holidays. Others have become predominantly secular, transforming their Jewishness into a set of ethical beliefs, a sense of peoplehood, the burden of 2000 years of oppression, or merely cultural artifacts like Jewish food or rituals to be enjoyed on a "pick and choose" basis. Thus for many, ethnic identity has been relegated to a peripheral or at most secondary position in their lives. There is, finally, a growing population of individuals of Jewish descent who today know nothing of their heritage and feel little connection to it. At present, intermarriage rates among Jews average around 50%, in some regions as high as 80%. It is nothing short of ironic that here in America, where Jews, like other White ethnics, have experienced more material and social success and have been more able to assimilate than ever before, there is a greater danger of disappearing as a group than ever before in history.

A cultural legacy of literacy, achievement orientation, and hard work combined with light-colored skin allowed Jews to quickly climb the socioeconomic ladder, primarily via professionalism and business. Like other White ethnic groups, most willingly took on the privilege of Whiteness and its attendant racism, while at the same time retaining a strong sense of social justice. Many, in fact, actively supported and identified with the plight of African Americans and their movement for civil rights. But the connection has not been mutual, and since the 1980s Jewish–African American relations have reached an all-time low. In many ways, this tension epitomizes the psychological plight of Jewish and White ethnicity in America. Its essence is well captured by Memmi (1965), when he described Jews as both the oppressor and oppressed at the same time. For many African Americans, Jews have become a symbol of White oppression and privilege. They are seen and experienced as very White.

Most Jews, on the other hand, perceive themselves not as White, but as Jewish. Although certainly part of this has to do with the invisibility of White privilege, it is equally fed by the experience of feeling culturally different from America's Northern European majority, not to mention a collective history of oppression, continuing anti-Semitism (though it differs in intensity and pervasiveness from that which existed in Europe), and anti-Israel sentiment.

Question: Are there any things that are important to understand about the nature of family, community, and culture among American Jews that have relevance for human service providers?

Diller: It is critical, first of all, to realize that American Jews, like all White ethnic groups, have their own unique cultural values and worldview. Just as there is enormous diversity in cultural content across Communities of Color, so too do White ethnics differ culturally from each other and from mainstream Northern European culture. It is in fact compelling to assume that White ethnics possess the same cultural patterns and traits as majority Whites, since they bear such a close physical resemblance. But this is just not the case, and White ethnic cultures, such as that of American Jews, are unique in their own structure and style.

Rosen and Weltman (1996) point to four central values that define and infuse Jewish culture (and much of what I am sharing is drawn from their work). These central values include:

- Centrality of the family
- Chosenness and suffering as a shared value
- Intellectual achievement and financial success
- Verbal expression of feelings

Jewish social existence is organized around these values, and the Jewish psyche is socialized to support and internalize them.

- Jewish tradition is highly family-centered. Unmarried men and women and childless couples are seen as incomplete; intermarriage and divorce are looked down upon and viewed as violations of family togetherness. Sex and family roles are fairly rigid and remain so throughout life within both the primary and extended family. High expectations are placed on children as well as adults, and socialization is accomplished through the threat of withdrawal of love and the engendering of guilt. The basic building block of Jewish life is, thus, the family as opposed to the individual, and there are strong pressures for family members to place the well-being of the family and the community before personal needs. Strong boundaries around the family protect Jewish ethnicity.

  Movement away from ethnicity is experienced and reacted to as rejection of the family. Within the family itself, relations are very close, often with unclear boundaries. Children are afforded higher status than in most other groups. They are expected to give their parents pleasure by way of their accomplishments and to remain within the family complex throughout life. Traditionally, the sexes tend to be segregated, yet there exist within the Jewish family very strong ties and conflicts between fathers and daughters and mothers and sons. Owing to these complex interactions, Jewish men are often described as distant and dependent, and Jewish women as intrusive and controlling.

- Jews tend to view suffering as a basic part of life. Jewish history has so often been characterized by persecution and oppression that the expectation of suffering, attitudes of cynicism and pessimism, and even paranoia have become a central aspect of the family's ethos. Suffering also serves as a shared basis for group belonging, as does the experience of slavery for African Americans.

  In other words, it is seen as an intrinsic part of Jewish history. Suffering is seen as something that is visited upon the Jew from outside as opposed to being a punishment for one's sins. Dwelling on suffering and life's negatives often has the consequence of eclipsing the experience of happiness and pleasure, and it is not uncommon for Jews to find it difficult to enjoy life without concurrently accomplishing something. Similarly, the focus on suffering is probably related to a high incidence of hypochondriasis among Jews. Such patterns are especially evident in families of Nazi Holocaust survivors in which parental suffering overwhelms and incapacitates children and where feelings of loss are too strong to talk about.

- Jews also place a high value on intellectual achievement and financial success. Historically, religious learning and scholarship were the primary sources of prestige and status in the Jewish world. A man learned, and all other aspects of family endeavor served to support that learning. As Jews assimilated into the gentile world, non-Jewish standards of success including money, professional status, and secular educational accomplishment grew increasingly important. The support of intellectual achievement within the family made success in these new secular activities easily transferable.

  With assimilation, a growing conflict emerged between family and success. Especially for men, becoming successful meant less time available in the home for family activities and interaction. As an oppressed minority, Jews also tended to push harder to succeed and prove themselves equal to or better than majority group members.

  Within the family itself, there is enormous pressure on children and spouses to achieve. In exchange for their special status and treatment, children are expected to perform, often at unrealistically high levels. The perfectionistic demands of the family can easily create a sense of failure irrespective of one's actual accomplishments. Such demands and their attendant sense of failure can also lead to competition among family members and the devaluing of each other to bolster self-esteem. This cycle of unrealistic demands, failure, and mutual criticism leaves family members wounded emotionally and permanently poised against attack. Also related to success is the high value placed on helping others and taking care of one's own. Traditionally, success is viewed as carrying with it an obligation of charity and generosity. Doing good deeds and giving to those in need are considered highly meritorious.

- Verbal expression is highly prized in the Jewish world. The ability to articulate thoughts and feelings and a passion for ideas are encouraged and rewarded within the family. All members including children are expected to express themselves verbally, and it is not unusual for the intensity of interaction to escalate as passions rise. Jewish couples tend to deal with conflict openly and directly. They increasingly seek verbal resolution and understanding as arguments and disagreements intensify. Of course, external circumstances can do much to alter such family value patterns. For example, in the well-known silence of Holocaust survivors and their offspring, verbal expressiveness has been limited by the trauma of their experience.

  The characteristics of heightened self-expression, achievement orientation, and adroit verbal skills often fuse in North American Jewish families to predispose its members to initiate verbal attacks when threatened. Aggressive language is used to express anger. Complaining, nagging, and criticism are means of controlling the behavior of others and at the same time venting frustration. Anger tends to be carefully controlled in the Jewish psyche and expressed only verbally or indirectly in action, but seldom spilling over into overt violence. It is important to realize that inherent in these seemingly aggressive acts is a component of caring which can make such interaction extremely confusing. Also relevant here, given Jews' long history as an oppressed people, is the possibility that some anger reactions may derive from a dynamic of identification with an oppressor.

Question: Let's switch our focus and begin to look at issues related to help giving and treatment. What factors influence how American Jews go about seeking help, and what kind of problems are they likely to present with?

Diller: Jews, like other White ethnics, exhibit unique patterns of help-seeking and attitudes and behaviors toward mental health issues. Generally, Jews tend to seek treatment earlier than other ethnic groups and to present with less severe neurotic symptoms. They tend to be more accepting of emotional symptoms and less so regarding symptoms of disordered thought. In general, they exhibit a low incidence of alcohol and drug problems. They are comfortable seeking mainstream professional treatment and prefer psychotherapy as opposed to shorter-term solutions. Families tend to seek help for aspects of their children's behavior, especially poor academic performance, lack of achievement, and problems in separation and leaving home. When marital therapy is sought, it is usually presented in terms of communication problems that classically translate into the husband being too distant and unaffectionate and the wife either sexually frigid or withholding. Problems with extended family, in-laws, and dealing with elderly parents are also frequent sources of difficulty. Counselors unfamiliar with Jewish culture may initially have problems dealing with a family's resistances to changing patterns of enmeshment, engaging distant Jewish men, dealing with demanding and assertive Jewish women, or misreading the use of verbal aggression.

It has been suggested that there is a strong relationship between Jews and psychotherapy. Jews are in fact overrepresented within the ranks of mental health practitioners and also as psychotherapy clients. There are various explanations for this connection. First, the roots of mental health treatment go back to Freud, who was himself a strongly identified cultural Jew. In Vienna where Freud practiced, psychoanalysis was referred to as the "Jewish science." Ernest Jones, his primary biographer, described the psychoanalytic movement as "very Jewish" in nature. Freud was actually fearful that his work would be rejected because of anti-Semitism and actively recruited Carl Jung and his Swiss Christian followers to give it a more international favor. Also, the growth of the mental health profession in the United States coincides quite closely with the assimilation and professionalization of Jews after World War II. Second, psychotherapy itself may be more familiar to those of Jewish descent. In my book *Freud's Jewish Identity* (Diller, 1991), I argue that certain aspects of Freud's theory—for example, the strong bonds between mother and son and father and daughter, tensions between same-sexed parents and child, repressed sexuality, strict incest taboos, and the inferiority of women—were modeled after his own experience of the Eastern European Jewish family. The emphasis in psychotherapy on verbalizing feelings, shared suffering, talking and insight as a means of resolution, and reliance on authoritative expertise also fit especially well with Jewish cultural patterns as described earlier.

Question: Could you talk more about issues of identity and group belonging as they affect members of the American Jewish community?

Diller: Jews, like other White ethnics, often report difficulties in group identity development. Some research findings might be helpful. In her research on Jewish identity and mental health, Klein (1980) found that of the 120 young Jewish adults from the San Francisco Bay Area tested, approximately 15% could be classified as positive identifiers, 15% as negative identifiers, and 70% as ambivalent identifiers. This means that 85% of the Jews tested voiced some inner conflict and discomfort with their ethnicity. These numbers are rather shocking and indicative of the extent of identity problems that still exist among White ethnic populations. What such statistics seem to show is that ethnic identity conflicts are slow to disappear, even with significant reductions in hostility and intergroup hatred. Rather, they are passed on from generation to generation as part of family dynamics. It has also been found that self-awareness of ethnic identity increases with perceived anti-Semitism and racial hatred. American Jews, for example, report growing discomfort and vulnerability as Jews as Israel has been increasingly criticized for its role in the Middle East conflict.

Question: What factors do you see as important in assessing American Jewish clients?

Diller: As I said before, in general, Jews tend to seek psychological help when they experience difficulties in their lives. Perhaps more so than any other ethnic group. But this does not mean that they will present initially with problems related to ethnicity, even if those are central to what has brought them into treatment. Conflicts around ethnicity tend to be avoided and remain unconscious even if they are actively shaping one's life course. So it is always useful to explore cultural and ethnic material—the role of Jewishness in one's family of origin, in growing up, in relationships, and in one's current life—when taking a personal history. Also, be prepared for some resistance in doing so. A common symptom of identity conflict is avoidance of ethnic material.

I would also like to say something about avoidance of ethnic material among providers. I do a lot of training of Jewish therapists about working with Jewish clients. What I find is that their own ethnic identities often dramatically shape how they work with their fellow Jews. If a therapist is conflicted around his or her own Jewishness, they will tend to avoid, distance, or manage discussions of the client's ethnicity in therapy. I remember back in the 1960s and 1970s, when there was a rebirth of interest in Jewish ethnicity and religiosity that paralleled the Power movements among People of Color, many of the Jewish therapists I knew were reporting the same phenomenon. "The strangest thing has been happening in my therapy with Jewish clients. All of a sudden, they are talking about being Jewish." Jewish therapists, like therapists of any race or ethnicity, can also internalize negative stereotypes of members of their own group and unconsciously bring these into treatment.

Question: Are their any subpopulations among American Jews that you feel deserve special comment?

Diller: Yes, first I would like to say something about survivors of the Nazi Holocaust and their families. The Holocaust is a critical issue to Jews, like slavery to African Americans, the Turkish genocide among Armenians, and the stealing of ancestral lands for Native Americans. It has been clearly shown that the trauma of the Holocaust crosses generations and is still very much evident psychologically in the children and grandchildren of survivors. Yellow Horse Brave Heart's (1995) idea of unresolved trauma and historic grief, reviewed in chapter 9, is very applicable here. Children raised by traumatized parents often become traumatized themselves. The unresolved grief is passed along, as is the sense of continual danger and loss. In Holocaust families the separation of children is especially difficult because it is so evocative of previous loss. Going back to the question of assessment, it is always critical to ask American Jewish clients about family history, proximity to the Holocaust, and the experience of anti-Semitism in their own lives.

A second subpopulation that providers should be aware of is Israelis living in the U.S. Israelis represent a very different Jewish culture than American Jews. It is a Middle Eastern culture. It is a majority, rather than a minority culture. It is a culture that has lived its entire history under the shadow of war. Secular Jews who live in Israel, which is the vast majority, identify themselves most prominently as Israelis, not as Jews. There is in fact a thread of "anti-Jewish" or identity conflict running through Israeli secular society. Anthropologist Stanley Diamond (1957), who studied the first kibbutzim (socialist communities) in Israel, sees the kibbutz structure as intentionally antithetical to Eastern European Jewish culture. Each value of Eastern European "ghetto" culture was turned upside down. The tight bond between parent and child was replaced by communal childrearing, religion and materialism were rejected, physical labor was valued over book learning and intellectualism, and self-defense, rather than blindly submitting to the will of God, became the way of dealing with a hostile world. Tensions also exist between Israelis and Diaspora Jews (Jews living in the dispersion). Israel sees itself as a protector of world Jewry as well as the proper and appropriate home, and only safe haven, for all Jews. U.S. Jews in turn feel that they insure Israel's survival by influencing American economic and military support. They view this role as crucial to Israel's existence and as a justification for remaining in Diaspora. U.S. Jews sometimes view Israelis as abrasive and haughty. Israelis in turn see U.S. Jews as soft and materialistic.

A central issue for Israelis living in the U.S. is their loyalty and responsibility to the State of Israel. All young adults are expected to serve in the army, and lack of service, for whatever reason, is looked upon with suspicion. Many Israelis experience feelings of guilt at residing outside of Israel. This is especially true during times of war or national threat. In order to deal with such feelings, the individual will often view their stay here as temporary, even if they have been here for 20 years and have no intention of going back. The downside of such a psychological strategy is the inability to mourn or grieve the loss associated with immigration. Attachments in the Israeli family are also very strong and separating from parents, friends, and even the land is often a difficult and painful process.

Lastly, two Jewish subgroups, Jewish women and gays and lesbians, often feel less than comfortable with their treatment in traditional Jewish culture. Many women believe that their role in traditional Jewish culture is demeaning and second-class. This has led to a strong feminist voice in the Jewish world, especially in the United States Jewish gays and lesbians, in turn, find their lifestyles unacceptable according to biblical law and thus find themselves alienated from their Jewishness.

Question: Can you make any suggestions for developing rapport with American Jewish clients?

Diller: Yes, several things. First, I find Jewish clients extremely verbal, cognitive, and desirous of discussing process in treatment. They prefer to be active collaborators in the therapeutic process and tend toward psychodynamic as opposed to behavioral forms of therapy. Any efforts you can make to reinforce these tendencies will be helpful. There is also high value placed on questioning and being verbally challenging in Jewish culture. This should not be routinely interpreted as aggression, although that may very well be present as well. I am reminded of an intermarried couple who sought treatment because of the wife's reaction to her Jewish mother-in-law. Having spent several years overcoming verbal abuse in her own family of origin, it was hard for her to tolerate and not react explosively as a result of interacting with her mother-in-law. She felt that she was once again being abused. We spent a significant amount of time looking at differences in cultural style and meaning between the world in which she was raised and the Jewish world she had recently entered. Therapy also involved encouraging the rather passive husband to be more supportive of his wife and to intervene in interactions with his mother.

Question: Finally, could you share some case material with us that shows how some of the various issues you have described in working with American Jewish clients come together in treatment?

Diller: I would like to share with you some case material that has been excerpted from sessions of an ethnotherapy group with Jews run by Klein (1981). The term *ethnotherapy* was coined by Cobbs (1972) to describe a therapeutic group method developed to explore and change negative attitudes about one's own race and ethnicity. Members joined the group because of strong feelings of alienation from their Jewish roots. In order to more directly experience some of the specific inner conflicts they had internalized, group members were asked to participate in an exercise Klein called "I Am a Jew." Each took a turn (and as much time as needed) standing in front of the group and repeating the phase: "My name is Jerry Diller, and I am a Jew." They keep repeating it until feelings, memories, or images begin to flow. Here are several examples:

- "My name is Beverly, and I am a Jew. I am a Jew. I am a Jew. The more I say it, the more nervous I get. I am a Jew. I am a Jew. It gives me the chills. It's not a strong word. It's too short, and I have to stand real tall. But it's not enough. It's as if someone is going to shake me. I realize that I've never let anyone insult me as a Jew. My trick is that I make it known from the beginning, so they wouldn't dare make any anti-Semitic remarks in front of me. But I know deep down that I am really afraid. Afraid that someone is going to come in and destroy me."

- "My name is Marlene, and I am a Jew. I am a Jew. I am a Jew. I want to tell my father. I am a Jew. My father grew up in a wealthy home in New Jersey. He always felt self-righteous about it. Always felt better than my mother, and she was the Jewish one. She and my grandmother spoke Yiddish to each other. It was because of her that I grew up in a Jewish home which my father never respected. As a child, I remember my mother cooking kippered herring, and my father complaining about the smell. I remember his comments. And I am ashamed of being a Jew. Especially with men. Dad, I am a Jew. And I am going to be a Jew if you like it or not. I am a Jew. Just like my mother. I am a Jew. I wouldn't care if I was Chinese. I just want to like what I am."

- "My name is George and, believe it or not, I am a Jew. I am a Jew. I am a Jew. Oy, am I a Jew. I am a dirty, #$%@& Jew. I am a Jew. I am a Commie, pinko, Jew. I am just beginning to get some of those feelings again. There was a lot about being a Jew in my childhood. I never felt that I was a good Jew. I can see myself having stones thrown at me as a kid, because I was dressed in regular clothes. It was Easter and all the Catholic kids were dressed in their best clothes. I was called a dirty Jew a lot. We fought the Italian kids a lot. That is just how it was. I want to keep saying it. I am a Jew. I am a Jew. (very loudly) I am a Jew. Can you hear me out there?"

The experience is a very powerful one. Beverly was able to identify the basic terror she felt about being a Jew and the strategies she used to avoid anti-Semitic comments. Marlene was able to confront her father, acknowledge her shame about being Jewish and her attraction to anti-Semitic men, and bond more positively with her "Jewish" mother. And George was able to re-experience childhood conflicts and overcome long-standing feelings of alienation in order to assert his Jewishness before the group.

According to Klein (1980), such experiences and the opportunity to explore personal feelings about ethnic identity and belonging are highly therapeutic and "overwhelmingly positive." Her postgroup research showed increases in self-esteem and ethnic identification and a decrease in social alienation. By way of summary, Klein (1981) suggests, "For minority group members group pride and self pride are inextricably bound. Struggling with and resolving conflicts in Jewish identity release tremendous energy formerly stifled by ambivalence and disaffiliation. This energy can be a potent source of self-acceptance and acceptance of one's own kind."

15 Some Closing Thoughts

You began your odyssey into the world of cross-cultural service delivery with an anecdote about Asian students who refused to avail themselves of mental health services at a college counseling center because its hospital-like setting reminded them of death. Such cultural "disconnects," which are still far too common in the human services, did not occur because of any lack of clinical expertise or caring. Quite the contrary, the staff of the counseling center where it happened boasts many skilled and dedicated clinicians. Rather, it occurred because of a lack of basic attention to the cultural dimensions of the world of their clients. In chapter 4 the concept of "paradigm" was introduced, referring to the worldview or perception of reality that a science or a practitioner has learned to adopt. It was suggested that paradigms shape perceptions and what one sees and doesn't see. The counseling center staff's shared paradigm did not allow them to see the cultural messages about death and avoidance that were so immediately obvious to the Asian students.

But paradigms can change and broaden, and that is what pursing cultural competence is all about. To reiterate the model found in Cross et al. (1989) (presented in chapter 2), cultural competence involves a series of five skills:

- Awareness and acceptance of cultural differences
- Self-awareness of one's own culture and cultural blind spots
- Understanding and working with the dynamics of cultural difference
- Gaining knowledge of the client's culture
- Adapting skills to cultural contexts

Hopefully, through your reading and study of this text, you have begun to see and acknowledge the importance of culture in working with clients.

You should by now have gained a good basic understanding of concepts such as cultural competence, racism, prejudice, privilege, and culture (chapters 1–4); insights into the psychological world of People of Color (chapters 5, 6, 7, and 9); a sense of how to get started (chapter 8); and introductory information on working with clients from the four Communities of Color as well as White ethnics (chapters 10–14). It is likely that you have been emotionally, as well as intellectually impacted by this material, have had some personal attitudes and beliefs challenged, and have become at least a bit more culturally open and less ethnocentric. And, although knowledge is no substitute for experience, you should have at least a beginning sense of whether working with culturally different clients is suited to your interests and temperament. If not, that is very important information to have. The rigor and demands of cross-cultural service delivery are not for everyone, and such work should be a matter of choice, not a matter of happenstance or default. In any case, you will find that what you have learned through this text will make you a better clinician no matter who your clientele is. Each client after all has his or her unique cultural background, which must be respected and viewed as the starting point for effective service delivery.

If you find yourself excited by the prospect of cross-cultural work and intend to pursue it further, I applaud your intentions. But remember what was said in chapter 2 about becoming culturally competent. It is no simple task, and it cannot be accomplished by reading a book or two, taking a seminar, or working with a few culturally different clients. It is instead a long-term, maybe lifelong process—one that never really seems to end. It is as much about learning about one's own internal processes as it is about gaining external knowledge. It is also cumulative and based on actual clinical work with diverse populations. Yet, it often seems, when first encountering clients from a cultural group with whom one has never worked, like "starting from scratch." Finally, moving toward cultural competence is highly developmental and growth-producing. You will likely be as changed by it as are your clients, perhaps even more so. As suggested in chapter 2: "This book is only a beginning. What happens next— what additional learning experiences you seek and the extent to which you seriously engage in providing services cross-culturally—is up to you" (p. 28).

So where to next? The following sections contain suggestions you might find useful by way of further preparation, as a means of gaining support (because such work can be isolating), and in helping to allay some of the natural anxiety you may experience in contemplating or actually beginning crosscultural counseling.

■ Gaining More Knowledge

It is necessary to continually broaden and update your education about cultural diversity. The more you can learn about the general topics of racism, culture, diversity, cultural competence, and cross-cultural service delivery as well as specific knowledge about individual groups and their cultures, the more comfortable and conversant you will become. Again, this book is only a foundation upon which to build. Since the late 1980s, there has been an explosion of good material in this area and a dramatic increase in excellent training opportunities. You should take advantage of these whenever possible.

Continuing education implies several kinds of knowledge. First, it means keeping current on racial and ethnic politics. The world of race and ethnic relations is an ever-changing kaleidoscope. History is not static, and once sensitized to the existence of race-related phenomena, it is hard to avoid the realization that racial and ethnic tensions are a central theme in our society. Witness, for example, the dramatic increase in hate crimes against Arab, Muslim, and Sikh communities in the United States since September 11, 2001. According to the U.S. Justice Department, more than 170 investigations of hate crimes were undertaken in the first month after the attacks. Muslim civil rights groups estimate the numbers of such hate crimes in excess of 1,000 and see this figure as very conservative given the fact that most incidents are never reported. A Western European socialist journal, *Committee for Workers International* (CWI, 2001), documents some of the most extreme reactions.

> A Sikh gas station attendant is murdered for wearing a turban in the Midwest. A Somalian is stabbed to death in Minneapolis. A Muslim man with an Arab name is found stabbed to death in Seattle. A man is murdered in Fresno, California, for looking Middle Eastern. A Salvadoran man screams for help in Spanish as a gang of five white youngsters beats him for being "bin Laden's next of kin." A Nicaraguan woman is assaulted in Los Angeles for her Turkish features. A mob attacks two Afghan teenagers in Prince William County, near Washington, DC. An angry mob of 300 "patriots" marches through a Chicago neighborhood chanting anti-Arab slogans and threatening local mosques with fiery destruction. A mosque in Central Kentucky is reduced to ashes by a fire bomb. Businesses with Arab or Muslim owners are threatened in New York, Detroit, San Francisco, Portland, Chicago, etc. Some are firebombed, others have windows broken or their storefronts decorated with the Neanderthal poetry of hate. (p. 2)

Such events have dramatic impact on all culturally different clients, not just those who are Arab or Muslim. They create an atmosphere of fear and danger that cannot help but bring back past memories of experiences of racial hatred. Clients will bring such reactions into sessions with them, and it is critical that they be acknowledged and processed.

Or consider the growing demand among African Americans for reparations from the U.S. government for slavery and its aftermath of racism. Chapter 10 describes reparations as part of the healing process following mass violence such as in South Africa and its Truth and Reconciliation Commission. It also points out the sad state of efforts to gain reparations for slavery in the U.S. Robinson (1999) calls it the "debt that America owes." African American scholars estimate the cost of unpaid wages during slavery and lost resources due to racism at at least 4 trillion dollars. Precedents for such reparations have been paid to Japanese Americans for incarceration and loss of property during World War II, Native Americans for lost land rights, and to European Jews for forced labor. And Michigan Congressman John Conyers has been introducing a bill, HR 40 (nicknamed "40 Acres and a Mule" after Civil War General Sherman's proposal of what each freed slave be given by way of compensation) to study the concept of reparations to Black Americans since 1989. Though Conyers' bill has never passed, and may never garner enough congressional support to do so, it is still a very real issue in the African American community and for many African American clients. Reparations for slavery and racism are not merely about money. Rather, they are symbolic of much more: the acknowledgment of an historic injustice, a means of healing the past and "leveling the playing field," a step toward reconciliation between Black and White America, and a matter of ethnic identity and pride.

Second, it means being aware that cross-cultural counseling and service delivery is a relatively young discipline in the helping services and, therefore, particularly prone to changing ideas, theories, and new research. State-of-the-art knowledge changes much more quickly than in established disciplines, and this calls for a much closer scrutiny of the emerging literature. The following are topics that I believe will emerge as particularly important in the near future for providers of cross-cultural service:

- Ethical guidelines for cross-cultural work. Although there have increasingly been efforts to enumerate behavioral standards for cross-cultural service delivery in all of the helping professions, these efforts have focused primarily on defining the skills necessary for culturally sensitive practice. You learned about three examples in chapter 2. The thrust of such work is based on the idea that it is unethical to offer services to culturally different clients without cultural competence. What is still lacking however are more substantive discussions of the specifics of appropriate and inappropriate behaviors by practitioners in the cross-cultural setting.
- Current definitions of general ethical standards, typically based on Northern European worldview and value systems, are often culture-bound and lead to conflicts between practitioner expectations and client's culturally prescribed behavior and style. Raising such issues is also at times experienced as an assault on the very heart of one's profession. Two good examples are professional boundaries and the confidentiality of personal information. Neither of these professional values are necessarily subscribed to or given the same degree of importance among non-mainstream cultures.
- Models of racial and ethnic identity development. Increasingly, researchers are realizing the great value of assessing and matching the level of racial and ethnic identity development (see chapter 6) of both providers and clients. In the future, such models will become more sophisticated and more fully enumerated for various ethnic and racial as well as for mainstream White subgroups. In addition, there will be more detailed work on the consequences of matching providers and clients who are at different levels of development.
- Countertransference in cross-cultural service delivery. There has been, over time, a growing awareness of the impact of countertransference in cross-cultural work. *Countertransference* is a psychoanalytic term that broadly refers to the personal attitudes and issues that color and shape a provider's reaction to individual clients. Becoming aware of one's own "baggage," especially around ethnicity, has increasingly been acknowledged as critical in the development of cultural competence. Future work will explore the impact of a provider's racial attitude (beliefs and stereotypes) toward a client's racial or ethnic group; ethnic identity, personal experience with "difference"; awareness of the communal dimension of a client's culture; and awareness of privilege and the power dimension of the therapeutic relationship.
- Bicultural clients and interethnic group relations. To a large extent, cross-cultural work has been defined in a binary fashion, that is, in relation to

the interaction of Whites and non-Whites. There has been, and will continue to be, increased interest and research in working with clients from bicultural and multicultural backgrounds. Similarly, there has been growing attention paid to the relationships among Cultures of Color.

- Transpersonal and spiritual dimensions of culture. Unlike mainstream European culture, Cultures of Color and certain White ethnic cultures tend to place higher value on the transpersonal or spiritual dimensions of reality. This can be seen, for example, in the different ways healing and mental health are defined. In conventional Western medicine, dysfunction is defined primarily in physical and psychological terms. The body and mind are seen as separate, and transpersonal experiences tend to be pathologized. Traditional cultures tend to be more holistic and view spiritual dimensions of healing as critical. As mainstream society becomes more interested in religion, spirituality, and other forms of nonrational experience, more attention will be paid to traditional healers and the transpersonal beliefs and worldviews of Cultures of Color.

Third, familiarize yourself with all forms of diversity. Although this book focuses on issues of racial and ethnic diversity, it is critical to be aware of the impact of differences in age, class, gender and sexual preference, language, and religiosity on human behavior. Each characteristic has been a source of bias and discrimination in our society, and although all share certain commonalities vis-à-vis the internal psychology of oppression, each has its own dynamics and characteristics. All represent sources of enormous variation and diversity within racial and ethnic groups. For example, age is defined, valued, and ascribed very different roles across cultures. In general, the elderly are revered, listened to, respected, and afforded high status among Communities of Color and White ethnic groups; quite the opposite occurs in Northern European culture, where youth is emphasized and aging is dreaded. It is suggested that you consider taking a separate course or reading a good text on each of the forms of diversity to familiarize yourself with their unique psychologies and how they interact with culture. In the "Selected Bibliography on Diversity" you will find a list of suggested readings in relation to each form of diversity.

■ Learning About Client Cultures

It is critical to prepare for work with clients from a particular ethnic group by doing research on that group's culture, history, and health care issues. This can include not only academic and professional reading and web searches, but also novels, biographies, social histories, and travel accounts as well as movies, videos, theater, art exhibits, lectures, and so forth.

A valuable supplement to such cognitive learning is various degrees of immersion in the client's culture. This can range from attending celebrations, cultural events, political rallies; eating regularly at ethnic restaurants; and patronizing community businesses to more sustained contact such as volunteering in the community, learning the language in programs in the community, and traveling to countries of the client's origin. One graduate program with which I was associated valued cross-cultural training to such an extent that it required its students' first field placement to be in a setting serving clients who were culturally different from themselves. As a learning strategy, students were responsible for gaining entry into these settings on their own.

This provided valuable, although sometimes frustrating, insights into cross-cultural interactions and cultural variation in organizational dynamics. Such cultural encounters and the cultural knowledge they impart are seen as so important that Coleman and Gates (1999) have added it as a sixth skill component of cultural competency in their extension of Cross et al.'s model.

■ Finding Support for Cross-Cultural Work

It is also a useful idea to find a "cultural consultant," a professional who is indigenous to the community with whom you will be working to consult on a regular basis. As a beginner to cross-cultural work, it is particularly helpful to discuss all cases, especially early in your training, with someone who is knowledgeable about the workings of the client's culture. With more experience and comfort, one might feel the need for consultation only in more difficult or problematic cases. Agencies should also establish ongoing consulting relationships with indigenous cultural experts from all groups that they serve.

One might also consider establishing a peer study/supervision group with other providers who are involved in cross-cultural service delivery. Regular meetings can involve discussing shared readings, presenting cases, having guest experts, and the like. Such a group can provide opportunities to share resources and knowledge, receive supervision and support when helpful, and remain focused on the cultural dimensions of cross-cultural service delivery.

A final suggestion is to join local ethnic provider groups and networks. Often, providers who work extensively with a specific population join together as a means of sharing information and resources, advocating for the needs and rights of clients, and keeping knowledgeable on current research and trends in providing services to the population of interest. Active participation in such a group is an excellent way to learn more about a client population, connect with other providers who might serve as valuable resources, and demonstrate interest and commitment to cross-cultural service delivery as a career focus.

■ Summary

The case of the Asian students who refused to seek services at a university because it reminded them of a hospital and a place of death, with which this book begins, is reviewed along with Cross et al.'s model of cultural competency skills for professional helpers. Readers are asked to review what they have learned and whether they feel ready or interested in pursuing further learning toward cultural competency. For those who wish to continue, suggestions are offered for gaining more knowledge (keeping current with racial and ethnic politics and emerging and changing ideas about cross-cultural service delivery); becoming more familiar with all forms of diversity; learning from immersion in client cultures; and developing support systems to facilitate further skill development and guidance. I sincerely hope that reading this text has been a satisfying, enlightening, and growth-producing experience for you.

■ Activities

1. *Review of learning experiences.* Review in your mind the most important learning experiences you had during the course in which you are enrolled. Describe each briefly in regard to what happened, how you felt as a result of the experience, and what you learned. You might find it interesting and informative to categorize each learning experience in relation to the professional skill development models we reviewed in chapter 2. What would you say is the single most important concept you learned during the course and from this textbook?

2. *Enjoy a career fantasy.* Project yourself 10 years into the future. Envision a hypothetical work situation that incorporates all of the fantasies you have about the kind of helping services work you would like to be doing in 10 years. What kind of agency or setting are you in? What kind of tasks are you involved in? Who is your client population? What kinds of cross-cultural work are you doing? What levels of cultural knowledge and skill have you developed over the past 10 years? What experiences in the interim have contributed to your growth in cross-cultural skills? How are you feeling about your cultural competency?

A Case of Elena

Before proceeding to an exploration of the social and cultural issues possibly related to this 17-year-old Mexican American female, it is important to note the enormous diversity that can exist within the Mexican American community. In the case that follows I will explore certain *possible* dynamics related to culture and ethnicity that have been reported in relation to the psychology of Mexican Americans as well as other immigrant communities. It is the therapist's job to assess whether they are being appropriately applied in a specific case. Such hypotheses are psychic possibilities that must be confirmed by the data one collects clinically.

Elena's distress seems to derive more from cultural conflict than inherent psychopathology. It is important to understand that her stress and conflicted feelings about going to college versus staying home and caring for her mother (family vs. self), not being understood by anyone, and the relative importance of her ethnicity, relate to a pattern frequently observed within immigrant families, that is, intergenerational conflict between parents and children over the retention of traditional values and ways as opposed to acculturation to "White European" American values. Immigrants' children who are born in the United States are acculturated much more quickly than are their parents, through schools, peers, and the media, and they typically take on the contemporary American styles and values, many of which are in direct conflict with traditional family values. At the same time, such children, quicker to take on English, often serve the role of cultural brokers (translating, explaining things, helping to make family decisions) and in the process tend to accumulate more personal power in the family than is typical in the native culture. Based on this expanded sense of power, they often challenge the traditional family structure.

Such a dynamic may be playing itself out within the conflicts Elena describes. Role prescriptions in traditional Mexican culture would require Elena to suppress her needs and desires in service to the family and so become a caretaker to her mother. The role expectation for children in the European family model is quite different; one is expected to separate from the family in order to become autonomous and prepare to live independently. Some theorists have referred to this cultural variation as the extended self as opposed to the individual self. Elena has internalized both definitions of self and vacillates between them, unable to decide which set of values to actualize. Her ambivalence reflects a classic approach-avoidance conflict because the two dictate opposing behaviors.

Elena's ethnic identity is conflicted as well; that is, there are traits related to being Mexican American that she has learned to experience as negative and thus difficult to internalize as positive aspects of self. Examples include her loss of Spanish language and how its use was taboo in the home, the ways in which she feels oppressed by traditional values, and her embarrassment at her parents "old world" ways and inability to understand the American norms, especially those that afford children greater freedom and autonomy. An important barometer of her ethnic conflict is her choice of White peers rather than Mexican American or a mixed group of friends. One is led to ask why she has made this choice, especially in light of the fact that she does not feel that these friends or their parents understand or value her situation or cultural background. This choice can thus be seen as an effort to escape aspects of who she is ethnically.

Research has generated several models of assimilation and acculturation relevant to Elena's situation. One model holds that acculturation (that is, the taking on of cultural artifacts and values from another group) is unidimensional. As one takes on aspects of a new culture, it is necessary to (consciously and unconsciously) give up aspects of the old that are found to be in conflict with it. This approach suggests that marginality and isolation are the most typical psychic outcomes for such a conflicted individual, where sufficient inner and outer changes have been made so that the person is comfortable in neither culture. One certainly sees such alienation in Elena's situation. An alternative theory holds the possibility of a person becoming "bicultural," that is, being comfortable, unconflicted, and able to move with ease between cultures. For Elena to move in such a direction, she must first resolve the conflicts she feels toward both cultures, acknowledging and accepting the values she has derived from each. A similar process of positive identity development must occur in biracial and biethnic children as well. It is important to understand that Elena's cultural conflict and sense of marginality, exclusion, and isolation are exacerbated by strong pressures being exerted both by her family in favor of adopting traditional Mexican American behaviors and values and by her peers and their parents in favor of European American cultural style and values. Each side is in its own way addressing issues of group and cultural survival: guarding and protecting group boundaries and trying to keep the individual within the group. Elena has internalized parts of each culture but finds it impossible to integrate them, especially under the pressure that both are simultaneously exerting. She also intimately feels the rejection of aspects of her "bicultural self" by both sides, making it difficult for her to feel fully at home and at peace in either "camp." This is the source of her sense of aloneness and isolation. Perhaps it is best captured in the distance she feels from her boyfriend. She feels pressed by his demand that she decide in favor of going to college and is very much put off by his bad manners, inconsiderateness, and prejudice against her parents as "stupid and ignorant." It certainly must be disquieting for Elena to hear such remarks directed toward parents whom she does deeply love and respect (in spite of the anger and frustration she currently holds toward them) and to realize that they are simultaneously being leveled at her and her own Mexican American identity.

Elena's feelings about her identity conflict are fueled by both the structure of the traditional Mexican American family in which she grew up as well as the ways in which her parents and siblings have adjusted to their new home in America. The Mexican American family is highly role-prescribed though less so than the traditional Mexican family. There is no question about her brother's attending college because he is the oldest male and must serve as a breadwinner. Her older sister, because of her rebellion, drug abuse, and rejection of the family, has become an antimodel and reinforcement of her parents' worst fears about what can happen to their children in America, thus making it even harder for Elena to break away. Traditionally, younger Mexican girls were not necessarily expected to marry, but rather to enter monasteries and dedicate themselves to God (among the wealthier) or to remain in the home and care for parents as they aged. Elena's parents, having experienced much discrimination upon entering the United States, especially in the form of language difficulties, refused to speak Spanish in the home as a means of protecting their children from what had happened to them. But in so doing, they unwittingly robbed the children of an important connection to their identities, a factor that would further alienate Elena.

Again, these are all hypotheses that must be checked out in the context of ongoing work with the client.

B Case of Theo

Before proceeding to an exploration of the social and cultural issues possibly related to this 22-year-old African American male, it is important to note the diversity that can exist within the African American community. In the case that follows I will explore certain *possible* dynamics related to culture and ethnicity that have been reported in relation to the psychology of African Americans as well as to other ethnic communities. It is the therapist's job to assess whether they are being appropriately applied in a specific case. Such hypotheses are psychic possibilities that must be confirmed by the date one collects clinically.

Because of a long history of experiencing personal and institutional racism, Clients of Color may exhibit initial mistrust and suspicion toward culturally different (and especially White) therapists, whom they regard as symbols of an oppressive society. They may also attempt to provoke and test the therapist as a means of assessing trust and safety. Such reactions, especially common in mandated treatment situations, should not in and of themselves be pathologized. We see some of this discomfort in Theo early in the session and might liken the reason he has come to therapy to being mandated, that is, as the result of a threat by his girlfriend Tamia.

Theo's anger must be understood not only psychodynamically but also in its sociocultural context. African American men are at particularly high risk for both physical and emotional stress reactions and diseases. Problems with rage and anger management are not uncommon. Theo's size and comportment, especially if he is much of the time consumed by anger and rage, may be off-putting to many, especially those who hold prejudicial attitudes, have limited contact with African American culture and style, and have learned to fear African American men. Such reactions are especially common in the largely White worlds of his current college and middle and secondary schools. They may well be responsible for some of the social isolation and rejection he is experiencing (whereby growing frustration and anger leads to increasing negative reactions and rejection by others, etc.). It is also important to realize that persons who feel powerless in their lives tend to develop an interpersonal style that gives them feelings of power and agency. Such behavior, as when a physically large individual uses size to intimidate or when someone controls others through dependency, often becomes counterproductive and isolating.

Additional sources of stress to explore include: Theo's family's relocation from a rural Texas town to a metropolitan area (possibly located in a non-Southern region), their rise to middle-class status, and a likely move to a more interracial and integrated neighborhood in which Theo found himself with fewer Black children and more of an isolated minority. Each event demands increased amounts of assimilation and acculturation into the White world, as well as possibly evoking feelings of not belonging, being different, being in danger, being expected to perform at higher levels, or being perceived by aspects of the African American community as non-Black or as turning one's back on the community. It has also been found that minority group members in primarily White jobs and schools (especially if they are the first members of their family to reach such statuses) often experience high levels of stress over their performances. Such situations can cause serious threats to self-esteem, especially in those with conflicted ethnic identities.

There is possible evidence of negative aspects of ethnic identity in Theo's history and behavior, that is, some discomfort with his own "Blackness." His anger and frustration at his parents' "yelling and throwing objects" may be partially fueled by internalized negative stereotypes of "African American" patterns of communication and interaction styles. Related may be his decision to go to a predominantly White college, when his parents wanted him to attend an historically Black college. By refusing to follow in their footsteps and thereby rejecting what they represent, he may be distancing himself from aspects of Blackness as well as "a lot of fighting and yelling."

His anger at his parents, which verges on total rejection (or at least in fantasy, as in joining his brothers as the family unit of importance), may also be related to issues of family structure. His brother, for example, to whom he is very attached, seems to play the role of the parentified child and caregiver and peacemaker in the family. Such patterns are especially common in lower socioeconomic families where both parents may have to work to survive or in upwardly mobile ones where making it is paramount.

Theo's anger and frustration seem directed especially toward women, as exemplified in his relations to girls in high school and his current girlfriend Tamia. It is important to note that (especially in primarily White settings) the entrance into adolescence and sexuality often marks a dramatic increase in separation between racial and ethnic groupings. This dynamic hits isolated Children of Color especially hard because often they find themselves rejected by previous friends of the opposite sex, often without explanation. We do not know Tamia's ethnic background, but can make a guess that she is African American also, given the information we have about her church membership. We do know that they share interests in the same type of colleges (predominantly White) as well as national issues (which may well include similar attitudes toward the importance of ethnicity and perhaps similar attitudes toward ethnic identity).

Tamia's discomfort with her sexuality seems problematic, especially in light of the duration of their relationship. We know little about Tamia's history or family drama, but she attributes her discomfort to fear of pregnancy, religious values against premarital sex, and excessive guilt. Her strong reaction to Theo's viewing of pornography perhaps is a related clue. It is also possible (and should be explored by the therapist) that her fear is in part related to issues of ethnic identity and internalized negative stereotypes of loose sexuality and unmarried pregnancies among African American youth. In that she seems to exhibit some evidence of distancing herself from the African American community and identity, such a guess may be worth pursuing.

Again, these are all hypotheses that must be checked out in the context of ongoing work with the client.

Selected Bibliography on Diversity

Ablism and Disability

Bragg, L. (2001). *Deaf World*. New York: New York University.

Charlton, J. I. (2002). *Nothing About Us Without Us: Disability Oppression and Empowerment*. Berkeley, CA: University of California.

Dorris, M. (1989). *The Broken Cord*. New York: HarperCollins.

Hockenberry, J. (1995). *Moving Violations: War Zones, Wheelchairs, and Declaration of Independence*. New York: Hyperion.

Keith, L. (1996). *What Happened to You: Writing by Disabled Women*. New York: New Press.

Murphy, R. F. (2001). *The Body Silent*. New York: W. W. Norton.

Neer, F. N. (2000). *Breaking Barriers: The Extraordinary Stories of Uncommon People*. Berkeley, CA: Creative Arts.

Potok, A. (2000). *A Matter of Dignity: Changing the World of Disability*. New York: Bantam.

Shapiro, J. P. (1993). *No Pity: People with Disabilities Forging a Civil Rights Movement*. New York: Three Rivers.

Shaw, B. (1994). *The Ragged Edge*. Louisville, KY: Avocado.

Aging

Creagan, E. T. (2001). *Mayo Clinic on Healthy Aging*. Rochester, MN: Mayo Clinic.

Doress-Warters, P. B., & Siegel, D. L. (1994). *Ourselves, Growing Older: Women Aging with Knowledge and Power*. New York: Touchstone.

Friedan, B. (1993). *The Fountain of Age*. New York: Simon & Schuster.

Gillick, M. R. (2001). *Lifetimes: Living Longer, Growing Frail, Taking Heart*. New York: W. W. Norton.

Ilano, J. A. (1998). *As Parents Age: A Psychological and Practical Guide*. Acton, MA: VanderWyk & Burnham.

Mace, N. L., & Rabins, P. V. (1999). *A Family Guide to Caring for Persons with Alzheimer's Disease*. Baltimore, MD: Johns Hopkins.

Marcell, J. (2001). *Elder Rage*. Irvine, CA: Impressive.

Nelson, T. D. (2002). *Ageism: Stereotypes and Prejudice Against Older Persons*. Cambridge, MA: MIT Press.

Olshansky, S. J., & Carnes, B. A. (2001). *The Quest for Immortality: Science at the Frontiers of Aging*. New York: W. W. Norton.

Pogrebin, L. C. (1996). *Getting Over Getting Older*. New York: Berkeley Books.

Schacter-Shalomi, Z., & Miller, R. R. (1995). *From Age-ing to Sage-ing: A Profound New Vision of Growing Older*. New York: Warner.

Snowden, D. (2001). *Aging with Grace: What the Nun Study Teaches Us About Living Longer, Healthier, and More Meaningful Lives.* New York: Bantam.

Classism

Dalrymplem, T. (2001). *Life at the Bottom: The Worldview That Makes the Underclass.* Chicago, IL: Ivan R. Dee.

Duncan, C. M. (2000). *Worlds Apart: Why Poverty Persists in Rural America.* New Haven, CT: Yale University.

Ehrenreich, B. (2001). *Nickel and Dimed: On (Not) Getting By in America.* New York: Henry Holt.

Fussell, P. (1992). *A Guide Through the American Status System.* New York: Simon & Schuster.

Grusky, D. B. (2001). *Social Stratification: Class, Race & Gender.* Boulder, CO: Westview.

Holloway, S. (1997). *Through My Own Eyes: Single Mothers and the Culture of Poverty.* Cambridge, MA: Harvard University.

Katz, M. (1989). *The Undeserving Poor: From War on Poverty to the War on Welfare.* New York: Pantheon.

Lewis, O. (1975). *Five Families in Mexico: Case Studies in the Culture of Poverty.* New York: HarperCollins.

Mills, C. W. (2000). *The Power Elite.* New York: Oxford.

Mills, C. W. (2000). *White Collar.* New York: Oxford.

Gender

Adoras, R., & Savran, D. (2002). *The Masculine Studies Reader.* Malden, MA: Blackwell.

Anzaldau, G. E., & Keating, A. (2002). *This Bridge We Call Home: Radical Visions of Transformation.* New York: Routledge.

Chessler, P. (1997). *Women and Madness.* New York: Avon.

De Beauvoir, S. (1980). *The Second Sex.* New York: Random House.

Estrich, S. (2000). *Sex and Power.* New York: Riverhead.

Faludi, S. (1992). *Backlash: The Undeclared War Against American Women.* New York: Doubleday.

Friedan, B. (1997). *Feminine Mystique.* New York: Norton.

Galliano, G. (2003). *Gender: Crossing Boundaries.* Belmont, CA: Wadsworth.

Gilman, C. P. (1999). *The Yellow Wallpaper.* New York: St. Martin's.

Hooks, B. (2000). *Feminist Theory: From Margin to Center.* Cambridge, MA: South End Press.

Lay, M. M., Monk, J., & Rosenfeld, D. S. (2002). *Encompassing Gender: Integrating International Studies and Women's Studies.* New York: Feminist Press, City University of New York.

Miller, S. B. (1999). *In Our Time: Memoir of a Revolution.* New York: Delta.

Millet, K. (2000). *Sexual Politics.* Urbana, IL: University of Illinois.

Pipher, M. (1994). *Reviving Ophelia: Saving the Selves of Adolescent Girls.* New York: Ballantine.

Sexual Orientation: Gay, Lesbians, Transsexuals

Barrett, B. (2002). *Counseling Gay Men and Lesbians: A Practice Primer.* Belmont, CA: Wadsworth.

Clark, D. (1997). *Loving Someone Gay.* Berkeley, CA: Celestial Arts.

Daly, M. (1996). *Surface Tension: Love, Sex and Politics Between Lesbians and Straight Women.* New York: Simon & Schuster.

Duberman, M. (2002). *Cures: A Gay Man's Odyssey.* Cambridge, MA: Westview.

Fone, B. (2000). *Homophobia.* New York: Henry Holt.

Morrison, J. (2001). *Broken Fever: Reflections on Gay Boyhood.* New York: St. Martin's.

Myerowitz, J. (2000). *How Sex Changed: A History of Transsexuality in the United States.* Cambridge, MA: Harvard University.

Nestle, J., Howell, C., & Wilchins, R. (2000). *Gender Queer.* Los Angeles: Alyron.

Savin-Williams, R. C. (1996). *Lives of Lesbians, Gays, and Bisexuals: Children to Adults.* Belmont, CA: Wadsworth.

Glossary

Acculturation   A form of assimilation wherein an ethnic group or individual takes on the cultural ways of another group, usually that of mainstream culture, often at the expense of traditional cultural ways.

Acculturative stress   Stress and emotional distress, and at times trauma, caused by acculturation.

African Americans   A diverse array of Americans of African descent—including those born in the United States, Africans, and individuals from the West Indies and Central and South America.

Alloplastic   An approach to personal change that involves altering the external environment to fit the needs of the individual.

Ambivalent ethnic identification   An inner sense of group belonging in which positive ethnic experiences co-exist alongside negative and rejecting ones, leading to a vacillation between positive and negative identification. Also referred to as internalized racism, internalized oppression, and racial self-hatred.

Apology   A formal statement of regret that includes acknowledgment of the facts, acceptance of responsibility, expression of sincere regret, and promise to not repeat the offense. An aspect of reparations.

Asian Americans   A diverse array of Americans of Asian and Pacific Islander descent representing 43 distinct Asian and Pacific Islander ethnic groups.

Assimilation   A process whereby a previously distinct ethnic group merges socially into another group, usually dominant or mainstream society. Forms of assimilation include acculturation, structural assimilation, marital assimilation, and identificational assimilation.

Authoritarian personality   A psychological theory of prejudice derived from the work of Adorno, Frandel-Brunswik, Levinson, and Sanford (1950), that views prejudice and racism as one of various characteristics of a global bigoted personality type.

Autoplastic   An approach to personal change that involves adapting the self to the external environment.

Axiology   A dimension of culture that describes the interpersonal values that a cultural group teaches.

Bicultural families   Families in which individual members descend from two or more cultures or racial groups. They can be formed either by parents from different cultures or through adoption.

Biculturalism   The belief that it is possible to live and function effectively in two cultures.

Concept of self   A dimension of culture that refers to whether group members experience themselves as separate beings (individual self) or as part of a greater collective (extended self).

Concept of time A dimension of culture that describes how time is experienced within a cultural group.

Cross-cultural Referring to different cultural backgrounds.

Cross-cultural service delivery The provision of human services in a situation where provider and client come from different cultural backgrounds.

Countertransference A psychoanalytic term that refers to a therapist's unconscious personal reaction to aspects of the client.

Cultural ally A White person who actively works to eliminate racism.

Cultural case formulation A framework, included in DSM-IV, to be used in assessing and the diagnosis of culturally different clients. It highlights areas of functioning where cultural characteristics may alter appropriate diagnosis, assessment, and treatment planning.

Cultural competence The ability to effectively provide services cross-culturally.

Cultural diversity The array of differences that exist among groups of peoples with definable and unique cultural backgrounds.

Cultural racism The belief that the cultural ways of one group are superior to those of another.

Culturally different Individuals (e.g., providers or clients) who come from culturally diverse and distinct backgrounds. Used synonymously with *cross-cultural*.

Culture The conscious and unconscious content that a group learns, shares, and transmits from generation to generation that organizes life and helps interpret existence.

Deficit theories Theories within the social sciences that purport to explain differences among racial and ethnic groups on the basis of cultural rather than genetic deficiencies.

Emic Viewing a culture through a perspective that is indigenous to it.

Empowerment A helping strategy that involves supporting, encouraging, and giving clients skills to become their own advocates.

Epistemology A dimension of culture that describes a cultural group's preferred way of gaining knowledge and learning about the world.

Ethnic conflict Repeating cycles of violence between two groups whereby acts of retribution by one side are answered with acts of violence by the other. Ethnic conflicts tend to spiral and are characterized by tunnel vision, historical grievances being perceived as if they were current, double victimization, lack of empathy for the other, and group chauvinism.

Ethnic group Any distinguishable group of people whose members share a common culture and see themselves as separate and different from the majority culture.

Ethnic identity or identification The aspect of personal identity that contributes to one's self-image as a member of an ethnic group; the nature of one's sense of belonging to an ethnic group—how one thinks, feels, and acts in relation to one's ethnic group membership.

Ethnic psychology Psychological dynamics that are peculiar to the experiences of People of Color and other oppressed ethnic groups. See also ethnic-specific "psychologies" in chapter 4.

Ethnocentrism Assessing, interpreting, and judging culturally different behavior in relation to one's own cultural standards. Such behaviors are acceptable to the extent that they are similar to one's own cultural ways.

Ethnorelativism Assessing, interpreting, and judging culturally different behavior within its own cultural context. Such behaviors are neither good nor bad, only different.

Ethos   A dimension of culture that refers to the basic values, assumptions, and beliefs that are held within a cultural group and that guide social interactions.

Etic   Viewing a culture through a perspective that is external to it.

Extended self   Ego development typical of ethnic group members who conceive of themselves not as individuals, but as part of a broader collective.

Forgiveness   An internal process of healing within the victim whereby she or he is able to disconnect from self-destructive defenses and reactions, such as anger and guilt, brought to bear interpsychically in reaction to a traumatic event, so as to move on toward a healthy lifestyle.

Frustration-aggression-displacement theory   A psychological theory of prejudice that holds that racial hatred derives from frustration, which leads to aggression, which in turn is displaced onto more vulnerable ethnic or racial group targets.

Genocide   The extermination and/or massive death of such magnitude that a group ceases to continue as a distinct culture and collectivity. A distinction is made between complete and partial genocide.

Historic trauma response   Brave Heart's description of psychopathology among Native and other ethnic groups who have experienced trauma repeatedly across generations and have also lost their traditions of grieving.

Historical trauma and unresolved grief   The damage that ethnic and racial communities may suffer from psychological violence that is passed on from generation to generation.

Human service providers   Professional helpers (e.g., counselors, therapists, psychologists, social workers) who provide social and emotional advice, resources, and education to those in need, most often on a one-to-one basis.

Iatrogenesis   Sickness or pathology that results from medical or psychological intervention and treatment.

Identity   An inner sense of self that reflects a stable perception of who a person is individually and socially.

Individual racism   The beliefs, attitudes, and actions of individuals that support or perpetuate racism (Wijeyesinghe et al., 1997, p. 89).

Institutional racism   The manipulation of social institutions to give preferences and advantages to Whites and at the same time restrict the choices, rights, mobility, and access of People of Color.

Justice   An inner sense of fairness that requires retribution for wrongs done to oneself, other individuals, or groups including one's people. Justice, after a violation, tends to be experienced when there is physical or psychic retribution, the perpetrator is seen to suffer, and it is perceived that the perpetrator has learned a moral lesson.

Latinas/os   A diverse array of Americans who descend from ethnic heritages that share Spanish as a primary language, Roman Catholicism as a religion, and various cultural values.

Learning styles   Preferred modes and styles of learning; children from different cultural groups internalize, become proficient at, and become increasingly more comfortable with various learning styles as they are socialized. Individual learning styles are culturally informed.

Locus of control   A dimension of worldview, suggested by Sue and Sue (1990), that reflects whether individuals feel in control of their own fate (internal control) or feel controlled externally by environmental forces (external control).

Locus of responsibility   A dimension of worldview, suggested by Sue and Sue (1990), that reflects whether individuals believe they are responsible for their fate (internal responsibility) or cannot be held responsible because there are more powerful forces at work in their lives (external responsibility).

Logic   In reference to culture, a dimension that describes the kind of reasoning and intellectual processes that a cultural group adopts.

Native Americans   A diverse array of Americans descended from tribes indigenous to North America including both American Indians and Native Alaskans.

Negative ethnic identification   An inner sense of group belonging that is typified by primarily negative ethnic experiences, which are rejected or disowned, thus remaining unintegrated into a coherent sense of self. Also referred to as *internalized racism, internalized oppression,* and *racial self-hatred.*

Ontology   A dimension of culture that describes how a cultural group views the nature of reality.

Paradigm   A set of assumptions and beliefs about how the world works that structures a person's perception and understanding of reality. Personal paradigms of reality are largely shaped by the culture in which one is raised.

Parental child   A child who has been given responsibilities or a parental role before he or she is emotionally prepared to fill it.

People of Color   A collective reference to Groups of Color in the United States, including African Americans, Asian Americans, Latinos/as, and Native Americans. Used synonymously with the term *non-White.*

Positive ethnic identification   An inner sense of group belonging that is typified by primarily positive ethnic experiences, which are integrated into a coherent sense of self.

Post-traumatic stress disorder (PTSD)   A mental disorder listed in DSM-IV that involves an extreme internal reaction to a traumatic experience and that includes symptoms of hyperarousal, intrusion of thoughts and memories, constriction of affect and other response systems, and social disconnection.

Power   The capacity to produce desired effects on others.

Powerlessness   The inability to influence others.

Prejudice   An antipathy or negative feeling, either expressed or not expressed, based on a faulty and inflexible generalization that places a group of people at some disadvantage not merited by their actions.

Psychobehavioral modality   A dimension of culture that refers to the mode of activity most preferred within a cultural group.

Race   Biological group differences that derive from an isolated inbreeding population with a distinctive genetic heritage.

Racial classification ability   The first step in the process of the development of racial identity, it involves the child learning to apply ethnic labels accurately to members of different groups.

Racial evaluation   The third step in the process of the developing racial identity, it involves the creation of an internal evaluation of one's racial group.

Racial identification   The second step in the process of the developing racial identity, it involves learning to apply the newly gained concept of race to oneself.

Racial identity   The aspect of personal identity that contributes to one's self-image as a Person of Color. Evolves in relation to the sequential acquisition of three learning processes. See *Racial classification ability, Racial identification,* and *Racial evaluation.*

Racial identity development   The series of predictable stages that People of Color go through as they struggle to make sense out of their relationship to their own cultural group as well as to the oppression of mainstream culture.

Racism   The systematic subordination of members of targeted racial groups who have relatively little social power by members of the agent racial group who have relatively more social power (Wijeyesinghe, Griffin, & Love, 1997).

Rankism   The persistent abuse and discrimination based on a power differential in rank or hierarchy.

Reconciliation   As it relates to cultural groups, efforts to bring about peaceful and nonviolent relationships between ethnic groups previously in conflict as well as between perpetrators and victims.

Reparations   Acts of compensation offered to victims in an effort to restore what has been lost. An aspect of the restorative justice model.

Restitution   The return of property, things, and even human remains to their rightful owners. An aspect of reparation.

Restorative justice   Justice defined by restoring the social order. It seeks to repair social connections and establish peace between parties rather than focus on punishment of the offenders, through truth-telling, public acknowledgement, and reparations to the victims.

Retributive justice   Justice defined by retribution and punishment of the offender.

Trauma   An extraordinary psychological experience—caused by threat to life or bodily safety or personal encounter with violence and death—that overwhelms ordinary human functioning.

Ubuntu   An African concept or value, called forth by Nelson Mandela in an effort to reinstate people and justice in South Africa after the end of apartheid, that emphasizes the interconnection of all people and beings.

Vicarious traumatization   Trauma caused by being in close emotional contact with a traumatized individual. Also known as secondary traumatization.

White   Individuals whose cultural origins are Northern European. Also refers to majority and mainstream group members as well as majority providers and clients.

White ethnics   National immigrant groups of Eastern and Southern European descent who share a common experience of immigration to the United States and a history of oppression. Included are Italians, Poles, Greeks, Armenians, Jews, Irish, and various ethnic groups making up the Russian Republic (Czech, Lithuanian, Russian, Slovak, Ukrainian).

White identity development   The series of predictable stages that Whites and White ethnics go through as they struggle to make sense out of their own Whiteness and its relationship to Communities of Color.

White privilege   The benefits that are automatically given to White Americans of European descent on the basis of their skin color.

References

Aboud, F. (1987). The development of ethnic self-identification and attitudes. In J. S. Phinney & M. J. Rotheram (Eds.), *Children's ethnic socialization: Pluralism and development* (pp. 32–55). Newbury Park, CA: Sage.

Aboud, F. (1988). *Children and prejudice.* Oxford: Blackwell.

Aboud, F., & Doyle, A. B. (1993). The early development of ethnic identity and attitudes. In M. E. Bernal & G. P. Knight (Eds.), *Ethnic identity: 1. Formation and transmission among Hispanics and other minorities* (pp. 46–59). Albany: State University of New York Press.

Adorno, T. W., Frankel-Brunswik, E., Levinson, D. J., & Sanford, R. N. (1950). *The authoritarian personality.* New York: Harper & Row.

Allport, G. W. (1954). *The nature of prejudice.* New York: Doubleday.

American Counseling Association. (1995). *Code of ethics and standards of practice.* Alexandria, VA: American Counseling Association.

American Psychiatric Association. (1994). Outline for cultural formulation, Appendix. In *Diagnostic and statistical manual of mental disorders* (4th Ed., Rev. Ed.). Washington, DC: American Psychiatric Association.

American Psychological Association. (2002). *Guidelines on multicultural education, training, research, practice, and organizational change for psychologists.* Washington, DC: American Psychological Association.

Anderson, J. A., & Adams, M. (1992). Acknowledging the learning styles of diverse student populations: Implications for instructional design. In L. L. B. Borders & N. Van Note Chism (Eds.), *Teaching for diversity* (pp. 5–18). San Francisco: Jossey-Bass.

Arendt, H. (1964). *A report on the banality of evil. Eichmann in Jerusalem.* New York: Penguin.

Arredondo, P., Toporek, R., Brown, S. P., Jones, J., Locke, D. C., Sanchez, J., & Stadler, H. (1996, January). Operationalization of the multicultural counseling competencies. *Journal of Multicultural Counseling and Development, 3,* 42–78.

Atkinson, D. R. (1983). Ethnic similarity in counseling psychology: A review of research. *The Counseling Psychologist, 11* (3), 79–92.

Atkinson, D. R., Brown, M. T., Casas, J. M., & Zane, N. W. S. (1996). Achieving ethnic parity in counseling psychology. *The Counseling Psychologist, 24*(2), 230–258.

Atkinson, D. R., Casas, J. M., & Wampold, B. (1981). The categorization of ethnic stereotypes by university counselors. *Hispanic Journal of Behavioral Sciences, 3,* 75–82.

Atkinson, D. R., Morten, G., & Sue, D. W. (1993). *Counseling American minorities: A cross-cultural perspective* (4th ed.): Dubuque, IA: William C. Brown.

Atkinson, D. R., Whitely, S., & Gin, R. H. (1990, March). Asian-American acculturation and preferences for help providers. *Journal of College Student Development, 31,* 155–161.

Austin, G. A., Prendergast, M. L., & Lee, H. (1989). Substance abuse among Asian American youth. *Prevention Research Update No. 5* (pp. 1–13), Portland, OR: Northwest Regional Educational Laboratory.

Bay Area Association of Black Psychologists. (1972). Position statement on use of IQ and ability tests. In R. L. Jones (Ed.), *Black psychology* (pp. 92–94). New York: Harper & Row.

Bell, L. A. (1997). Theoretical foundations for social justice education. In M. Adams, L. A. Bell, & P. Griffin (Eds.), *Teaching for diversity and social justice* (pp. 3–15). New York: Routledge.

Bennett, M. B. (1993). Towards ethnorelativism: A developmental model of intercultural sensitivity. In R. M. Paige (Ed.), *Education for the intercultural experience* (pp. 1–51). Yarmouth, ME: Intercultural Press.

Bernal, M., & Castro, F. (1994). Are clinical psychologists prepared for service and research with ethnic minorities? *American Psychologist, 49,* 797–805.

Bernard, B. (1991, April). *Moving toward a "just and vital culture": Multiculturalism in our schools.* Portland, OR: Northwest Regional Educational Laboratory.

Black, L. (1996). Families of African origin: An overview. In M. McGoldrick, J. Giordan, & J. K. Pearce (Eds.), *Ethnicity and family therapy* (pp. 57–65). New York: Guilford.

Bollin, G. G., and Finkel, J. (1995). White racial identity as a barrier to understanding diversity: A study of preservice teachers. *Equity and Excellence in Education, 28*(1), 25–30.

Boyd, N. (1977). *Perceptions of black families in therapy.* Unpublished doctoral dissertation, Teacher's College, Columbia University, New York.

Boyd, N. (1982). Family therapy with black families. In E. E. Jones & S. J. Korchin (Eds.), *Minority mental health* (pp. 227–249). New York: Praeger.

Braginsky, B., & Braginsky, D. (1974). *Methods of madness: A critique.* New York: Holt, Rinehart & Winston.

Brave Heart, M. Y. H. (1995). *The return to the sacred path: Healing from historical trauma and historical unresolved grief among the Lakota.* Unpublished doctoral dissertation, Smith College School of Social Work, Northampton, MA.

Brave Heart, M. Y. H. (2004). The historic trauma response among Natives and its relationship to substance abuse. In E. Nebelkof & M. Phillips. *Healing and mental health for Native Americans: Speaking in red.* Walnut Creek, CA: Alta Mira Press.

Brodkin, K. (1998). *How Jews became white folks and what that says about race in America.* Piscataway, NJ: Rutgers.

Broverman, I. K., Broverman, D. M., Clarkson, F. E., Rosenkrantz, P. S., & Vogel, S. R. (1970). Sex-role stereotypes and clinical judgments of mental health. *Journal of Consulting and Clinical Psychology, 34*(1), 1–7.

Brown, M. T., & Landrum-Brown, J. (1995). Counselor supervision: Cross-cultural perspectives. In J. P. Ponterotto, J. M. Casas, L. A. Suzuki, & C. M. Alexander (Eds.), *Handbook of multicultural counseling* (pp. 263–287). Thousand Oaks, CA: Sage.

Burroughs, M. (1968). *What shall I tell my children who are black?* Chicago: M.A.A.H. Press.

Canino, I., & Zayas, L. H. (1997). Puerto Rican children. In G. Johnson-Powell, J. Yamamoto, G. E. Wyatt, & W. Arroyo (Eds.), *Transcultural child development: Psychological assessment and treatment* (pp. 61–79). New York: Wiley & Sons.

Cardinal, M. (1984). *The words to say it.* London: Picador.

Carrasquillo, A. L. (1991). *Hispanic children and youth in the United States*. New York: Garland.

Carrillo, C. (1982). Changing norms of Hispanic families: Implications for treatment. In E. E. Jones & S. J. Korchin (Eds.), *Minority mental health* (pp. 250–266). New York: Praeger.

Casas, J. M., & Pytluk, S. D. (1995). Hispanic identity development: Implications for research and practice. In J. P. Ponterotto, J. M. Casas, L. A. Suzuki, & C. M. Alexander (Eds.), *Handbook of multicultural counseling* (pp. 155–180). Thousand Oaks, CA: Sage.

Churchill, W. (1994). *Indians are us? Culture and genocide in Native North America*. Monroe, MA: Common Courage Press.

Clark, C. (1972). Black studies or the study of black people. In R. L. Jones (Ed.), *Black psychology* (pp. 3–17). New York: Harper & Row.

Clark, K., & Clark, M. (1947). Racial identification and preference in Negro children. In T. H. Newcomb & E. L. Hartley (Eds.), *Readings in social psychology* (pp. 169–178). New York: Henry Holt.

Clark, K. B. (1963). *Prejudice and your child*. Boston: Beacon Press.

Cobbs, P. (1972). Ethnotherapy in groups. In L. Solomon & B. Berzon (Eds.), *New perspectives on encounter groups* (pp. 383–403). San Francisco: Jossey-Bass.

Coleman, D., & Gates, H. (1999). Seven elements of cultural competency. In *The way of cultural competency: A conceptual framework*. Madison, WI: Mental Health Center of Dane County.

Collett, J., & Serrano, B. (1992). Stirring it up: The inclusive classroom. In L. L. B. Borders & N. Van Note Chism (Eds.), *Teaching for diversity* (pp. 35–48). San Francisco: Jossey-Bass.

Committee for Workers International. (November 2001). Hate crimes on the rise. *Justice: The papers of the U.S.-Section of CWI.*

Costello, R. M. (1977). Construction and cross validation of an MMPI Black-White scale. *Journal of Personality Assessment, 41*, 515–519.

Cross, T. L. (1988, Summer). Services to minority populations: What does it mean to be a culturally competent professional? *Focal Point.* Portland, OR: Research and Training Center, Portland State University.

Cross, T. L., Bazron, B. J., Dennis, K. W., & Isaacs, M. R. (1989). *Towards a culturally competent system of care*. Washington, DC: Georgetown University Child Development Center.

Cross, W. E. (1995). The psychology of Nigrescence: Revising the Cross model. In J. P. Ponterotto, J. M. Casas, L. A. Suzuki, & C. M. Alexander (Eds.), *Handbook of multicultural counseling* (pp. 93–122). Thousand Oaks, CA: Sage.

Cross, W. E. (1971). The Negro-to-black conversion experience: Toward a psychology of black liberation. *Black World, 20*(9), 13–27.

Curry, N. E., & Johnson, C. N. (1990). *Beyond self-esteem: Developing a genuine sense of human value*. Washington, DC: National Association for the Education of Young Children.

Daly, A., Jennings, J., Beckett, J. O., & Leashore, B. R. (1995). Effective coping strategies of African Americans. *Social Work, 40*, 240–248.

Dana, R. H. (1988). Culturally diverse groups and MMPI interpretation. *Professional Psychology, 19*(5), 490–495.

D'Andrea, M. (1992). The violence of our silence. *Guidepost, 35*(4), 31.

D'Andrea, M., & Daniels, J. (1995). Promoting multiculturalism and organizational change in the counseling profession: A case study. In J. P. Ponterotto, J. M. Casas, L. A. Suzuki, & C. M. Alexander (Eds.), *Handbook of multicultural counseling* (pp. 17–33). Thousand Oaks, CA: Sage.

Devore, W., & Schlesinger, E. G. (1981). *Ethnic-sensitive social work practice.* St. Louis: C. V. Mosby.

Diamond, S. (1957, Fall). Kibbutz and shtetl: The history of an idea. *Social Forces, 5,* 71–99.

Diamond, S. (1987). *In search of the primitive: A critique of civilization.* New Brunswick, NJ: Transaction.

Diller, J. V. (Ed.) (1978). *Ancient roots and modern meanings: A contemporary reader in Jewish identity.* New York: Bloch.

Diller, J. V. (1991). *Freud's Jewish identity: A case study in the impact of ethnicity.* Cranbury, NJ: Fairleigh Dickinson University Press.

Diller, J. V. (1997). *Informal interviews about self-esteem and racism with people of color raised outside of the United States.* Unpublished notes, Conference on Race and Ethnicity in Higher Education, Orlando, FL.

Dollard, J. (1938). Hostility and fear in social life. *Social Forces, 17,* 15–26.

Draguns, J. G. (1981). Dilemmas and choices in cross-cultural counseling: The universal versus the culturally distinct. In P. B. Pedersen, J. G. Draguns, W. L. Lonner, & J. E. Trimble (Eds.), *Counseling across cultures* (pp. 3–22). Honolulu: University of Hawaii Press.

Dupree, D., Spencer, M. B., & Bell, S. (1997). African American children. In G. Johnson-Powell, J. Yamamoto, G. E. Wyatt, & W. Arroyo (Eds.), *Transcultural child development: Psychological assessment and treatment* (pp. 61–79). New York: Wiley & Sons.

Duran, E., & Duran, B. (1995). *Native American postcolonial psychology.* Albany: State University of New York Press.

Epstein, H. (1998). *Children of the Holocaust.* New York: Penguin Putnam.

Erikson, E. (1968). *Identity, youth, and crisis.* New York: Norton.

Falicov, C. J. (1986). Cross-cultural marriages. In N. Jacobson & A. Gurman (Eds.), *Clinical handbook of marital therapy* (pp. 429–450). New York: Guilford.

Fleming, C. M. (1992). American Indians and Alaska natives: Changing societies past and present. In M. A. Orlandi (Ed.), *Cultural competence for evaluators: A guide for alcohol and other drug abuse prevention practitioners working with ethnic/racial communities* (pp. 147–171). Rockville, MD: U.S. Department of Health and Human Services.

Fogelman, E. (1991). Mourning without graves. In A. Medene (Ed.), *Storms and rainbows: The many faces of death* (pp. 25–43). Washington, DC: Lewis Press.

Freedman, D. G. (1979, January). Ethnic differences in babies. *Human Nature,* 36–43.

Fuller, R. W. (2003). *Somebodies and nobodies: Overcoming the abuse of rank.* Gabriola, BC: New Society Publishers.

Gallimore, R., Boggs, J., & Jordan, C. (1974). *Culture, behavior and education: A study of Hawaiian-Americans.* Beverly Hills, CA: Sage.

Garcia, E. E. (1995). Educating Mexican American students: Past treatment and recent developments in theory, research, policy, and practice. In J. A. Banks &

C. A. McGee Banks (Eds.), *Handbook of research on multicultural education* (pp. 372–387). New York: Macmillan.

Garcia Coll, C. T. (1990). Development outcome of minority infants: A process oriented look into our beginnings. *Child Development, 61,* 270–289.

Garcia-Preto, N. (1996). Latino families: An overview. In M. McGoldrick, J. Giordan, & J. K. Pearce (Eds.), *Ethnicity and family therapy* (pp. 141–154). New York: Guilford.

Gaw, A. C. (1993). *Culture, ethnicity, and mental illness.* Washington, DC: American Psychiatric Press.

Gobodo-Madikezela, P. (2000). On trauma and forgiveness. In F. Reid & D. Hoffman. *Long night's journey into day* [documentary], *Facilitator Guide,* San Francisco, CA: California Newsreel, p. 19.

Gobodo-Madikezela, P. (2003, January 10). The roots of Afrikaner rage [Op-ed]. *New York Times,* p. A23.

Goodman, M. E. (1952). *Race awareness in young children.* London: Collier.

Gordon, M. (1964). *Assimilation in American life.* New York: Oxford University Press.

Graham, J. R. (1987). *The MMPI: A practical guide* (2nd ed.). New York: Oxford University Press.

Grant, D., & Haynes, D. (1995). A developmental framework for cultural competence training with children. *Social Work in Education, 17,* 171–182.

Green, J. W. (1982). *Cultural awareness in the human services.* Englewood Cliffs, NJ: Prentice Hall.

Grieger, I., & Ponterotto, J. G. (1995). A framework for assessment in multicultural counseling. In J. P. Ponterotto, J. M. Casas, L. A. Suzuki, & C. M. Alexander (Eds.), *Handbook of multicultural counseling* (pp. 357–374). Thousand Oaks, CA: Sage.

Grier, W., & Cobbs, P. (1968). *Black rage.* New York: Basic Books.

Grinberg, L., & Grinberg, R. (1989). *Psychoanalytic perspectives on migration and exile.* New Haven, CT: Yale University Press.

Group for the Advancement of Psychiatry, Committee on Cultural Psychiatry (1984). *Suicide and ethnicity in the United States.* Series No. 128. New York: Brunner/Mazel.

Gushue, G. V., & Sciarra, D. T. (1995). Culture and families: A multicultural approach. In J. P. Ponterotto, J. M. Casas, L. A. Suzuki, & C. M. Alexander (Eds.), *Handbook of multicultural counseling* (pp. 586–606). Thousand Oaks, CA: Sage.

Hacker, A. (1992). *Two nations: Black and white, separate, hostile, unequal.* New York: Ballantine.

Hale-Benson, J. (1986). *Black children: Their roots, culture, and learning styles.* Baltimore, MD: Johns Hopkins University Press.

Hampden-Turner, C. (1974). *From poverty to dignity: A strategy for poor Americans.* Garden City, NY: Anchor Press.

Hardiman, R., & Jackson, B. W. (1992). Racial identity development: Understanding racial dynamics in college classrooms and on campus. In M. Adams (Ed.), *Promoting diversity in college classrooms: Innovative responses for the curriculum, faculty, and institutions* (pp. 21–37). San Francisco: Jossey-Bass.

Hardy, K. V., & Laszloffy, T. A. (1995). The cultural genogram: Key to training culturally competent family therapists. *Journal of Marital and Family Therapy, 21*(3), 227–237.

Hauser, S. T., & Kasendorf, E. (1983). *Black and white identity formation.* Halabar, FL: Kreiger.

Hayner, P. (2000). The truth and reconciliation commission. In F. Reid & D. Hoffman. *Long night's journey into day* [documentary], *Facilitator Guide,* San Francisco, CA: California Newsreel, p. 10.

Healey, J. F. (1995). *Race, ethnicity, gender, and class: The sociology of group conflict and change.* Thousand Oaks, CA: Forge Press.

Helms, J. E. (1985). Cultural identity in the treatment process. In P. Pedersen (Ed.), *Handbook of cross-cultural counseling and therapy.* Westport, CT: Greenwood Press.

Helms, J. E. (1990). An overview of black racial identity theory. In J. E. Helms (Ed.), *Black and white racial identity: Theory, research and practice* (pp. 9–32). Westport, CT: Greenwood Press.

Helms, J. E. (1995). An update of Helms's white and people of racial identity models. In J. P. Ponterotto, J. M. Casas, L. A. Suzuki, & C. M. Alexander (Eds.), *Handbook of multicultural counseling* (pp. 181–198). Thousand Oaks, CA: Sage.

Herman, J. (1989). *Trauma and recovery: The aftermath of violence—from domestic abuse to political terror.* New York: Basic Books.

Hill, R. (1972). *The strengths of black families.* New York: National Urban League.

Hilliard, A. G. (1995). *The maroon within us.* Baltimore: Black Classic Press.

Hines, P. M., & Boyd-Franklin, N. (1982). Black families. In M. McGoldrick, J. K. Pearce, & J. Giordano (Eds.), *Ethnicity and family therapy* (pp. 84–107). New York: Guilford.

Ho, D. R. (1994). Asian American perspectives. In J. U. Gordon (Ed.), *Managing multiculturalism in substance abuse services* (pp. 72–98). Thousand Oaks, CA: Sage.

Ho, M. (1987). *Family therapy with ethnic minorities.* Newbury Park, CA: Sage.

Ho, M. K. (1992). *Minority children and adolescents in therapy.* Newbury Park, CA: Sage.

Hollingshead, A. B., & Redlich, F. C. (1958). *Social class and mental illness.* New York: Wiley.

Holtzman, W. H., Diaz-Guerrero, R., & Swartz, J. D. (1975). *Personality: Development in two cultures.* Austin: University of Texas Press.

Hoopes, D. S. (1972). *Reader in intercultural communication* (Vols. 1 & 2). Pittsburgh, PA: Regional Council for International Education.

Hsu, F. (1949). Suppression vs. repression: A limited psychological interpretation of four cultures. *Psychiatry, 12,* 223–242.

Hudson Institute. (1988, September). *Opportunity 2000: Creative affirmative action strategies for a changing workforce.* Washington, DC: Employment Standards Administration, U.S. Department of Labor.

Institute for the Healing of Memories (2004, April). *Journey to healing and wholeness* [Conference report] Robben Island, Capetown, SA: Institute for the Healing of Memories.

Ignatiev, N. (1995). *How the Irish became white.* New York: Routledge.

Jacobs, J. H. (1977). *Black/white interracial families: Marital process and identity development in young children.* Unpublished doctoral dissertation, The Wright Institute, Berkeley, California.

Jacobs, J. H. (1992). Identity development in biracial children. In M. P. P. Root (Ed.), *Racially mixed people in America* (pp. 190–206). Newbury Park, CA: Sage.

Jensen, A. R. (1972). *Genetics and education.* New York: Harper & Row.

Jewell, D. P. (1965). A case of a "psychotic" Navaho Indian male. *Human Organization, 11*(1), 32–36.

Jones, A., & Seagull, A. A. (1983). Dimensions of the relationship between the black client and the white therapist: A theoretical overview. In D. R. Atkinson, G. Morten, & D. W. Sue (Eds.), *Counseling American minorities: A cross-cultural perspective* (2nd ed., pp. 156–166). Dubuque, IA: William C. Brown.

Jones, E. E., & Korchin, S. J. (1982). Minority mental health: Perspectives. In E. E. Jones & S. J. Korchin (Eds.), *Minority mental health* (pp. 3–36). New York: Praeger.

Jones, J. M. (1972). *Prejudice and racism.* Reading, MA: Addison-Wesley.

Jones, R. L. (1972). *Black psychology.* New York: Harper & Row.

Jones and Smith 2001

Jung, C. G. (1934). On the present situation of psychotherapy. In *The collected works of C. G. Jung* (1953–1979) (Vol. 10, pp. 157–173). Princeton, NJ: Princeton University Press.

Kagen, S., & Madsen, M. (1972). Experimental analysis of cooperation and competition of Anglo-American and Mexican-American children. *Developmental Psychology, 6,* 49–59.

Kardiner, A., & Ovesey, L. (1951). *The mark of oppression.* Cleveland, OH: World Press.

Kendall, F. E. (1997, June). *Understanding white privilege.* Paper presented at the National Conference on Race and Ethnicity in Higher Education, Orlando, FL.

Kerwin, C., & Ponterotto, J. G. (1995). Biracial identity development: Theory and research. In J. P. Ponterotto, J. M. Casas, L. A. Suzuki, & C. M. Alexander (Eds.), *Handbook of multicultural counseling* (pp. 199–217). Thousand Oaks, CA: Sage.

Kich, G. K. (1992). The development process of asserting a biracial, bicultural identity. In M. P. P. Root (Ed.), *Racially mixed people in America* (pp. 304–317). Newbury Park, CA: Sage.

Kim, U., & Berry, J. W. (1993). *Indigenous psychologies.* Newbury Park, CA: Sage.

Kivel, P. (1996). *Uprooting racism: How white people can work for racial justice.* Gabriola Island, BC: New Society Publishers.

Klein, J. (1980). *Jewish identity and self-esteem: Healing wounds through ethnotherapy.* New York: Institute on Pluralism and Group Identity.

Klein, J. (1981). Ethnotherapy with Jews: Discussion Guide for Videotape Presentation. New York, The American Jewish Committee, Institute of Human Relations.

Klor de Alva, J. J. (1988). Telling Hispanics apart: Latin sociocultural diversity. In E. Acosta-Belen & B. R. Sjostrom (Eds.), *The Hispanic experience in the United States* (pp. 107–136). New York: Praeger. References **267**

Kohout, J., & Pion, G. (1990). Participation of ethnic minorities in psychology: Where do we stand today? In G. Stricker, E. Davis-Russell, E. Bourg, E. Duran, W. R. Hammond, J. McHolland, K. Polite, & B. E. Vaughn (Eds.), *Towards ethnic diversification in psychology education and training* (pp. 105–111). Washington, DC: American Psychological Association.

Kohout, J., & Wicherski, M. (1993). *Characteristics of graduate departments of psychology: 1991–1992.* Washington, DC: American Psychological Association.

Kramer, M., Rosen, B., & Willis, E. (1972). Definitions and distributions of mental disorders in a racist society. In C. V. Willie, B. Kramer, & B. Brown (Eds.), *Racism and mental health* (pp. 353–360). Pittsburgh: University of Pittsburgh Press.

Kroeber, A. L. (1948). *Anthropology: Race, language, culture, psychology, prehistory.* London: Harrap.

Kroeber, A. L., & Kluckhohm, C. (1952). *Culture: A critical review of concepts and definitions.* Cambridge, MA: Papers of the Peabody Museum No. 47.

Kuhn, T. S. (1970). *The structure of scientific revolutions.* Chicago: University of Chicago Press.

Kunjufu, J. (1984). *Countering the conspiracy to destroy black boys.* Chicago: Afro-Am Publishing.

Kupers, T. A. (1999). *Prison madness: The mental health crisis behind bars and what we must do about it.* San Francisco: Jossey-Bass.

Landau, J. (1982). Therapy with families in cultural transition. In M. McGoldrick, J. K. Pearce, & J. Giordano (Eds.), *Ethnicity and family therapy* (pp. 552–572). New York: Guilford.

Larsen, J. (1976, October). *Dysfunction in the evangelical family: Treatment considerations.* Paper presented at the meeting of the American Association of Marriage and Family Therapists, Philadelphia.

Lee, C. C., & Armstrong, K. L. (1995). Indigenous models of mental health intervention: Lessons from traditional healers. In J. P. Ponterotto, J. M., Casas, L. A. Suzuki, & C. M. Alexander (Eds.), *Handbook of multicultural counseling* (pp. 441–456). Thousand Oaks, CA: Sage.

Lee, E. (1996). Asian American families: An overview. In M. McGoldrick, J. Giordan, & J. K. Pearce (Eds.), *Ethnicity and family therapy* (pp. 227–248). New York: Guilford.

Legters, L. H. (1988). The American genocide. *Policy Studies Journal, 16*(4), 768–777.

Lewin, K. (1948). *Resolving social conflicts: Selected papers on group dynamics.* New York: Harper & Row.

Lifton, R. (1986). *The Nazi doctors: Medical killing and the psychology of genocide.* New York: Basic Books.

Linton, R. (1945). *The cultural background of personality.* New York: Appleton-Century-Crofts.

Lum, D. (1986). *Social work practice and people of color: A process-stage approach.* Monterey, CA: Brooks/Cole.

Lum, R. G. (1982). Mental health attitudes and opinions of Chinese. In E. E. Jones & S. J. Korchin (Eds.), *Minority mental health* (pp. 165–189). New York: Praeger.

Lusker, F. (1999). Training materials. www.learningtoforgive.com.

Luskin, F. (2002). *Forgive for good.* New York: HarperCollins.

Manson, S., & Trimble, J. (1982). American Indians and Alaska Native communities: Past efforts, future inquiries. In L. Snowden (Ed.), *Reaching the underserved: Mental health needs of neglected populations* (pp. 143–163). Beverly Hills, CA: Sage.

Marin, G. (1992). Issues in the measurement of acculturation among Hispanics. In K. F. Geisinger (Ed.), *Psychological testing of Hispanics* (pp. 235–252). Washington, DC: American Psychological Association.

Marin, G., & Marin, B. V. (1991). *Research with Hispanic populations.* Newbury Park, CA: Sage.

Marshall, L. M. (2002). *Cultural diversity in our schools.* Belmont, CA: Wadsworth.

McAdoo, H. P. (1985). Racial attitude and self-concept of young black children over time. In H. P. McAdoo & J. L. McAdoo (Eds.), *Black children: Social, educational, and parental environments* (pp. 213–242). Newbury Park, CA: Sage.

McDougall, W. (1977). *Is America safe for democracy?* New York: Ayer.

McGoldrick, M. (1982). Normal families: An ethnic perspective. In F. Walsh (Ed.), *Normal family processes* (pp. 399–424). New York: Guilford.

McIntosh, P. (1989, July/August). White privilege: Unpacking the invisible knapsack. *Peace & Freedom*, 10–12.

McWilliams, N. (2004). *Psychoanalytic psychotherapy: A practitioner's guide.* New York: Guilford.

Meadow, A. (1982). Psychopathology, psychotherapy, and the Mexican-American patient. In E. E. Jones & S. J. Korchin (Eds.), *Minority mental health* (pp. 331–361). New York: Praeger.

Memmi, A. (1965). *Dominated man: Notes towards a portrait.* Boston: Beacon Press.

Memmi, A. (1966). *The liberation of the Jew.* New York: Grossman.

Milgrim, S. (1974). *Obedience to authority: An experimental view.* New York: Harper & Row.

Minow, M. (2000). The hope of healing: What can truth commissions do? In R. I. Rotberg & D. Thompson (Eds.), *Truth v. justice: The morality of truth commissions* (pp. 235–260). Princeton, N.J.: Princeton University Press.

Minuchin, S. (1974). *Families and family therapy.* Cambridge, MA: Harvard University Press.

Minuchin, S., Montalvo, B., Guerney, G., Rosman, B., & Schumer, F. (1967). *Families of the slums.* New York: Basic Books.

Mosby, D. P. (1972). Towards a new specialty of black psychology. In R. L. Jones (Ed.), *Black psychology* (pp. 33–42). New York: Harper & Row.

Moynihan, D. P. (1965, March). *The Negro family: The case for national action.* Washington, DC: Office of Policy Planning and Research, U.S. Department of Labor.

Myers, H. F. (1982). Stress, ethnicity, and social class: A model for research with black populations. In E. E. Jones & S. J. Korchin (Eds.), *Minority mental health* (118–148). New York: Praeger.

Myers, H., & King, L. (1985). Mental health issues in the development of the black American child. In G. J. Powell, J. Yamamoto, A. Romero, & A. Morales (Eds.), *The psychosocial development of minority children* (pp. 275–306). New York: Brunner/ Mazel.

Nobles, W. W. (1972). African philosophy: Foundations for black psychology. In R. L. Jones (Ed.), *Black psychology* (pp. 18–32). New York: Harper & Row.

Norton, D. G. (1983). Black families' life patterns, the development of self and cognitive development of black children. In G. J. Powell, J. Yamamoto, A. Romero, & A. Morales (Eds.), *The psychosocial development of minority children* (pp. 181–193). New York: Brunner/Mazel.

Obgu, J. U. (1978). *Minority education and caste: The American system in cross-cultural perspective.* New York: Academic Press.

Oetting, E. R., & Beauvais, F. (1990). Orthogonal cultural identity theory. The cultural identification in minority adolescents. *International Journal of Addiction, 25,* 655–685.

Omar, D. (1996). Introduction by Minister of Justice, Truth and Reconciliation Commission. www.truth.org.com

Parham, T. (1992). *The white researcher in multicultural counseling revisited—Discussions and suggestions.* Paper presented at the annual meeting of the American Psychological Association, Washington, DC. Quoted in D'Andrea, M., & Daniels, J. (1995).

Promoting multiculturalism and organizational change in the counseling profession: A case study. In J. P. Ponterotto, J. M. Casas, L. A. Suzuki, & C. M. Alexander (Eds.), *Handbook of multicultural counseling* (pp. 17–33). Thousand Oaks, CA: Sage.

Pearl, A., & Reismann, F. (1965). *New careers for the poor: Nonprofessionals in human service.* New York: Free Press. References **269**

Perkins, M. (1994, March 17): Guess who's coming to church? Confronting Christians' fear of interracial marriage. *Christianity Today*, 30–33.

Petersen, P. B., Draguns, J. G., Lonner, W. J., & Trimble, J. E. (1989). *Counseling across culture.* Honolulu: University of Hawaii Press.

Pinderhughes, E. (1982). Afro-American families and the victim system. In M. McGoldrick, J. K. Pearce, & J. Giordano (Eds.), *Ethnicity and family therapy* (pp. 108–122). New York: Guilford.

Pinderhughes, E. (1989). *Understanding race, ethnicity, and power: The key to efficacy in clinical practice.* New York: Free Press.

Pollard, K. M., & O'Hare, W. P. (1999, September). America's racial and ethnic minorities. *Population Bulletin, 54*, (3).

Ponterotto, J. G. (1988). Racial consciousness development among white counselor trainees: A stage model. *Journal of Multicultural Counseling and Development, 16*, 146–156.

Ponterotto, J. P., Casas, J. M., Suzuki, L. A., & Alexander, C. M. (Eds.). (1995). *Handbook of multicultural counseling.* Thousand Oaks, CA: Sage.

Poussaint, A. F. (1972). *Why blacks kill blacks.* New York: Emerson Hall.

Powell, G. J. (1973). The self-concept in white and black children. In C. V. Willie, B. Kramer, & B. Brown (Eds.), *Racism and mental health* (pp. 299–318). Pittsburgh: University of Pittsburgh Press.

Powell, G. J., Yamamoto, J., Romero, A., & Morales, A. (1983). *The psychosocial development of minority children.* New York: Brunner/Mazel.

Proshansky, H., & Newton, P. (1968). The meaning and nature of Negro self-identity. In M. Deutsch, I. Katz, & A. Jensen (Eds.), *Social class, race and psychological development.* New York: Holt, Rinehart & Winston.

Reynolds, C. R., & Kaiser, S. M. (1990). Test bias in psychological assessment. In T. B. Gutkin & C. R. Reynolds (Eds.), *The handbook of school psychology* (pp. 487–525). New York: Wiley.

Riche, M. F. (2000, June). America's diversity and growth: Signposts for the 21st century. *Population Bulletin, 55* (2).

Robinson, R. (1999). *The debt: What America owes to blacks.* New York: Dutton.

Rochlen, A. B. (2007). *Applying counseling theories: An online, case-based approach* (1st ed.): Upper Saddle River, NJ: Pearson Education.

Rokeach, M. (1960). *Beliefs, attitudes, and values.* New York: Basic Books.

Rosen, E. J., & Weltman, S. F. (1996). Jewish families: An overview. In M. McGoldrick, J. Giordan, & J. K. Pearce (Eds.), *Ethnicity and family therapy* (pp. 611–630). New York: Guilford.

Rosenberg, M. (1979). *Conceiving the self.* New York: Basic Books.

Rosenhan, D. L. (1975). On being sane in insane places. In D. L. Rosenhan & P. London (Eds.), *Theory and research in abnormal psychology* (pp. 254–270). New York: Holt, Rinehart & Winston.

Rosenthal, D. (1976). *Experimenter effects in behavioral research.* New York: Halsted Press.

Rosenthal, R., & Jacobson, L. (1968). *Pygmalion in the classroom: Teacher expectations and pupils' intellectual development.* New York: Holt, Rinehart & Winston.

Rowe, W., Behrens, J. T., & Leach, M. M. (1995). Racial/ethnic identity and social consciousness: Looking back and looking forward. In J. P. Ponterotto, J. M. Casas, L. A. Suzuki, & C. M. Alexander (Eds.), *Handbook of multicultural counseling* (pp. 218–235). Thousand Oaks, CA: Sage.

Russo, N. R., Olmedo, E. L., Stapp, J., & Fulcher, R. (1981). Women and minorities in psychology. *American Psychologist, 36,* 1315–1363.

Saeki, C., & Borow, H. (1985). Counseling and psychotherapy: East and west. In P. B. Pedersen (Ed.), *Handbook of cross-cultural counseling and therapy.* Westport, CT: Greenwood Press.

Scanzoni, J. N. (1971). *The black family in modern society.* Chicago: University of Chicago Press.

Scarr, S. (1993). Biological and cultural diversity: The legacy of Darwin for development. *Child Development, 64,* 1333–1353.

Seifer, R., Sameroff, A., Barrett, L., & Krafchuk, E. (1994). Infant temperament measured by multiple observations and mother report. *Child Development, 65,* 1478–1490.

Singer, D., & Seldin, R. (1994). *American Jewish yearbook, 1994.* New York: American Jewish Committee.

Smolowe, J. (1993, November). Intermarried . . . with children. *Time, 142* (21), 64–65.

Snowden, L., & Todman, P. A. (1982). The psychological assessment of blacks: New and needed developments. In E. E. Jones & S. J. Korchin (Eds.), *Minority mental health* (pp. 227–249). New York: Praeger.

Soriano, F. I. (1994). The Latino perspective: A sociocultural portrait. In J. U. Gordon (Ed.), *Managing multiculturalism in substance abuse services* (pp. 117–147). Thousand Oaks, CA: Sage.

Spenser, M. B., & Markstrom-Adams, C. (1990). Identity processes among racial and ethnic minority children in America. *Child Development, 61,* 290–310.

Stack, C. (1975). *All our kin: Strategies for survival in a black community.* New York: Harper & Row.

Stonequist, E. V. (1961). *The marginal man: A study in personality and culture conflict.* New York: Russell & Russell.

Straker, G. (1999). An interview with Gillian Straker on the Truth and Justice Commission in South Africa. *Psychoanalytic Dialogues, 9*(2): 245–274.

Sue, D. W., Arredondo, A., & McDavis, R. J. (1992). Multicultural counseling competencies and standards: A call to the profession. *Journal of Counseling and Development, 70,* 477–486.

Sue, S., & McKinney, H. (1975). Asian Americans in the community mental health care system. *American Journal of Orthopsychiatry, 45,* 111–118.

Sue, S., McKinney, H., Allen, D., & Hall, J. (1974). Delivery of community health services to black and white clients. *Journal of Consulting Psychology, 42,* 794–801.

Sue, S., & Zane, N. (1987). The role of culture and cultural techniques in psychotherapy: A critique and reformulation. *American Psychologist, 42,* 37–45.

Sue, S. W., & Sue, D. (1999, 1990). *Counseling the culturally different: Theory and practice* (2nd & 3rd eds.). New York: Wiley.

Sutton, C. E. T., & Broken Nose, M. A. (1996). American Indian families: An overview. In M. McGoldrick, J. Giordan, & J. K. Pearce (Eds.), *Ethnicity and family therapy* (pp. 31–44). New York: Guilford.

Suzuki, L. A., & Kugler, J. F. (1995). Intellectual and personality assessment: Multicultural perspectives. In J. P. Ponterotto, J. M. Casas, L. A. Suzuki, & C. M. Alexander (Eds.), *Handbook of multicultural counseling* (pp. 493–515). Thousand Oaks, CA: Sage.

Takaki, R. (1993). *A different mirror: A history of multicultural America.* Boston: Little, Brown.

Tatum, B. D. (1992, Spring). Talking about race, learning about racism: The application of racial identity developmental theory in the classroom. *Harvard Education Review, 62* (1).

Tatum, B. D. (1997). *"Why are all the black kids sitting together in the cafeteria?" and other conversations about race.* New York: Basic Books.

Thompson, C. (1949). The Thompson modification of the Thematic Apperception Test. *Journal of Projective Techniques, 13,* 469–478.

Thompson, V. (2005). What is a multicultural ally? Curricular material developed for Multicultural Awareness Course. Berkeley, CA: The Wright Institute.

Thornton, M. C., Chatters, L. M., Taylor, R. J., & Allen, W. (1990). Sociodemographic and environmental correlates of racial socialization by black parents. *Child Development, 61,* 401–409.

Tong, B. R. (1981). *On the confusion of psychopathology with culture: Iatrogenesis in the "treatment" of Chinese Americans.* Unpublished manuscript. Berkeley, CA: The Wright Institute.

Torrey, E. F. (1986). *Witch doctors and psychiatrists: The common roots of psychotherapy and its future.* New York: Harper & Row.

Trawick-Smith, J. W. (1997). *Early childhood development: A multicultural perspective.* Upper Saddle River, NJ: Prentice Hall.

Trawick-Smith, J. W., & Lisi, P. (1994). Infusing multicultural perspectives in an early childhood development course: Effect on the knowledge and attitudes of inservice teachers. *Journal of Early Childhood Teacher Education, 15,* 8–12.

Turner, J. R. (1985). *Differential treatment and ethnicity.* Unpublished notes. Berkeley, CA: The Wright Institute.

United States Bureau of the Census (2000). *Profile of selected social characteristics: 2000.* Washington, DC: Government Printing Office.

Valentine, C. A. (1971). Deficit, difference, and bicultural models of Afro-American behavior. *Harvard Educational Review, 41,* 135–157.

Vontress, C. E. (1981). Racial and ethnic barriers in counseling. In P. B. Pedersen, J. G. Draguns, W. L. Lonner, & J. E. Trimble (Eds.), *Counseling across cultures* (Rev. ed., pp. 87–107). Honolulu: University of Hawaii Press.

Wampold, B., Casas, J. M., & Atkinson, D. R. (1982). Ethnic bias in counseling: An information-processing approach. *Journal of Counseling Psychology, 28,* 489–503.

Wechsler, H., Solomon, L., & Kramer, B. (1970). *Social psychology and mental health.* New York: Holt, Rinehart & Winston.

Weinstein, G., & Mellen, D. (1997). Anti-Semitism curriculum design. In M. Adams, L. A. Bell, & P. Griffin (Eds.), *Teaching for diversity and social justice* (pp. 170–197). New York: Routledge.

Weissmark, M. S. (2004). *Justice matters: Legacies of the Holocaust and World War II*. New York: Oxford University Press.

White, J. (1980). Towards a Black psychology. In R. Jones (Ed.), *Black psychology* (pp. 43–50). New York: Harper & Row.

Wijeyesinghe, C. L., Griffin, P., & Love, B. (1997). Racism curriculum design. In M. Adams, L. A. Bell, & P. Griffin (Eds.), *Teaching for diversity and social justice* (pp. 82–109). New York: Routledge.

Williams, J. E., & Morland, J. K. (1976). *Race, color, and the young child*. Chapel Hill: University of North Carolina Press.

Williams, R. M. (1947). The reduction of intergroup tensions. *Social Science Council Bulletin, 59*, 119–127.

Wolkind, S., & Rutter, M. (1985). *Sociocultural factors in child and adolescent psychiatry*. Boston: Blackwell Scientific.

Wright, M. A. (1998). *I'm chocolate, you're vanilla: Raising healthy black and biracial children in a race-conscious world*. San Francisco: Jossey-Bass.

Wylie, R. C. (1961). *The self-concept*. Lincoln: University of Nebraska Press.

Yamamoto, J., & Acosta, F. X. (1982). Treatment of Asian-Americans and Hispanic-Americans: Similarities and differences. *Journal of the Academy of Psychoanalysis, 10*, 585–607.

Yamamoto, J., James, O., & Palley, N. (1968). Cultural problems in psychiatric therapy. *Archives of General Psychiatry, 19*, 45–49.

Yehuda, R. (1999). *Risk factors for posttraumatic stress disorder*. Washington, DC: American Psychiatric Press.

York, S. (1991). *Roots and wings: Affirming culture in early childhood programs*. St. Paul, MN: Redleaf Press.

Index

327